Social Anthropology of Work

Association of Social Anthropologists
A Series of Monographs

A.S.A. MONOGRAPH 19

Social Anthropology of Work

Edited by

SANDRA WALLMAN

SSRC Research Unit on Ethnic Relations
University of Bristol
Bristol, England

1979

ACADEMIC PRESS

A Subsidiary of Harcourt Brace Jovanovich, Publishers

London　New York　Toronto　Sydney　San Francisco

ACADEMIC PRESS INC. (LONDON) LTD.
24/28 Oval Road,
London NW1

United States Edition published by
ACADEMIC PRESS INC.
111 Fifth Avenue
New York, New York 10003

British Library Cataloguing in Publication Data
Anthropology of Work *(Conference), University of York, 1979*
    Social anthropology of work. – (Association of Social
Anthropologists of the Commonwealth. Monograph; 19).
    1. Economic anthropology – Congresses
    2. Work – Congresses
    I. Wallman, Sandra   II. Series
    301.5′5   GN448   79-41277
    ISBN 0 12 733250 2
    ISBN 0 12 733252 9 Pbk.

Printed in Great Britain by
Whitstable Litho Ltd., Whitstable, Kent

PREFACE

The papers which make up this volume were circulated in draft and presented to the A.S.A. Conference 1979, "The Anthropology of Work". It was held at Derwent College, University of York. The local Organiser was Anne Akeroyd. Only one of the papers presented is not included: Jonathan Parry's complex analysis of the work of funeral priests in Benares will appear somewhat later than this volume goes to press. I am grateful to the other contributors for making their papers available for publication within two months of the conference. The A.S.A. now normally aims to produce each monograph within a year of the occasion at which the collection was presented. In this case we were concerned to do so for two additional reasons. One is that many of these papers constitute reports of work in progress which will lose credence and point if too long delayed in the pipeline. The other is that there is a marked resurgence of popular interest in the topic "work" at this time. While some A.S.A. conference topics are esoteric to the profession, others are "folk" notions reflecting the concerns of ordinary people and in some historical phases, of politicians and policy makers. Work is one of these latter notions and this is one of those periods. Discussions of incentives, occupational identity, labour organisation, industrial action, unemployment and the "threat" of new technology crop up in the mass media as often they do in social scientific publications. Various "futures of work" are prophesied, some glowing, some gloomy, all of them implying change of the present circumstances and of the needs, constraints and opportunities which structure the business of livelihood.

In this sense the question of work has become the stuff of political and economic debate — at least in industrial countries, and quite often in the so-called "developing world". Closest to home, both the recent British election campaign and the European parliamentary elections which followed immediately after it have been "about" unemployment, pay restraint and the ownership of resources on the one hand, and "about" national regional and occupational status on the other. On the local level, similar issues arise: the efficiency of agricultural and industrial production, and the provision of personal and social services seem more and more directly to hinge on questions of incentives to work, the just reward for labour, and the scope for individual initiative and autonomy in particular work processes or in the political economy at large.

The debate is heated and confused; two fundamental human issues are involved. While the preoccupations of work are directly concerned with the work of making a living, they are indirectly but equally concerned with the work of personal and group identity. If these issues loom largest in industrial societies it may be only because our habits of self-examination are more explicit and our means of communication more elaborated: the organisation, the experience and even the classification of work are matters of moment to people in a variety of social and technological settings.

This small collection includes examples from pre-industrial, industrialising and late industrial "stages of development". Because the same problems occur across the range, a comparative analysis of the dimensions of work and of variations in the relations between them cannot but be interesting. It may even be useful. And if, as social anthropologists, we claim to have insights relevant to contemporary social issues, then we should not be coy about entering contemporary debate — even if with an imperfect script. The mood of the conference was exploratory but positive. Accordingly, this volume is offered as the preliminary statement of an anthropology of work; the final word may follow later.

The editorial framework imposed on these separate cases is built around two very simple questions. Firstly: what is "work" about? Secondly: what does social anthropology have to say about it that has not already been said?

Pursuing the first question, the conference solicited views from three widely different other disciplines — biological anthropology, psychiatry and economics. We are indebted to Geoffrey Ainsworth-Harrison, Leonard Fagin and Walter Elkan for agreeing to venture across the boundaries of their respective disciplines in order to contribute to *our* professional conference. Their respective short statements have served to broaden the perspective of our discussions. Certain aspects and anomalies of work which arise in the social anthropological contributions have been signalled from outside social anthropology; views from other disciplines are neither less relevant nor less exotic than views from other societies. To counter the argument that other practitioners of other professions should also have been asked to state their views, we can only state the pragmatic constraints: virtually every academic discipline shows or has shown serious interest in the topic; no single conference could reasonably hope to cover every aspect. This volume does not therefore purport to review the field of work studies or the many theoretical issues raised in the literature. The references following each contribution do, however, provide specialist bibliographies to the subject matter.

Here it should be noted that the topic is not new to social anthropology either. Indeed the 1979 "Work" Conference took place forty-seven years after the publication of Audrey Richards' classic *Hunger and Work in a Savage Tribe* (London, Routledge 1932) — one of the first of many intricate analyses of work organisation and process in non-industrial societies. It may be that this Conference has extended the anthropological range by including industrial societies within the same rubric as the "savage". It is this extension which requires us to pose the second of our two questions: What does social anthropology have to say about work that has not already been said?

No single answer will speak for the whole discipline, nor even for the few cases presented here, but a number of characteristic social anthropological approaches can be used, in combination, to indicate what a social anthropology of work might be about. These are: (i) social anthropologists take a comparative perspective and so recognise that not everyone classifies the same world in the same way; (ii) we pay particular attention to context and to the systematic relation between elements of culture, structure and organisation — which is only to say that we tend to ask "what else is happening?" when seeking to understand social events; (iii) we are able to visualise the innumerable sub-systems of culture, structure and organisation as domains or spheres — whether of activity, exchange, or meaning — to which particular kinds of resources pertain, and between which they can be transposed when conditions are appropriate; and (iv) this perception allows us to notice, if not to account for contradictions of value, and the ordinary anomalies of ordinary life. Because the understanding of *Work* will be advanced by these perspectives, then we may claim to have something useful to say about it.

This volume begins with views of work from biological anthropology, psychiatry and economics, then takes up the two questions posed here in relation to the social anthropological contributions which follow.

S. Wallman

ACKNOWLEDGEMENTS

It is inevitable that many people who contribute to a conference volume of this kind are not cited in the text. We would like to acknowledge the role of participants to discussions at the conference, both in and outside the formal sessions; to thank Richard Werbner, Jeremy Boissevain, Adrian Mayer and Lorraine Baric for chairing those sessions so ably; and to record that Marianne Heiberg prepared the Index of Names at the end of the volume.

It is, however, unusual for an ASA Conference volume to owe as much to the Local Organiser of the conference as this one owes Anne Akeroyd. The editor is particularly indebted to her, — not simply for carrying the brunt of reading and correcting the proofs of the book, but for doing so with such extraordinary thoroughness, generosity and speed.

CONTENTS

INTRODUCTION

SANDRA WALLMAN

A Social Anthropology of Work?

Within any society, "work" has a number of very different meanings. When the word is used in English, only the personal or professional interests of the speaker provide the gloss. It can be analysed in terms of physical transformations, social transactions, economic activities or personal identities. For the worker himself it is both a psychic necessity and the cause of pain and alienation. It makes no sociological sense without reference to control and the division of labour, no physical sense unless the level of technology available for its performance is considered. Across cultures, those activities that are called "work" (or by the word which is translated as "work") change, and the component parts of work processes appear in different combinations and with different significance. A comparative perspective on work must therefore take into account not only what is done, how it is done and who does it, but also how and by whom it is evaluated.

In each of these respects, work is 'about' control — physical and psychological, social and symbolic. The primaeval purpose of work is the human need to control nature, to wrest a living from it and to impose culture on it. By definition there is no social group that does not "work" at this level. Because the business of controlling nature is a matter of technical ingenuity, it is both eased and complicated by inventions of culture and patterns of organisation. The control of nature is therefore transposed into a more general need to control the environment and the business of livelihood. Central to the rubric of this volume is the fact that the working relationship between man and nature is never unembroidered; and that much of the social-cultural embroidery on work tends to be concerned with the control of one person or category of people over another — whether direct control by means of command over the actions of others, or indirect control achieved either by limiting their access to resources and benefits (cf. Nadel 1957), or by devaluing the resources and benefits which they have. These resources may pertain to any or all aspects of work.

In the loosest possible sense, people can.be said to "make" others work just as they "work" machines, but the analogy is limited by three particular considerations. Firstly, because work is 'about' social transaction as much as material production. Indeed its significance is more often seen to lie in the *quality of the relationships* involved in the allocation, production or distribution of resources than in the bald facts of material survival (Firth 1967: 4). Secondly, work controls the identity as much as the economy of the worker, whether as an individual or as the member of a caste or an occupational group. Being (also) a psychological matter, it is both more and less than economic activity; however instrumental or impersonal the attitude of others to his work, it is, for the worker, a personal experience, his relation to the reality in which he lives. At the same time it is only a tiny part of the wider processes of the environment and must be understood in an economic framework. We may say that work is 'about' the physical and psychic energy a worker puts into producing, maintaining or converting economic resources; but that the choices, decisions and rewards of the worker are constrained by the logic of the system in which he works. Thirdly, the control of work entails not only control over the allocation and disposition of resources, it implies also control over the values ascribed to each of them: Giriama feel in control of the value of wage labour, Melanesians of unpaid work (Parkin, Schwimmer, this volume). Classification of the activities and achievements of others is more subtle than the physical constraint of their actions, but it is no less controlling for that. Most of us are not conscious that we evaluate the environment within frames we learned from our parents. The categories of any culture feel so natural and unquestionable to the "members" of that culture that changes in evaluation are hard to accept and slow to come about. So it is with the meaning of work. We need not only to ask what activities are called "work" and how their economic value is computed in that setting; we need also to know which forms of work are, in that setting, thought to be socially worthy and personally fulfilling.

Criteria of control provide the base for a cross-cultural overview of work, but the comparative perspective does not of itself resolve the anomalies of classification. It has been observed, for example, that specific hunter-gatherer peoples make no distinction between work and non-work activities (Sahlins 1974). The same may be true of artists (Schwimmer, this volume). Concepts of leisure are specific to rare contexts of time and place (Parkin, Schwimmer, this volume); and in any society the boundaries between work and non-work or between sub-categories of work, are not always drawn in the same place or in the same terms (Cohen, Murray, Parkin, Schildkrout, Schwimmer, Searle-Chatterjee, this volume). A peasant pauses in the hard labour of hoeing to say: "I see no work between here and the grave . . . " (Wallman 1969): "work" is what he gets paid cash to do (Murray, Parkin, this volume). An actor by contrast "rests" between contracts by taking a paid job: "It's not work, it's only for money": "work" is what he identifies with. The Japanese are said to work at leisure; and the English to play at work. Jogging is work *or* recreation, sometimes it is both work *and* recreation. And three similar questions asked of members of the tribe *Nacirema* would elicit three quite different answers: "What's your job?" "What do you do?" "What are you into?" Non-member outsiders would not even recognise that three questions all apply to work and to work of very different sorts.

It is clear the variation within and across cultures is very great. We might choose either to conclude simply that work means different things to different people and so to call the discussion to a halt (which is what our detractors inside and outside the profession probably expect us to do), or to prolong it until we have pulled a new and all-purpose definition of work out of the cross-cultural hat (which, no doubt, is what our more loyal supporters and debating partners would like us to do!). Insofar as our professional addition to the debate lies exactly in recognising that the world is both simpler and more complex than it appears (Firth 1967), neither course is satisfactory. The first implies that work is too trivial or too general a notion to bother about, or that *notions* of work are anyway beside the point: if all livelihood is controlled by structures of power and exploitation — sexual, local or international — then the real meaning of work is governed by larger and more inevitable processes than those analysed by the methods of social anthropology. The second underestimates the complexity of systems called work and of the variations in organisation, meaning and function that occur from one system of work to another. It will be clear to lumpers and splitters, formalists and substantivists alike, that neither stance will, in pure form, solve the problems of work. It is heuristically useful instead to proceed by compromise. If we can first chart the elements involved, one layer at a time, we can then attempt to monitor the relations between them. It is in terms of the relations between constituent dimensions of systems of work that social anthropology is most likely to inform both the practical and the theoretical issues.

In the following discussion the order in which the dimensions of work are mentioned should not be read as a ranking of their importance; each depends on every other. The final section deals explicitly with the multilineality of relations between them.

Energy

Work is the application of human energy to things; which application converts, maintains, or adds value to the worker, the thing worked on, and the system in which the work is performed. This physical definition can deal with the work of economic sectors and occupational groups as much as with individual workers. It could even be made to take in the work of managers, brokers, intermediaries, artists, ritual specialists — all those whose work cannot be measured by its material product or "use value" (Firth, this volume). In physiological terms, each is expending energy and is therefore altered by the work effort; even psychic energy burns calories (Harrison, this volume). And if "the thing worked on" can be read to include non-material resources (institutions, symbols, information), then all systems of work are energy systems. At a base line, this must be correct. But work can never be understood as a mechanical function of energy expenditure: human work is energy directed to more or less explicit goals.

Incentive

In Tikopia as in business economics an element of purpose is contained in the simplest definition of work: work is the expenditure of human energy, to accomplish ends, with some sacrifice of comfort and leisure (Firth, this volume). We can agree, however, that the ends or objectives of work vary. Despite the heat generated by wage bargaining in democratic industrial systems, few would seriously argue that the maximisation of money or other material gain is the sole form of rational economic behaviour or the only incentive to effort. By the same token, work is not only "economic" activity: it has more 'reasons' than that. "Work is at one time an economic, political and religious act, and (it) is experienced as such" (Godelier 1972: 266).

Incentives to work are embedded in a total set of norms. There is, in real life, relatively little autonomy for economic objectives, or for economic criteria of evaluation *alone*. Economic purposes are "hemmed in by the social prescription of means and ends", by other-than-economic assessments of what is and should be happening — although in industrial society, in particular spheres of economic

activity, the social is said to be kept out of account (Cohen 1967:
112—3). It is hard to accept that this could ever be so. Studies of
"informal" organisation within "formal" institutions demonstrate
that social, symbolic, existential or "non-economic" purposes are
essential parts of their operation. The most rational and impersonal
bureaucratic procedures always leave room for particularistic
criteria and often depend on personal relationships (Wadel, this
volume. See also Flett 1979). Strike action is as often about the
dignity of working conditions as it is about wage rates; some
people go into factory work "only" because it is more sociable
than being in an office or at home, or because they want to be with
their friends (see e.g. Klein 1976; Beynon and Blackburn 1972;
Saifullah Khan 1979). In this latter respect at least, the incentives
of industrial workers are not unlike those of Melanesian gardeners
(cf. Schwimmer, this volume). Certainly the most serious implications
of "the silicone chip revolution", human redundancy and unemployment in industrial process are not the narrowly economic (Richard
Harrison 1976; Marsden and Duff 1975). But because the
dominant definitions of this society equate "work" with a job in
the formal economy (Elkan, this volume), the question "What is
work about?" can be approached by asking what it means to be
unemployed (Fagin, this volume). If we visualise a circumstance in
which the State (or the extended family) pays the basic bills so
that the absence of a job has no monetary implications, we may
then begin to see other-than-economic incentives in perspective;
to know what work *apart from a job* is necessary to livelihood.
The "work" of maintaining social status and personal esteem is
most often reported as paramount, whether the focus is on authority
within the family or credibility in the community (Fagin, Wadel,
this volume; Wadel 1973). The incentive to regain formal employment is hard to distinguish from a pressing need to put structure
and purpose back into everyday life (see Time, Identity, below).

   Incentives to employment, however they are distinguished from
incentives to work, are not the same for everyone: formal employment means quite different things in different settings. The job
comes closest to being an end in itself in those rare cases where
people are paid to do what they would do "at leisure" — i.e. if
they could choose. Usually it is experienced as a means to other
ends, at least until the job is lost. And as the ends of employment
vary, so do incentives to it. Both Giriama and Basotho people
migrate to wage work to meet an immediate need for cash. But the
former see "a job" as a means to better control over the uncertainties
of the future (Parkin, this volume), the latter use it to shore up the

traditional system at home (Murray, this volume). Whalsay islanders are markedly more affluent than Basotho but express similar incentives to wage work: it allows them to continue the now uneconomic traditions of crofting (Cohen, this volume). Similarly, young Moslem girls in one part of Kano work as street or market traders for the explicit purpose of making money, but the incentive to their doing so is the desire to accumulate the dowry to make a good marriage. Moslem girls in another part of the same town use a different means to the same end: they stay out of the public arena and work at getting educated (Schildkrout, this volume).

The incentive to take up a particular kind of work or even to work at all has a logic distinct from incentives to working *well*. Most obviously, people are inspired to make the extra effort necessary for a better performance by the promise of extra reward. It need not of course be material reward: in industrial society personal satisfaction is said to be better than money in the bank. In many economies as well as in societies where money values are beside the point — either because there is no currency or because money is used only in very limited spheres of life — the incentive to a specially good performance or product may be its extra value in use or in direct exchange, but it is probably as often the kudos or "differentials" gained from special skill or the satisfaction of having created something with which one is quite simply proud to be identified (Firth, Ortiz, Schwimmer, this volume).

Questions about incentive are usually of the kind: How can people be persuaded to work? What gives them the incentive to work especially well at particular tasks and to take pride in the work they do? How is work to be rewarded when subsistence is anyway assured — whether because nature provides warmth and fish and fruit, or because a reasonable minimum wage is guaranteed by an affluent state? Incentives to work are built up of the dimensions of work itemised in the sections following. They depend particularly on the complex relations between resources, values and identity structure. But the really interesting question turns the problem of incentives around: how come people tend to work as much or as little when they are not forced to, as when they are?

Resources

Even a job in the formal economy of an industrial society has other than monetary value and implications for other than formal economic activity (Elkan, this volume). Other-than-economic resources are a necessary part of getting and performing a job; other-than-economic criteria will be used in the worker's (and in society's) assessment of how good that job is (Beynon and Blackburn 1972; Klein 1976; Terkel 1977; Willis 1977).

By the same token, the loss of any work may cause the loss of necessary non-economic resources, notably of identity, status and the structure of time (Jahoda *et al.* 1972; Wadel 1973). It is bound to entail changes in the way those resources are managed. Consider: when people of working age in a wage economy are not "at work", what are they doing instead? Improving their property or their minds? Looking for or travelling to formal employment? Living off the land and barter? Watching television or tending the garden? Baking bread or finding out where to buy it? Relating to their children? Dealing with the bureaucrats that give them unemployment benefit? (Wadel, this volume). How far do segments of a single population differ in these respects? (Gershuny 1978). Does it mean the same to be out of a job in the 1970s as it did in the 1930s?

We can begin to assess "what they are doing instead" if it is recognised that both in and outside the formal economy, work is the performance of necessary tasks, and the production of necessary values — moral as well as economic. The task of meeting obligations, securing identity, status and structure, are as fundamental to livelihood as bread and shelter. On this basis, work may be defined as the production, management or conversion of the resources necessary to livelihood — "the sum total of capital, skills and social claims" (Frankenburg re: Barth 1966). These will vary according to environment and technology and, of course, according to what is regarded as "necessary": the notion presents the same difficulty as Malinowski's "basic needs". But for the moment let us assume the necessary resources to be six: the classical trio, Land, Labour and Capital (or their equivalents) are joined by Time, Information and Identity. Each can be used for or converted into the other. Work is then not only 'about' the production of material goods, money transactions and the need to grow food and to cook the family dinner. It must equally be 'about' the ownership and circulation of information, the playing of roles, the symbolic affirmation of personal significance and group identity — and the relation of each of these to the other.

Value

Each system of work involves the management of resources and the ascription of value to those resources. These two processes are ultimately what work is about. Its value may be assessed in social, personal or economic terms and measured by moral or material criteria. Nor are the weights of these values fixed: the relative value of any resource depends on what it is being measured against; its converted value on the technical processes applied to it; its added or "surplus value" on the structure and state of the market (see Firth, this volume). None of these value dimensions is autonomous: in any one system, the value of particular forms or aspects of work, even of work itself, depends on other elements in that system. This is as true for individuals as for social forms. The extent to which a person values one kind of work above another depends not only on the values of the society in which he lives, but on other things happening at the time — other options, other constraints, other obligations. The evaluation of work therefore changes with historical and social context but also with personal circumstances. It is necessary to be clear whose evaluation is at issue, the context to which it pertains, what *kind* of evaluation it is — whether the criteria used are economic or social or personal, and what dimension of work is the focal point of assessment.

Even from the limited evidence of this volume it is obvious that the variation of value across cultures is very great and that both the concept and the value of work change with historical, technical and social process in particular cultures (Cohen, Firth, Gudeman, Parkin, G. Mars, Ortiz, Schwimmer, Searle-Chatterjee, this volume). Changes in the relations, the means and the techniques of production and distribution affect relations between worker and work, worker and product, skill and status, means and ends, incentive and effort "on the ground", and must affect the organisation and evaluation of various forms of livelihood (Wadel, this volume).

But the evaluation of work will vary within one culture at a single point in history as well as between cultural systems. A number of reasons for internal variation can be designated. Firstly, whatever the central measure of work, the assessment of efficiency, productivity, worthiness, value itself, must depend on where, in any system, the actor sits. This is most obviously crucial because structural or status position governs the resources at his/her disposal. It is also crucial because the assessment of values is an assessment of *relative* worth. The value that I put upon my work is in some part a function of what else I could be doing; what I see others doing; what I expected to be doing at or by this time; what I expect to do next year; whether my position has changed and whether that change is for the better (Harrison, Fagin, this volume; Wallman 1977, 1979a); whether I am prepared to sweat for the sake of my own or my children's future benefit, or I must have my returns *now* (compare e.g. Kosmin 1979 with Willis 1977). Migrants in any system are said to work harder and to put up with conditions that no indigenous worker would tolerate, exactly because they tend to be future oriented and to see conditions "away", however inhospitable, as somehow better than conditions at home (Murray, Parkin, this volume; Wallman 1979b). All these values are governed by other things happening, or more directly, by what particular categories of people know about or think about what is happening. The (relative) value of work is therefore a function of its *opportunity costs*. What am I giving up to achieve this end? And of its *alternative costs*. How else could I achieve it? Could anyone else do it for me? One recent study used this last notion as the defining feature of work itself. It is called "the third person criterion": if I could pay someone else to do this task, then this is *work* . . . (Hawlyryshyn 1978). This definition does not fit the frame of this volume, but it does indicate that, insofar as the value of work depends on what else one could be doing it is a function of information systems and creative imagination as well as of the strictures of power and competition (Gudeman, Loudon, this volume).

Secondly, endogenous valuations of work will vary because work is not always assessed by comparable elements in the work process. This may be because not all the possible dimensions pertain to every kind of work — certainly not to all "occupations": most work can be assessed by the value of its product, but the products of social workers, service employees and politicians are always intangible and commonly without cultural definition. These products in effect depend on a recipient client in order to exist at all: in a system of work in which a person *qua* client is "the thing worked on", the value of the work depends not only on the client's assessment of its success, but even more fundamentally on his playing of the client's role (Fred, G. Mars, L. Mars, Wadel, this volume). Sometimes one dimension of work is subsumed in or identified with another (Gudeman, this volume). Some evaluations, apparently for no systematic reason, focus on one aspect of work to the exclusion of others — on the performance rather than the product; on the product's beauty or efficiency rather than on the time or the energy invested in its making (compare Ortiz, Schwimmer with Harrison, all this volume).

Thirdly, work is, even in a single culture. not always evaluated by the same criteria. This may be because the different kinds of work are so unlike: subsistence work and social work, artistic work and drudgery, marriage and management are comparable but not similar activities. More important, the ordinary anomalies of the system can only be made tolerable by the shifting of values. This can be achieved by denying the moral contradictions of everyday life and concentrating on the "higher" and more cohesive values of ideology or tradition (Cohen, Gudeman, Loudon, Schildkrout, this volume). Sometimes contradictions are built into the organisation of the work process itself and the shift of values occurs in a tidy cycle over predictable periods of time (G. Mars, L. Mars, this volume). Since different kinds of value pertain to different contexts, contradictions are resolved to the extent that the context of valuation can be clearly bounded and held distinct. There are numerous cases in which economically worthless work is personally highly valued (Cohen, Schwimmer, this volume), or socially despised tasks are a source of personal pride and identity (Searle-Chatterjee, this volume). Similarly the fact that works of art and ritual performances are neither useful nor negotiable in exchange does not preclude their being of immense personal or social worth (Murray, Schwimmer, this volume).

Time

The concept and value of work vary according to when it is done: "overtime" can be paid at the value of "time-and-a-half" only if it has been agreed that a specific quantity of time is worth more at particular moments in the daily, weekly or annual cycles (L. Mars, this volume). On a different time dimension, personal age or "time of life" is pertinent too, in two respects. One is that some tasks become easier with experience, others harder with age; it was observed in the conference discussion that activities designated pleasure and play in youth may turn, in time, into laborious obligations. The other is that the perception of amounts of time and so of time cost is not consistent throughout a lifetime: a young child feels the year between Christmases like a century; his grandmother insists that "the days drag and the years fly". The difference is due in some part to changes in biological process, but it must also reflect patterns of livelihood. In some cultures, at least in the performance of some tasks, no time cost is computed — i.e. time, *as such*, appears to have no value (Schwimmer, this volume. See also Wallman 1965, 1969). From this perspective the scope for using time as a measure of value in economic spheres without a money currency is very limited (see Belshaw 1954, and the discussion in Firth, this volume). Even where money values pertain, time and money belong to different work equations: work structures time; money rewards (some) work. Remember the unemployed man in Marienthal in the 1930s whose day had no time structure and so was "empty". Remember too that he reported talking to his wife as an obligation, along with waking his children for school, fetching wood and eating a midday meal (Jahoda *et al.* 1972: 68). It is as though, in the absence of formal employment, other activities took up the function of giving shape and purpose to his day — they "became work" — although not in this case satisfying work. We could argue that they already were "work" on the grounds that they were necessary to livelihood, but Wadel has demonstrated (this volume) that while the value of even the most essential tasks remains unacknowledged, "hidden", those tasks will not be dignified by the status of work and their performance will score no points, neither social nor existential, for the worker. We might also ask how and how far the various activities of livelihood can be computed along a single time dimension. Does less time spent at one mean more time available for another? How elastic is the time curve? Does the unemployed man at home *in fact* spend more time tending the garden or relating to his wife and children than he did when he had a job which kept him out of the house all day? (Fagin, this volume).

Levels of energy govern both the perception and the productivity of time. These are not strictly a matter of kilo calories or kilo joules (*pace* Harrison, this volume). Consider: when my partner is away for days or weeks I have many more household tasks to perform. Logically, I must be "spending" his share of task time as well as my own. But if he is absent I can spend no time at the work of relating to him. The balance of the day's work is therefore altered — more household tasks, less affective energy. The number of working *hours* in the day is not significantly changed. Do I spend more or less energy than usual? Do I have more or less to spend? At what point is the lack of emotional re-charge reflected in overt energy levels?

Ideally, if we want to know the relation between time and work we should know not only who does which necessary tasks and how long each takes, but also who chats to whom; how much time each parent spends (or thinks it spends?) with its partner, with each child . . . While X was doing the cooking or tending the garden, what else was happening (Schwimmer, this volume). It is not hard to ask an informant who plants the yams and who tends the garden. Should we not ask also who else was at home and what they were doing at that time?; and was anyone else in the garden, not helping with hoeing, but relating to the gardener? (Cohen, Firth, Loudon, Murray, Wadel, this volume).

Work in a sociable atmosphere or work which, while accomplishing

economically necessary tasks, also fulfills specific *social* obligations
— what Murray (this volume) has called "the work of custom" — is
in some languages distinguished from work which has no explicit
social dimension (e.g. Ortiz, this volume). Perhaps the distinction
signifies that the time spent on such work is doubly valuable,
much as the French talk of industrial overtime as extra quality
time because it occurs in what should be social periods (Grillo,
personal communication), and shift workers have peculiar wage
rates to compensate for "unsocial" hours — i.e. for timetables of
work which disrupt normal social life — although there is evidence
that shiftwork timetables actually increase the "social" options of
some categories of shiftworker (Clark 1979). Clearly the social
debits and credits accruing to time spent in particular forms of
work alter the value of that time and so the value of the work itself.

Place

Similarly it often matters very much *where* work is done. In some
cases the work is so closely identified with a particular place that
the place becomes the means of its performance (Gudeman, Cohen,
this volume). In others it is the purposes or the technicalities of the
work process which require particular *kinds* of setting: dockers
need ports (G. Mars, L. Mars, this volume), bureaucrats need
offices (Fred, this volume), farm labourers farms (Loudon), market
vendors markets (Schildkrout) and migrant wage workers need
industries to migrate to (Murray, Parkin, this volume). In this sense
some places are peripheral to the market nexus, although of course
the true measure of peripherality to any system is a measure of
distance from the centre of power (Murray, this volume). Sometimes
the jural right to work is restricted to particular places (Loudon,
Searle-Chatterjee, this volume), but legislation is not always a
necessary condition of labour immobility: workers made redundant
by the closing of mines or plants in one part of Britain are often
fiercely reluctant to move to work — even the same work — offered
elsewhere. In Melanesia, people are paid to do work outside the
village which they are not paid to do in it, but work outside they
do not control and cannot identify with (Schwimmer, this volume.
See Identity and Alienation below).

The most common evaluation of work by the place in which it is
done pertains to the place in which women most often work,
whether in "traditional" or "modern" societies: home-centred
work, household production and housework are defined by the
place of performance and are economically undervalued, sometimes
given no formal economic value at all (Murray, Schildkrout, Wadel,

this volume. See also Gershuny 1978). The same work performed outside the home is evaluated quite differently. Outworkers or home-workers are invariably paid below factory rates for doing essentially the same as factory work, yet for some the lower money returns of their work are more than compensated by social or cultural advantages accruing to staying at home (Saifullah Khan 1979). The fact that work is done outside one's *own* home also makes a difference to its value, even to the criteria by which it is evaluated. In this society cleaning and caring done by a woman in her own home are not formally paid tasks because they are not, in the terms of this society, "economic" (Wadel, this volume). The same tasks performed in someone else's home are evaluated like work done in a public institution. Similarly, Italian women find the political work that they do in other women's homes existentially more valuable than in their own (Piccone-Stella, personal communication).

Person

In the latter example most cogently it can be seen that the value of work also varies with the person of the worker. Some work is more highly valued when performed by one category of person than by another. It should go without saying that this is not always because the performance of the work, the quality of the product or the amount of time and energy invested in it differ. (See Harrison's reference to Brooke Thomas, this volume.) It is more often the (relative) value imputed to the worker which governs the (exchange) value attributed to the work (Firth, Loudon, Murray, Searle-Chatterjee, Schildkrout, this volume). Some work is appropriate only to particular kinds of people, either because the "real" requirements of its performance demand strengths, skills or talents that only they have, or because it is restricted by custom, by right or by obligation to particular social categories.

Specialisation on any basis is both a bind and a privilege. The right to work at a particular task fixes both identity and livelihood — however lowly the task or meagre the livelihood it provides. Two effects follow. One: a person identified with or by a particular kind of work cannot lose or change it without loss of social and psychic esteem. Both the reluctance of workers made redundant by changes in industrial process to re-train into other jobs of equal status and difficulty, and the existential trauma of retirement, whether from professional employment or agricultural labour, show this very clearly. Two: if no one else may or can do my work then I *must*. Exclusive right is also binding obligation. However exalted the work and the position of the worker in any hierarchy, this paradox of specialisation pertains. It is particularly important because readily overlooked as an aspect of the work of individuals or status groups at the top of hierarchies of privilege or power, and in the analysis of exploitation. In this volume, its effect is explicit in two discussions of the work roles of traditional rulers (Firth, Schwimmer, this volume), and in a sensitive and controversial exposition of relations between white farmers and black farm labourers in South Africa (Loudon, this volume).

People can be specialised into forms of work by very different criteria. Specialisation on the basis of physical characteristics like sex (see Murray, Parkin, Schildkrout, this volume and the extensive literature on the position of women), age (Schildkrout, this volume. See also La Fontaine 1978), and nationality, "race" or caste (Fred, Loudon, Murray, Searle-Chatterjee, this volume) seems most fundamental: specialisation or discrimination on these bases is indeed justified by "natural" laws of ability and appropriateness. But since much of the significance of physical characteristics is a function of the social status ascribed to them, changes in their significance do occur (as Wallman 1979a, 1978) – even to the extent that, in some contexts of time and place they count for nothing. They tend nonetheless to govern patterns of access to work: status ascribed by inheritance of one kind or another facilitates or restricts access to capital means of production (Cohen, Gudeman, Loudon, Ortiz, Schwimmer, this volume); to information essential to the getting or the performance of work (Fred, Gudeman, Loudon, G. Mars, L. Mars); to the necessary skills – whatever combination or training or talent they represent (Firth, Ortiz, Schwimmer, this volume); and even to work itself (Loudon, Murray, Searle-Chatterjee, Schildkrout, this volume).

The "causes" of a specialised division of labour are neither plain nor autonomous, but three degrees of constraint can be distinguished for the sake of analysis. The most stringent we may call *specialisation by decree*. Examples of this are less common than in previous centuries, but they are not made less appalling by anachronism. The conference included two papers dealing with different aspects of apartheid job reservation in southern Africa (Loudon, Murray, this volume) and two on the hereditary restrictions of caste in India (Parry, forthcoming; Searle-Chatterjee, this volume). These four cases demonstrate anomalies of hierarchy which call into question the possibility of the total constraint of work by decree, but the lack of flexibility in the *formal* structure of work is in all of them indisputable; it is outside or in cracks within the formal structure that individuals or groups find room for "informal" manoeuvre (Wallman 1979b). (Formal economics, we may note, does not or cannot adequately deal with systems of work that are not part of formal economic organisation. See Elkan, this volume). It might be expected that *specialisation by custom* would give the individual worker more scope, but in fact it does not. In the cogent case of women's work: even in settings which do not legislate against women in politics, banking or engineering, or forbid *by decree* their handling cattle, ploughing fields or slaughtering animals, social (or socio-biological?) forces designate categories of "women's work" and assume it specialised to women whatever the empirical evidence to the contrary. By a similar logic, when work which falls outside the customary frame of women's work is done by women, either the work or the sex of the worker can be conceptually and politically invisible (Murray, Parkin, Schildkrout, Searle-Chatterjee, Wadel, this volume. See also Wallman 1978). Given the power of custom and practice, the notion of *specialisation by choice* rings a trifle hollow. Nevertheless it is clear that individuals *do* choose the work they do, however limited the options open to them. They certainly can choose how well they do it (Cohen, Firth, Ortiz, Schwimmer, this volume) and how closely they identify with it (see Identity, below). The way in which a whole category of people becomes "by choice" specialised is less clear. Can we say that American blacks "chose" to become specialised as musicians and sportsmen? No measure of choice makes anthropological sense without reference to those elements of the social system which structure its scope.

Technology

The division of labour concept is useful to us only if we give it a time dimension, and if we recognise that labour is an expenditure of time and energy on all kinds of work — instrumental, social, symbolic, existential. Similarly a realistic assessment of the time values of work cannot be made without reference to the technology used in the performance of that work. This technology counts in a number of ways. The most obvious is the crudely instrumental: tools extend the efficiency or the energy of the worker; the better the tools the better the performance. A given piece of work done by hand costs so much time and energy, although these costs vary with the strength and the skill of the worker (Harrison, this volume). If a machine is bought to do the same task, (some) human energy is replaced by machine energy and the input of time is reduced. The scope for conversions of this sort is by definition extended by "advances" in technology, but it is not easy to calculate, even in a money economy. The debate between economists concerned to distinguish proportions of time and money spent on services rather than goods and on goods that are brought to replace services, and to use the ratios as indicators of "the future of work" in industrial society makes the difficulty plain (Gershuny 1978). In this line of argument the discussion of technology merges with the discussion of opportunity costs. It is not unreasonable to assume either that the first level explanation of any form of work (as of any other activity) lies in the relative costs and benefits of alternative forms (as Harris 1979), or that people will choose to do or to use what they think is best for them out of the options available at the time (as Barth 1966), but it should be noted that these arguments are circular unless dimensions of value are inserted (Paine 1974). What, otherwise, is the measure of "appropriate" technology?

Whether for this reason or by coincidence, none of the papers submitted to the A.S.A. Conference and presented in this volume makes technology central to the analysis of work: there is more frequent reference to the relations than to the means of production (but see Firth, Gudeman, Ortiz, Searle-Chatterjee, Schwimmer, this volume). Where objects of technology are at issue it is implied that they are not simply instruments of production or tools of work. Other meanings are ascribed to them: they have other uses. People define themselves as owners of particular tools or types of tool and they may identify with material items or technical processes as strongly as they do with places or people (Cohen, Gudeman, G. Mars, L. Mars, Ortiz, Searle-Chatterjee, this volume). Objections to changes in technology are not therefore explained by the fear of redundancy alone. A change in the technology used at work may constitute a change in and so a threat to the concept of self. Conversely people are not only "social" resources or the focus of affect in work systems. Exploitation consists in making people stand in for instruments in the production of "use values" (Firth, Ortiz, Schwimmer, this volume). Where the worker is converted into an item of technology, he can be said to be totally alienated from the work he does.

Identity and Alienation

The extent of individual or group identification with one kind of work or one aspect of work rather than another ultimately depends on the structure and the values of the society of which that work is a part. Since the social system is in process, so must be the identity investment in work. Some changes in identity patterns occur through historical time, usually following developmental changes in technology or organisation such that the economic value of particular forms of work is altered. Often there is a lag in the change. People may find the new forms threatening and so continue to identify with work that has lost economic significance (Cohen, this volume; Wallman 1977). Sometimes the significance of new forms of work is "hidden" by a general unwillingness to recognise that change has occurred (Wadel, this volume), or obscured by lack of definition (Fred, this volume): either way, such work will probably not "satisfy" the worker. The "identity crisis" of service workers whose economic role in late industrial societies has increased enormously over the last few years is a useful case in point.

Historical development apart, patterns of identification with work shift with changes in situation or circumstance. Total and unwavering identification with one kind of work must be rare, even for people whose caste identity might be expected to dominate their lives (as Parry, forthcoming; Searle-Chatterjee, this volume), or whose formal work obligations tend towards obsessive (Fred, Loudon, G. Mars, L. Mars, this volume). Where "over-identification" occurs in industrial society it is diagnosed as pathology: anyone too closely identified with work is "workaholic", bound to be neglecting other obligations (Wadel, this volume), and probably suffering from stress (Harrison, this volume). The normal balance in any society would seem to be a spread of identity investment across all of livelihood so that each role gets and gives its due. Very likely the balance is easier to maintain in those settings — usually smallscale but not necessarily rural — in which role frames tend to be overlaid and relationships "multiplex": a person brings all his identities to bear in each context, or finds them made relevant by others who "know all about him" willy-nilly (Firth, Gudeman, Ortiz, Schwimmer, this volume). In such settings the likelihood of *anomie* is remote; so is total identification with a single work role.

The reverse of identification with work or aspects of the work process is alienation from it (Schwimmer, this volume). Just as complete identification is unlikely, so is total alienation: logically it would mean the worker being — not just being treated like — a machine. Degrees of alienation are greatest where the worker has negligible control over the value and the disposition of his product, least where he initiates the work effort, organises time, place, person — all the elements of the work process, and can identify with the product and the values of the product.

The relationship of the worker to the product is most often used to assess the extent of his identification/alienation with work. The product, in effect, is a projection of the self, its value an extension of the value of the worker. If the product is taken from him, he loses part of himself and is presumably diminished unless that value is returned, perhaps in some other form, in exchange, or is replaced by the satisfaction of using it, or using it up (Firth, Ortiz, Schwimmer, this volume). It is difficult to generalise with any conviction since it is seldom clear how use value and exchange value are to be distinguished and who gets which (Firth, this volume); or which value the worker-as-producer is identifying with or alienated from (Schwimmer, this volume). Nor is it easy to say how far the value of the product is self-projected and independent of the assessments of others (Schwimmer, Wadel, this volume). It seems to matter whether the product is consumed directly or recycled in distribution — both for dock worker trade unionists (G. Mars, this volume), and for funeral priests in Benares (Parry, forthcoming). Perhaps it matters whether it is to be used for subsistence or for ceremony, at least to the extent that the worker may identify with more immediate returns if he is producing food for himself and his family and more deferred returns if he is producing it to placate the Gods. Murray (this volume) argues that so firm a distinction cannot be made since the two kinds of work are closely integrated, but whatever the analytic evidence it is likely that the worker identifies with one aspect over another in the course of any one transaction: however hard the early Protestants worked in this world, they identified with or were said to identify with the value of the reward they could expect in the next.

In all these cases the character of the product is important. Is it efficient or only beautiful? A work of art has no value in use and often as little in exchange, yet the artist identifies and is identified more strongly with his product than the producer of much more "valuable" items. Is the product tangible at all? The product of many kinds of work, even work in the narrow sense of occupation, is ephemeral. This is true of all services, brokerage and management, and of academic or intellectual pursuits (Piccone-Stella 1969; see also Schwimmer, this volume). The worker must therefore be identified with or alienated from other dimensions of the work process — with the personal satisfaction or the social rewards he gets for performing. Still he has no control over the value of such work; it cannot be self-projected because it depends on the evaluations of clients, audiences, customers. It is *their* work (Wadel, this volume). Perhaps for this reason those whose product is not subject to standardised evaluations are most likely to feel ambivalent about identifying with the work they do, or with social assessment of it (Fred, Loudon, Schwimmer, Wadel, this volume).

An alternative may be to identify with a generalised status or lifestyle: the efforts of white collar workers to preserve differentials of salary and patterns of consumption are made unusually desperate by the fact that their occupations have no explicit locus of identity. In the terms of this volume, they (therefore) identify more importantly with other kinds of work (Wadel, this volume). A similar adaptation would be one of the better possible outcomes of a future without jobs; there is no reason why the jobless could not build integrity and identity on the work of running a family and participating in community life, once these kinds of work were recognised to be socially and economically valuable. There is already massive evidence to show that some forms of "informal" economic activity fulfil these functions for some people (Elkan, this volume).

The individual can identify with a particular domain or sphere of livelihood and minimise or deny his investment in others; and he can shift his identity investment from one domain to the other according to the relative value of each, and to the opportunities and constraints of circumstance. The shift is easiest in "complex" industrial society where the domains of livelihood are curiously discrete. But each needs "work" if the composite identity structure of the individual is to be sustained: occupational status is not ascribed, it must be "achieved"; marriage must be "worked at"; concern should be "demonstrated". On the other hand, alienation in one sphere need not tarnish identity in another. An explicit illustration of this comes from a study of bread salesmen who "fiddle" on the job: " . . . what they do and how they feel at work has no relevance to the 'real me' that is constructed out of working hours" (Ditton 1977: 118).

Finally, the worker may identify with one dimension of the work which becomes for him its defining feature. Thus: Melanesians prefer to work "for nothing" in the village to doing exactly the same work "for money" outside: the work is defined by the place in which it is done (Schwimmer, this volume). Panamanian shifting cultivators (in one phase) identified pieces of land with the person who worked them and accordingly identified themselves with the means of production (Gudeman, this volume). Giriama fishermen, defining themselves in relation not to fishing but to wage work, identify with the predictability of cash returns as though the wages as such are their product and the locus of their identity (Parkin, this volume). And sweeping in Benares is only polluting if it is done for others; the work is defined not by the agent, but by the client or the consumer of its value (Searle-Chatterjee, this volume).

Domains, Spheres, Systems

A model of society as a single and notionally static structure is suited neither to the analysis of process occurring within that structure, nor to the unravelling of the organising principles by which that process is articulated (cf. Elkan, this volume). For our present purposes we need a model which allows us to recognise that not all the elements of systems of work are organised in the same way, for the same reason, or by using the same resources; and that each is nonetheless complementary to every other. Unless this logic is recognised, there is no way to account for the contradictions of behaviour and evaluation inherent even in those variations on the theme of work which make up this volume.

We have defined "work" as the production, management and conversion of the resources necessary to livelihood and constituted a rough list of six: land, labour and capital, time, information and identity. We have indicated that each resource may be assessed in terms of its economic, social or personal value, and that resource value is by no means a measure only of utility or material worth. Here enters the matter of spheres or domains — whether of activity, exchange or meaning — to which particular resources or kinds of resources pertain, and between which they can be transposed under particular conditions of constraint or opportunity.

In the first respect, systems of inheritance are cogent: certain kinds of resources are passed to one category of kin, other kinds of resources to others (see e.g. Leyton 1970). In some studies it is possible to follow the process by which a wholly new sphere of inheritance is generated by changes in economic production and opportunity (as Hill 1963). Similarly with ethnic niches: they are generated by the "arrival" of an economic opportunity which converts "cool" cultural variables or traditional loyalties into "hot" marketable economic resources (Wallman 1979b *passim*). In the second respect, the classic example is that of the man who makes himself a successful entrepreneur by converting status resources from the social sphere into economic resources in the business sphere (Barth 1963). Working the same theme we may add that he does so by managing, negotiating, investing in the sound information and good political connections entailed by his particular social position (see also Clark 1979a).

Distinctions between spheres (or domains) of activity, exchange or meaning, and "conversions" between resource systems are ultimately what work is 'about' from the perspective of social anthropology. No description of the control, evaluation or organisation of any dimension of work makes sense unless account is taken of its other dimensions and of other things happening in other domains of livelihood. This is never easy to do: the more complex the overall social system, the more diversified the spheres of work: it is impossible to take "everything" into account. A total system of work begins even before energy is expended and continues after production through distribution, consumption, reproduction — and so around again (cf. Harrison, this volume). Each of these papers can therefore be said to deal only with *particular* aspects of work — often on those which informants themselves observe most keenly, sometimes on anomalies raised by theoreticians; occasionally the preoccupations of the two coincide.

Some papers deal with the conceptual change of gear which accomplishes the shift from one domain to another: in these the articulation of spheres of resources is plainest. The examples are diverse: a man unemployed in the formal economy may be paying his bills on the dole, defining himself by growing roses, and at last have the time to be productively involved in local politics (Wadel, this volume; Marsden and Duff 1975). The commercial work of Muslim girls in Kano is defined apart from the personal domain in which the principal incentive to work is a good marriage. The chances of making such a marriage are enhanced by money, but the activity of making money is itself unacceptable. The contradiction of value is contained only because the distinction between the commercial and personal domains is held firm (Schildkrout, this volume). The move up a Union hierarchy in Newfoundland also involves shifting between different domains of value — here the moral and the legal — but in this case the boundary is imperfect: behaviour in one is invariably tainted by contradictory behaviour in the other (G. Mars, this volume). This "no win" outcome may be typical of "democratic hierarchies" in which the aspirant to office or occupation cannot avoid contravening important values either way (Fred, G. Mars, L. Mars, this volume). Some systems deliberately compensate the worker for bad conditions or low status by paying him disproportionately high wages or allocating special areas of autonomy (G. Mars, this volume), i.e. a negative value in the personal sphere is recompensed by a positive economic good — although neither economic compensation nor power seem to reduce the physiological stresses entailed by alienation (Harrison, Loudon, this volume). Satisfactory identity in another domain apparently does: sweepers in Benares do not identify with the polluting aspects of their occupational role but with the strength and courage that are said to be characteristic of the caste (Searle-Chatterjee, this volume). In the same analysis lowly status itself brings at least bargaining power since no one else will do such lowly work. Garbage collectors in the United Kingdom and in Benares have this backhanded power in common, despite the fact that their lives are very different in most other respects.

The domain of work with which a person identifies is, as we have noted, not consistent. Even less is it predictable: he who makes good money as a fisherman may prefer to define himself as a crofter (Cohen, this volume), or as a wage worker (Parkin, this volume). Wage work itself is alienating insofar as it involves being controlled by others, outsiders (Murray, Schwimmer, this volume), but it is a locus for identity insofar as it assures a regular cash income and allows planning for and control over the future (Parkin, this volume). It is the domain of work over which the worker has or thinks he has most control that seems to become the focus of his most positive identity. If he is in control of nothing, then he is totally alienated. The unemployed man who appeared earlier in this section will come apart if he has no control over the paying of his bills, no roses to grow, no community to join – if all his resource systems are in the single domain of formal employment.

The fourteen papers which make up the body of this volume are presented here in the order in which they are delivered. The first three (L. Mars, Schildkrout, Loudon) were grouped as *Systems of Organisation and Authority*; the next four (G. Mars, Fred, Firth, Ortiz) as *Systems of Value and Values*; the following three (Gudeman, Cohen, Searle-Chatterjee) as *Systems of Identity* (Parry's paper, which is to appear elsewhere, was delivered in this session); and the final set of four under the title *Concepts of Work*. The groupings were to some extent arbitrary; all the papers inform each of the topics in some way. The significance of work in each case is a function of the proportions of time and energy spent on all kinds of work; of the balance of values – instrumental, social, symbolic, existential – by which work is measured; and of the systems of production, access, distribution and consumption which determine who gets what.

References

Barth, F. 1963. Introduction to *The role of the entrepreneur in northern Norway*. Oslo: Scandinavian University Books.
——— 1966. *Models of social organization*. R.A.I. Occasional Paper No. 23. London: Royal Anthropological Institute.

Barth, F. 1967. Economic spheres in Darfur. In Firth (ed.) 1967, cited.

Belshaw, C. 1954. *Changing Melanesia*. Melbourne: OUP.

Beynon, H. and Blackburn, R.M. 1972. *Perceptions of work: variations within a factory*. Cambridge Papers in Sociology No. 3. C.U.P.

Clark, D. 1979a. Politics and business enterprise: limits on the scope of ethnicity. In Wallman (ed.) 1979b, cited.

—— 1979b. Production workers on shifts: ethnic difference in South London. *New Community* (forthcoming).

Cohen, P. 1967. Economic analysis and Economic Man: some comments on a controversy. In Firth (ed.) 1967, cited.

Ditton, J. 1977. *Part time crime: an ethnography of fiddling and pilferage*. London: Macmillan.

Firth, R. (ed.) 1967. *Themes in economic anthropology*. ASA Monograph 6. London: Tavistock.

Flett, H. 1979. Bureaucracy and ethnicity: notions of eligibility to public housing. In Wallman (ed.) 1979b, cited.

Frankenburg, R. 1966. British community studies: problems of synthesis. In *The social anthropology of complex societies*. ASA Monograph 4, M. Banton (ed.). London: Tavistock.

Gershuny, J.I. 1978. *After industrial society: the emerging of a self-service economy*. London: Macmillan.

Godelier, M. 1972. *Rationality and irrationality in economics*. London: NLB.

Harris, M. 1979. *Cultural materialism: the struggle for a science of culture*. Westminster, Maryland: Random House.

Harrison, R. 1976. The demoralising experience of prolonged unemployment. *Department of Employment Gazette*, London: April, 339–48.

Hawlyryshyn, O. 1978. *The measurement of household production*. Ottawa: Statistics Canada.

Hill, P. 1963. *The migrant cocoa farmers of southern Ghana*. Cambridge: C.U.P.

Jahoda, M., Lazarsfeld, Paul F. and Zeisel, Hans. 1972. *Marienthal: the sociography of an unemployed community*. London: Tavistock.

Klein, L. 1976. *New forms of work organisation*. Cambridge: C.U.P.

Kosmin, B. 1979. Exclusion and opportunity: traditions of work among British Jews. In Wallman 1979b, cited.

La Fontaine, J.F. (ed.) 1978. *Sex and age as principles of social differentiation*, ASA Monograph 17. London: Academic Press.

Leyton, E. 1970. Spheres of inheritance in Aughnaboy. *American Anthropologist* 72, 1378–88.

Marsden, D. and Duff, E. 1975. *Workless: some unemployed men and their families*. Harmondsworth: Penguin.

Nadel, S.F. 1957. *The theory of social structure*. London: Cohen and West.

Paine, R. 1974. *Second thoughts about Barth's models*, R.A.I. Occasional Paper No. 32. London: Royal Anthropological Institute.

Parry, J.P. forthcoming. In *Man*.

Piccone-Stella, S. 1969. Rapports sugli intellettuali italiani: le condizioni di lavoro. *La Critica Sociologica* **10**, Summer.

Sahlins, M. 1974. *Stone age economics.* London: Tavistock.

Saifullah Khan, V. 1979. Work and network: South Asian women in South. London. In Wallman (ed.) 1979b, cited.

Terkel, S. 1977. *Working.* Harmondsworth: Penguin.

Wadel, C. 1973. *"Now, whose fault is that?" the struggle for self-esteem in the face of chronic unemployment.* St. Johns, Newfoundland: Memorial University I.S.E.R.

Wallman, S. 1965. The communication of measurement in Basutoland. *Human Organisation* **24**, 236–43.

—— 1969. *Take out hunger: two case studies of rural development in Basutoland*, L.S.E. Monographs No. 39. London: Athlone.

—— (ed.) 1977. Introduction to *Perceptions of development.*Cambridge: C.U.P.

—— 1978. Epistemologies of sex. In L. Tiger and H.P.T. Fowler (eds.), *Female hierarchies.* Chicago: Aldine.

—— 1979a. Refractions of rhetoric: evidence for the meaning of 'race' in England. In *Politically speaking*, R. Paine (ed.) (forthcoming).

—— (ed.) 1979b. Introduction to *Ethnicity at work.* London: Macmillan.

Willis, P. 1977. *Learning to labour.* Farnborough: Saxon House.

VIEWS FROM THREE OTHER DISCIPLINES:

(i) ECONOMICS: WALTER ELKAN

Almost everything in economics to do with work can be fitted into one of three categories. First, the relationship between work and output. Secondly, being in or out of work, i.e. being employed or unemployed. Thirdly, the allocation of time between work and leisure and the economic factors which determine it.

Between them, these three categories comprise almost the whole of economics, because economics is centrally concerned with output and how more of it could be produced and with how what is produced is distributed or allocated to those who have participated in the process — i.e. *worked* or facilitated more productive work for others.

In this sense one might argue that whereas in social anthropology and in the other social sciences work is one of several concerns — which also include kinship, political organisation, religion, magic and so forth, for economics work is the core or central concern, albeit sometimes fairly remotely as when we occupy ourselves with forecasting — a very popular pre-occupation at present and perhaps more properly the pursuit of those interested in magic than in economics, but too profitable to be easily abandoned!

I want briefly to look at these three categories which most directly bear on work, to try to give some idea of the sort of questions economists ask. The relationship between work and output was virtually the starting point of economics. Adam Smith's *Wealth of Nations* was primarily concerned with the conditions under which a given number of people would produce more or less, or would work more or less productively. Today, economists are inclined, wrongly, to put the major stress on how much equipment and other forms of capital goods people have at their disposal in finding the explanation for different degrees of productivity. Adam Smith placed much more emphasis on having a framework of institutions, as well as attitudes, which maximised the effort people were willing to make by linking the rewards for effort closely to

what they contributed to output. The failure in the low income
countries today to increase output proportionately to capital
investment and accumulation has caused many of us to go back to
Adam Smith for instruction. People will work harder and produce
more if the rewards accrue to *them* rather than their landlords or
the State, and that often implies reform of the terms on which land
is held, and of the system of taxation rather than the application
of more machinery and equipment, or, what we call 'capital
formation'. In Britain today, too, it is commonly said that output
is failing to increase because of lack of capital formation
in manufacturing industry, whilst manifestly the real problem is
deliberate and conscious restriction of output either for lack of
buyers or through restrictive practices on the part of employees,
or lack of incentive to work more, or just plain demoralisation,
boredom or idleness – call it what you will. Most economists are
frightened to say outright that the reasons why the Germans
produce more than the British is that they work harder, and likewise that the Chinese in Hong-Kong, Singapore and Taiwan are
making much greater progress than are India or Bangladesh,
because the former are more hard-working. That is either a
racialism and therefore not kosher or it is a 'sociological factor'
requiring sociological or anthropological methods of investigation,
and therefore not the proper study of economics. Unfortunately
for economists, the other social sciences are not always prepared
to pick up the tasks allotted to them by economists, as they may
have other interests to which they attach greater importance.
Areas crucial for economics therefore remain insufficiently
researched.

The second category of economics concerned with work covers
employment issues:– being in or out of work, employed or unemployed or, as we must increasingly think of it, being or not
being 'gainfully occupied'. This comprises the whole field of macro-
economics that made Keynes famous. Keynes showed that the
heavy *un*employment which prevailed between the wars could be
overcome by more appropriate Government policies. It remains
the principal piece of economic apparatus that we have for
explaining fluctuations in employment though it no longer does
so satisfactorily. The trouble is that we have become so mesmerised
by the torrent of official statistics that now deluges us, that we
never enquire whether the greatly increased unemployment that
they have recorded in recent years actually exists other than in the
official statistics. We might learn here from the Third World countries.
It used to be thought that there was large-scale urban unemployment

in the Third World — 20%—30% were often quoted — because one knew that the towns were growing rapidly and that enumerated or recorded employment was not. From this it seemed reasonable to infer that the difference between the two sets of figures constituted the unemployed. It never occurred to anyone to ask how all those unemployed were supporting themselves in countries lacking government social security provisions. The question was brushed aside with vague references to the extended family and going to sponge on more fortunate relatives already there, who had the luck to have a job. The most elementary arithmetic should have disclosed that there was 'no way' (as Americans say) that the rapidly increasing numbers in the towns could be thus accommodated and absorbed! It was that which eventually led to the recognition that there was something which was then labelled the Informal Sector — and which provides large numbers with work. The Informal Sector — for those who are not familiar with this term — is simply the myriad of very small scale activities — making simple furniture or paraffin lamps from re-cycled scrap materials, hawking, carrying water from the stand-pipe to peoples' homes, or carrying the people themselves by rickshaw or rickety old taxi to where they want to go, selling charcoal for cooking, repairing bicycle punctures, shining shoes, begging for old clothes to flog them to the poor, plus activities of a rather different kind such as petty thefts, illegal distilling and commercial sex. In all these ways and hundreds of others people earn money:— they are 'gainfully occupied' to use the old-fashioned but very apt term that has been used in English population censuses since they first began in 1801. In the advanced industrial countries, as we call them, earning a living has come to be regarded as virtually synonymous with being employed, and if some-one is *not*, then it is assumed that he must be *un*employed. The trouble is that the international transfer of categories can be dis-astrously misleading, and we have here an excellent example of a case in point. If one insists on using the distinctions 'employed or unemployed', and thinks of being employed as having a job that pays a wage or salary, then one is looking at one world through the conceptual categories of another. We have, of course, always known of, and recorded the existence of the *self*-employed — doctors, architects, shopkeepers and farmers. But they have seemed to become an unimportant minority of no great economic significance, and so we forget our own past and instead we view Third World societies through what are for them largely irrelevant statistical distinctions. The German words *Arbeiter* and *Arbeit* have at least the advantage of reminding one that being employed has something to do with work which the words employment and unemployment do not. Hence my preference for 'gainfully occupied'.

This brings me back to my starting point, which was unemployment in our own country and other advanced industrial countries. Is it actually true, as I suggested a moment ago that in the advanced industrial countries, earning a living has come to be virtually synonymous with being employed? Clearly not. Here too we have been mesmerised by official statistics and ignored the new reality that now stares us in the face, viz. that large numbers now earn a living in not dissimilar ways from those which are described as the Informal Sector in Third World countries, except that what takes place is altogether more sophisticated and productive. We call it moonlighting or the Hidden Economy, to use the title of an admirable study by the Outer Circle Policy Unit, or the 'black' economy. It ranges from the plumber or electrician who puts a card through your letter box via the mini-cab driver to the surgeon who prefers to be paid in cash. There may however be a crucial difference between the Informal Sector of the Third World and our own Hidden Economy. The latter has probably grown up largely in order to avoid income tax and social security contributions, both of which now make heavy inroads into declared incomes. Also to supplement unemployment benefits. Victor Keegan of *The Guardian* (28/3/1979) reported recently that Marks & Spencer had been puzzled by booming sales in areas of high unemployment and found on further investigation that many of the registered unemployed were substantially supplementing their unemployment and supplementary benefits by earnings in the Hidden Economy. Indeed, Sir William Pile, Chairman of the Inland Revenue Board told a House of Commons Committee a week or two ago that it was "not implausible" that the amount of output produced in the Hidden Economy amounted to 7½% of the total output of the economy, or GNP. In Italy the figure is thought to be much higher. The chief executive of Fiat is reported to have said that he thought GNP would be 30% greater than the official estimate if the Hidden Economy were added (*The Guardian* 4/4/1979).

It is generally assumed that the Hidden Economy exists because people prefer the greater risks of self-employment to the certainty of high deductions from their pay packets. It is quite possible however that we have exaggerated the tax and social security reasons for its existence and that people may in any case prefer to work 'for themselves' and now increasingly have the opportunity to do so in many parts of the country. It is further assumed that the Hidden Economy, whilst sizeable in the numbers who are

engaged in it, produced much less per person than the Open
Economy. Even if not all the unemployed are actually unemployed
in the sense in which they manifestly *were* between the Wars, they
are said to be engaged in activities of much lower productivity than
those who have a regular job. Even that may be a myth. The assumption rests on the tenet that production per man in a factory with a
lot of machinery or other equipment must be much higher than
production per man with no more than a set of tools. This ignores
two relevant facts which few would dispute. First that in British
industry there is gross over-manning of which, of course, the
reciprocal is rather low output per man. Whether one takes the
overmanning from statistical comparisons with industry in other
countries, or from watching Peter Sellers in *I'm Alright Jack* is
immaterial, but output per head in manufacturing industry and
most other parts of the Open Economy is low. The other relevant
fact is that people working 'for themselves' (as they say) work
infinitely harder, for longer hours and for many more days in the
year. It is therefore by no means to be *assumed* that those in the
Hidden Economy are necessarily less productive. We have all seen
houses painted — and *well* painted and at breathtaking speed, by
people who have neither a bank account nor a VAT registration
number. In the Open Economy the pace tends to be altogether
slower.

Someone may well retort that there is a crucial difference
between the Informal Sector and the Hidden Economy in that the
latter comprises a great many for whom earnings in the Hidden
Economy are a supplement rather than an alternative to regular
wage employment. Dustmen who finish work at 11 and drive
mini cabs for the rest of the day are the popular and topical example.
But that is also true of the urban and rural informal sectors in the
underdeveloped countries. Activities in all countries are a good
deal easier to classify than people who have an awkward propensity
to move about from one activity to another in ways that defy
statistics, and especially official statistics.

That brings me to my third and last category of economics as it
relates to work: the allocation of time between work and leisure.
For the sake of simplicity economists have tended to assume that
people divide their time between these two and that time not
spent at work was leisure. We have then gone on to postulate that
to varying degrees people prefer leisure to work and need therefore to be induced to work. Years ago it was alleged that there was
a crucial difference between Western, Protestant, White men and
the rest, in that when offered higher pay, the former would work

harder and longer and more people would seek work whilst the latter had a high leisure preference and very limited wants, so that the sooner these wants were satisfied the sooner people would knock off from work. Higher wages or higher prices for produce, would simply cause fewer people to work for fewer hours for fewer months. We now know that this is no more true in the underdeveloped countries than elsewhere.

The dichotomy between work and leisure was intended to facilitate analysis of the effect of wage changes or tax changes on the number of hours people are prepared to work. But even that dichotomy may prove to be a mirage, if what people do when they go home from their wage jobs is *not* to engage in leisure, but either to continue work in the Hidden Economy or to 'do it yourself', i.e. to do at home what they can no longer afford to have done for them by specialist painters, plumbers, electricians, builders, car mechanics and so forth. The latest round of the General Household Survey reveals that two thirds of all men between the ages of 25 and 44 engage in Do It Yourself activities (Frances Cairncross, *The Guardian* 29/3/1979.) On Hidden Economy activities it is of course silent.

To conclude: economics is centrally concerned with work, but as with other disciplines, we have sometimes been a little slow in accommodating our analytical framework to changing circumstances. The fundamental concepts of economics can however be very powerful in explaining phenomena and in solving problems when we take care to look at them unblinkered by preconceptions.

VIEWS FROM THREE OTHER DISCIPLINES:

(ii) PSYCHIATRY: LEONARD FAGIN

Our interest in this field stems from a current project studying the effects of unemployment on family life. Working as a psychiatrist, I have observed the distress and major upheavals caused by unemployment and have been surprised at the lack of interest that the medical profession has given to this topical issue. But then, few in our profession bridge the gap between socio-political reality and health. Although some studies have described the psychological 'stages' individuals go through in chronic unemployment (Eisenberg *et al.* 1938; Hill 1977) few researchers have recently looked at families of the unemployed.[1] In my clinical experience I have seen that not only does unemployment have a major effect on family relationships, but also that the changes it provokes are of a permanent nature and sometimes transmitted across generations. This is particularly observed in those families where the working husband exerts his authority through the family's financial dependency on him. When he becomes unemployed the family responds with dramatic role changes (e.g. wife becoming more assertive in decision making) which will not be relinquished even if the husband regains employment (see Komarovsky 1940).

From the psychological viewpoint, unemployment is a crisis. The individual and the family are faced with a previously unencountered situation which requires that psychological adaptive mechanisms be set in motion (see Caplan 1964). The way in which it is handled will depend on the individual's coping abilities and experience in dealing with previous crises, the availability of alternative solutions present in his environment, and the extent of change produced by the new situation. Crises are usually seen as negative occurrences, but they can also be of a positive nature (such as promotion, a new relationship, a house move) which also test the capacity for resolution. Crises offer the individual an opportunity for personal growth if the end result is felt to be appropriate and enhancing, but they can also determine maladaptive responses with much personal

handicap and distress. In this sense, unemployment is by no means
necessarily a psychological 'evil'. On the contrary, many people on
losing a job are able to break from an alienating working life into a
productive and meaningful unemployed existence. It is not uncommon to find people saying that they only realised how they
detested work after they became unemployed. Work, therefore, is
of vital psychological importance, as is seen when it is lost through
unemployment. But what is it exactly that is lost? Or, more
precisely, how does work influence psychological and emotional
life?

In this paper I will attempt to describe some of the psychological
consequences of work. Work is here defined as all those activities
which an individual is involved in on a regular basis and for which he
receives direct financial reward. This usage approaches Prof. Elkan's
definition of work as "gainful employment". I am aware that some
of the contributors to this conference have broadened the term to
include the energy expended in maintaining social, familial and
political relationships, and even of identity structures as such, and
that even on the psychological level "unconscious work", as for
example, in the dream resolution of emotional conflict could be
fitted into a work rubric. But while an expanded meaning of work
has the advantage of giving relevance to the *affective* as well as the
physical aspects of virtually all spheres of life, it leaves us without a
frame of reference by which distinctions between work and rest
and leisure can be drawn. As I am concerned with the ways in which
work influences identity formation, time orientation and interpersonal relationships in London, I have found it necessary to
establish an arbitrary boundary on its definition: the "work" here,
refers to "a job", and pertains to formal employment in industrial
society. Even with these restrictions, the meaning of 'work' is
neither static nor universal.

Work as a Factor which Structures Personality

We use work to identify ourselves, as a calling card to the rest of the
world. In many ways, our personalities are intimately bound with
our work. When the possibility of choice exists, adolescents will
try to enter jobs which they consider complementary to the way
they see themselves (see Erikson 1956). Problems arise when this
self-perception or the job are, for example, idealised, leading to a
clash between real job requirements and individual limitations.

It is important to describe what, to coin a phrase, may be called
the 'psychopathology of work'. The working situation can complement and support personality features and vice versa. Some

obsessional qualities are of benefit if the job requires meticulous and repetitive checking of data (e.g. an archivist, proof-reader, ledger clerk).

Similarly, a tendency to be extrovert, manipulative and boisterous may be useful in the acting profession. Conversely, one sees the difficulties encountered by people who use their work to channel unresolved anxieties, which may not necessarily belong to the job, and which allows them temporarily to avoid painful issues. Many workers in the 'helping professions' disguise their own needs for affection and their hostile impulses in their jobs, sometimes leading to over-involvement or to harmful interactions with their clients. In terms of mental health and the job/personality fit, there is ample evidence that work can be 'therapeutic', just as it can be alienating and soul-destroying, especially if it is used as a psychological defence.

The personalities of individuals are also shaped by their work. This is seen not only by the changes that individuals go through as they adapt to their work, but also in their reactions as they move along the hierarchy. These changes may account for some of the homogeneity of personality types associated with a particular job and status, which are usually stereotyped by outside observers.

All these points probably apply more to the professional people and higher ranks of the working class than to semi-skilled or unskilled labourers for whom identification through the job is probably less important. Work, however, is also used to identify what one is not, and this determines role boundaries, group and class identities.

Work Determines the Quality and Intensity of Relationships

The work situation has an important influence on the quality of inter-personal relations. Sociological studies in different areas of production in an industrial setting show how within the same factory, the diverse working environments determine the quality of communication and bonds between workers (Seglow 1970). Family relationships are also affected, although less clearly, by the special tie between the worker and job. The role of 'breadwinner' has obvious psychological meaning for the family. It is not uncommon, as we have mentioned above, to see the financial standing of each individual in the family determining the quality of relationships and hierarchy within it. Families as a whole also use the work of the main breadwinner to identify themselves in the community, and many of the social ties are based on common work-identity. In small towns and villages, where employment is concentrated on one or two industries, the whole social relationship network is rooted in work experience.

Work also permits acceptable distancing. The temporary separation associated with work allows an emotional outlet in family relationships as well as providing other sources of interpersonal interaction. A common complaint from the wives of the chronic unemployed men is 'that they get under our feet!'

The Psychological Meaning of Work is in the Process of Continuous Change

The concept of work is not a well defined, rigid entity but dependent on the stages of personal development and society's historical moment. Work identity in this society is already established in school life, where obligation and tasks are set out by 'elders' which must be completed following determined criteria, and which later are rewarded or criticised (Neff 1968). At this stage, competitiveness is encouraged and work is not associated with survival but with achievement and progress. In adolescence, at the time of the first job, work is a step towards independence and identity formation. For the adult, work tends to be bound to family responsibilities and preparation for the future, and in this regard the financial reward can become as important as job satisfaction. Work, therefore, means different things at different times; its meaning is in a process of continuous change, sometimes imperceptible, sometimes with marked fluctuations, sometimes occupying peripheral importance, at others in the centre of the emotional stage.

This dialectical model of work, as seen by each individual, is influenced by the social, political and economic reality, by the traditional and moral values attached to work by his own culture. Nothing more graphic than this is seen in countries at war or in the process of revolutionary change, where the concept of work transcends its restricted meaning to become a collective endeavour with communal goals. Work here becomes identified with the individual's contribution to change, and fervour and self-sacrifice is given without consideration. In our own society, in economic recession and with an increasing number of unemployed, the financial aims take priority, a job becomes 'only a job' and the individual prevents himself from establishing emotional ties with his work as he is always in danger of losing it.

Work Structures Psychological Time

A usual feature of prolonged unemployment is the sense of timelessness, empty periods which are blotted out by excessive sleep or dissociation from external events. Work organises time, giving it structure and organising it in relatively well-defined compartments of work and leisure. When at work or in any form of activity, time is felt to 'fly by' while in enforced inactivity it drags on: there is social pressure to 'fill it and to occupy one's time constructively'. In some of the unemployed families we have interviewed, whole days are forgotten; there is nothing in them to remember them by.

Work Gives Meaning to Leisure

The concept of control seems to be psychologically crucial when one is looking at the distinction between work and leisure. What appears to be characteristic of leisure is the feeling of greater control over one's activity. Whether this is corroborated or not in reality, there is an assumption that leisure implies doing what one wants to do, whatever the external restrictions imposed on one's 'free time'. One deduces from this that in work one hands over control over activities to other agencies. Is this a characteristic of exploited labour in capitalist societies or does this remain constant in societies with different economic structures? And does the distinct difference between work and leisure disappear when control is in the hands of the worker?

What appears to be clear is that the psychological value and meaning of leisure in our own society depends on how the individual relates to his work. Leisure must be distinguished from non-work (for example the enforced inactivity seen in some people due to unemployment, old age or disability). In this there is a total loss of control over one's activities, with the resulting inability to master any situation, inducing lethargy and hopelessness.

From this it becomes evident that work does not imply a total loss of control, but is more like an exchange. The control over one's work is sacrificed to obtain in return financial gain which offers the possibility of control over one's leisure and future. With increasing unemployment, shorter working hours and technological advances, leisure is a topic in the near rather than distant future. How man uses and relates to his leisure time is an important field for anthropological as well as psychological research (Fagin 1978).

In this short paper there is an obvious gap. The psychological essence of work is not fully discussed, only hinted at. The question, 'Why do people work?' is a complicated one to answer, if one leaves aside issues of physical survival. We are only able, for the moment, to approach what work means to individuals and their families by observing its effect on their lives and their views of the world surrounding them. What is clear is that, in our society at least, work is central to both these issues.

Notes

1. Notable exceptions to this neglect are the superbly detailed studies of an unemployed community by Marie Jahoda and others (1933), the family relationship study by Komarovsky (1940) and more recently the vivid sociological descriptions by Marsden and Duff (1975).

References

Caplan, G. 1964. *Principles of preventive psychiatry*. New York: Basic Books.

Eisenberg, P. and Lazarsfeld, P. 1938. The psychological effects of unemployment. *Psychological Bulletin* **35**, 358–390.

Erikson, E.M. 1956. The problem of ego identity. *Am. J. of Psychoanalysis* **4**, 56–121.

Fagin, L. 1978. The psychology of unemployment. *Medicine in Society* **4**, 2.

Hill, J.M.M. 1977. The social and psychological impact of unemployment. *Tavistock Institute of Human Relations*. London.

Jahoda, M. *et al.* 1933. *Die Arbeitslosen von Marienthal*. Leipzig: Hirzel. (Repr. as *Marienthal: sociography of an unemployed community*. London: Tavistock, 1972.)

Komarovsky 1940. *The unemployed man and his family*. Dryden Press.

Marsden, D. and Duff, E. 1975. *Workless: some unemployed men and their families*. Harmondsworth: Penguin.

Neff, W.S. 1968. *War and human behaviour*. New York: Atherton Press. Quoted in M. Argyle (1972) *The social psychology of work*. Harmondsworth: Pelican.

Seglow, P. 1970. Reactions to redundancy: the influence of the work situation. *Industrial Relations Journal* **1** (Pt. 2), 7–22.

VIEWS FROM THREE OTHER DISCIPLINES:

(iii) BIOLOGICAL ANTHROPOLOGY: G. AINSWORTH HARRISON

I find it very formidable to address a meeting of social anthropologists after a long career in biological anthropology, or
physical anthropology as some of you may know it. This is the
first occasion that I have been called upon to speak professionally
to social anthropologists. It actually represents some liberalization
of social anthropology and some liberalization of biological
anthropology. One hopes it is a joint movement in the same
direction.

The two aspects of work that I would like to present to you
as a biological anthropologist are firstly: that area of biological
anthropology which is concerned with bio-energetics − which I
would call, rather naively, a sort of economic model; and
secondly, the area of associations between various aspects of
lifestyle and occupation or work and health and well being. I
have more firsthand experience with the latter than with the
first.

There is, in biological anthropology, a growing interest in the
energetics of work. And to a biological anthropologist I think
"work" would be defined simply as the expenditure of energy.
Any form of energy expenditure is a form of work. In this sense
the only time that we stop working is when we die because it
requires work just to keep alive − that is to say it requires an
energy expenditure. For an adult male of average size, about
70 kilo calories per hour are required just to keep alive. There is
quite a lot of variation by age and by sex and size is critical,
but this sort of figure is the basal level. (I hope there are no
purists amongst you because if there are I should be speaking in
terms of *kilo joules* rather than *kilo calories*, but I think that
calories are more familiar to most people than joules.)

We obtain these figures for energy expenditure essentially by
a physiological means of indirect calorimetry; i.e. by the measurement of heat. Energy is ultimately reflected in heat and if we

could measure heat production during the course of different types of activity we would be measuring work. In fact heat production is difficult to measure, and what is formally measured instead is oxygen consumption because to burn things up to provide energy requires oxygen. So the traditional physiological way of measuring work is to measure oxygen consumption, and to measure the products of combustion — particularly carbon dioxide in exhaled air. That is the simple way that a biological anthropologist would go around measuring the amount of work that an individual undertakes.

As I said, even just sleeping or lying around requires about 70 kilo calories an hour. There is a broad spectrum of energy expenditure related to activity. Most of it is of course muscular activity. Walking involves an expenditure of about 110 kilo calories per hour. The most arduous tasks, things like chopping wood, cutting down a forest, cost about 450 kilo calories per hour.

Most activities lie between these limits. One can calorie cost every activity in which human beings are engaged, and indeed over the last ten or fifteen years or so, a very large number of activities have been so costed, particularly those that are concerned with primary production in traditional society. One important aspect of energy expenditure is the amount of energy that an individual has to expend to get more energy, the so-called productive ratio. This varies greatly by ecosystem and even more so by economy. To understand it fully one needs to measure not only energy expenditure but also energy production and energy consumption.

A number of studies have now been undertaken to ascertain energy ratios. One of the earliest was undertaken by Ronald Fox among Swidden Cultivators in the Gambia in the 1950s. In this study he did not make very precise measurements of energy expenditure and energy production, but he did observe food production throughout the year, and the comparative amount of energy expended on agriculture over the whole year too. He noted that in this particular Swidden society the maximum amount of work occurred at a time when there was the least amount of food. He observed in consequence that if you followed a characteristic, like body weight, throughout an annual cycle, there was a period when body weight continuously dropped for about six months because the population was in "negative energy balance". People were expending more energy on their activity than they had available to sustain it, and of course they were relying on stores of energy in their body, particularly on body fat. Then there was a period of affluence, when the harvest was in and there was relatively little activity, but an abundance of energy. At that time, body weight restored itself. That example very forcibly demonstrated that if you were examining work in any society which had this sort of seasonality to its food supply and to its activity, you could only get any real insight if you observed it over a full annual cycle. If you looked at only one time of the year, you might well get the impression that the population was achieving the impossible.

Since the pioneering work of Fox, many more sophisticated studies have been made. I would like to draw your attention to one by R. Brooke Thomas (1976), formerly of Pennsylvania State University, now of the University of Massachusetts, who did an extremely detailed energy flow study of Quechua Indians in the High Andes at Nuñoa in Peru. Thomas measured the amount of energy that is required by an average family, for cultivating cereals, for cultivating tubers, for herding sheep, and herding llamas and herding alpaca and so on; and also determined the calorie returns from these various activities. He further identified the strategies that the family can adopt at certain places in the flow system where they have the opportunity of choice. In many of the situations and procedures they do not have much choice at all; but whether, for example, people use dung for fertiliser or dung for fuel is open to choice on the part of the family and it has considerable economic consequences to that family. Likewise, the extent to which they invest in crops as against the extent to which they invest in pastoralism has implications, because the energy expanded in pastoralism gives a poor calorie return in itself, as compared with the investment in crops. However, they can export the animal products and, from the cash that they obtain from those exports, invest in high energy food crops of an agricultural kind. That is an important decision "available" to the family within this flow system.

One other point made in Brooke Thomas' article is relevant here. It concerns the energy expenditure of a boy involved in herding, and the energy cost of herding for a man. Apparently if a herd is less than a hundred animals a boy can do the work as well as an adult man. Brooke Thomas calorie costed all the activities of this herding and related them to a particular time budget, the amount of time spent in lying, sitting and standing, in walking moderately, walking up and down hills and so on. On this basis he showed that the energy cost for that herding was 685 kilo calories over an eight hour period for a boy, and for an adult man over the same period,

it was about 982 kilo calories. So the calorie cost of the job done by
a boy was only about two-thirds of the cost of the same job done
by a man. This he argues might be one of the reasons why large
families were desired amongst the Quechua.

I think that is probably the best model that has so far been
worked out in human biology, but a number of others are currently
underway. The reason for looking at human populations in this
context is that they clearly indicate the relationship of the human
individual, the human family or the human population with its
environment, within the framework of its particular technology.
They indicate the places where strategy decisions can be made and
where in effect the flow system can be changed or influenced, and
perhaps most meaningfully from the biological-anthropological
point of view they indicate the forms of direct or indirect competition which can occur between individuals or families and thereby
provide the sort of opportunities in which natural selection can act.
I do not mean by that to imply any genetic determination of these
capacities at all, though of course the genetic determination would
be a pre-requisite for their evolution.

That is as much as I feel I ought to say at this juncture about the
bio-energetic models. The other type of concern of biological anthropologists in work is, as I have said, in the associations, particularly
the lifestyle associations, which occur with particular occupations.
In these, we have tended to move from the traditional societies
where bio-energetic models are relatively simple — though complicated enough, and difficult enough in terms of man-power and
effort and cost — to societies more like our own. In our department
in Oxford, we have been concerned over the last two or three years
with examining the effects of different work patterns and different
occupations upon lifestyle and health in a group of Oxfordshire
villagers in the Otmoor region. It happens that amongst these
villagers there are approximately a third of the people still living
fairly traditional types of agricultural existences; about a third of
the people working as skilled and unskilled manual workers, many
of them in British Leyland for example; and the other third, amongst
the males anyway, tend to be professionals of one kind or another.
We have been doing a house-to-house study of this population,
attempting to examine all males and females between the working
ages of 16 and 65. The general framework of the study is to examine
the effects of lifestyle, particularly a job, upon three measures of
well-being. One is a morbidity history in a traditional medical sort
of way; the second is quality and quantity of sleep; the third is output of stress hormones, particularly the catecholamines noradrenalin

and adrenalin which are excreted in the urine. We have been collecting urine for such analyses.

So far, we have taken the analysis of sleep further than any other. In relationship to jobs, we have looked at the number of hours slept by individuals and also their perceived quality of sleep — whether they think it is very good, good, poor or very poor and so on. I can report to you a few of those findings. On the whole we find little relationship between sleep and people's perceived satisfaction levels with, for example, pay or hours of work. There is a slight relationship between sleep and the extent to which people think they enjoy their work, in that those who tend to dislike their work intensely, tend to sleep rather badly. If you look at the extent of what we call job or work attachment, we have asked people whether or not they would wish to change their particular job or specific things that they are doing in their work, or change their employer, or change the very type of work which they are doing, and indeed we find a relationship between the amount of sleep that a person has and their wish to change: if they wish to change their job, or if they wish to change their type of work they have fewer hours sleep than if they do not wish to change. Another measure of this is whether or not they have changed their job or their employer or their type of work. Again, those who have changed within the last twelve months tend to have fewer hours sleep than those who have not changed. We can combine these two characteristics — a wish to change and whether a change was actually made — into a fourfold comparison: those who have changed and would still wish to change, as compared with the other extremes of those who would not wish to change and have not changed. Again sleep hours show a profound relationship between the four categories. Those who have not changed their job or their employer or their type of work, sleep longer than those who have and would still wish to change. We have also looked at particular groups of people according to the environment in which they work. For example, people who work out of doors tend to sleep longer hours than do those who work indoors. Drivers of almost any category, whether they are sales representatives, or long distance lorry drivers, or whether they drive specialist vehicles off the road like JCB's and so on, tend to have short hours of sleep in the working week. There are quite a lot of very subtle relationships between job and the number of hours that are slept. I could go on with lots of other relationships that we found between sleep hours and forms of life-style, but they are not specifically connected with work and therefore not relevant here.

Just to conclude, if I have not already taken too much time, we have done a provisional analysis on stress hormones, as excreted in the urine, and find that on weekends (on non-working days), people who are manual workers and people who are non-manual workers excrete similar levels of adrenalin and noradrenalin. But on work days, in the midday sample and in the evening samples, non-manual workers excrete very significantly higher levels of adrenalin than do manual workers. If you use these stress hormones as a measure of occupational stress, then you may conclude that the non-manual workers are more "stressed" in the course of their working day than are the manual workers.

I have already taken up too much of your time, but I have tried to summarise two of the main interests in work in biological anthropology.

Reference

Thomas, R.B. 1976. Energy flow at high altitude. In *Man in the Andes*, P.T. Baker and M.A. Little (eds.). Dowden, Hutchinson and Ross.

LEARNING THE ROPES
The Politics of Dockland[1]

LEONARD MARS

Introduction

This paper arises out of an article[2] written in January 1976 and based on fieldwork carried out in Israel in 1970–71. In that article I examined the power of a committee of shop-stewards which had assumed office in 1969 and which subsequently had consolidated its position after a series of biennial elections. That committee had the backing of most workers, the support of management, and was recognized by the *Histadruth*[3] both locally in Ashdod, and nationally at Head Quarters in Tel Aviv where it was especially favoured by the Secretary-General of the Labour movement.

In short, I considered that the committee was well-entrenched in office and likely to remain there for a considerable period. But even when I was writing that paper an opposition was forming which later that year succeeded in toppling that committee. In this paper I shall discuss both the established committee and the emergence of the opposition, its organisation, and its transition from opposition to office. Moreover, since this new committee in turn has been deposed, I shall analyse its demise. The analysis will focus mainly on the interplay between three sets of relationships: firstly, port management; secondly, the leaders of the dockers; and thirdly, rank and file workers. I shall examine the way in which bureaucratic relationships and the system of personal relationships are inter-twined in the operation of the port. In particular, I shall show the flexibility of bureaucracy in contrast to the conventional wisdom that stresses its rigidity and I shall demonstrate how a cyclical pattern of *proteccia* (patronage) gives way to bureaucracy which in turn reverts to *proteccia.*

The work force that I examine in this paper, dockers, represents a sector of the working class which, together with miners and railway-men, is usually associated with a tradition of militancy. To some extent this reputation for militancy derives from their organization in the work place, their long history of involvement in industrial society and their patterns of residence in tightly-knit communities. The dockers that I examine undoubtedly enjoy a reputation for militancy in Israel, but they certainly lack a tradition in dockwork, neither do they live in residential communities segregated from their fellow townsfolk, but dwell side by side with them mainly in new blocks of flats.

The residential dispersal of dockers in Ashdod, together with the segregation of the field of work from other social fields (e.g. kinship, religion and politics) typical of city life, involved a methodological move away from the traditional anthropological study of groups linked by ties of residence and of kinship and marriage, to the study of relationships that derived from the work situation itself.[4] In short, I was not studying "the whole" social life of port workers but was concerned with the way in which relationships emerged and developed on the waterfront in what was largely a novel situation: a new port administered by a new bureaucracy, in a new town settled by new immigrants. Each of these elements was itself in the process of establishing a stable form, and in so doing was establishing relations between itself and the other elements. What was happening was the development of a social system. The social groups corresponding to these elements were each feeling their way in their relationships with other groups. These explorations in some cases took the form of severe trials of strength that led to modifications in the division of labour and authority between management and workers, and eventually produced dock leaders of national rather than of local importance (Mars, L., forthcoming).

Before discussing in detail the position of the shop stewards' committee, I present material on the history of the port and on the Israeli Ports Authority (I.P.A.); demographic, economic and political material on the town; data on the growth of the port and the expansion of its labour force; and the occupational structure of the Operations Department.

The Israeli Ports Authority and the Port of Ashdod

The port of Ashdod, which is located twenty-five miles south of Tel Aviv, was opened in November 1965. Its opening resulted in the closing of two of the country's small Mediterranean ports, Jaffa, which had been in operation for at least 3,000 years,[5] and Tel Aviv, which had begun operations in 1936. Haifa, hitherto Israel's only large port, situated in the north of the country also felt, though less drastically, the impact of Ashdod's competition, since it suffered an immediate decline in the volume of cargo that it handled.

The first men to be employed as permanent port workers in

Ashdod were recruited from two different backgrounds: firstly from the defunct ports of Tel Aviv and Jaffa, and secondly from the ranks of the labourers who had been employed by the building contractors, Solel Boneh,[6] during the four years that it had taken to construct the port, and who had been transferred to the I.P.A. after going on strike shortly before the completion of the port's construction.

The I.P.A. which is a state-owned corporation, was established in 1961 after the Israeli Parliament had passed the Ports Authority Law earlier that year. Although responsible to the Ministry of Transport, the I.P.A. is independent of it in its finances and operations. Statutory requirements demand that the I.P.A. manage its three ports, Ashdod, Eilat and Haifa as a profit-making concern without recourse to government subsidies. The I.P.A.'s tariffs can only be increased with the approval of the Government since this is one of the basic issues pertaining to the I.P.A. on which the Government retains the final say. The Government also appoints the members of the I.P.A.'s board, the Director of the I.P.A., and the managers of the various ports.

Hence the same statute that grants the I.P.A. independence also restricts that autonomy by its definition of basic issues which are reserved for the Government. Apart from these statutory limitations on its independence the Authority is also susceptible to the influence and to the policies of the Government and to pressures that groups and organizations can exert on the Government, so that in fact the I.P.A. becomes a government agency. Thus the wider national interests that the Government has to take into consideration may further infringe what senior officials of the Authority regard as their prerogatives (Mars, L. 1978a).

Because of the need for regular consultations between the I.P.A. on the one hand and government ministries, banks, the *Histadruth*, and clients on the other, the headquarters of the I.P.A. are located in Tel Aviv. Proximity to these bodies is indicative of the role of headquarters in relation to its constituents, the three ports. Although each port is independent in its operations, and is free to compete with the other ports in attracting clients, headquarters determines development projects, manpower policy, wage policy, and budgets and therefore requires close and immediate contact with the institutions that deal with these matters.

The Town of Ashdod

The town of Ashdod, established in 1956, experienced rapid growth, especially after the decision had been made to construct a deep-water port there. From a figure of 4,600 in 1961 the population rose to 23,300 in 1965, to 38,000 in 1971[7] and to 52,500[8] in 1975. Most of this increase was due to immigration, particularly of new immigrants. Thus in 1965 over half of the population, 12,000, had immigrated to Israel since 1961. Not only were the town's inhabitants new immigrants but they were young, one half below the age of 19 and two-thirds below the age of 30 years. Thus Ashdod was and is a rapidly growing new town populated mainly by young immigrants and their numerous children.

As the largest single employer in the town, the port and its workers are of great concern to local politicians who see it as a strong base for their parties and who also show interest in its affairs. Since 1969 the town council has been controlled by the *Likud* coalition dominated by Menahem Begin's party, but the Labour party, through its domination of the Ashdod Labour Council (the local branch of the *Histadruth*), has effective political and economic control over many organisations in the town. These include those owned or administered by the *Histadruth.* Examples are *Kupat Holim*, the *Histadruth* Sick Fund, which provides medical care to most of the town's residents, and the sports and youth club which attract many of Ashdod's youth. Ashdod port workers sit on the Labour Council as the representatives of political parties. The Labour Council has a department concerned with trade union affairs which has the authority to declare a strike legal, thereby granting official *Histadruth* support to the striking workers. Consequently their roles as port workers and Council members may come into conflict.

In 1971, the manpower resources of the Ashdod Labour Council were so limited that one official dealt full-time with all the works committees in all the enterprises in Ashdod including the six committees in the Port of Ashdod. Because of the local and national importance of the port, this local official and even his superior, the secretary of the local Labour Council, are often bypassed when disputes óccur in the port, since local workers may appeal directly to officials at *Histadruth* H.Q. in Tel Aviv, and to government ministries in Jerusalem.

In short, because of the divided allegiance of its members, its inadequate manpower resources, and the strategic national importance of the port leading to the direct involvement of national bodies, the local Labour Council is weaker than its nominal inferior, the local committee of dock workers.

The Growth of the Port

The opening of Ashdod port, which expanded rapidly, reduced not only the volume of trade passing through Haifa port[9] but also diminished the political power of Haifa port workers. When the ports of Tel Aviv and Jaffa were the only rivals of Haifa, the latter's workers did not need to seek an alliance with the men from the southern ports since they were unequal in the competition for cargoes: Tel Aviv and Jaffa were lighterage ports and for that reason only handled a few ships per month. However, when the Haifa men went on strike after Ashdod had commenced operations, they appealed to the Ashdod workers not to accept ships diverted from their port.

One outcome of rapid expansion[10] and subsequent opportunities for promotion was that expectations of advancement in the workplace became to be considered the norm and this led to disappointment by 1971 when workers who had been employed a few months less than their workmates felt their promotion prospects to be blocked. Promotion was not confined to rank and file workers, since their elected leaders, members of the Operation Workers' Committee, also benefited and became foremen. Thus the first three men to hold the office of Secretary of the Workers' Committee of the Operation Department gained promotion between 1965 and 1967 as did other members of their Committees. Changes in the membership of the Operations Workers' Committee affected relationships between the Committee and port management, especially when one committee refused to acknowledge agreements reached by its predecessor. Managerial positions also expanded with the growth of the port and new posts were created which were filled by men with limited administrative experience.

Rapid expansion created a situation of fluidity both within the ranks of the workers and in their relationships with management. As far as management was concerned, the turnover in leadership among port workers created problems about continuity and predictability in relationships so that management itself became interested in the establishment and maintenance of a stable leadership for port workers. That stability was maintained until 1976 when the Committee of shop stewards was overthrown by a revolt of the rank and file led by instructors from the Training School.

The port of Ashdod is divided into five departments as revealed in Table 1.

By far the largest is the Operations Department whose main task is the loading, unloading and storage of cargo. Space precludes a long description of the occupational complexities of this department (cf. L. Mars, forthcoming). Suffice it to say that the basic work unit is the gang of stevedores, assisted by winchmen or coastal crane

TABLE I

Permanent employees in Ashdod port per department as on 31.3.70.[11]

Adminis-trative	Engin-eering	Finance	Marine	Operations	Total
52	97	74	111	1,167	1,501

operators, and by forklift truck operators whose work is co-ordinated by the gang leader, known as the signaller, all of whom are supervised by a foreman, A fundamental distinction in this department is that between the cargo handling men and the mechanical equipment operators, namely the forklift drivers and the coastal crane operators.

The gang is not a stable unit since its composition may be modified by technological factors, e.g. the type of crane employed, by the nature of the cargo that is worked, which may require more or fewer workers, and by workers' norms, e.g. the principle of seniority which is critically relevant when work is scarce so that junior signallers may have to stand down and their gangs be dispersed (L. Mars, forthcoming).

The basic cause of fluctuation in the composition of the work gang is the seasonal flow of work. In 1970 the permanent work force was sufficient to man 45 work gangs per day; at the height of the citrus season between 65/67 gangs were required. This total was achieved by the recruitment of temporary labourers from the labour exchanges in and around Ashdod. During the peak season winchmen become signallers, and stevedores with winchmen's certificates move up on deck and in turn are replaced in the hold by temporary unskilled workers. In 1974 the employment of temporary workers was terminated and several score were granted permanent employment by the Government, who forced the I.P.A. to accept these men, most of whom were immigrants from Georgia, U.S.S.R.

The Operations Department is characterised by its dominance within the port, by the transience of its basic unit, and by the high degree of segmentation among the department's workers which derives from the diversity of occupations. Thus the department contains three separate works committees, one for foremen, one for warehousemen, and one for the men who work in gangs assisted by the crane and fork-lift operators. This last committee, which is styled the Operations Committee, itself represents a wide range of occupations.

Against this background of transient working relationships, we have one relatively stable group, the Operations Committee, to which the dockers can turn when they have problems, whether about pay, conditions of employment, promotion, and, in some cases, domestic life. The position and strength of the Operations Committee in the port, which arises out of the segmentation of its workers, is enhanced by the status which management accords it in dealing with those workers and their problems.

Management has acquiesced to the incorporation of the Operations Committee into the administrative organisation of the port. This incorporation was only achieved as a result of a series of confrontations between management and workers, as a result of which management lost what it considered to be some of its prerogatives, e.g. complete control over the recruitment of labour, control over the promotion of workers and of managerial officials, and control over the timing and holding of occupational courses (cf. Mars, L. 1978a).

The Workers' Committee of the Operations Department (*va'ad tif'ul*) 1970–76

In the previous sections I have documented the dominance of the port in the economic life of the town of Ashdod and I referred to its political importance which is based on that economic strength. Apart from its local economic and political importance, the port is of national significance since it plays a vital role in the country's economy which is based largely on international trade, almost all of which passes through the ports of Haifa and Ashdod.[12] Because of its importance it is a major concern of several government ministries e.g. Agriculture, Development, Finance, Labour, Trade and Commerce, Transport, and consequently these ministries become involved when disputes occur in the ports. Apart from government ministries, the *Histadruth* becomes involved at the national level, as well as locally through the Labour Council; Government ministers and senior *Histadruth* officials, therefore, express interest in the affairs of the port and are able to put pressure on officials of the I.P.A., which pressures involve national considerations rather than those seen by the I.P.A. as issues about local relations between labour and management.

The Committee elected in 1971 consisted of thirteen members, six of whom represented the Mechanical Equipment section of the cargo handling men and seven of whom came from occupations representing the gangs of workers. The workers themselves refer to these separate sections as Mechanical Equipment and the Operations section, although according to port management the term 'Operations' applies to all workers in that department and subsumes operatives in the Mechanical Equipment section. It will be appreciated that the distribution of Committee members by no means represents the numerical supremacy of the Operations men who outnumber Mechanical Equipment by a ratio approximately three to one (687 compared with 221).[13] Although workers elect committee members from two separate lists of candidates, one representing Mechanical Equipment and one representing Operations, all workers irrespective of the section they work in, are entitled to vote for each list. Men from Operations vote for Mechanical Equipment candidates and workers from the latter section vote for Operations candidates. The dual list acknowledges the differences of interest between the two sections whilst the undifferentiated franchise signifies the unity and common interests of the electorate, and their representatives.

Although the Committee of 1971 was unbalanced in terms of its composition, that imbalance was less remarkable than the fact that not one stevedore was a member of the Committee though stevedores constitute over half the electorate. Indeed of the thirty one candidates only two were stevedores. How does one explain this situation?

Firstly, the stevedores tend to be relative newcomers to the port and less experienced in its affairs. They see themselves as such, and are viewed in that light by others including their fellow stevedores. They have not yet learned the ropes, both metaphorically and literally. They are aware that they have sectional interests of their own but consider that these are satisfactorily served by experienced men with higher occupational qualifications. They are egalitarian and are reluctant to elevate one of their peers to a position of formal leadership. This egalitarian ethos is also associated with the holding of a negative self-image characterised by a denigration of the status of stevedore which, lacking prestige, is held to preclude a man from even seeking, let alone attaining, office. One view often expressed was that if a man would not advance from the ranks of stevedore, he could not aspire to be a member of the Committee.

Secondly, in terms of their social situation in Ashdod port, stevedores lacked social ties gained either from previous experience in the Ports of Tel Aviv and Jaffa or from the construction company that built Ashdod Port which could serve as a solid electoral base from which votes could be expected. In the port they had little chance to establish an *esprit de corps* since they moved from gang to gang and from gang leader to gang leader.

In occupational terms, the Committee of 1971 comprised one coastal crane driver, five fork lift drivers, five gang leaders and two winchmen who had passed courses in signalling and therefore could on occasions assume the position of gang leader.

The over-representation of men from Mechanical Equipment is related to the position of the Secretary of the Committee. It was, and still is, the Secretary who, in presidential style, selected a list of running mates to serve with him on the Committee. This list is circulated to the electorate by a band of canvassers either a day or two before or on the day of the elections, and on the whole is voted for en bloc by the majority of the workers. Thus if a candidate is on the Secretary's list then he is almost automatically guaranteed election so that rival candidates who recognise the fact hand voters lists of candidates purporting to be that of the Secretary. At that time the Secretary was Yehoshua Peretz, the acknowledged leader of the port workers. Peretz was a fork lift driver, originally employed on the construction of the port. He was generally popular and polled more votes than any other candidate. His power base was located in Mechanical Equipment.

The disproportionate representation of Mechanical Equipment on the Committee was also reflected in the executive body of that Committee which is known as the Secretariat (*mazkirut*), to which Peretz appointed three representatives from Mechanical Equipment and two from Operations. The Secretariat is the group that usually sits with representatives of the I.P.A. either at local or national level and that meets with officials from the *Histadruth*. Its members tend therefore to become white-collar officials who spend less time on the waterfront in their occupation than other members of the Committee who are released less frequently from their work on the docks.

The Secretary of the Committee is a full-time white-collar worker, whose office is located on the ground floor of the main administrative building in the port and not in the Operations Department over half a mile away. He employs a full-time secretary/typist, and a staff recruited from the members of the Committee. He represents and promotes the interests of workers in his department, but public opinion in the country tends to regard him as the leader of all port workers in Ashdod. Although the elected leader of the dockers, his salary is paid by the I.P.A., his employer, which in fact pays the salaries of the secretaries of all works committees in the port though none of these devote all their time to committee affairs, and none has secretarial assistance.

As the only secretary of any committee who works full-time as a workers' representative, he is thrust into a quasi-managerial role.

Management permits and encourages him and his staff to deal with matters to do with the workers he represents, particularly with queries about salaries and problems of discipline between workers.

As they become involved in the administrative organization of the port, the Secretary and the other members of the Committee gradually adopt behaviour which is characteristic of management in its relationships with workers. Thus in late 1970 workers were requested to consult the Secretary in his office at fixed hours whereas previously they were free to enter whenever they chose (except during meetings of the Committee). Moreover, they were now enjoined, by a notice fixed to the door, to enter the office decently attired in a shirt instead of stripped to the waist as used frequently to be the practice. Likewise, the behaviour of Peretz, then the Secretary, towards fellow members of the Committee resembled that of a superior to his staff rather than that of *primus inter pares* which was his formal position. He was apt to hand the keys to a cabinet which stands against the wall opposite him to a member of the Secretariat who was seated beside him and order him to take out and to bring him a document. His position as a superior was recognized by Committee members who referred to him as 'my boss', both when he was present and when he was not.

The members of the Committee of 1971 who had little formal education and who had little experience of the operation of a bureaucracy until their employment by the I.P.A., were obliged to learn the role of procedure and of rules as they progressed. None of them had been a labour leader before his employment in the port and many of them owed their position to the fact that their predecessors had been promoted to foremen. Thus they had to grope and feel their way in their new positions. To some extent they were assisted by the *Histadruth* which holds courses on Labour Laws, trade union history and structure, labour agreements, pensions and so forth. The Committee members often played competitive games in the form of betting who knew sections such and such of the Labour Agreement. They poked fun at the legal terminology and deliberately mispronounced words for comic effect, e.g. 'rubric', pronounced as 'republic'. They jocularly threatened each other with disciplinary hearings for minor mistakes. The self-conscious, half-embarrassed manner in which they engaged in these activities indicated that the Committee members were coming to terms with practices, procedures and rules which were strange and new to them but which they were obliged to follow in their dealings with management and workers in the port and which had been thrust on them by virtue of their incorporation in the administration of the department.

So far I have examined the situation as it was in 1970/71 and as it obtained until the beginning of 1976. I now propose to examine the emergence of an opposition which was to overthrow that Committee.

Before I discuss the emergence of the opposition to the strongly entrenched committees I should say a few words about external objective factors that affected political relationships within the port. The main external factor was the decline in the volume of cargo that passed through Israeli ports during 1975/76. This decline affected the port of Ashdod more than it did Haifa[14] which is Israel's only other Mediterranean port. The loss of trade resulted in a major loss of earnings for most port workers, since a considerable proportion of a worker's wage is based on bonuses for work actually performed. In effect workers enjoy a low basic rate which is supplemented by incentive payments for exceeding production norms that are calculated for each cargo.

The underemployment or unemployment of most dockers increased their militancy against senior men who, by virtue of the principle of seniority, were always guaranteed work with the benefit of bonuses. These unemployed men who lacked leaders were brought into contact with instructors from the Training School who, during periods of unemployment, laid on courses for idle dockers. Thus the Instructors were brought into a position where they could activate the latent opposition to the Committee, an opposition based on diverse segments of the labour force hitherto relatively isolated from each other. The instructors who formed the core of the faction that had been latent were able to extend their networks as a result of the external situation and the way in which it affected the alignment of forces in the port. The instructors who enjoyed high status because of their technical skills, formed an alliance with the low status and numerically dominant stevedores whose votes were essential to ousting the Committee.

In addition, in July 1975, the arbitrary behaviour of Peretz, the Secretary of the Committee, who refused to show his identity card to a border policeman who was on duty at the port entrance, resulted in the closure of the port, and encouraged shippers to divert their vessels to Haifa since they considered Ashdod unreliable when it could be closed at the whim of a dock worker, albeit the Secretary of the Committee. This impulsive action of Peretz, for which he was subsequently put on trial and convicted, further reduced the earnings of port workers.

The decline in trade and consequently the loss of earnings suffered by dockers were not in themselves enough to topple the Committee but they did activate the hitherto latent opposition. What was absent was some organisation of this opposition. I now turn to consider the basis of the opposition.

The Opposition

The very closure of the gates by Peretz and his immediate associates on the Committee indicated the lack of any organised opposition among the ranks of the dockers. The Committee itself was solidly behind the Secretary since the few independent-minded members that I knew in 1971 had become foremen in 1974, leaving behind a Committee composed of men who seldom if ever dissented from their leader's views.

That Committee, the Secretariat of which had held office from 1969 to the beginning of 1976, was well entrenched, self-confident, perhaps even complacent. Its composition did not reflect the various occupational groups among the dockers, for example the stevedores, although the largest category of workers, had not one of their number on the Committee. Provided they were ensured régular employment they were not concerned with their lack of representation; on the whole they were relative newcomers to the port, and lacked the strong ties and solidarity that veteran dockers had made through previous employment in the ports of Tel Aviv and Jaffa, or the bonds that were established by the labourers who had built the port and who had been granted employment as dockworkers. These stevedores, numerically strong, but unorganized, had to be mobilized by anyone or any group that intended to oppose the Committee, and such mobilisation would not be easy since the stevedores voted solidly for Peretz who was a 'man of the people', who had attained a position of national importance, and with whom they identified. He was a simple, uneducated man of Moroccan origin who rubbed shoulders with government ministers, and who spoke strongly on T.V. and to the press about port workers' grievances. He was one of the boys who had made it.

Apart from a few isolated individuals, whom I shall describe shortly, opposition to the Committee was weak during the period of prosperity, since discontent was limited; with the sharp decline in the volume of work in 1975/76 conditions arose which gave rise to dissatisfaction that could be exploited. The men who were to exploit that dissatisfaction were the instructors of the Training School.

The Training School for port workers is located in a single-storey building away from the quayside and from the administrative buildings of the port. Geographically it is isolated and self-contained; workers do not go there unless they are on a course. The instructors, eight skilled workers, are full-time teachers who occasionally, during the citrus season, work a shift or two to supplement their income, which is much higher than rank and file workers since they are on the same pay scale as foremen. Training courses are fewer than during the early days of the port, for example between 1971 and 1977 there was only one course for foremen which lasted ten weeks and was held in 1974. Instructors are therefore men with time on their hands, which time they employ in discussing current affairs and port matters.

The Leader of the Opposition

The leader of the opposing faction, Eli Maman, is a short, squat, tough man. At the age of seven he was sent alone by his family, who came from Morocco, to live in Israel. There he was brought up by ultra-orthodox Jews in a boarding school from which he later ran away; at about fifteen he went to a *kibbutz* which he subsequently left after completing army service at the age of twenty-one. He moved to Ashdod and was employed as a building worker on the construction of the port. Very much a loner, unlike Peretz, who was fond of company, he lacked close friends in the port. But he was known to be opposed to Peretz and was waiting his chance to overthrow him. However he was unable to act alone, and even among his fellow instructors he was isolated. They supported Peretz and actively campaigned for him. After Peretz had closed the port, however, and because of other aspects of his highly personal, and what they considered tyrannical rule, some of these instructors became disenchanted and turned to Eli Maman in the hope, as they saw it, of restoring freedom of speech to the port, eradicating corruption and getting a fairer allocation of work. Thus three other instructors joined with Maman as the nucleus of an opposition.

One of these, who defected from Peretz, was a man called Maurice Duq. He had been a member of the first Committee from 1965—67 but thereafter had withdrawn from port politics — his defection from Peretz was publicly significant since he had always acted as chairman of the Election Sub-Committee which, though technically responsible for holding the biennial elections, was in fact in business to secure the re-election of Peretz. Duq was known as a quiet, thoughtful, responsible and upright person whose word carried weight, so that he became influential both in converting others to his viewpoint and as a symbol of rectitude. When workers saw Duq turn against Peretz's Committee, though not against Peretz, they were more ready to accept the need for changes in the Committee.

Of the two other instructors at the core of the faction one had played football for Ashdod Hapoel F.C. and had several kinship connections and footballing acquaintances in the port, whilst the other was a popular member of the group of marchers that the port workers had formed, and which I discuss below.

The Training School therefore provided the nucleus of the opposition to the Committee — the instructors had time to prepare their plans and they also had occupational prestige. They had moreover experience of committee work, of organization, and of experience at communication through public speaking. In their leader, Eli Maman, they had a person of considerable intelligence, a very capable organiser, and a man who was dedicated to the overthrow not only of the Committee but ultimately of Peretz.

The sport of marching is very popular in Israel and most large places of employment have teams of marchers which compete in local, regional and national competitions. Ashdod Port also has its team which numbers thirty members. One of these, as already mentioned, is a Training Instructor. Another, the leader of the marchers, is a senior crane driver. The crane drivers, about sixty in all, represent the élite of the Mechanical Equipment workers who had as far back as 1971 attempted to form an opposition but who had failed. Combining his occupational and his sporting links the leader of the marchers had a ready-made organized basis of opposition which was readily mobilised for the forthcoming political struggle.

Thus at this stage of the analysis we have an amorphous mass of stevedores, a close-knit nucleus of instructors, and a group of marchers who come from all sections of the port, but have links with crane drivers, who though relatively few in numbers are of a prestigious occupation. As I have described elsewhere (Mars, L. 1978b) this opposition succeeded, after a fierce struggle, in gaining office after two elections that were held in 1976.

Maman's group conducted a campaign that stressed the corruption and moral deficiencies of its opponents. They wished to show how they would and could avoid the contamination that office brings to all men but especially newcomers most of whom who had never held office before. Of the committee of eleven, only Maman, Duq, and a veteran from Tel Aviv port had ever sat on the Committee previously.

Maman wished to show that impartiality and fairness were the hallmarks of his Committee; that all sections of the work-force were truly represented; that his colleagues were not workshy and that lazy and ill-disciplined workers were not going to be tolerated. The purity of the Committee and the raising of work standards all round were stressed. His goal was to improve the image of Ashdod port workers and to attract more work to the port since the major problem that he faced was lack of employment in the port. In fact Maman had gained office at a very difficult period, during a recession, when management was in a more advantageous position than workers so that as a negotiator, he was not likely to be able to exert much pressure on the I.P.A.

Symbolic, Economic, Political and Administrative Changes

I divide the reforms introduced by Maman's Committee into symbolic, economic, political and administrative — these are not necessarily exclusive. By symbolic I mean 'intended to express the values and ethos of the Committee', and designed to distinguish this new Committee from its predecessor — the values stressed were diligence, honesty, impartiality and justice, values that Maman's group claimed had been ignored by Peretz's Committee.

The first symbolic change that Maman introduced was that all but four of the Committee should return to full-time dock work instead of all eleven becoming fulltime officials. The four posts devoted to Committee work were those of the Secretary, the Treasurer, the Supervisor of the Works Allocator which was a key position, and one post without a portfolio to be held by Duq, who was competent to handle any problem that might arise. In fact, no sooner had they gained election than Committee members found themselves involved in negotiations for the new biennial Labour Contract which was due for renewal so that several days per week more members of the Committee were released in order to take part in these discussions.

A second symbolic change involved the renaming of the fund into which workers' dues were paid. In Peretz's day this fund, quite accurately in the light of the *Histadruth*'s subsequent report on its administration, was called the "Committee's Fund" and indeed such it became, as members lined their pockets from it, including paying themselves for time involved in attending Committee meetings for which they were already paid by the I.P.A. Maman renamed this fund 'the Workers' Fund'.

These symbolic changes expressed the honesty of the Committee but they did not do much to satisfy the grievances of the majority of

workers whose pay had been reduced by the decline in the amount
of trade handled by the port. This decline was part of a national
and international recession about which Maman could do little
except to improve Ashdod's competitive position *vis-à-vis* Haifa —
through his stress on improved discipline at work, reduction in
damage to cargo, and the belated opening of Ashdod's Container
Terminal, which had been held up by Peretz for eighteen months.

What he could do within the port was to allocate work more
equitably. Limits on the earnings of senior men were imposed in
order that junior men might earn more. In negotiations about the
new Labour Contract he endeavoured to raise basic pay without
affecting the basis on which bonuses were calculated. In this he
was less successful since management struck a very hard bargain
which he felt he could not accept.

Inside the port Maman rewarded his supporters, many of whom
were junior men, by imposing a modified form of rotation so that
they would each get a chance to earn some bonuses. He did not
introduce complete rotation since he would have alienated senior
and influential workers who had also supported him.

The system of rotation differed between the two halves of the
Operations Department. In Mechanical Equipment where individual
operators were attached to gangs a ceiling of 150 hours bonus per
month was imposed. Senior men were allocated work first but as
soon as they reached 150 hours bonus they were withdrawn from
the work roster and replaced by junior men who in turn were allowed
to reach that figure whereupon senior men would be restored to
the roster. The assumption behind this was that there would be
sufficient work for men to reach 150 hours. When work was really
scarce some senior men might have difficulty reaching that target.
However this scheme did prevent the inequity of one man earning
perhaps 300 hours or more and another gaining nothing or a
pittance.

In the Cargo handling section of the port where men worked in
gangs, implementation of the 150 hour rule would have caused
administrative chaos for the Works Allocator (*sadran avodah*) and
would probably have meant that workers would have absented
themselves from unprofitable cargoes such as sacks. Thus a system
of rotation was introduced whereby senior men were allocated
priority in the first three days of the week and full rotation applied
for the remaining three days — so that in effect senior men obtained
four or five days work and junior men only one or two.

Whereas senior men lost some of their privileges by the restrictions
on their earnings, they were rewarded in another area by guarantees

of promotion when posts became available. The only criterion, after medical considerations, was seniority. Management was presented with lists of senior workers by the Committee and told that those were the men for the vacant jobs. This clear cut rule also demonstrated the new Committee's impartiality in stark contrast to the previous one which had favoured its own clients.

The Opening of the Container Terminal

One major change which had symbolic, economic and political significance was the opening in July 1977 of Ashdod's Container Terminal which was marked by a formal ceremony attended by local politicians, senior officials of the I.P.A., representatives of the central and local *Histadruth* and, significantly, dock workers from Haifa as well as from Ashdod.

The opening of the Terminal had been delayed because the previous Committee, with the support of the Ashdod Labour Council, had been unwilling or unable to reach agreement with the I.P.A. on the problem of manning the Terminal which had remained idle for eighteen months, and was costing Ashdod port considerable sums of money in maintenance. Moreover during that period Haifa was operating its own terminal and obtaining much business that otherwise might have fallen to Ashdod.

Maman's Committee co-operated with Ashdod Port management and with I.P.A. Head Office in the opening of the terminal so that Ashdod Port would be able to compete successfully with its rival, Haifa. Maman hoped that its opening would attract more trade to Ashdod and also enable some workers to be trained to operate the new equipment and thereby gain promotion. He recognised however that this new method of handling cargo would require a reduction in the port's manpower and was prepared to consider redundancies if phased over a period of time. Indeed after his election over one hundred men accepted offers of an early pension or compensation to leave the port.

A further reason for his opening the terminal was to increase unity among all of Israel's port workers, indeed he hoped to establish a National Union of Portworkers, a move strongly opposed by the *Histadruth* which in its monolithic manner represented all port workers together with most of Israel's labour force.

The opening of the terminal was also a major achievement in terms of public relations since it portrayed Maman and Ashdod port workers as public-minded citizens in contrast with the negative image that the port had acquired under Peretz's leadership. However the fact that Maman's Committee was eager to co-operate with the

I.P.A. did not mean that he would do so at all costs as his leadership
of the first national dock-strike in Israel's history demonstrated.

The national dock strike was not against the I.P.A. but against
the Government and its pay policy and indirectly against the
Histadruth which was a part to that policy. The Ashdod port
workers had accepted a settlement within the government's guidelines for production workers, but shortly afterwards professional
and white-collar workers had breached the pay code and so Maman
engineered, with Haifa's support, the dock strike which also brought
benefits to all production workers both inside and outside the
ports. This achievement in the face of opposition from the
Histadruth brought him into national prominence. Moreover, this
strike, unlike those local strikes led by Peretz, did not arouse the
hostility of the media and the public. For example, the *Jerusalem
Post*, usually hostile to Ashdod port workers, and a strong supporter
of the Government, produced a sympathetic editorial in favour of
the dockers. However, because the strike lacked the support of the
Histadruth, and was therefore unofficial, dock workers lost money
for the duration of their stoppage.

Relations with the Histadruth

The new Committee's relations with the *Histadruth*, as can be seen
from the unofficial national strike, are based on reluctant cooperation. The co-operative element recognised the strength and
power of the *Histadruth* especially since the election of a government led by Prime Minister Begin which is dominated by a free-
enterprise party, so that the *Histadruth* has a much greater role as
a form of political opposition than it had under the successive
governments led by the Israel Labour Party. However, in so far as
the *Histadruth* resists the establishment of an independent port
workers' union, Maman and his committee are reluctant to rely
solely on the *Histadruth*. One manifestation of his reluctance is
the hiring of a private, independent, labour lawyer, the country's
leading expert in that field, to handle all issues pertaining to the
Labour Contract. This man is paid a retainer of IL.5,000 per
month from port workers' funds even though the *Histadruth* has
its own permanent staff of labour lawyers whose services can be
called on free of charge. Maman's claim is that the *Histadruth*
officials are concerned with a whole range of different cases and
lack the special concern, interest and expertise that a private
professional man has towards his client. The point is that Maman
reduced his links with, and dependence on, the *Histadruth* and
thereby alienated a source of external support in his struggles with

the I.P.A.

Relations between the Committee and the I.P.A.

I have briefly discussed some of the relationships between the Committee and local management in my discussion of the Container Terminal and of the National Dock Strike. In this section I shall refer briefly to local management in Ashdod. Ashdod port management was used to negotiating with Peretz on a personal basis, and indeed to attending night clubs with him and enjoying his hospitality. Maman adopted a more formal, bureaucratic approach — he put an end to the entertainment of management and, so he informed me, refused to accept phone calls at his home from management officials. Management had to readjust to the new style and methods of Maman's Committee. One result of this was that Ashdod's port manager, who had held office since 1973, was replaced in July 1977. To some extent this change was the outcome of changes at Head Office where a new Director of the I.P.A. took office in February 1977 and decided to institute changes in senior positions but it also represented the decline of the Peretz era during which the port manager and his acting deputy had been closely identified with Peretz. Maman attempted to exert pressure for the removal of the acting deputy port manager who was the Head of the Administrative Department. He was unsuccessful at first but he did succeed by preventing his permanent appointment to the post of Deputy Port Manager when the new Port Manager, who assumed office in July 1977, refused to confirm his appointment. Later, early in 1978, this official was appointed to Head Office.

Maman's election was not welcomed by the most senior port managers because it disrupted their relationships with workers whose compliance could be relied on if Peretz requested it, but Maman's election was appreciated by middle and mid-senior managers who welcomed his concern with efficiency, respect for foremen, punctuality, diligence and indeed the managerial ethos with which both they and Maman were imbued. One index of Maman's bureaucratic and impartial approach was the readiness with which he, or rather his representatives in that forum, punished workers who appeared before disciplinary hearings (*birurim*) on grounds of late arrival at work, failure to wear safety boots, striking or insulting foremen and other breaches of discipline or work regulations. Peretz's representatives rarely agreed to reprimand or punish workers so that foremen and managers in fact ceased to report cases of ill-discipline because of the futility of so doing.

In adopting a bureaucratic ethos that stressed the maintenance of boundaries between private and public life, Maman may have been adhering to a Weberian notion of bureaucracy but he was rejecting the Israeli bureaucratic style that combined the formal and the informal in its bureaucratic culture (Marx 1975; Mars, L. 1976). He was in short, cutting himself off from casual, unofficial meetings where much business was conducted between leaders of management and of workers.

The Demise of the New Committee

The demise of Maman's Committee is attributable to several factors and a combination of diverse forces. Firstly, the economic climate did not change and unemployment or underemployment persisted in the period 1976/77 and early 1978. Modifications to the system of rotation did not significantly affect the earnings of junior men, who remained dissatisfied. Furthermore though many of the rank and file had supported Maman in his campaign against Peretz and were aware that he rejected the idea of *proteccia* by which supporters were rewarded in the Peretz era, they nevertheless thought that their turn to benefit from office had arrived and they expected special treatment for their support. Maman's strict bureaucratic ethos was alien to their expectations. Indeed the gulf between Maman and the rank and file is, that while workers saw him as the leader of a faction who represented sectional interests, he saw himself as a representative of all workers.

Whilst the earnings of most dockers declined during the recession, the income of the Training Instructors, who, as mentioned, enjoyed the pay-scale of foremen, remained constant and high by the standards of stevedores. This grievance was exploited by a member of Maman's Committee, Jossi Atias, who remained close to Peretz and who held the position of supervising the job of the work Allocator (*sadran avodah*). Atias by virtue of his office was close to the rank and file, and favoured the return of Peretz, who in fact had voluntarily transferred after his defeat to another department (marine) and was therefore out of the political race, but who was attempting to return to the Operations Department with the support of the Ashdod Labour Council and with the backing of what remained of his followers among the dockworkers. A petition calling for fresh elections was organized by Atias; elections were duly held and though Maman was re-elected the rest of his Committee, with one exception, refused to stand for office with him. Their refusal was based on what they termed the increasingly personal rule of Maman. They saw him as another Peretz, another 'boss', who though different in style, nevertheless dominated the Committee instead of being one among equals; they sought by their abstention to teach him a lesson. Maman was particularly vulnerable to with-drawal of support by his core supporters since he had deliberately avoided alliances with senior management and with the *Histadruth*. Thus internal dissension among Maman's closest supporters was another factor in the fall of his Committee.

Another element in the overthrow of Maman's Committee was the role of the Ashdod Labour Council where the new holder of the trade union portfolio felt threatened by Maman's attempt to form a separate trade union for dockworkers and whom Maman treated with disdain. This trade union official joined the opposition to Maman. He worked with Atias among the dockers and with the head of the Administrative Department of the port, who had collaborated with Peretz when the latter held office, and though they failed to remove Maman from the Committee completely they did succeed in isolating him on the new Committee that took office after fresh elections were held.

Conclusions

This paper has examined work in one development town, Ashdod, in one modern nation-state, Israel. The study of Israeli development towns was part of the Bernstein Research Project (Marx 1975) that examined the diverse ways in which State bureaucracies interacted with their various and varied clientele in both rural and urban areas. In the urban studies two clear problems emerged: firstly, the relation between municipal and national politics (Aronoff 1974; Deshen 1970), and secondly, the provision of welfare services (Handelman 1977; Marx 1976). These studies, in their different ways, examine the nature of dependence on state organizations, attempts to resist such dependence, and endeavours to exploit that dependent relationship. But Ashdod differs significantly from the towns studied by Aronoff, Deshen and Marx. Because of its key national economic position, its dependence on state bureaucracies, national and political parties and the *Histadruth* is considerably altered. Ashdod, because of its port and the industry which has been attracted to the port, has prospered and is not a depressed town from which folk seek to escape; on the contrary its growth has been spectacular.

The dockworkers in the early years of Peretz's regime and even before he assumed office (Mars, L., forthcoming) had attempted to gain control over their own position in the economy and to resist the control of the I.P.A., the *Histadruth* and the government. At the same time, of necessity, they co-operated with these organizations.

The result of this complex interaction was a series of compromises whereby both the power of the I.P.A. and of the local branch of the *Histadruth* were diminished *vis-a-vis* port workers.

As Peretz's Committee became entrenched in office, so it worked more closely with local management, or rather with the upper echelons of that management. That Committee became incorporated into the administration of the port and though it became bureau-cratized to some extent, it also acted as a patron to its supporters in the field of promotion in the granting of loans, and in protection in disciplinary hearings. It also punished opponents by denying them promotion and on some occasions unilaterally suspending them from work. Although individual opponents existed during the Peretz era, concerted, organised opposition did not exist mainly because relative prosperity was enjoyed by all workers since work was plentiful. Only when the slump occurred in 1975/76 did an opposition develop and later emerge publicly.

This opposition adhered to a bureaucratic ethos, stressing universalistic criteria and eschewing patronage. This stance alienated not only senior management which, through Peretz's Committee, had operated a system of patronage, but also rank and file workers who had expected to receive rewards for their support. Further opposition to the new Committee came from the *Histadruth* which did not wish to see one of its major constituents break away to form a separate trade union. As the slump continued and as the renewed Labour Contract brought no major increase in basic rates of pay, so the configuration of forces outside the Committee and dissension within brought about its downfall.

What has emerged from this presentation is that a variety of groups are engaged in continuous conflict and competition for control over the domain of work in the modern nation-state. Firstly there is the State itself, which as Emanuel Marx (*op. cit.*, p. 136) pointed out, is not a monolithic giant but is composed of numerous organizations, each internally divided and each with its own personnel, organization and aims. Whilst Government appoints the Director General of the I.P.A. and the individual managers of the ports, these men both co-operate and conflict with government ministers, *Histadruth* officials, and party politicians over such issues as pay policy and the recruitment of labour in a State which attempts to maintain full-employment during a recession and which encourages immigrants to enter the country who have to be found employment.

The variety of interests that characterizes the State is also found at that level of organization in the port which is designated 'management'. Managerial tasks are performed not only by administrators and their subordinates who appear on the chart that represents the formal organization of the port, but are carried out by the Committee which is elected to represent the interests of workers, but in fact controls them as much as it serves them. Management too is not monolithic — departmental and sub-departmental interest groups exist and interact in various ways with diverse sections of the work force. Thus the foremen, the lowest rank of management, welcomed Maman's Committee as did middle-management, but the most senior managers preferred Peretz's Committee with which they had co-operated for several years.

The range of interests found in both the State and in management is also found within the work force itself, not only in the number of committees of shop stewards that exist within the port but within the Operations Committee itself. The diversity of occupations produces a prestige system which is reflected in the composition of the Committee. Maman's Committee which consciously sought to include stevedores only recruited two from their ranks, neither of whom was on the Secretariat. The structural diversity of the work force is reflected culturally. Whilst Maman's Committee stressed bureaucratic themes, the rank and file favoured a system of patronage. Here there is an interesting similarity to and difference from management. Whereas top management favoured patronage, lower management preferred bureaucracy; on the other hand, workers' leaders on the new Committee espoused bureaucracy and the rank and file favoured patronage. Maman and his closest supporters were obliged to adopt, and did believe in, a bureaucratic position opposed to that of Peretz in order to emerge as an opposition. This same stance jeopardized the links cultivated by top managers with the Committee, which links had been converted into a system of patronage since these senior managers were not as constrained by rules as were their subordinates who were obliged to refer to their superiors for any departure from their bureaucratic brief. This common perspective of senior management and rank and file, together with the defection of Atias who mobilised the latter, and with the withdrawal of support by members of his Committee, resulted in Maman's fall. By focussing on the systematic features of these data we can see that the political process has involved an oscillation between systems based predominantly on patronage and on bureaucracy.

Notes

1. The research on this paper was carried out in 1970/71 on Research Grant 779/1 of the Social Science Research Council of Great Britain. A further

grant, HR5209 from the SSRC enabled me to pursue à limited follow-up
study in the summer of 1977. I acknowledge the discussion of Dr. Gerald
Mars and his seminar in the Centre For Occupational Studies, Middlesex
Polytechnic where I delivered an earlier version of this paper. I also
thank my Swansea colleagues Dr. C.C. Harris and Dr. J.K. Hutson for their
comments on this paper.

2. This is to be published shortly. See L. Mars (forthcoming).
3. *Histadruth* — The General Federation of Labour, a federation of trade
unions which is also one of the largest employers of labour in Israel.
4. For a discussion of the problems of urban anthropological research among
dockworkers see G. Mars (1972).
5. Jaffa ('Joppa' in Greek), 2 Chronicles Chap. 2 v 16 and Ezra Chap. 3 v 7.
6. Solel Boneh — the largest construction company in Israel, owned by the
Histadruth (the General Federation of Labour).
7. Ashdod Labour Council Records.
8. Ministry of Social Welfare (1976).
9. Indeed it was not until 1969/70 that Haifa exceeded the amount of cargo
that it had handled in 1965/66.
10. *Growth of the labour force 1966–76.* Source: *Annual Reports* of the I.P.A.

1965/66	701	1966/67	933	1967/68	965
1968/69	1154	1969/70	1504	1970/71	1552
1971/72	1654	1972/73	1755	1973/74	1880
1975/76	2063				

11. Personnel Section Ashdod Port.
12. 93% of Israel's tonnage was handled by the Mediterranean ports of Ashdod
and Haifa in 1969/70 (*Year Book of Israel Ports Statistics*, 1969/70, Table
4.3).
13. Source: Operations Department Ashdod Port.
14. Ashdod declined by 21.2%; Haifa by 6.5%. In fact Ashdod's tonnage for
1975/76, 3,052 m. tons was its lowest total since 1971/72, 2983 m. tons,
a situation further exacerbated by the growth in the labour force over that
period. Source: *Annual Report* of the I.P.A. 1975/76.

References

Aronoff, M. 1974. *Frontiertown: the politics of community building in Israel.*
Manchester University Press.

Deshen, S. 1970. *Immigrant voters in Israel.* Manchester: University Press.

Handelman, D. 1977. *Encounters among the aged: the social organization of
interaction in a Jerusalem setting.* Amsterdam.

Israel Ports Authority 1970–76. *Year book of Israel ports statistics,* 1969–70;
1975–76. *Annual Reports,* 1969–70; 1975–76. Tel Aviv.

Mars, G. 1972. *An anthropological study of longshoremen and of industrial
relations in the port of St. John's, Newfoundland, Canada.* Unpub. Ph.D.
thesis. University of London.

Mars, L. 1976. The position of the administrator in a Israeli cooperative
village. *Sociologia Ruralis* 16, no. 1–2, 41–55.

—— 1978a. Politics and administration in the Israeli port of Ashdod. *Institute of Development Studies Bulletin* **9**, no. 3, 33–38.

—— 1978b. Report to the SSRC on grant number HR5209. *Shifts in political leadership among Israeli dock workers in Ashdod Port.* Available from British Lending Library, Boston Spa.

—— (forthcoming). Leadership and power among Ashdod Port workers. In *A composite portrait of Israel*, E. Marx (ed.). London: Academic Press.

Marx, E. 1975. Anthropological studies in a centralized state: the Bernstein Research Project in Israel. *Jewish Journal of Sociology* **17**, no. 2, 131–150.

—— 1976. *The social context of violent behaviour.* London: Routledge.

Ministry of Social Welfare, Israel 1976. *Social profile of settlements in Israel.* (In Hebrew). Jerusalem.

WOMEN'S WORK AND CHILDREN'S WORK:

Variations among Moslems in Kano[1]

ENID SCHILDKROUT

Economic Roles of Women and Children

The notion of the division of labour has several aspects of socio-logical interest: the categorization of different types of work in particular societies; the comparison of societies with different classifications of work; and consideration of modes of recruitment of persons into roles as workers. In addition, as anthropologists, we inevitably focus attention on the cultural values which validate categorizations of work and modes of recruitment into work roles. A study of work-related values — what one might call the "culture of work" — includes consideration of how the definition of work and the allocation of economic roles relates to values in other cultural domains such as religion, ethnicity, class, age and sexual stratification.

Among the modes of labour recruitment given most attention in discussions of the division of labour is ascription based on class, caste, ethnicity and sex. Age has been virtually ignored, undoubtedly because of the relative insignificance of children and older people in the labour force in modern western industrial society. In dealing with countries with rapidly changing economic and demographic structures, this gap is significant, for it leads to ignorance of the economic contribution of large segments of the population. An emphasis, particularly among economists, on the formal sector of the economy also contributes to an underestimation of this portion of the labour force.

This paper is an attempt to examine aspects of the division of labour by age and sex in Hausa society in Kano city. It deals exclusively with Hausa people in an urban setting. Even so, within this limited context, men, women and children are by no means monolithic categories in regard to their economic activities. The high degree of occupational specialization among men in Hausa society has often been noted, and several detailed studies of particular occupational groups have appeared (Jaggar 1973; Tahir

1976). Occupational specialization among men relates closely to
social status, for a man's position in society is in many ways,
although not entirely, defined by his occupation (Smith, M.G.
1959).

The economic roles of Hausa women have not gone unnoticed
(Barkow 1972; Bashir 1972; Hill 1969; Smith, M. 1954), although
discussion of women's economic roles aré inevitably subsumed under
discussions of marital status. Although occupational roles are varied
among women, they do not define women's status to the extent
that they do that of men. The emphasis on Islamic values in defining
the position of women; the importance of the institution of marriage,
and seclusion, or purdah, within marriage; the dominance of men in
marriage and in political life – all obscure the significance of
women's economic roles. Consequently, variations in these roles
and the factors which lead to occupational choices and income
differentials among women – including age, class, marital status,
child-bearing history, and husband's occupation have not been
given much attention.

Among children, too, there are significant variations in economic
activities, depending upon age, class, birth order, family size,
parents' occupations and education. Adults in Hausa society, particularly women in purdah, are dependent upon children in many
ways. Changes now taking place in the economic roles of children,
mainly as a result of the spread of western education, have far-
reaching implications – not only for the future of the children
themselves, but for the adults dependent upon children's economic
services.

Kano City

The research on which this paper is based was conducted in two
wards[2] in Kano city between 1977 and 1979. There are many
similarities between the populations in the two neighbourhoods:
both have been settled for many generations by Hausa speakers,
all of whom today are strongly committed to Islam. Most of the
inhabitants of one ward, Kofar Mazugal, trace their ancestry to the
original Habe inhabitants of Kano; while those in the other, Kurawa,
trace theirs to the Fulani invaders who seized political control of
the state in the early nineteenth century. There has been so much
social and cultural integration between these segments of the society,
that the ethnic distinction has only minimal significance today, as
one among many markers of identity (Paden 1970). It is reflected
primarily in a continuing distinction in occupational roles between
the inhabitants of the two wards. Most of the adult males of Kurawa

are currently in salaried civil service jobs, many of them messengers and clerks; formerly many of them were palace officials — from district chiefs to servants in the Emir's palace. The men of Kofar Mazugal are today, as in the past, engaged primarily in mercantile activities.

Both wards are similar in their inhabitants' commitment to a common set of values with regard to the status of women. These values stipulate early marriage, high fertility, submission to male authority in decision making in the domestic and political domains, polygamy, and seclusion, or purdah, in marriage. Women's occupational activities, while of considerable social and economic importance, are subordinated to other social considerations as indicators of status. There are very few women in Hausa society who do not rely on men in some way for economic support: married women receive housing, some food and some clothing from their husbands; elderly women who have sons rely on their sons, usually more than on their husbands, for support in old age; divorced or widowed women often rely on gifts from men in exchange for sexual favours. This male economic support — its source and extent — is very important in defining a woman's social position. A woman who receives no support from or through men also lacks a certain form of social support — she may work as a housemaid, beg, pound grain, or fetch water — but her status and usually her income are far lower than those of women who are in some ways dependent on men.[3] Those women who are, at least partially, financially and socially dependent on men, are nevertheless able to pursue economically remunerative occupations. These occupations are highly significant in economic terms — often paying for most of a woman's clothing, some of her food, some of her children's living expenses including much of their bridewealth and dowry, gifts for exchange with other women, medicines and luxury goods. Nevertheless this income plays little part in determining status; economic "independence", even relative wealth obtained from a woman's occupation, does not in itself imply high socio-political status for women in Hausa society. There are constraints on the status of women which limit the transferability of economic gain into social or political advantage.

There are also many similarities between the two wards with regard to values about children. Filial piety, first-child avoidance, an increasing separation of the sexes with maturity — accompanied by a strong emphasis on the notion of *kunya*, or shame — are important in all Kano Hausa families.[4] Children are expected to accept increasing responsibility in household tasks from a very young age: there is no notion that "work" is the exclusive prerogative of adults. This is particularly evident in the domain of housework, where women's and children's work is intimately connected. Women in purdah are extremely dependent upon children's services for performing essential household tasks, including shopping, communicating with others outside their houses, removing refuse, caring for younger children, escorting women when they leave the house to go for medical services or to visit friends or relatives on ceremonial occasions. Except in the wealthiest families where some, but not all, of these tasks are performed by servants, children's services are absolutely essential for performing basic housework, not to mention the necessity of assistance from children in helping women with their income-earning activities. All children spend some time every day helping women with various kinds of housework, although there are differences in amounts and types of work done by different children. In addition, all children are expected to attend Qur'anic school, where verses from the *Qur'an* are memorized and the basic obligations of the Muslim person are learned. Most of the boys in both wards attend "*boko*" or secular school.[5]

A striking difference between the two wards which will be discussed in much of the remainder of this paper concerns the education and work of girls. While most girls in Kurawa are now attending "*boko*" school none in Kofar Mazugal are doing so. The girls in Kofar Mazugar are actively involved in street trading, or *talla*, while those in Kurawa rarely do *talla*. There are corresponding differences in the roles of the women in the two wards: while most women in Kofar Mazugal trade, few in Kurawa do so.

Given the broad cultural similarities between the two wards outlined above, how are we to explain these differences? As we have said, the populations of both wards are Muslims and both accept the same Islamic prescriptions regarding the status of women; both stress early marriage for women, male dominance, high fertility and purdah. Yet the attitude towards work, towards what is an acceptable occupation for women and girls, differs markedly in the two wards, as does the attitude towards western education for women. Thus beneath the ideological commitment to Islam, the common use of the Hausa language, and the cultural integration that has occurred among the various segments of Hausa society, differences persist in the domain of the "culture of work" which reflect a long history of economic specialization. The roles of women and young girls not only reflect the Islamic ideals of early marriage and purdah, they also are complementary to male economic roles and reflect a similar divergence. However, only among men is the occupational specialization acknowledged and translated into socio-political status. The ideology of purdah ignores the economic roles of women, which have been aptly termed the "hidden trade" (Hill 1969). Unlike male economic activities, female trading, including the street trading of young girls, is justified by the actors not as an end in itself, not as means of "making a living", but as a means towards the attainment of the ideal status of the Muslim woman — a status which denies and restricts these very activities: women's need to work. Thus the street trading of young girls or the occupations of married women are not seen as means of subsistence, but rather as means of obtaining dowry for the young girl — the *sine qua non* of entry into purdah. In Kurawa, where street trading is rare, dowry and marriage are no less important. There, school attendance has become an alternate means to attaining this end. For young Hausa girls, school attendance and street trading are different kinds of work: both preparatory to entry into purdah — the status in which, ideally, women need not work, but which in reality requires them to work to obtain the means for their daughters' entry into the same status.

Kurawa

Kurawa is near the Emir's palace, and many of the present inhabitants trace their ancestry to the Fulani invaders who, following 'Uthmān dan Fodio, seized political power in the early nineteenth century. Except for claims to certain traditional offices which are based on descent, this ethnic status has little contemporary political or economic significance.

In the last century most of the men in Kurawa had employment within the Emirate administration (see Bashir 1972). Relatively few were traders or craftsmen. The women, most but not all of whom also claimed Fulani descent, practised spinning and embroidery, and specialized in making *jalala* or embroidered saddle covers which are part of the regalia associated with chieftancy. They also embroidered men's trousers and boots. Although in the past, as today, they claim to have kept their earnings separate from the household economy, it is important to note that most of the occupations they pursued were ones which were related to the occupations of the men. The men were the market for women's income-producing activities, while the women supported male status by manufacturing the finery which expressed this. All of these occupations were done from within purdah, as they are today, with men and children assisting women in purchasing supplies and marketing the final products.

Purdah was well established in urban Hausaland by the nineteenth century. In his teachings on women 'Uthmān dan Fodio complained (quoted in Hodgkin 1975: 225) about the abuse of purdah before the *jihad* of 1807. He lamented that men "locked their women up in ignorance, subjected them to the oldest women in the house like 'slaves' ", and kept more than four wives. He certainly did not suggest that women should be removed from seclusion, but rather than men should be concerned with women's religious education within purdah. He emphasized that women should not go out to market if someone else could go for them, although it was appropriate for them to pursue business activities from within the house; they should attend funerals only of close relatives, and they should not attend mosque or court (Ogunbiyi 1969). What was novel about 'Uthmān dan Fodio's teachings about women was his emphasis on education: restricted as it was to the basic tenets of Islam, the notion that women should have some knowledge of written law set a precedent which is cited today when people accept western education for women. As with Muslim education in the past, this˙ is not seen to be in conflict with the ideals of Muslim marriage.

A concern with literacy and education is also evident in the occupations of men in Kurawa. Today, the majority of men are in various civil service occupations, mainly in the Local Government Authority which is, basically, the traditional Emirate administration incorporated into the modern municipal and state government system. All of the Kurawa men have some formal Islamic education, and many are partially literate in Arabic. Some of the older men, over age forty, have studied English at night school or have attended some primary school. All, of course, have attended Qur'anic school. Reflecting the general level of western education in northern Nigeria, very few have attained literacy or fluency in English, but most recognize that their careers would be enhanced by these skills. The relatively low level of western education here, as elsewhere in the north, has kept the income and status level of wage earners down. In Kurawa, the wealthiest families are members of the few trading families who live there, for among traders income is not as dependent upon western education as it is with wage earners. Nevertheless, because of their traditional political status and because of the length of time these families have been settled in Kano, most families are not exclusively dependent upon wages for income. Most houses are privately owned and most families receive some income from family farms outside the town. The inhabitants of the ward (the estimated population of which is about 800) as a whole vary considerably in income and are not clearly distinguishable from other wards in the old city of Kano in terms of a simple notion of economic class. Many of the inhabitants of the ward do, however, have some common identity as members of an occupational category.

The attitude towards western education among men in this ward is evident in the seriousness with which sons are now sent to school. With the exception of *almajirai* (Qur'anic students living with malams) and boys working as servants (none of whom are living with their own families), the male children in Kurawa are in primary school. Some older sons have now finished secondary school. The only girls not attending primary school were ones who lived in female-headed households: girls whose mothers were divorced or widowed, and who needed help from their daughters in procuring the basic means of subsistence, one girl who was a foster child living with relatives, and one girl, age ten, who was married and in purdah.

Kofar Mazugal

The other ward, Kofar Mazugal, is one of the oldest wards in Kano. Most of the men, like their fathers, are traders, many in the cattle trading and butchering businesses. Today trade in manufactured goods, transport, and building contracting are also important occupations. Very few of the older men have any western education and only a few can speak English. Few of them see western education as a means to occupational advancement although most have complied with the Federal Government's policy of universal primary education by enrolling their sons in primary schools.

In Kofar Mazugal, as in Kurawa, there is a gradation in wealth from fairly wealthy to poor. Many houses are privately owned, but there are more renters than in Kurawa. (The ward is also three times larger.) Houses can be found adjacent to one another whose inhabitants vary greatly in income, even though most are traders. Many of the families also receive some produce from family farms, although these are often at a greater distance from Kano city.

The women in Kofar Mazugal, also in purdah, are involved in trade as are their husbands. They trade in raw food stuffs, cooked food and manufactured goods. Many receive initial or periodic help from their husbands, fathers or brothers, mainly in the form of credit or loans. Most of the women trade in items that can be sold in very small quantities and children are extremely important in commodity distribution. Selling is either done from within the house, in which case children come as buyers, or outside, in which case children are both sellers and buyers. Depending on the nature of the commodity, children either take the wares to one place outside the house, or hawk their wares in the street on head trays. Some children, whose mothers do not use their services, trade for other women or for men, receiving either a ten percent commission or a fixed rate of pay.

As in Kurawa, women are dependent on children for carrying on daily household activities. In Kofar Mazugal, however, the role of children in enabling women to carry on their income-producing activities is more noticeable. While dependence on children for either household tasks or income-producing activities is ubiquitous, the extent of this dependency and the nature of children's activities varies with a number of factors: the wealth of the family — especially the presence of servants or clients, the size of the household, the numbers and ages of the children, and the occupations of the women. In both wards children help women in their occupations by purchasing supplies and delivering or selling goods. But in Kurawa, given the nature of women's occupations, these are not necessarily daily activities. In Kofar Mazugal, women work with perishable ingredients and rely on child labour on a daily basis.

Women's pursuit of various types of trade and the level of their investment is thus related to the availability of children between the ages of five and fourteen years. Women's individual occupational histories show changes in activities to be correlated with the birth, growth, and fostering of children. There is no evidence that the need for children in trade is related to decisions about bearing children — for there are many other social and cultural pressures which foster the ideal of high fertility, but the practice of fostering, common in Kano as in many parts of West Africa (see E. Goody 1969, 1971; Oppong 1965; Schildkrout 1973), is clearly correlated with women's economic investments as well as with their child-bearing histories.

Because of their heavy involvement in trade, the incomes of the women in Kofar Mazugal are considerably higher than those in Kurawa. A preliminary survey of data on 83 women indicates that incomes are generally three times higher in Kofar Mazugal. Due to the centrality of marriage in defining female status, these variations in income do not directly alter a woman's socio-economic position. However, high income can facilitate mobility out of one marriage and into a more successful one. Within marriage, there is little conjugal pooling of resources (in either ward), but the extent to which a woman uses her income to feed and clothe her family does depend on the husband's income. Ideally, Hausa husbands provide housing, at least one meal per day, at least one new set of clothes per year for each wife and child, and educational and medical expenses.

Women's income is used to help with subsistence if necessary; if this is not necessary it is reinvested in business, used to purchase luxury items, or invested in gift exchange (*biki*) with other women. The *raison d'être* for some women working for income at all, however, is the expense involved in their children's marriages, much of which is borne by women themselves.

Marriage

Marriage is the most important *rite de passage* in the life of a Hausa person, male or female.[6] First marriage marks the transition to full adult status. The ideal age of marriage for girls is just before puberty, in other words, as soon as the girl is reproductively mature. Most girls are married at about fourteen, but many are married younger, even at age ten. With western education beginning to change the nature of childhood, a small minority of girls delay their marriage until late teens. Boys marry later, usually not until they are economically productive. For boys, there is a long transition period from childhood to adulthood, during which time new occupational skills are learned. Marriage symbolizes the attainment of adult status for the man, but the ability to be economically productive is the necessary condition for this status change. Thus, wealthier men marry younger. For girls, there is no transition period between child-hood and adulthood: marriage and reproductive capacity are in themselves marks of maturity, and as noted earlier, a woman's non-domestic economic roles are irrelevant in defining her status as an adult. In fact, since girls participate fully in housework and in women's income-producing activities from a very young age, and also sometimes carry on small businesses of their own as children (see Schildkrout 1978: 128), there is no transition period in which adult economic roles, distinct from the economic roles performed in childhood, are learned. For boys, who grow up in the sphere of women, initiation into adulthood requires a transition period in which masculine productive roles are learned. Many of these require the acquisition of skills that differ from those acquired in the course of childhood work.

The expenses entailed in getting married, especially for first marriages, are considerable for the families of both bride and groom. Both girls and boys are expected, except in the wealthiest families, to contribute to their marriage expenses, but boys even more so than girls.

Bridewealth, dowry and what J. Goody (1973) refers to as indirect dowry are all involved in the long series of gift exchanges between spouses and their families. The groom must give the bride gifts during courtship; a sum of money is paid to the bride's family when the marriage arrangements are finalized; a formal payment is made to legalize the marriage under Islamic law; and large quantities of cosmetics and clothing are given to the bride during the course of the betrothal and ceremony. The bride's family must reciprocate with a dowry consisting of household goods, provided mostly by the bride, her mother and other female relatives, and furniture and linens, provided by her father. After the marriage and at the birth of each child, but especially after the first birth, the bride's family gives the couple a gift, known as *gara*, consisting of food-stuffs and cash, part of which is distributed to the groom's family. In total, these expenses often far surpass a year's income for any of the parties concerned, and they vary greatly depending upon the wealth of the families involved.

For women, the major part of the marriage expense is entailed in the purchase of that part of the dowry known as *kayan daki*, literally, "things of the room". *Kayan daki* consists of enamel, brass, and glass bowls; pots and platters of many size, shapes, and designs; tea-sets and ornamental glassware; and cooking utensils. All of this is conspicuously displayed in the bride's room and is a sign of the status of the bride's family. In case of divorce, the bride keeps these things. She may sell them if necessary (very occasionally women sell part of their *kayan daki* to raise business capital) and they are eventually passed down to her daughters, although all marriages also require the purchase of new *kayan daki*. In the past, *kayan daki* consisted of brass bowls and calabashes. With the general increase in cash and manufactured goods, the perceived need for large quantities of enamel bowls and glassware has increased. Bashir (1972) reports that poor women will borrow bowls from others to save face at their daughters' marriages, for during the ceremony many women visit and inspect the quantity and quality of a girl's dowry. They do the same thing with the gifts of cosmetics and clothing from the groom. Among women with some western education, the custom of *kayan daki* has not ceased, but the content is changing. There are fewer glass trinkets and enamel bowls, and more electric appliances and china dishes.

In Kofar Mazugal the cost of *kayan daki* is met mainly through the activities of the female children themselves. The income brought in by street trading, or *talla*, except in the poorest families where part of it may be used for food or clothing, is saved for the purchase of *kayan daki*. Men in Kofar Mazugal are generally supportive of their wives' trading activities, often helping them procure supplies or credit. They do not see street trading as a violation of purdah, since women do not enter purdah until after marriage. Most of the young girls in Kofar Mazugal spend between four and eight hours a day engaged in street trading. The profit they earn is kept by their parent or guardian for their marriage, and even before a spouse is selected, the mother uses this income to purchase *kayan daki*. This process may take several years. Girls supplement their earnings from street trading with money they get as gifts from suitors; and delaying the final choice of a husband can be a way of accumulating money for dowry.

If street trading is so important in accumulating dowry, the question arises as to how this expense is met in Kurawa, where most girls do not do *talla*, and where women, who still must bear a large part of their daughter's marriage expenses, have lower incomes. As I have noted, their lower incomes are related to the absence of children — children who are in school, who could otherwise help in their income-producing activities, and to their reliance on low-income occupations such as embroidery or hair-plaiting. Part of the answer to the question of how Kurawa women meet these expenses lies in western education itself, for at present, among those who are not resistent to western education for women, the expenses are often met by the grooms, indirectly, through the larger courting gifts they make to prospective brides. It is common for civil servants, and for businessmen who have some appreciation of the advantages to be gained by acquiring literacy in English, to want to marry women with some western education. While the girls are still in school, suitors give them significant gifts in cash which go towards the purchase of dowry. Men often want to marry women with some western education because of a general sense of the value of education — more prevalent in some sections of the population than in others, or because they feel the educated wife may help them in business. But very few of the men who desire educated wives expect the women to work outside of their homes after marriage. Despite the willingness of some to send their daughters to primary school, in very few cases have expectations of women's roles after marriage changed. Western education thus can be seen as an economic asset for girls, comparable to street trading, within the traditional marriage system and within the traditional definition of female roles. Compared to street trading, it is an economic activity for the same end, the accumulation of dowry, but utilizing different means. Seen in this way, the significance of the income differential between women in the two wards fades. True, women in Kurawa have lower incomes without the help of their daughters to trade; yet since their daughters are engaged in other activities —

i.e. school attendance, which also lead to the accumulation of
dowry, the necessity of high incomes is reduced.

In searching for an explanation of the different attitudes towards
street trading and education for women, we run into difficulty if we
start by examining peoples' attitudes to these alternate activities.
By those opposed to one or the other activity, the same explanation
is given: both western education and street trading are said to lead
to "immorality". Parents fear that their daughters will "be spoiled"
in either case. Fears about the loss of virginity before a girl's first
marriage, and fears about pre-marital pregnancy are great, and these
are the most frequent explanations for opposition to either activity:
street trading or western school. The early age of marriage for girls
is explained in the same way: it is a means of ensuring that the girl
will not risk losing a husband by waiting too long, until she is
"spoiled". A frequent complaint of educators in the north is the
common withdrawal of girls from school for marriage. On the
other hand, for advocates of either school attendance or street
trading, these activities are seen as means of attracting husbands
and accumulating dowry. Except in the wealthiest families where
marriages are often arranged, it is important for a young girl to be
seen in public to attract suitors.

The Work of Boys

Up to this point, I have dwelt primarily on the income-producing
economic activities of women and girls, and the ways in which these
activities relate to the expense of marriage. As we have seen, with
girls, different children pursue different types of activities, the main
dichotomy being between those who attend school and those who do
not. All girls, whether in school or engaged in street trading, also
engage in a large variety of domestic chores, including child care,
shopping, errand running, delivering messages for women in purdah,
escorting women when they go out, sweeping, and helping with
food preparation. Besides these activities, some engage in street
trading, and others do not: this being a function of income (a
minority of girls in the very poorest families engage in street trading
for subsistence) and of the value orientation of the parents regarding
western education.

Among boys, children can also be categorized according to
different work roles, but there is, as well, a temporal categorization
which is not relevant in the case of girls. Young boys help in
domestic work, including child care, shopping, delivering messages,
cleaning house, and washing clothes. Less often than girls — usually
when girls are unavailable, they help with food preparation and

escorting women outside the house. All of these activities, whether done by boys or girls, like the housework of women, must be considered "economic". Were family members not to perform these tasks, outside help would·have to be hired. And, in fact, in wealthier Hausa families, some of these tasks are performed by hired help including washmen and housemaids.

There are fewer boys than girls who do not attend primary school. The majority of these are the *almajirai*, Qur'anic students, who spend all of their time studying the *Qur'an* with a particular malam or teacher. Many of them come from rural areas and stay in Kano during the dry season, returning home to help with farmwork when the rains appear. While they are in town, these boys are usually self-supporting.[7] Some support themselves through begging, a not unprofitable job given the Islamic injunction to give alms, through odd jobs such as cleaning gutters or portering, by embroidering caps, or by doing *talla*, for a commission or for subsistence. Other boys who do not attend primary school include crippled children, who beg, or children whose parents adamantly oppose western education. These children are either in Qur'anic school full time, or are apprentices to their fathers or to other men in particular trades. Until these boys are old enough to be useful as apprentices, they may help their mothers by performing *talla*. For most boys there are several changes in work roles before adulthood: domestic tasks, within the female domain, dominate early childhood; school attendance or apprenticeship in a "male" occupation dominate the period after puberty and before marriage.

Conclusion

In looking at variations in the roles of women and children in urban Kano, I have noted that these variations fall into a pattern, corresponding to residence in particular wards. The categorization of wards according to men's occupations has long been noted (see Paden 1973), but the corresponding variation in the roles of women and children has not been studied. The variations in male occupational roles can easily be traced back through history, to the point where what are today simply occupational roles formerly corresponded to ethnic and cultural differences. But today the cultural differences have virtually disappeared: certainly they have disappeared in terms of the way in which the position of women is defined in the society as a whole.

Islamic ideology, with its acceptance of male dominance, polygamy, and seclusion in marriage dominates the attitude toward women in both wards. Yet the conceptualization of women's and children's (particularly girls') economic roles in the two wards is clearly different. These differences are related to the different traditions of men's work. Thus, beneath or within a homogeneous religious ideology there exist different "cultures of work", resulting from varying historical experiences. Today these historical experiences are reflected in different attitudes about the relationship between time, labour, income, and aspects of personal status including age and sex roles. Consequently, purdah has a different expression for the wives of civil servants claiming aristocratic background than it does for the wives of traders or butchers, regardless of their incomes, and regardless of the ubiquitous enforcement of seclusion. Children's roles also differ according to the differing ways purdah is interpreted, for in order to enforce purdah, and at the same time allow women to trade, children must participate directly in these trading activities as they do in Kofar Mazugal. But these economic activities on the part of both women and children, geared as they are to the marriage system, are understood not as occupations but as a means towards the realization of Islamic and Hausa ideals regarding marriage and the family. In the same way, western education is accepted for women not as a harbinger of a new definition of femininity but as an alternate means to a traditional end.

The definition of female status, based as it is on sexuality and the reproductive role of women, takes little account of variations in the lives of women within purdah. But as I have shown, these variations are considerable, even though they do little to alter the status of women *vis-à-vis* men, that is, in the socio-political structure of the society as a whole. In looking at the variations in women's economic activities, I have noted that the income from women's occupations is always kept separate from the household budget: housework and income-producing activities are clearly conceptualized as separate domains of female activity, even in those instances where the actual work — food preparation, for example — is identical. Because the incomes of some women, like those in Kurawa, are lower than the incomes of others, some women are economically more dependent upon their husbands than others. In this sense, one could argue that although the ideal of purdah is ubiquitous, it is more strictly enforced in those wards where female occupations are limited, in particular where street trading among young girls is prohibited and, ironically, where western education for women has been accepted. But as we have seen, these differences are negated by the impossibility of women doing little with their income other than investing it right back into the marriage system.

Purdah is said to be a sign of the high economic status of the husband since it indicates his ability to support his family without his wife needing to work. When this refers to agricultural work in a rural context, the connection between female employment and seclusion has a different meaning than it does in an urban context. Thus many writers (Smith, M.G. 1954; Hill 1972; Barkow 1972) have noted that at the end of farm slavery in Hausaland, rural women embraced purdah as a means of freeing themselves from arduous farm labour and as means of allowing them to pursue cash-generating trading occupations. In an urban context the relationship between purdah, the economic status of husbands, and the economic activities of wives is more complicated, since in any case, the arduous work of agricultural production is not an option. As I have shown, in urban Kano, purdah takes many forms. In all wards, many families are only able to adopt purdah because children work and help secluded women perform household tasks which necessitate communication with the outside world. In some wards, such as Kofar Mazugal, women actively trade, with the result that they are even more dependent on their children. In other wards, such as Kurawa, women are somewhat less dependent on their children but more dependent, financially, on their husbands. Thus purdah may cut across class lines if one judges this by examining the economic status of the men whose wives are in seclusion. But it does this by increasing the economic differentiation among women and children, including their access to education and the amount of work they perform.

Looked at from the point of view of the economy as a whole, women and children perform a very large variety of labour roles which tend to be overlooked. As women's work moves away from agricultural production — where its significance has also long been underestimated — it tends to be less and less recognized as work. Thus, we have the common stereotype of women in purdah, like housewives the world over, as being women who do not work. Children's work, crucial as it may be in commodity distribution and in the domestic economy, is often seen as education rather than work. In a sense, women and children can be said to do work, but not to have occupations. Their economic roles are not the primary means of defining their persistently sub-ordinate social positions. This may account, as well, for the typically low status evaluation in most societies of certain types of work including food preparation, child care, and petty commodity production and distribution.

Notes

1. The research on which this paper is based has been supported by the National Science Foundation, the Wenner-Gren Foundation, the Social Science Research Council and the American Museum of Natural History. Institutional support was also offered by the University of Lagos, and Bayero University, Kano.
2. Wards are administrative units of the *birni* or old city of Kano. There are at present 132 wards.
3. This does not necessarily imply emotional dependence. The structure of Hausa marriage and the great separation of male and female domains leads to a high degree of emotional independence among Hausa women *vis-à-vis* men.
4. See Schildkrout (1978) for a more detailed discussion.
5. In Hausa, both Arabic school and western school are known as *makaranta*, distinguished as *makarantar Arabia* and *makarantar boko*. This dualism in the educational system of the north is a result of the imposition of the colonial system on a highly developed traditional system, and the preservation of the latter. Attempts are being made to expand and unify the system. For the history of education in the north, see Hiskett (1975), Hubbard (1975), Ogunsola (1974), and Fafunwa (1974).
6. For boys, circumcision, performed at about age 6, is also very important.
7. In rural areas, *almajirai* work on the farms of their malams, or teachers.

References

Barkow, J. 1972. Hausa women and Islam. *Canadian Journal of African Studies* 6 (2), 317–328.

Bashir, M.K. 1972. *The economic activities of secluded married women in Kurawa and Lallokin Lemu, Kano City*. B.Sc. thesis. Ahmadu Bello University, Zaria.

Fafunwa, A. Babs. 1974. *History of education in Nigeria*. London: George Allen & Unwin Ltd.

Goody, E. 1969. Kinship fostering in Gonja. In *Socialization: the approach from social anthropology*, P. Mayer (ed.). ASA Monograph 8. London: Tavistock, 51–74.

—— 1971. Forms of pro-parenthood: the sharing and substitution of parental roles. In *Kinship*, J.R. Goody (ed.). London: Penguin Modern Sociology Readings.

Goody, J.R. 1973. Bridewealth and dowry in Africa and Eurasia. In *Bridewealth and dowry*, J.R. Goody and S.J. Tambiah (eds.). Cambridge Papers in Social Anthropology 7. Cambridge: Cambridge University Press, 1–58.

Hill, P. 1969. Hidden trade in Hausaland. *Man* 4 (3), 392–409.

—— 1972. *Rural Hausa, a village and a setting*. London: Cambridge University Press.

Hiskett, M. 1975. Islamic education in the tradition and state systems in northern Nigeria. In *Conflict and harmony in education in tropical Africa*, G.N. Brown and M. Hiskett (eds.). London: George Allen and Unwin.

Hodgkin, T.H. 1975. *Nigerian perspectives*, 2nd edition. London: Oxford University Press.

Hubbard, J.P. 1975. Government and Islamic education in Northern Nigeria (1900–1940). In *Conflict and harmony in education in tropical Africa*, G.N. Brown and M. Hiskett (eds.). London: George Allen and Unwin.

Jaggar, P.J. 1973. Kano city blacksmiths: precolonial distribution, structure and organisation. *Savannah* 2 (1), 11–26.

Ogunbiyi, I.A. 1969. The position of Muslim women as stated by ʿUthmān b. Fūdī. *Odu* (New Series), 2, 43–61.

Ogunsola, A.F. 1974. *Legislation and education in northern Nigeria*. Ibadan: Oxford University Press.

Oppong, C. 1965. *Some sociological aspects of education in Dagbon*, M.A. thesis, Legon, Ghana.

Paden, J. 1970. Urban pluralism, integration and adaptation of communal identity in Kano, Nigeria. In *From tribe to nation in Africa: studies in incorporation processes*, R. Cohen and J. Middleton (eds.). Scranton, Pennsylvania: Chandler.

—— 1973. *Religion and political culture in Kano*. Berkeley: University of California Press.

Schildkrout, E. 1973. The fostering of children in urban Ghana: problems of ethnographic analysis in a multi-cultural context. *Urban Anthropology* 2 (1), 48–73.

—— 1978. Age and gender in Hausa society: socio-economic roles of children in urban Kano. In *Sex and age as principles of social differentiation*, J.S. La Fontaine (ed.), ASA Monograph No. 17. London: Academic Press, 109–138.

Smith, M. 1954. *Baba of Karo*. London: Faber.

Smith, M.G. 1954. Introduction. *Baba of Karo*. M. Smith. London: Faber.

—— 1959. The Hausa system of social status. *Africa* 29, 239–252.

Tahir, I. 1976. *Scholars, sufis, saints and capitalists in Kano 1904–1974*. Ph.D. thesis, Cambridge University.

WORKERS, LORDS AND MASTERS:

The Organization of Labour on South African Farms

J.B. LOUDON

Introduction

Labour conditions on South African farms are remarkable for their
diversity. Nevertheless it is possible to distinguish three main
varieties of White-owned farm in terms of the composition of the
Black work-force. First there are what may be called 'plantations'
where various kinds of crops are cultivated, including sugar, citrus
fruit and commercial timber. Such farms, employ, usually on an
annual contract basis, large numbers of temporary male migrants
from the so-called Black homelands. F. Wilson (1977) has described
them as 'labour-mining farms', since the men live in compounds
and work for wages on much the same terms as in the gold mines,
without their employers having any need to take responsibility for,
or indeed even think about, the dependants of their workers or the
communities from which they come. On the Natal sugar belt, for
example, where large numbers of such migrant workers are employed,
wages in fact follow closely behind developments in the gold fields
which provide the main alternative source of wage-labour for these
men.

A second variety, found in many parts of South Africa, consists
of farms where the resident Blacks comprise only those regular male
workers actually required by the farmer, together with what is usually
described as a 'reasonable' number of women and children, but with
no other dependants. Although these workers and their immediate
families usually live on the farms continuously for a number of years,
and may therefore be said to have their homes there, they are not in
general permitted to cultivate land or graze their own stock; nor
can they often expect the relative security of hoping to continue
living there when the head of the household is no longer able to do
a full day's work.

The third variety consists of what have been called 'labour
reserve farms', since the ratio of dependants to regular workers on
such farms is usually very high and the overflow of labour tends to

seep into other agricultural areas or into industry. They are better described as 'labour tenant farms', since they have their origin in the labour tenancy system characteristic of those parts of South Africa, such as Natal and the Eastern Cape, which were already thickly populated by Blacks when the first White settlers came in the first half of the nineteenth century. By most of their Black inhabitants these farms tend to be regarded as home from cradle to grave; the people live in their own kraals and each household may expect to have customary rights to graze a specified number of livestock and to cultivate as much land as they wish. Apart from certain crucial restrictions, together with the obligation to provide labour for the farmer, living conditions in Black households on these farms bear some superficial resemblance to those applying in 'tribal' areas in the past and also to those found in Black homelands today.

This essay is about status relations in the context of work on certain South African farms of this third kind.[1] The material to be presented was collected in an area of Natal which I shall call Izolo.[2] The farms in question are owned and managed by White English-speaking South African farmers; the workers on the farms are Zulu-speaking Blacks.[3] The large-scale national setting consists of a super-structure based upon a long-standing ideology of enforced separation between Whites and Blacks and on machinery designed to place power and authority firmly in the hands of the dominant White minority. The culture is one in which interaction between Whites and Blacks is public and instrumental, and is pitched almost exclusively in terms of work. By contrast, the small-scale local setting is that of a collection of large, contiguous, privately-owned estates, on each of which relations between individual Whites and individual Blacks are frequently highly personalized. Even though interaction commonly occurs in the context, and through the idiom, of work, on most occasions explicit definition of the situation in terms of employer-employee relations is avoided by both parties. Behaviour tends to accord with ideas of White hegemony, involving accepted notions of ostensible inequality; but this shared view of their social world is conceptualized by both Whites and Blacks as one involving dyadic relationships between master and servant, patron and client, lord and retainer, and generally finding expression in terms of command and deference.

Farm People – Black and White

Remarkably little is known about the details of social relations on White-owned farms in South Africa, apart from what may be inferred from macroscopic studies and from a mass of notoriously unreliable statistics and official reports. There are also a few isolated case studies; but the best of these remain those carried out more than forty years ago by Hunter (1936 and 1961, 1937) and twenty years later by Roberts (1958).[4] Most studies of South African agriculture take the sociography of White employers almost as a given, above or beyond serious consideration. This is understandable. The most important problems — human, practical and theoretical — concern Black farmworkers. But, as Malinowski wrote more than forty years ago, "the modern ethnographer cannot ignore" the Whites who (as Malinowski put it) "play their own cultural game in Africa". The ethnographer (he wrote) "must know the home foundations of European institutions and movements. And this general knowledge he must then check by fieldwork on Europeans in Africa" (Malinowski 1938). This is especially important where, as seems to be the case in Izolo, the Blacks' self-image is substantially affected by White constructions of past events and present circumstances, and where the formal structure of work arrangements derives from exclusively White control of resources, particularly time and capital investment. Thus there seemed to be good grounds for redressing the more usual emphasis and writing rather more fully about the Whites of Izolo than about the Blacks. Anyone who finds, with Malinowski, that 'the concept of Africans and Europeans . . . leading a contented tribal existence suffers from a taint of smugness and sense of unreality' (ibid.) is clearly either unwilling or unable to read between the lines of what follows.[5]

The total White population of South Africa is expected to reach about four and a half million by 1980; of these, over one and a half million will be Whites whose first language is English, roughly ninety-five per cent of whom will be living in urban areas. Throughout this century White English-speaking South Africans have been an overwhelmingly urban population. In rural areas Whites whose first language is Afrikaans outnumber their English-speaking counterparts by more than three to one. But it should be noted that the number of English-speaking Whites in rural areas, although relatively small, has remained remarkably constant when compared with the growing White population of urban areas in South Africa generally and with the steadily declining proportion of Afrikaans-speakers who have their homes in rural areas.[6] English-speaking Whites in rural areas today probably total about 80,000 over half of whom live on farms in Natal, many of them in scattered local communities similar to that which is the subject of the present study.

Izolo is a locality in the Natal Midlands, south of the Tugela river and roughly midway between the Indian Ocean and the Lesotho border in the Drakensberg Mountains. It consists of a valley about thirty kilometres long and ten kilometres wide, lying about 3,500 feet above sea level, and enclosed on three sides by hills rising in places to an altitude of some 6,000 feet. The climate is temperate in comparison with that of Durban and the coastal belt of Natal; the summers are warm and wet, the winters dry and bracing. In spite of having relatively distinct physical boundaries, Izolo has never had any administrative identity. Today it has about 2,500 inhabitants, of whom about 180 are English-speaking Whites, mostly farmers and their families; the remainder are Zulu-speaking Blacks, mostly farm-workers and their families, living in their own kraals on land owned by their employers. In one instance a farm also has a compound for migrant workers. Two farmers also employ Asian mechanics who live with their families in houses provided by their employers; but these two households, the only Asian households in the valley, number in all less than a dozen persons.

In 1950—52 there were twenty-one farms in Izolo. By 1977 several changes had occurred in the size and boundaries, and in the ownership, of a number of the farms. The net effect of a series of adjustments is that there are now twenty-eight farms, with an average size of about 1,000 hectares, ranging from three farms of over 2,000 hectares to a number of only about 100 hectares or less. The larger farms are all concerned with timber production, cattle rearing or dairying — with wide variations of emphasis. Some of the smaller farms concentrate on pig production, poultry rearing, fruit and vegetable growing or producing honey, though they usually combine two or more activities.

The size of the Black workforce, and the varieties of skilled and unskilled labour required, varies considerably from one type of farm to another. This in turn affects the composition of the workforce and the structure of social relations between White farmers and their Black labourers. At one extreme for example, is a farm with an area of about 2,500 hectares and a total Black population of about 800 men, women and children. The farm is run as a partnership by three White farmers with a White farm manager; its success depends on the ability of the Whites to delegate detailed authority over work gangs to Black *indunas* or 'headmen' and to retain the services of sufficient skilled and trusted Black workers to keep various departments of a relatively massive enterprise running smoothly and profitably. At the other extreme, a small farm of about 100 hectares, specializing in intensive pig rearing and fattening, can operate with a very small workforce; but the success of the undertaking depends on close working relations between the

White farmer and his wife and a few trusted Black workers who can
be relied upon to take a good deal of initiative and responsibility
and also work regularly for long hours and at weekends. The same
is true on all farms in respect of certain key workers, who must be
capable of being left to get on with their jobs without constant
supervision by their employers. Such work carries higher prestige,
and often higher wages, than other less responsible jobs. On large
dairy farms this applies to men responsible for calf rearing and, in
particular, to those in charge of complex milking machinery and
its care and cleaning. It used also to be true of other men dealing
with cattle, especially those in charge of trek or draught oxen. Nowadays this responsibility for transport and haulage has been largely
relegated to an even more prestigious group, tractor drivers, who
are regarded, as much by their employers as by themselves and
their fellow workers, as the élite among Blacks working on farms.

In 1937 there were about 120,000 regular Black workers resident
on White-owned farms in Natal. At the present time the number is
probably about 150,000. In addition there are about 90,000 Black
workers on Natal farms who are categorized as 'casual workers' or
'domestic workers'.[7] Most of these are almost certainly members
of the households of regular workers. When due allowance is made
for those dependants of regular workers who live with them,
whether or not they are themselves employed as casual or domestic
workers, the total Black population resident on White farms in Natal
is probably in excess of one million. Unlike the other three provinces
of the Republic (i.e. the Cape, the Transvaal and the Orange Free
State), where the average percentage drop in regular farm workers
between 1961 and 1973 was of the order of eighteen per cent, their
numbers in Natal have dropped over the same period by less than
one per cent. The numbers of domestic workers on farms have
dropped over the same period by about twenty-five per cent in all
four provinces. But, when it comes to casual workers on farms,
Natal is again the exception; in the other provinces the number of
casual workers has dropped by an average of about fourteen per
cent, whereas in Natal the number of casual workers has shown a
marked increase.[8]

A number of Dutch place-names in the District serve as a
reminder of the fact that this wholly English-speaking 'white rural
area' was once part of the short-lived Boer Republic of Natalia,
established by Voortrekkers from the Cape in 1839. It was under
the Republic that Izolo and many similar areas in the midlands of
Natal were first surveyed and carved up into large plots for White
settlers. But Natal became a British colony in 1843 and most of the

Voortrekkers departed. The lands left empty were before long taken over by British settlers, the first big waves of which arrived in 1849 and 1850. By 1856 Natal had a White population of 8,500; almost all were English-speaking and most lived in what were than still rural areas. Durban and Pietermaritzburg were at that time little more than overgrown villages.[9] After the creation of the British colony certain areas were set aside for occupation by the native Black population. Chiefly situated in southern Natal, but including one not far from Izolo, these areas were then known as 'locations', the word still most commonly used by local Whites to refer to them; later they became 'Reserves' and are now parts of the Black 'homeland' of KwaZulu. Zululand itself did not become an administrative part of Natal until annexation in 1879. Most of it remained in the hands of Blacks; but considerable areas, notably almost the whole of the fertile coastal sugar belt, were later transferred to White ownership.

When the Union of South Africa was established in 1910 the rights of Blacks to occupy land were very different in the four constituent provinces and were nowhere clearly defined. The Natives Land Act of 1913 aimed at a stable and uniform policy; though initially regarded as a temporary measure designed to maintain the status quo, the situation established at that time laid the main foundations for the present situation and remained unaltered for almost twenty five years. The Act began by clearly demarcating Reserves for Black occupation and by forbidding the transfer of such land by sale or lease to Whites. But a further provision forbade the purchase of land by Blacks outside the Reserves, except in the Cape Province. This last-named exception was cancelled by the Native Trust and Land Act, introduced in 1936 as an integral part of the South African government's segregation policy. No Africans thereafter had the right to purchase land outside Reserves. By 1945 the latter comprised about ten per cent of the land surface of the Union of South Africa; the addition of some areas has brought the Black homelands (as the former Reserves are now called) up to about twelve per cent of the land surface of today's Republic, including those parts known as the Transkei and Bophuthatswana, which were granted spurious independence in 1976 and 1977 respectively.

When we come to examine the position of Blacks on White-owned land in Natal (the situation in the other three provinces was very different), we find that there has never in effect been any limit to the number of families that might be resident on a European-owned farm. Before 1913 there was also no general restriction upon the acquisition of land by native Blacks. But the vast majority of Blacks living in Natal outside the 'locations' or 'reserves' fell into one or other of two categories — 'squatters' and 'labour tenants'. Squatters were Black tenants living with their families on White-owned land and paying to their landlord a rent in cash or kind for the right to have access to a defined plot. They were under no obligation to work for their farmer-landlord. Many in fact did so on a casual basis; but others nominally living in White rural areas used them as a base, leaving their families there while they worked in towns; many of them were more or less permanent migrant labourers who were away from home for long periods. Others managed to scrape a living (and their rents) by working as peasants cultivating their patches as cash-tenants, often combining this with periods of migrant labour elsewhere. Labour tenants were those who agreed with a farmer to provide him with labour, either their own or that of members of their family or both, for a limited period of the year, in return for the right to live on the farmer's property, cultivate a portion of land, and graze a specified number of stock.

Up to the 1914—1918 war full-time wage-paid labour was almost unknown on Natal farms. Labour was provided by labour-tenants and their dependants (particularly their sons), who usually worked for six months of the year, either unpaid or for very low wages; while actually working they were also provided with rations. Wives and daughters were also expected to work on a casual basis as required, and as domestic servants for specified periods, usually for six months at a time. Many labour tenants and some of their dependants also worked for more than the compulsory six months' period; they were then paid a wage at least double that paid before. Full-time wage labour, provided by men who lived on the farm and worked throughout the year for wages in cash and kind, did not usually involve the farmer in providing accommodation for a man's family or allowing him to cultivate land or graze stock. By the outbreak of the 1939—45 war it is estimated that about 30 per cent of farm-labour in Natal fell into this category: but full-time wage labour was found mostly in southern parts of the Province and on sugar estates along the coastal belt. A high proportion of these wage-labourers were 'foreign' migrant workers; among them were many from Central Africa, Basutoland (now Lesotho) and the Eastern Cape (cf. Murray, this volume).

In 1950 almost all farm work on private European-owned farms in Izolo and other parts of the midlands of Natal was done by labour-tenants and their dependants, on much the same basis as that which had prevailed for two or more generations. Elsewhere in South Africa there were increasing complaints from farmers that labour on the mines and in the towns, most of which (other than 'foreign' migrant workers) had previously been drawn from the Reserves, was now being provided from among the most active young men on the farms. Farmers saw themselves in danger of becoming the unwilling landlords of the elderly relatives and wives and children of men most of whom worked elsewhere for wages higher than they could get on their home farms. By the 1960s, large numbers of squatters throughout South Africa had been removed from White-owned land; and most labour-tenants and their dependants were either evicted or, more often in Natal, converted into full-time wage labourers. By 1976 labour tenancy in South African agriculture had in effect vanished; this was largely the direct or indirect result of state intervention designed to establish a more stable relationship between urban industry and farming as far as the supply of labour was concerned. By 1977, however, increase in unemployment had produced a situation in which, as far as farms in Izolo were concerned, there was no great shortage of unskilled workers; but increased mechanization and greater sophistication in agricultural techniques, together with in many cases the substitution of Black semi-skilled labour for the skilled labour of Asians, had the effect of creating a scarcity of the most highly valued Black workers. The best men tended to leave the farms. The clearest example is that of tractor drivers, especially those sufficiently trained to carry out servicing and minor repairs on the farm. By 1976 it is reckoned that farm mechanization in Izolo had increased by something like six hundred per cent compared with 1950. As we shall see, tractor drivers and others responsible for using and maintaining expensive capital equipment earn substantially higher wages than most other farm workers. At the same time the extremely low level of education among farm workers, combined with the need on each farm for at least a few labourers able to read, write and do simple arithmetic, led to readiness on the part of farmers to permit the setting up of government-supported farm schools for the elementary education of the children of workers, among whom would be found the tractor drivers of the future. In addition, they believed that the most able, progressive and skilled farm workers were likely to be encouraged to remain on the farm if they knew that their children were going to obtain an education there which they might not get elsewhere.

But by 1977 the reality was that former labour-tenants on most Izolo farms retained many of the advantages (such as they were) of

labour-tenancy, despite having been transformed into full-time
wage labourers, paid in cash and kind, with two weeks paid leave
per annum on basic wages, plus rations, grazing for their stock, land
to cultivate and a number of other perquisites, unobtainable in most
other kinds of job. Many continued to live on the land which their
ancestors had occupied and in which they, like their fathers and
grandfathers before them, expected to be buried. They worked for
employers who were the sons or grandsons of men for whom their
forebears had worked in their time and for whom their mothers or
fathers' sisters had acted as nurse-girls. They knew the families of
their employers, and their employers knew their families, to an
extent undreamt of among White employers and Black workers in
urban industries. The other side of the coin included the fact that
some of them were either in more or less permanent financial debt
to their employers, or dependent upon their employers for the
possibility of credit, provided that their industriousness and regularity
at work were deemed reasonably satisfactory and that their personal
relations with their employers remained good. At the informal level,
if not otherwise, the situation on many of the long-established
farms is probably nearer to that of the tenant-labour system of the
past, with the coercion applied not so much by the world outside
the farm as by the ties within it, than it is to that of the modern
capitalist enterprise, characterized by more or less impersonal
relations between employer and wage-labourer, which at first sight
some farms appear to be. In other words, from the Black point of
view, provided you did what was expected of you, at work and
otherwise, and kept on good terms with your employers, and
provided he neither sold the farm nor died without an immediate
heir, you were all right; but if these conditions failed to apply, you
had nowhere to go apart from the overcrowded and unfamiliar
towns and reserves, to neither of which could you take your stock
in the hope of getting grazing land, and in neither of which could
you reasonably hope to obtain a house site with a plot for
cultivation. Obtaining another job on another farm depended
partly on the possession of a good reputation, preferably with at
least some special skills or experience, and partly on not being
encumbered with too many dependants to accommodate and
support.

In Natal today there are increasing numbers of landless and jobless
Blacks, searching for a living and, if possible, for security. Their
situation is reminiscent of, and yet very different from, that of the
farmworkers' forebears who first came to Izolo in the middle years
of the last century. It seems clear that most of the Blacks living on

Izolo farms in the later part of the nineteenth century, from whom most of the present inhabitants are descended, were there as a result of the movement onto them of Zulu-speaking people from other areas, seeking security and a living under White protection. But there is also a local tradition among both Blacks and Whites that a small number of indigenous Zulu-speaking people managed to remain in the area despite the fact that most of them were wiped out during the *Mfecane*, the violent upheavals accompanying the emergence of the Zulu kingdom under Shaka and its later depredations under his successors. In the 1850s and 1860s, according to their descendants, Izolo farmers were well able to accommodate more Blacks than they needed for daily work on their land; a surplus of local labour, provided it was kept within bounds, served as a reservoir easily drawn upon as and when required. Farmers derived their income mainly from the sale of indigenous timber, and from raising cattle and sheep. But to a considerable extent they seem to have been self-supporting and self-sufficient, leading comfortable lives in a small community and in most cases lacking opportunity or ambition to become more prosperous. Their grandchildren speak wistfully of those days, contrasting what they see as their uncertain future, and their struggles in a competitive economy, with what they imagine to have been a time free from serious anxieties and forebodings.

The core of the present White population consists of second, third and fourth generation descendants of English-speaking settlers in the valley. The first of these arrived between 1849 and 1856, and were therefore among the original British settlers in Natal. Most of them were from Scotland and the north of England. Many of those who came to Izolo and other parts of the Natal midlands did so because they already knew each other in Britain or had mutual acquaintances; others seem to have become neighbours as a result of ties of friendship established during the voyage to South Africa or soon after arrival.[10] Mostly they had been farmers, tradesmen or members of the middle classes; there were also a few professional men among them and one or two younger sons of minor landed gentry. Their values and attitudes (and also perhaps their class identity) may be inferred from the fact that they were nearly all staunch Methodists and Presbyterians. The present Anglican church in Izolo was founded and built by Methodists; but the founders soon became Anglicans in most cases, and their descendants are virtually all Anglicans today.[11] The latter retain, however, many of the down-to-earth characteristics commonly attributed to Nonconformist Yorkshiremen and Presbyterian Lowland Scots. With the passage of time, and under the influence of those descended from minor landed gentry, they have tended to develop slightly inflated notions about the social standing in Britain of their founding settler forebears.

This is scarcely to be wondered at. While it would be a slight exaggeration to say that they live like lords on their estates, they are at home accustomed to deference and surrounded by servants, and able to give more time, thought, money and energy to leisure and sporting pursuits than is now possible for more than a tiny minority of British people. Few Izolo Whites have ever been overseas and even fewer have direct personal experience of modern Britain; the knowledge of those that have is based on brief holiday visits. The attitudes of all of them to that country, especially in relation to Rhodesia, are, to put it mildly, ambivalent. They vehemently insist on the fact that they are South Africans first and last. Yet, to an extent of which they themselves seem scarcely aware, they identify themselves in ordinary conversation as English; and, despite all evidence to the contrary, including the consistent emphasis by South African radio and television news programmes on the seamier sides of life in Britain and on the bleaker aspects of British weather and industrial relations, most Izolo Whites carry in their minds a sentimental vision of Britain that is at least forty years out of date. In so far as they identify themselves with any group in Britain, it is with a rural upper class of pre-war vintage; this is reinforced by the almost proprietary interest many, especially the women, take in the British Royal family, which they see presented as being, like themselves, much involved with dogs, horses and sport, especially polo.

For the Whites the locality forms the basis for a clearly defined community, with its own church, surrounded by a graveyard, a modern recreation hall and sports club with tennis courts and squash courts, a flourishing Women's Institute and a well-known local polo team. The annual Izolo gymkhana is an important equestrian and social event in the district. White households in the valley are all linked through the same local dirt road to each other's houses and to the newly-completed tarmac road at the bottom of the valley, so that it is virtually impossible to leave the place without at least some neighbours knowing. Furthermore, all houses are connected up to one or other of a small number of manually operated shared telephone circuits or 'party lines', through which those on one local 'party line' can communicate with each other without needing to go through the exchange in town. Whites visit one another constantly. They tend to travel even the shortest distances by car or truck, and think nothing of long journeys of hundreds of kilometres to shop or visit friends or members of their families. Few if any White households in Izolo have less than two motor vehicles available for family use; some have three or more. Very recently an unofficial walkie-talkie radio service has been set up in Izolo, as has happened in other remote localities in the region. This is ostensibly for use in case of emergencies such as forest fires; to some it is not unconnected with more serious events in other parts of Southern Africa, while for others it is simply one more medium for the exchange of practical jokes and gossip.

On all farms the extent to which Black servants play a part in the ordinary domestic life of the household is as natural and invisible to the Whites as the air they breathe. Blacks clean the house; polish the floors, the furniture and the silver; do the gardening; collect and chop firewood; stoke the boilers for hot water; lay, light and clear the fires; wash the dishes and the cars; do the laundry and the ironing; make the beds; do much of the minding of White children; and do most of the cooking. No White ever carries parcels or bags of shopping from the car into the house. Trays of refreshments are brought at least six times a day: early tea to each bedroom first thing in the morning; tea or coffee, with cake and biscuits, at about half past ten in the morning on the verandah; coffee after lunch; afternoon tea, with sandwiches and cake; drinks of various kinds soon after six o'clock in the evening; tea or coffee in the sitting room after the evening meal. Meals themselves in many households are lavish and formal affairs, at least by present day British standards, with two or more servants waiting at table, especially when visitors are present. Most White housewives on farms find themselves having to supervise a good deal of the work done by their servants, since the latter are mostly relatively untrained girls who only do two or three separate spells of six months domestic service before becoming pregnant or marrying, when they either leave the farm altogether or join the outside labour force in some capacity or other. On the other hand, cooks, gardeners and laundry women may spend a large part of their lives as domestic servants and, being trained and experienced, can to a great extent be left to do their work without close supervision. In such cases the housewife's main function with regard to them may only be to give general directions, arrange menus and hand out supplies from larders, store cupboards or deep freezes, all of which are kept locked to prevent pilfering.

A few Izolo farmers are members of the Victoria Club in

Pietermaritzburg; they use it as a place to meet friends or have lunch when visiting town. Its atmosphere and architecture are little different from those of one of the smaller London clubs; but outside its premises in one of the main streets of the provincial capital is a flag-staff from which the Union Jack is still flown every day. Certain protected species of antelope, such as the reedbuck in Izolo, are known as 'Royal Game' and the main annual agricultural show in Natal, held every year in Pietermaritzburg, is still entitled the Royal Show. Perhaps these trivial relics will survive as harmless reminders of an already almost forgotten Imperial past. Far more important, and far more likely to survive (if their present thriving condition is anything to go by), are the English-speaking South African boarding schools for boys. Two of the most prestigious of these are in Natal, within fifty miles distance from Izolo. They were founded in the last quarter of the nineteenth century and are ideologically indis-tinguishable from the English public schools on which they were originally modelled, as may be seen from the fact that their head-masters are still members of the Headmasters' Conference in London. In addition, there are in Natal a number of boarding preparatory schools for boys, and several boarding schools for girls, again in both cases modelled on similar schools in England. Virtually every White male and female in Izolo over the age of forty attended one or other of these schools; and most are enthusiastic members of old boys' or old girls' associations.[12] Of those under the age of forty, including today's children, the majority were, are being, or expect to be, educated at them, despite the fact that the annual fees are now in the region of R2,500 (equivalent to about £1,500) or more.[13] The continued existence in Britain of the originals on which these schools are based, together with their continued association with them through the Headmasters' Conference, is seen by Izolo Whites as one of the two most important aspects of the English tradition.

The other is sport, devotion to which is probably more intense and widespread among English-speaking Whites than among members of any other section of the South African population.[14] Izolo farmers and their families are no exception. Whether as spectators or participants, members of both sexes and all age-groups share a consuming interest in competitive outdoor games. Substantial amounts of money, energy and time are invested in sports as a leisure activity which in fact serves to underline certain key values in the community and to maintain its collective identity. In this respect polo and tennis are paramount. The calendar is full of local sporting fixtures at virtually all of which every White in Izolo at least puts in

an appearance as a matter of course. In addition, many of them
regularly travel considerable distances to meet each other, and also
friends from other areas, on school playing fields where they watch
their children and grandchildren at cricket, rugby and tennis
matches, swimming galas and other inter-school competitions.
There is more rejoicing and lamentation in White Izolo over the
sporting performances of the young, even if it is only in the seventh
school cricket eleven, than is ever heard over academic progress. It
would be unfair and inaccurate to dismiss them all as philistines;
but those who find that certain children appear to be keener on
reading than on sport express genuine concern at the possibility of
local offspring becoming what are referred to as 'bookworms'.
Cultural links with Britain and the United States, especially those
represented by the traditions of South African English-language
newspapers and by the English-speaking universities, do not loom
large in their thinking. Nor are they able to recognize how
unbalanced a selection of British and American television productions
appear on their screens. Those who occasionally ponder openly on
the vague possibility of emigrating think, not unnaturally, in terms
of Australia, New Zealand, Canada or Argentina rather than of
Britain or the United States. Membership on equal terms in an
international English-speaking world community is still taken very
much for granted.

Fundamentally, of course, their sense of identity as English-
speaking South Africans is the outcome of their own perception of
their position as an ethnic minority *vis-à-vis* Afrikaans-speakers
within a White minority in the country as a whole. Among Izolo
Whites this has past and present military and political implications
which can only be touched on briefly here. Many of the sons of
the original settlers in the valley were of an age to join one or other
of the locally raised units, such as the Durban Light Infantry, the
Natal Carbineers, and the Umvoti Mounted Rifles, and fight in
defence of their colony alongside British troops in the Anglo-Boer
War. Forty years later the sons of some of these men joined the
South African forces in support of the British and took a
prominent part in campaigns in East Africa, Ethiopia and Egypt.
Today the Natal Carbineers, commanded by a farmer from a
District not far from Izolo, take their turns in serving on what is
generally referred to as 'the border'. Fighting alongside Afrikaans-
speaking units, they now see themselves as defending their country
against an enemy in Angola and elsewhere whose attacks are
inexplicably tolerated or even (as they see it) condoned by the
British government. They feel that few English-speaking people

elsewhere in the world understand or care about their situation.

Although in the abstract very reluctant to admit to the possibility of class distinctions existing among Whites in South Africa, in very many contexts Izolo Whites manifestly see the boundary between themselves and Afrikaners as much in terms of social class as in terms of ethnicity.[15] The only Afrikaners in the District with whom they have any contact are mostly minor civil servants, stock inspectors, post office clerks, railway officials and members of the police force; most of their dealings with them are conducted perforce through the medium of English since, even though Afrikaans is a compulsory subject in schools, relatively few can apparently speak more than a smattering of it or, for example, understand more than the gist of Afrikaans news bulletins on television. And I am in no doubt that English-speaking children on the farms today are very much more open and vehement in their negative attitudes towards those to whom they refer as 'rocks' or 'hairies' than were their great-grandfathers, whom I remember in 1950—52 often speaking in terms of admiration about the qualities of the Boers against whom some of them fought in 1899—1900.[16]

The South African general election of November 1977 resulted in an overwhelming victory for the governing National Party led by the then Prime Minister B.J. Vorster. Analysis of the poll indicates that in most parts of the country many English-speaking voters must have supported the government and cast their votes for National Party candidates. As far as one can judge, most Izolo Whites, formerly loyal (if disillusioned) supporters of the now defunct United Party, voted for the successful local New Republic Party candidate, himself an English-speaking farmer from a neighbouring District and formerly the United Party local member of parliament. A few individuals were known or thought to be supporters of the Progressive Reform Party, supposedly rather more 'liberal' in its policies than the N.R.P. and now (through force of numbers) the official opposition in parliament. With very few exceptions, however, Izolo Whites approve the main outlines of present government policies. This does not stop them continually complaining about the effect upon them of particular administrative measures, especially in the fields of agriculture, transport and finance; nor do they hesitate to condemn and abuse the cabinet ministers responsible for them. At the same time most Izolo Whites grudgingly admired and tacitly supported the national leadership of Vorster himself, often with the clear idea that speaking against the Prime Minister was somehow unpatriotic if not subversive. One or two went further and hinted that they wished they had felt free to vote for a National

Party candidate; but they were able to take comfort from the fact that on most major issues their local member of parliament showed himself reluctant to oppose, as a matter of course, all government policies.

There is one general proposal of potential local importance against which Izolo farmers anticipate that their member of parliament would support them in making a clear stand. This is the suggestion to establish villages for farm workers. The notion would be to create, either within White rural areas or in areas adjoining them, separate rural settlements for exclusive occupation by Black farm workers and their families. Apart from domestic servants, no farm workers would then continue to live on the land of their employers. Such labour as was required on farms would either commute or be transported on a daily basis to and from their place of work. This proposal is not yet by any means official policy; but it is said to have support on a number of grounds from some of the government's advisers. For example, ease of surveillance by security forces would be one obvious advantage in the event of the outbreak of guerrilla operations similar to those currently taking place in many White farming areas in Rhodesia. Furthermore, it is felt that the establishment of farm worker villages might make it easier than it is at present to keep a tight check on the flow of Blacks from rural areas to the towns and elsewhere and to maintain a stable farm labour force.

Opposition by farmers to the creation of villages for farm workers has generally been strong in the past. Nevertheless such villages have in recent years been established in a few parts of the Cape, with apparent support from farmers and smallholders, particularly those concerned with fruit and vegetable growing and with forestry. The proposal also has qualified support from the other end of the White political spectrum; certain avowed opponents of the principle of apartheid think that "there are great advantages in developing villages throughout South Africa from which workers may find employment on farms and elsewhere" (M. Wilson 1977: 193). These advocates of farm villages regard certain conditions as essential elements in the scheme, though it is probably unrealistic to expect them to be fulfilled under present circumstances. They include some measure of security of tenure for villagers, together with freedom for the inhabitants to build houses for themselves, perhaps with a government subsidy. The chief advantage from the workers' point of view is seen as their greater independence and their possible consequent ability to exert pressure from the improvement of working conditions on farms. The advantage to employers would be the removal of their responsibility for providing houses and other facilities, and for caring for workers' dependants; in addition, for farmers needing seasonal labour, villages might provide a larger number of casual workers than can be drawn from the dependants of regular workers living on farms.

Izolo farmers dismiss such schemes as both impracticable and irrelevant to the needs of themselves and their workers. Apart from questions about the possible location of the villages and the methods to be used in organizing and supervising them, they foresee insuperable problems in attempting to run largescale agricultural enterprises with a non-resident labour force living some distance away, and with the inevitable consequent uncertainty about the regular daily attendance of key workers upon whom so much depends. In any case, as they see it, the farm villages which in effect already exist long established on their land provide living arrangements which are of the kind most generally acceptable to workers and employers alike. They firmly believe that Blacks living with their families in their own kraals on the farms already enjoy a combination of security, freedom and benevolent care infinitely preferable to anything they would be likely to get in 'official' villages built elsewhere. Although most farmers habitually complain about the burdens and anxieties imposed upon them by the present traditional arrangement which they have inherited, they say they can conceive of no better alternative and consistently play down its material advantages to themselves. They speak in terms of job satisfaction not simply of their work in any narrow technical agricultural sense but in broad terms, of being able largely unchallenged to run their estates in their own way and to manage their labour force in what they tenaciously maintain to be almost total freedom from interference. They justify this by their feeling that they 'know' Blacks as few of their White fellow citizens do; they are genuinely puzzled by occasional suggestions that, since they only know them as servants, their knowledge of Blacks is defective and partial, despite their lifelong fluency in the Zulu language. They strenuously deny that they exploit their workers and wryly complain that, on the contrary, they are themselves exploited by them, without apparently imagining for one moment that on both counts they may be deceiving themselves.

In addition, though few seem fully aware of it and even fewer are prepared to discuss it, the continuity and surface stability of the present labour system gives farmers and their families a sense of relative security, of independent stewardship, in a world which they acknowledge is elsewhere rapidly changing. On their own verandahs, with their own servants at beck and call, they are conspicuously assured, hospitable and courteous hosts to any White visitors. But, despite the fact that most of them have mixed with a variety of people at school and in the armed services, some farmers are noticeably ill at ease, uncertain or brusque in their dealings with strangers when they are away from Izolo and its neighbourhood, or from such familiar outside extensions of home territory as cattle sales, playing fields and the like. This is discernible not only or mainly when they are confronted by fellow Whites, be they city-dwelling sophisticates or waiters in fashionable restaurants, by whom they feel disconcerted; it is also palpable in relation to categories of Blacks with which they are largely unfamiliar and from which, especially in such instances as educated English-speaking Black civil servants or hospital nursing sisters, they do not necessarily receive the prompt compliance and easy-going vernacular deference to which they are accustomed when at home.

The Farms as a Community

I now propose to examine some of the details of labour organization on Izolo farms today by describing certain aspects of daily work on one reasonably typical example of a large farm in the locality. Middleldaal has an area of about 2,250 hectares and a resident population of 265 persons. The farm is owned by a private company, the active directors of which are two brothers named Smith, both of whom live on the farm in separate large houses with their wives and children. The other directors include their widowed mother, also living on the farm in her own house, and their three sisters, all of whom are married and live elsewhere. One sister is married to a chartered accountant in Pietermaritzburg, who is also a director of the company and in effect financial adviser to his brothers-in-law. The other two sisters are married to farmers, one living elsewhere in Natal and one living in Rhodesia; neither of these men is a director of the company or has any formal say in the running of Middleldaal.

George Smith, the elder of the two brothers, was born in 1939. His wife is the daughter of a farmer in the District; she is a trained nurse who also holds qualifications as a midwife. They have three children, a son aged 15 and two daughters aged 13 and 11. The younger brother, Robert, was born in 1946. His wife, the daughter of a business man in Johannesburg, was trained as a school-teacher. They have three daughters aged 7, 5 and 3. The father of George and Robert died in a motor accident in 1958 at the age of 56, when the brothers were aged respectively 18 and 10. His widow, the mother of George and Robert, was born in 1906, the daughter of a farmer in Izolo; her brother now runs the farm where she was born and brought up. She and her husband were both descended from British settlers who came to Natal in the 1850s. Middeldaal was bought in 1864 by John Smith, the great-grandfather of George and Robert; it was subsequently owned and farmed in turn by their grandfather and their father. The brothers concentrate on cattle breeding and forestry; they have diverse though complementary approaches to farming and very different interests in it. Robert, the younger brother, specialises in cattle and in those aspects of husbandry, such as crop growing, which are associated with fatstock rearing. George takes charge of forestry operations and is much more interested in entrepreneurship and the management of property and labour than in scientific aspects of farming. As a sideline he is one of the directors of a firm of dealers in agricultural supplies and machinery in town.

The only Whites on the farm to have been overseas are George, the elder brother, who visited Britain for three weeks some years ago as a member of a touring group of young farmers, and Robert's wife, who spent six months doing the 'grand tour' of Britain and Europe commonly undertaken by the daughters of prosperous English-speaking South Africans. Born and brought up in a city, she is the only member of the farm households with extended experience of the outside world; she is also the only one unable to speak Zulu with any fluency. All the others are almost as proficient in Zulu as a spoken language as they are in English, though generally this applies more to White males than to White females. George and Robert, in particular, give the impression of being more eloquent in Zulu than in their native tongue; they spend almost the whole of their working lives speaking Zulu and my impression was that they are both more at ease addressing in Zulu a large gathering of their workers than they are when, for instance, on their feet making a speech in English at a meeting of local farmers. In common with almost all local Whites, they were cared for by Black nursemaids when they were babies and toddlers; and, in their particular case, because of the age gap between them, they both as young boys depended to some extent on Black boys of the same age as themselves for companionship. To an important extent those Blacks are now among the key workers on the farm.[17]

Notwithstanding this lifelong knowledge, amounting in a very few cases to something not far removed from comradeship, between certain individual Blacks and Whites, particular category words serving to emphasize the gulf between the two groups remain of crucial importance in the recognition of fundamental aspects of the local social structure. For example, White farmers almost never use the nouns 'Africans' or 'Blacks' to refer to those they commonly describe collectively as natives, coons, nigs, kaffirs or munts (fr. Zulu *umuntu*, a person), depending on the context and the sensibilities of the audience. Some maintain, half-humorously, that they are themselves Africans; they regard the word 'Black' as a fashionably 'liberalistic' euphemism with political overtones. Individual Blacks of any age, particularly if they are domestic servants, are generally referred to in the singular as 'boy' or 'girl', though rather less commonly within earshot than used to be the case; and the same words are nowadays almost never used as a term of address to an adult Black whose name is unknown to the White speaker. On the farms Blacks are generally addressed by personal name, though often referred to by teknonymy; young male or female servants may be summoned by the Zulu words *umfana* or *intombi*, boy or girl.

Blacks on Izolo farms are not referred to collectively as 'workers' by their employers, nor do they describe themselves as such by the Zulu equivalent, *umsebenzi*, meaning a servant, employee or worker for wages. If forced to distinguish themselves from other sections of the Black population, they refer to their place of residence rather than to their occupation when they say they are people of *ipulazi*, farm people. Correspondingly, they never refer to or address either their employer or other White males by the term *ubasi*, boss or master, though this is the word used elsewhere, on plantations, among road repair gangs, in industry and (for example) at petrol filling stations — that is to say, wherever relations between White and Black, between White employers, supervisors or customers, and Black workers, are more or less impersonal. On the farms and elsewhere Blacks refer to Whites collectively as *abelungu*, usually distinguishing carefully between those they believe to be *amangisi*, English-speakers, and those they identify as *amabhunu*, Afrikaners. On Izolo farms, Blacks address White males as either *inkosi* or *inkosana*, depending largely on age and supposed status, these being Zulu words usually rendered into English as 'chief' or 'lord'; White females are addressed by the corresponding gender terms, *inkosikazi* and *inkosazana*. Blacks, when referring to individual Whites, either among themselves or sometimes in conversation with Whites, employ either teknonymy or modified terms of address or (most usually) what may very loosely be called 'nicknames' embodying aspects of physical appearance, personal character or typical behaviour. Significantly, as an indicator of lifelong acquaintance, many of these latter names refer to childhood characteristics which may no longer apply to the individuals concerned.

For most Blacks who live in Izolo, the significant local community
tends to consist of those who live and work together on one farm,
together with many of those who live on farms nearby. At weekends
Blacks continually come and go between farms and between each
other's homes. Ties of kinship and marriage, and those resulting
from long association and longstanding neighbour relationships, are
the most important bases of the exchange of visits, information,
opinions and a wide variety of services and commodities. The main
superficial difference between Whites and Blacks, as far as the network of exchange relationships is concerned lies in the part played
by physical distance; even here, however, important changes have
come about in the past twenty five years. On weekdays there is now
a daily bus service for Blacks between Upper Izolo and the local
towns, including Pietermaritzburg itself. At weekends, when there is
no bus service, Blacks generally travel on foot when visiting kin,
friends or neighbours in Izolo and adjacent areas, but many men,
now as in 1952, ride on horses or bicycles. The use and ownership
of motor vehicles among Blacks, even on farms, is growing: and visits
to or from friends living in urban areas all over Natal are now a
frequent occurrence instead of being the very rare events they were
a generation ago.

We have therefore seen that there are eleven Whites living in
Middeldaal, three males and eight females, outnumbered twenty-
three to one by the Blacks who live there. In March 1978 the resident
Black population of the farm was 254, of whom 129 were males and
125 females. Sixteen Blacks were in receipt of Government
pensions on account of old age and infirmity, supplemented in some
cases by additional pensions paid by the farmers. A further 112 were
children under the age of fourteen, including those attending the
farm school for Black children and those of pre-school age. The
remainder, sixty-two males and sixty-four females, make up the
actual or potential work force. Of the sixty-eight Black males over
the age of fourteen now on the farm, fifty-four were born there and
have lived there all their lives; in contrast, of the sixty-nine females
of the same age range only twenty-two have always lived there. Most,
but not all, married women come from other farms in the area.[18]
The importance of these simple demographic features lies in the fact
that the vast majority of the Blacks on the farm, together with
their parents, and in many cases their grandparents, together with
other relatives over at least three generations, are or were known
personally to George and Robert Smith or to their mother. Conversely,
most adult Blacks on Middeldaal know the majority of their White
employers' relatives living in the area, at least by sight; and most

long-established Izolo White farmers and their wives know, again at least by sight, the majority of adult Blacks living and working on farms in the neighbourhood.

Systems of Production and Payment

Middeldaal comprises several different types of land. Flat, well-watered or irrigable areas are used for winter grazing and for growing maize, root-crops, material for sileage, and hay. The lower slopes of the hills, where the houses of the Whites and the farm buildings are situated, together with the separate so-called 'native paddocks' occupied by Black homesteads, are mostly covered with plantations of conifers, blue gums and black wattles, none of which is a species of tree native to South Africa. In 1977–78 only the last named, *acacia mearnsii*, a fast-growing member of the mimosa family, was of great commercial importance on Middeldaal.[19] The upper steep slopes of the hills, making up about a quarter of the farm's total area, are covered with dense natural forest or 'bush'; apart from providing an emergency source of food for browsing cattle in the depths of the winter droughts, this part of the farm is now wholly unproductive. But it was from these slopes that the early settlers made most of their living, cutting out many thousands of indigenous hardwood trees for the building and furniture industries in the second half of the 19th century. Few mature specimens of these tree survive, all in inaccessible gorges; felling them is very strictly controlled by the authorities.

The tops of the hills, above the 'bush', form a rugged bare plateau, which provides summer grazing for cattle for about six months of the year, or a little longer if the season is favourable. There they are herded, moved from one fenced area to another, brought down for dipping, sorted out for sale, and otherwise attended to, by a small number of male Blacks who take little or no part in other labour on the farm. Some are youngsters; two are elderly men who spend almost all their time inspecting and repairing wire fences and gates. Kept in other more accessible paddocks are other cattle; there are two span of trek oxen, each of eight animals, used for hauling heavy loads under conditions or in places unsuitable for tractors; the breeding herds, four in number, are also kept separate from the fat cattle, as are the cows used to provide milk, butter and cream for the White households and to produce milk used in the preparations of free rations issued daily to all Blacks on the farm who are at work.

The overseer of all cattle keeping and breeding operations, working in close daily co-operation with Robert Smith, is an experienced and responsible man aged about forty, referred to in

English as the 'herd boy'. He is the eldest son, by his senior wife, of
the former 'herd boy', now semi-retired and working in his own
time as one of the two 'fence menders' mentioned above. At the
end of 1977 the 'herd boy' had charge of a total of nearly 600
head of stock, including calves; over the previous two years the
number of cattle owned by the Smiths and kept on Middeldaal
varied from a maximum of about 650 to a minimum of about 450.
In addition to the White-owned cattle, however, there are also a
number of Black-owned cattle, kept separate from the former and
grazed on the land set aside for Black occupation in the 'native
paddocks'. At the end of 1977 these Black-owned cattle numbered
about 170; over the previous two years the number varied from 120
to 270. At the end of 1977 they were counted as being the property
of thirty-one individual Blacks, an average of about five cattle per
owner, most of whom were heads of households. But the range in
the numbers owned by particular individual Blacks over the two
years 1975—77 fluctuated considerably, going as high as twenty-
five in the case of a few men who never over that period had less
than ten head, while there were those owning a few in 1977 who had
at times had none.

The 'herd boy' was consistently among those owning the largest
number of cattle. Unexpectedly, an owner with a steady average of
about seven head was a woman, aged about fifty and divorced some
time ago by a husband who had never lived or worked on the farm;
she is in effect the head of a household of nine persons, including
a married son aged about twenty-two and an aged widowed childless
aunt, her mother's sister, with whom she moved in when she was
divorced. This woman is one of a number of middle-aged Black
females, widows or divorcées, living on the farm and acting as heads
of household, something that was unheard of in Izolo thirty years
ago. They all have children and are all full-time workers in the wattle
plantations. Here again a change has taken place. Thirty years ago
women were employed on farmwork on an entirely casual basis;
they weeded and hoed the crops when required, and in the plantations
only worked at hoeing seedlings and collecting brushwood, again on
a casual basis and mostly in the dry winter season when no other
work was being done in the plantations as far as timber was concerned. The only women to be employed on a full-time basis in
those days were domestic servants, working in the households of
the Whites; and then, as now, those domestic servants who are young
girls only work 'inside' for six months at a time, though for that
period they may be regarded as full-time workers, living in the house,
taking all their meals there, and sleeping at night on the floor of the

kitchen.

Nowadays women work in the plantations both on a full-time basis and a part-time basis, depending on circumstances. Those with babies or young children may decide only to do light tasks as casual workers. Others, including young girls aged about sixteen who take turns at spending periods of six months 'inside' the houses of the Whites, are otherwise mostly full-time labourers. Women now do almost as much of the heavy work in the plantations as is done by men; and while officially they work under the supervision or direction of male Black 'foremen', they in fact operate in work gangs with their own female informal leadership patterns. But they have little or nothing to do with loading up lorries and trailers, mainly because this job needs considerable physical strength; and they never operate the chain-saws with which timber is felled and sawn into lengths, nor do they have anything to do with driving spans of oxen or with driving tractors or operating any kind of machinery, as (for instance) in harvesting, making sileage, cultivating, irrigating or spreading fertiliser.[20]

The work situation in the plantations in 1977—78 cannot be detached from the relative current profitability of the wattle industry; the amount of work available on farms and the level of wages paid on Middeldaal and other timber farms is a reflection of international demand for the products of the trees. Work and wages on the farms must also be compared with those of giant timber concerns, financed by the South African government and by international companies, whose plantations adjoin some of those of the private farms in Izolo and make them look relatively small by comparison. Formerly the wattle tree was grown for its bark, the extract of which was only used in the domestic leather tanning industry. There was virtually no market for the timber; smalltime Asian traders with lorries came out to Izolo to collect it for sale as firewood in urban areas, and it was used on the farms for the same purpose and for fencing. Otherwise most of it was left to rot when the bark had been stripped off. Nowadays the wattle tree growers are producing for a world market; the timber is exported to Japan in the form of chips and used in the manufacture of high quality glossy paper, while the bark extract is exported, as a powder or a resin-like solid, for use in the manufacture of new industrial plastics, adhesives and paint additives. The main markets for extract are in the United States, France, Italy and Britain. One of the latest applications of extract is in the manufacture of the plugs used to seal off bore holes made in the floor of the North Sea and elsewhere in explorations for oil and natural gas. South Africa is one of the world's most important producers of high quality wattle bark extract for these purposes.

On timber farms in Izolo roughly eighty per cent of the farm income is derived from wattle products. On Middeldaal the proportion is slightly lower. But less than eighty per cent of the working year is spent on felling wattle trees and stripping their bark. They are only cut during the wet summer months, from about mid-September to about the middle of April. From April to September work in the plantations is confined to repairing tracks for the next season, digging drains, and hoeing and thinning seedlings and young trees. Other departments of the farm's under-takings need more labour in the dry winter months, since grazing for the cattle is sparse. But the felling and stripping season is the time when workers are able to earn higher wages through the system of payment by results and by the payment of bonuses. Among the main limitations on earnings are those imposed by outside forces.

Wattle trees are felled when they are about ten years old, and about thirty to forty feet high; by that time most trees have a diameter near the base averaging about ten to twelve inches. Plantations are cut in sequences as they come to maturity; now-adays, on almost all farms in the district, there are usually rather more trees ready for felling than can be dealt with. The limitation here is not the size of the work force or the length of the cutting season so much as the quota system for bark; this is imposed on each independent farmer, all of whom belong to a timber co-operative which arranges the quota and represents the farmers in negotiations with outside industry. The details of the quota system are com-plicated; the main relevant points here are that the size of the farm's bark quota is related partly to past performance, partly to the quality of the material produced and partly to the regularity with which it is delivered in good condition to the rail-head and thence to the factory. It is taken to a depot twenty or more miles away by lorry or by tractor-drawn trailers, each having a Black driver and a small crew to help the driver and off-load the produce. These issues affecting the quota are themselves dependent upon the smooth-running reliability of labour operations on each farm, and on the efficiency with which each farm prepares the ground — both literally and metaphorically — for the production of good quality bark and, in the case of timber, logs of the right length and diameter and in the right condition, having no jagged branches, and being neither too dry nor too wet.

Trees are felled; the bark is stripped off and tied into bundles, each four feet long; the stripped tree trunks are sawn into eight foot lengths, and the residual brushwood cleared and burnt. All this is a major operation; it is done by gangs of men and women — sometimes mixed, more often separated by sex, depending on circumstances and on the kind of scale of work needing to be done. The operation is relatively dangerous, heavy and skilled, and it requires constant on-the-spot supervision and decision making, together with daily organization of the strategies to be employed: which trees to-day, which tomorrow, how many trees for this gang, and how many for that — and so forth.

Each gang of workers consists of about a dozen persons, supervised by a 'foreman'; but he is not known as such, or by any equivalent title, although he is generally accepted as the person responsible for immediate decisions and for acting to some extent as an intermediary between workers and employers. Each gang has trees felled and trimmed for it by one man with a heavy chain-saw, accompanied at all times by a 'mate' with a measuring stick who also assists the chain-saw operator in various ways and keeps watch that nobody is in the path of falling trees. Chain-saw operators are of necessity strong and mature young men; their 'mates' are either elderly men or youths. The noise is tremendous and goes on for hours at a time, with workers shouting to each other over the din. The stripped bark, tied in bundles, is collected by each worker into his or her individual piles; each individual has personal preferences about the size of bundles, size and distribution of piles, method of stripping, selection of trees, size of bark strips, whether to strip first and cut into lengths afterwards, or *vice-versa*, and many other points, including the mode of tying bundles, each worker having his or her individual mode and type of knot. At the end of each day this last idiosyncracy makes it easy for the 'foreman', with one or two other workers usually designated for the task, to weigh the bark stripped by each person and record the weight of each bundle. On some farms weighing of the bark is always done under the eye of the employer; on other farms this is left to be done by the workers themselves and it is rare for the farmer to be present at the bark-weighing. In the latter case any disputes there may be about weights and subsequent payments are ostensibly sorted out by the workers themselves.

On Middeldaal the weight of each bundle is recorded against the name of each worker and the list of names and weights taken to George Smith, either at the end of the day's work or first thing the following morning. The list is prepared by an elderly man known by virtue of this task as the *induna* or headman; he is in

fact in no other respect a particularly prominent figure on the farm
and is certainly not an *induna* or leader in any non-work context.
But he is trusted by both the farmer and the workers and is, of
course, literate. When he reports to George Smith he may be
accompanied to the back verandah of the farmhouse, where all such
transactions are conducted, by one or other of the *de facto*
'foremen' in charge of work gangs if there is anything particular
to report; but he often goes alone. The farmer then adds up the
totals for each worker and completes his own daily record, from
which at the end of each month the wages due to each worker
are calculated. The recording is done in this way, according to
George Smith, because none of the Blacks, including the *induna*, is
capable of doing the adding up; I do not know if this is true.

During the stripping season the wages paid to each man and
woman doing that work in the plantations are based on the weight
of bark stripped. In the case of men, however, a basic daily rate is
paid for an agreed task, consisting of a weight of (say) 800 lbs,
with an added piecework 'bonus' for every 100 lbs of bark in excess
of the target. Smaller excess weights, less than a complete 100 lbs,
are apparently accumulated for each individual and made into an
eventual total largely at the discretion of the farmer; each worker
appears therefore to be open to strict or generous treatment when,
at the end of the month, the moment comes for rounding up totals.

The task set for men varies according to conditions on a particular
day, as — for example — when the terrain in the plantation being
stripped is steep, rocky or otherwise difficult, or when the state of
the trees is poor, as it may be in some places on the farm as a result
of shallow soil, frost damage or some other factor. A lower target
may also be set for young and inexperienced men. In the case of
women no fixed target is set, each worker being paid entirely on a
piece work basis for every 100 lbs of bark at a rate different from
that paid to men as a 'bonus'. But women are expected to reach a
reasonable target of round about 200 lbs per day; otherwise they
may be told that they are not suitable for bark stripping and may
be given other less remunerative work. What is regarded as reasonable in this respect depends on a variety of factors; by and large it
depends on whether other members of the gang find the presence
of a slow or relatively unproductive worker interferes with their
own capacity to strip good quantities or with the gang's ability to
make progress. This in turn depends on whether a gang is working
on a broad or narrow front in the plantations; in the case of a
narrow front, when they may be working in cramped conditions,
it is important for all members of a gang to work together at roughly

the same speed, but when the front is broad and workers can choose their own speed because of the layout of the ground, the presence of a slow or inexperienced worker may not matter so much.

It will be clear that, in such operations as bark stripping, relations among the workers, between them and the 'foremen', chain-saw operators and bark-weighers, and between all of them and their employers, are crucial in getting steady supplies of top quality bark off the trees, onto the trailers or lorries, and down to the rail-head or directly to the factories. Usually four loads of bark are sent each week during the season, each load being of about 10,000 lbs weight. At the factory the bark is graded into one or other of three qualities, the price per ton in 1977—78 varying from R58 (about £34) to R62 (about £37), the latter being the price for 'prime' or top quality bark. Over an eight week period for which I have consistent records a total of about R8,000 (approximately £4,762) was due to Middeldaal as payment for bark sent to the factory.

When the work involved does not have an easily calculable piece-work basis, payment is at a set rate per day for tasks of a standard kind or tasks arranged and agreed with the 'foremen' and others. This applies particularly to regular workers, though much the same applies to casual workers on a more informal and *ad hoc* basis; but the types of work and the rates of pay are usually very different. For example, at one extreme a gang of regular male workers may be carting timber; at the other extreme a small party of women with babies on their backs may be hoeing vegetables or weeding flower beds in the farmer's garden. In the first case time may be of great importance to the workers and the farmer; in the second it may not matter to either side whether the set job is done in a few hours or a few days. The payment involved takes account of this difference, and of the other differences, including the sex of the workers and whether the work is regular or casual.

In the case of regular workers, failure to report for work on any particular day means loss of wages for that day; but in such circumstances as illness or some other good cause a more or less nominal retainer may be paid, especially if the illness or injury arose in the course of work, depending to some extent on the record, reputation and responsibilities of the worker concerned. Repeated failure to turn up for work without good cause not only means no wages but may also lead to dismissal, with all that means in terms of removal of a household from the farm; in practice no such case has occurred in Middeldaal for more than fifteen years, when the sacking of one man had disastrous repercussions, including the departure of three other households, among them that of a highly valued key worker. On the face of it the most likely source of disagreements over work and wages lies in the rule that failure to complete an agreed task results in reduced wages or none at all; in practice it seems that this very rarely happens and only when the reasons for failure are manifestly unjustifiable. Usually there are plausible explanations for a gang failing to complete a basic task, including mechanical breakdowns, weather conditions, emergencies of some kind or other. In the case of individuals (as opposed to gangs), failure to complete a set task seems to be relatively unusual; such evidence as was obtained suggests that fellow workers either do not allow an individual to fail to pull his weight in a joint task or make up an individual's task on a generally accepted reciprocal basis.

Shifting, loading, carting and stacking lengths of timber is paid for on a task basis. At certain times the task for a gang of men shifting logs was fixed, by agreement, at three tractor loads per day. Whether this is fair or reasonable depends on how tidily the logs have previously been stacked and whether they have been neatly stacked along the sides of tracks or scattered in piles throughout the stripped and felled plantations. If all is arranged carefully before-hand — which means on previous days while clearing up after a day of felling and stripping — it is reckoned that it takes two hours for a gang with one trailer and tractor plus driver to load up and carry logs to the co-operative depot about four miles down the road from the farm and load it off there onto enormous piles for collection by contractors' lorries. While engaged on log-hauling, a gang, including the crucial man, the tractor driver (since only a licensed driver is permitted to go onto the public roads, as opposed to driving on the farm), may decide for itself when to start work. If the gang members wish, for their own reasons, they may decide to start work at 2 a.m. and then, if the weather holds, their day's task is over by breakfast time at eight o'clock and they can have the rest of the day free. The value attached to this kind of work is not easy to calculate in monetary terms; but just as stripping good trees on a good day is enjoyed because of the money clocking up as they work, so a task which can be got over in their own time is appreciated even though it doesn't pay as well. These con-siderations — plus the money it is possible to earn in a few days and the leisure it is possible to earn by getting up early — do not apply to the key workers whose responsibilities are recompensed in other ways. These men work on a slightly different basis and, in most cases, for rather higher average wages throughout the year, to compensate them for having to work regular hours as well as for being on call for emergencies such as calving; they are also deprived of chances of making a lot of cash quickly on a good day's stripping. Such men get special privileges and perquisites. One of the most important of these is the availability of loans and cash advances. For them the farmer acts as a bank, only those who are credit worthy being able to draw money. In this way certain men have access to very considerable cash assets, usually denied to others. In some cases regular payments, deducted from wages, are made into a building society by the farmer as a kind of forced saving which the workers appear to value. One said that they know their wives would fritter the money away if they had it all in wages. Whether this is true or not I do not know; but this is clearly one of a number of ways of keeping good workers, since the farmer holds the deposit books and handles the accounting.

In addition, as already indicated, all workers get certain non-monetary payments, some of them, such as free rations, dependent upon the individual coming up to certain basic requirements as far as number of days worked per week is concerned. Other payments in kind include:— free housing; grazing for cattle and horses; free veterinary services (including dipping and artificial insemination, both being of importance to the farmer if his stock is not to be contaminated by the stock of his workers); free medical attention; basic pensions and rations for the old, sick and disabled; a farm school for the children, financed by the farmer with a government grant; and certain other items from time to time at bulk-buy prices, including tobacco, seed, and some groceries. Some farmers used to dole out tobacco on Monday mornings only, to ensure that workers turn up after festive weekends; this no longer seems to happen.

Perspectives on Five Households

Wages vary a good deal as between workers and between different seasons of the year, depending on the types of work available; they also vary between farms, though it proved impossible to get reliable figures of a systematic kind on this inter-farm variation. On Middeldaal the wages paid to individuals serve as a rough and ready indication of the hierarchy of jobs and workers; but the important issue, as far as the Blacks themselves are concerned, is the household income. This needs, of course, to be related to size of household and to the stage in the domestic life cycle reached in each case. In the following presentation I have selected five Black households on Middeldaal and attempted to estimate the monthly income in each case in cash and kind; in two cases the earnings varied slightly according to season, as indicated; in the other cases there was little or no seasonal variation on account of the jobs performed by the principal wage earners (see Table I).

Household A (Column 1) comprises a full-time tractor driver aged thirty-two, with his wife and five children and his wife's widowed mother. The wife works part-time as a laundry woman in one of the White houses; her mother received an old age pension, supplemented by an unofficial pension from the farmer since she was for many years a part-time worker. *Household B* (Column 2) is that of a 'stable boy' aged thirty-five with a wife and four children. The wife, half-sister to the tractor driver in Household No. 1, works full-time as a cook in one of the White houses, doing a five and a half day week of about forty-six hours. The eldest of the children does a small amount of casual work. *Household C* (Column 3) has as its current head the divorced woman aged fifty already mentioned as a cattle owner. There are nine persons in the household, including two pensioners and two young men working as regular full-time labourers. Column 4 shows the same household's earnings in the winter season. *Household D* (Column 5) comprises a chainsaw operator aged twenty-four with a wife and small child. The wife does occasional casual work in the plantations or in one of the farmers' gardens. *Household E* (Column 6) consists of a labourer aged twenty-eight and his wife, both of whom work as full-time regular hands. They have three children. Column 7 shows the same household's earnings in the winter season.

As will be seen, payments in kind are estimated to be basically the same for each household throughout the year, for lack of any evidence allowing a more sensitive analysis than may be achieved by averaging up. The total sum of R43 per month for payments in kind is made up as follows:—

(1) Rations purchased by the farmer and provided for each worker — R.8.50.

(2) Rations provided from farm produce, including free milk (not provided on many farms), mealie-meal drinks and porridge, vegetables and meat — R16.50.

(3) Housing and house sites (mostly wattle and daub huts built by the occupants from materials, including timber and thatch grass, freely available on the farm), together with a proportion of the value of the site provided for the farm school and its grounds, and for housing for the teachers — R3.50.

(4) Working clothes, including overalls, protective clothing, helmets, gloves, gumboots and certain other items — R1.00; many of these items remain the property of the farmer but

'disappear' in the course of time.

(5) Grazing land for a notional five animals (mostly cattle and horses) per household head; gardens and other land set aside for cultivation by Blacks; occasional aid with cultivation (loan of tractors and other equipment, use of farm tools, etc.) − R3.50.

(6) Sundry items, including the following:− firewood, frequent free transport, all medical expenses (with a few exceptions), most veterinary expenses (including dipping of cattle, inoculations, artificial insemination, medicines), subsidized ('bulk-buy') seed, tobacco and basic foodstuffs, gifts of clothing and certain other 'expected' gifts of extra rations on special occasions, including Christmas, weddings and other similar events − R10.00.

TABLE I

Monthly income of five households

	(A)	(B)	(C)	(C) winter	(D)	(E)	(E) winter
Payments in kind	43.00	43.00	43.00	43.00	43.00	43.00	43.00
Cash wage head of household	53.00	30.00	18.00	12.00	32.00	36.00	20.00
Cash wage other	7.00	22.00	42.00	32.00	2.00	21.00	12.00
Pensions	5.00	−	20.00	20.00	−	−	−
Total cash income	65.00	52.00	80.00	64.00	34.00	57.00	32.00
Total income	108.00	95.00	123.00	107.00	75.00	100.00	75.00

According to unreliable information from farmers, which I was unable to check, workers are not required to pay tax on their incomes if the monthly cash payments are below R30. No workers on Middeldaal paid tax, since none of them were shown on official returns as earning more than R29.99 in cash per month. This aspect of the workers' income is not allowed for in the Table.

To put these earnings into some kind of perspective, a few random comparisons may be made with earnings elsewhere, mostly from information I was able to obtain myself, although I cannot vouch for its accuracy in all cases. On one large cattle farm elsewhere in the District, where most of the labour lives not on the farm but in their own homes in a nearby 'location' the elderly *induna* or senior 'herd boy' was paid an official wage of about R80 per month; his employer usually made this cash wage up to about R120 per month through payments made 'round the back of the sheds', in order that others, including both the farmer's wife and other workers, would not know of the arrangement. When this *induna* retired from the farm two or three years ago his employer gave him a Toyota pick-up truck, with which he is now operating a private transport business with his son. I have little doubt that similar arrangements, perhaps not on quite so lavish a scale, are made on other farms, including some of those in Izolo.

The workers on the large-scale timber concerns already mentioned, which are only a short distance from Izolo, are mostly migrants housed in compounds without their families and without any payments in kind other than rations. Their average monthly cash wages for a fifty-hour week are said by Izolo farmers to be R66, a figure with which one farmer said it was impossible to compete. On a large sugar estate owned by an international combine and situated on the north coast of Natal, where the workers are all young migrants from the Transkei and adjacent parts of the Eastern Cape, housed in 'model' compounds and provided with all food and numerous recreational facilities, I was reliably informed that cane cutters were able in 1977 to earn up to R200 in cash wages per month. On a smaller privately-owned sugar farm some distance away, also employing the same sort of labour under less 'luxurious' conditions, cane cutters were able to earn cash wages of between R90 and R110 per month, for a period of about nine months a year. Payments in kind on this farm consist of free housing, rations, clothing and medical attention, together with schooling for those who are able to have women and children living with them. But there are no facilities for keeping stock, since these workers' permanent homes are elsewhere.

According to Lipton (1977), the wages paid to Blacks in construction work and manufacturing industry in South Africa in 1975 were in the region of R105 per month. In the only industrial undertaking within daily commuting distance by car from Izolo for which I was able to get figures, a small engineering firm specializing in the sale and servicing of agricultural machinery, jobs for Blacks were hard to get and very much sought after. Blacks taken on to do semi-skilled work in the repair shop started at a monthly wage of R160; if they proved satisfactory (and the Black labour turnover was very high) they were able to earn as much as R240. One worker in this undertaking told me that Asians in the same firm's employ earn between R250 and R400 per month, while White trainee salesmen start at about R600 (about £357) per month, the lowest salary paid to Whites in the firm.

Farmers and workers were very reluctant to discuss details of wage rates and farmers were evasive about the way in which payments were governed, if they were, by notions of skill, task and time. I never felt free to press for information which did not come easily. But the relation between these notions was puzzling at the time and still remains unclear. This is partly the simple matter of gaps in the material. But it was not just a matter of informants being reluctant to reveal things to a questioner from outside their world. Farmers keep the details of their management techniques very close to their chests among themselves; I repeatedly heard them presenting to one another grossly inaccurate and camouflaged versions of what went on, even when they were unconscious of my presence. When, as happened a number of times on different farms, there are disputes or difficulties between workers and farmers, the latter brush such things aside in conversation with neighbours, shrugging them off as the inevitable lot of anyone having to shoulder the burden of dealing with 'these people'; as often as not they keep their evident worries hidden, even from their own wives and families. But in many cases they were clearly deeply anxious about their capacity to manage their farms and handle their labour. In some instances, those with manifest signs and symptoms of moderately severe psychiatric disorders attributed them to the worries of their work.

Farmers told me repeatedly that the essence of their job was the organization and management of labour and only secondarily a matter of business skills and knowing a great deal about technical aspects of agriculture, forestry and stock-rearing. Here I think they did less than justice to their own abilities as farmers and concentrated attention on that aspect of their daily lives about which they were least trained but felt that they were best informed. There was a noticeable contrast between the modesty and eagerness with which they discussed technical details with each other and asked for and gave advice, and the reserve displayed when any aspect of work *arrangements* arose; it will be recalled that these are men who have lifelong intimate knowledge of one another, see each other constantly and in many cases are close friends and neighbours.

To a remarkable extent each farm appears to be a law unto itself in matters of management and wage rates, including payments in kind. Behind each others' backs they constantly complain that their neighbours over-indulge their workers. But I began to suspect that some of my problems in unravelling the interplay between the notions already mentioned, — skills, tasks and time — were due to uncertainty among farmers themselves about how the system really

worked, especially when they attempted to consider it in the abstract
rather than just leaving it to practical rule of thumb. Indeed I would
argue that their uncertainty, and that of their workers, is the
essence of the system. Contradictory or incompatible ideas about
how it operates give room for manoeuvre in particular situations
and a wide if not indefinite range of possible choices in different
contexts which each side is able to exploit. From the farmer's
point of view this means that he can stretch a point in relation to
some workers and some issues, and insist on the existence of customary rules in other instances, and on their observance. Perhaps this is
the gist of paternalism.

Boundaries, Information, and the Settlement of Disputes

Among the Blacks on each farm, and on occasions between farms,
job specialisation, together with appreciable differences between
household earnings and differential access to capital (such as
cattle and credit), clearly forms the basis for potential differences
in socio-economic status within an apparently undifferentiated
category of agricultural workers. What is clear is that they themselves have views about the relative importance and standing of
various named lineages and clans represented on farms, irrespective
of the jobs and wages of members. On Middeldaal the general
opinion seemed to be that members of at least two descent groups
long established on the place are regarded, by themselves and others,
as being in some respects superior to more recent arrivals. In part
this is a matter of rights of access to hut sites and the graves of
ancestors buried there. It is also related to the links members of
such groups have with Clan Chiefs in the District and region,
including the office of Chief's court messenger or *induna* (in the
context of the Zulu political system rather than that of the farm)
which was held by a senior member of one of them. Disputes,
including witchcraft accusations, seem to occur more commonly
across boundaries between groups of different standing. Newcomers were said to 'fear' the influence of long established groupings.
The picture is, however, much complicated by stereotypes and by
the extensive affinal links between most groupings on each farm
and between farms.

Regarding one matter, however, I feel on surer ground. This concerns the frequency with which men who are members of relatively
high status groups act towards their White employers as what I
propose to call 'monitors'. In no sense should it be thought that
this word has any connection with the idea of a school prefect; if
there were an indigenous term in either Zulu or English generally

used on Izolo farms to denote an almost universal informal role, I
would use it. In the absence of such a term I use 'monitor' to
indicate somebody maintaining surveillance, serving to select the
picture to be presented, detecting the first signs of contamination,
and listening to the reporting on communication systems. This
role, although performed by a mature man who is head of a household, is quite separate from more or less formal leadership roles,
whether within the farm system or the indigenous Zulu system.
At the same time, the role of 'monitor' often overlaps with that of
lineage head, 'foreman', key worker or *induna*; but I do not think
the formal and informal roles necessarily reinforce one another if
performed by the same actor. Nor should it be thought that a
'monitor' is neither more nor less than an informer, since a man
regarded by his fellow workers as a spy would be useless as a means
of communication employed equally by both Whites and Blacks.
What seems clear, and this was confirmed explicitly by a number
of them, is that every farmer who hopes to run a large farm and a
large labour force, the size of a village, without undue difficulty,
needs to have among his employees one or two men to whom he
can turn for confidential and even fatherly advice; indeed, in many
cases these men are old enough to have been household heads in
the time of the farmer's father. The farmer needs to have a channel
of communication which he can rely upon to transmit the climate
of opinion among workers and their families; it was on this basis
that one of them felt he knew what his workers felt about topics
as different as terrorism and the price of school exercise books.

The men I have described as 'monitors' are not only those who,
on the whole, are trusted by both sides, by farmers and workers;
they also tend to be possessed of certain qualities, crudely over-
simplified in such terms as detachment, lack of personal ambition,
a sense of their own worth, *gravitas* combined with a sense of
humour. Some are men who are often the butt of harmless and
even affectionate teasing; others are men at whom no one would
dream of laughing. Many labour problems on farms seem either
to be nipped in the bud or dealt with successfully through private
conversations between farmer and 'monitor'; or so most farmers
believe. By no means all disputes and difficulties can be dealt with
so painlessly, as I shall now demonstrate.

Disputes, misdemeanours, crimes and outbreaks of violence
occurring on farms in Izolo, and mainly involving only those who
live there, are dealt with in several different ways, depending on
the nature of the occurrence and the identity of those concerned.
In almost all cases both farmers and workers go to some lengths

to avoid bringing in outside authorities, especially the police; matters are only brought to the latter's attention when strangers are involved, or when matters are so serious that failure to report them may have grave consequences, or when things are getting out of control. In many cases, of course, the possibility of one or other party to a dispute reporting matters to the police is held in reserve and used, implicitly or explicitly, as a way of bringing pressure to bear.

Civil matters among Blacks, particularly disputes over marriage prestations or involving actual or potential marriage breakdown, are often taken to the local Chief's Court in town if no settlement is reached through negotiations or through the farm's own informal 'court' hearings. These farm 'courts' are presided over by senior heads of households; but the farmers themselves sometimes attend or take part in the proceedings, usually when asked to do so by those most closely involved, but sometimes at their own request when a dispute seems likely to disrupt the life and work of the farm.

Even though the power of the Whites in the national super-structure is overwhelming, whether exerted through money or guns, the extent to which farmers are able to exercise authority at the local level and on their farms is at first sight surprising, given the obvious but largely unrealized Black potential for simple dis-obedience or unobtrusive subversion. Take, for example, an entirely trivial matter such as the breaking of crockery by young Black female servants working in the kitchens of White's houses. As already mentioned, certain farm girls, the daughters of workers, are required to spend a period of six months 'inside', working for very low wages (usually about R7 per month or less) and their keep. On the whole girls appear to dislike the prospect of this work, however much they appear in fact to enjoy some of the perquisites, including the tips of overnight guests; often it seems that those selected by the farmers' wives as suitable for this work have to be coerced into it by their parents. On many farms, for every piece of china broken, the girls concerned are required to work without wages, in house or garden, for one day over and above their allotted span. In no case, as far as I could discover, did they ever refuse to accept a punishment which farmers' wives said was the most effective way of keeping breakages down to an acceptable level.

When the offence is rather more serious, though still too un-important for anyone seriously to consider calling in the police, various alternative modes of handling and punishing those involved may be employed. Take the case of a stolen fowl. At weekends girls working in the kitchen of one farmhouse are allowed to sleep at their homes on Saturday nights. Since by the time they have finished work it is already dark, they are fetched by a small party of brothers and other young boys and accompanied on the walk of a mile or more, since they would be frightened to go on their own. On one such occasion an elder brother of one of the girls, a married man aged twenty-four, induced his younger brother to steal a fowl from the farmer's poultry run on his way back with his sister and the other girl. Two days later the farmer's wife discovered the theft and the farmer conducted enquiries, in the course of which one of the young boys in the escorting party confessed his knowledge of the affair and identified the chief culprits. An informal 'court' was held at which the guilt of those concerned was established and admitted by them. The elder brother, the instigator, was offered by the farmer the choice between two alternative punishments: a public thrashing or a fine of R2. He accepted the latter penalty, the sum being deducted in due course from his wages. The younger brother was said to have been thrashed by his father; the youngster who had first confessed was forced to leave home for a week or two until the affair had blown over; and the two girls, both of whom at first denied all knowledge of the affair, were deprived of the privilege of sleeping at home on Saturdays for the remainder of their period of service, a punishment which was in fact suspended after a couple of weeks.

A very much more serious case on one farm involved two married men, both under the age of thirty, members of different lineages. One accused the other of committing adultery with his pregnant wife. After some days of mounting tension, a 'court' was held on the farm, at which the farmer and myself were asked to be present, and in the proceedings of which the farmer in due course took an active part. The hearing was presided over by three senior heads of households, representing both lineages concerned. A fine of R10 was imposed on the defendant, who reluctantly agreed, after long deliberations, that he was guilty of making improper advances to the woman by touching her on the knee. The plaintiff husband, dissatisfied with the defendant's demeanour in court, then attempted to attack him while the 'court' was still sitting and was restrained by, among others, the farmer. The 'court' then agreed that the plaintiff's behaviour justified a fine of R2. Both these fines were to be paid to the farmer, acting as an intermediary, on the understanding that, had they not been paid by the end of the month, the sums involved would be deducted from the two men's wages. The fines were paid within a few hours. Nevertheless all was not well, even though the matter had been declared as finished. Two weeks later there was a major outbreak of fighting between members of the two groups concerned, in which the mother of the defendant sustained serious head injuries from which she almost died, and in which a number of men on both sides in the dispute were seriously wounded. Yet again the police were not informed and the farmer did his best to keep knowledge of the affair from reaching his neighbours. A further 'court' was then held, again attended by the farmer and myself, at which a senior woman on the farm made an impassioned plea for a cessation of hostilities, saying the young men were "behaving like dogs". This seemed to have some effect, since no further fighting took place; but a feeling of disquiet continued for weeks, in the course of which some Blacks, including one of the tractor drivers, married to a full sister of the defendant (and hence a daughter of the injured woman), decided to leave the farm. This came to nothing in the end; but the farmer's anxiety at that time gave me considerable insights into the way in which the smooth and profitable running of a farm depended on the farmer being informed about, and able to control, personal relations among his employees. Covert recriminations between sections of the Black population had some effect on work arrangements. Suspicions of witchcraft, though kept short of open accusations, led to changes in the composition of gangs of men and women in the plantations. Three or four individuals declared that they were unable to work for varying periods on account of illness manifesting itself in relatively minor physical complaints associated with anxiety and depression. The farmer's attempts to keep the affair dark were predictably fruitless. The dispute had repercussions elsewhere; tractors and trailers carrying loads of bark to the depot, and manned by members of one of the groups involved, were stoned by adherents of the other group, mostly women living in *kraals* on a farm through which the road passed, one of whom was a half-sister to the defendant.

For some time these and similar incidents, most of them trivial, together with a general underlying sense of disquiet and uncertainty among the Blacks, were the cause of vexation to the farmers most directly involved. Although there was no serious interference with work on the farms, and no sign that they were ever in any way apprehensive about the possibility of an outbreak of violence beyond their power to control, some Whites became a little edgy for a while. On such occasions a link becomes strikingly clear

between the mood of some Whites and the apparent disposition of a
majority of their Black workers. Most farmers find it easy to deal
with declared grievances among their workforce and to cope, not
only with behaviour generally described as 'stroppy' and by no
means uncommon, but also with relatively rare instances of frank
insubordination. On the other hand, they find sullen acquiescence
by unsmiling workers much more disturbing and harder to tolerate.
Over and over again one finds that among the chief characteristics
leading to the choice of particular Blacks for certain jobs, especially
those involving frequent contact or communication with employers,
was that of being always cheerful. Living in such close and constant
proximity to a large population of Black men, women and children,
White farmers and their wives barely notice the expected display
of deference as they move about their property; but they are
quick to see a sour face, for — above all else — they like 'their
natives' to at least appear to be happy.

Conclusion: Authority and Dependence

Work and work relationships are the essence of a specifically South
African culture shared in by both Blacks and Whites. This essay has
been an extended demonstration of that fact. It has also been more
particularly concerned with the examination of a work situation
which has become atypical and anomalous by current South African
standards.[21] Features of the anomaly are indicated by the words
chosen for my main title.

Neither Whites nor Blacks on Izolo farms have much first hand
experience of any situation other than that tendentiously described
by some commentators as 'semi-feudal' or 'neo-feudal'. Despite
the virtual abolition of labour tenancy, many features of that
system persist and may rather be seen as an adaptation, over several
generations, of certain aspects of traditional Zulu institutions. Full-
time Black wage labourers and members of their families living on
the farms are still regarded, by themselves and their employers, as
tenants, dependants, clients, even subjects, as much as mere
workers. Farmers are accepted by their employees as lords, masters
and patrons rather than simply as employers. This emerges most
clearly in the preceding section of the essay where White farmers
are shown to be acting, with their employees' consent — even at
their invitation — in a quasi-judicial capacity, almost like petty
chiefs at the hearings of domestic disputes among their underlings.
In other contexts farmers act to protect their workers from the
police and from other agents of the State, be they game wardens,
tax officials and collectors of statistics. But in acting in these ways

farmers are under no illusions about it being part of their job as landowners and employers to do so. If there is little likelihood of particular affairs in which their workers are involved having any repercussions for the work of the farm, they usually ignore them.

Given that legislation has increasingly restricted the movement of rural workers, together with the fact that there has recently been a general increase in Black unemployment, it is perhaps no wonder that Whites and Blacks in Izolo appear to share an interest in maintaining the status quo. Farmers are able to pay relatively low cash wages and yet apparently remain competitive with other labour markets, including the towns. They provide facilities and perquisites which cost them very little but which are highly valued by their workers. These benefits, as already indicated, include payments in kind and the virtual certainty of selective extension of credit. In addition, many Blacks on Izolo farms undoubtedly derive a certain sense of security and modified independence from the relative absence of irksome supervision when at work. They frequently contrast the working arrangements on the farms, of which some account has already been given, with the situation of relatives and friends working in other less easy-going rural settings or in urban industrial areas. They recognize that they are free from too rigid a dependence on the clock. They balance the regular involvement of their employers in almost any aspect of their personal lives against the uncaring unpredictability of remote White supervisors in industry who (as one Black informant put it) do not know if you are married or not, nor how many children or other dependants you may have to support. They see a certain safety in being (as they think) removed from the harshest uncertainties of a competitive labour market. Wages may be low on farms; but Blacks in Izolo believe they would never be allowed to starve.

To the outside observer the situation in Izolo seems at first an assemblage of illusions and paradoxes. There are at least two ways of looking at some of the material I have presented. Personalized relationships between Whites and Blacks may be regarded as an essential ingredient of a system of tied labour and little more than the way in which the over-arching power structure is dressed up for local consumption. According to this view, the fact that farmers often bend over backwards to avoid involving the police or other agents of authority in disputes and other affairs on the farm is an indication of their determination to maintain the illusion about where power really resides. Here I would argue that few of those involved harbour such naïve ideas; rather I would tend to the view that both Blacks and Whites have much to gain and little to lose by fostering personalized relationships which happen to modify or mitigate some of the harsher realities of the social system. It may well be also that, by expecting Whites to involve themselves in many of their concerns, Blacks are seeking to reassure themselves that they read things all right, that the continued patronage of their employers ensures protection.

The dynamics of the situation may be seen as a product of the tension between dependence and authority. White farmers exercise authority, backed by overwhelming power upon which they are reluctant to draw precisely because to do so reveals the extent to which they are dependent upon Black labour. Blacks, on the other hand, are wholly dependent upon Whites for security if not survival; yet they hold reserves of power, including withdrawal of labour, which they barely recognize because, in present circumstances, they cannot draw upon them without themselves suffering more than anyone else. The central paradox here is that, despite the apparently overwhelming power and authority of the Whites over the work and the personal lives of their employees, the Whites themselves are highly vulnerable to informal aspects of the micro-system represented by their farms.[22]

When speaking of the personalization of relationships, more is implied than simply relationships between individuals rather than between members of categories. On the farms, as has been indicated, such relationships may involve a high degree of familiarity with each other's purely personal affairs and involvement in them. But here the paradox to be noted is that familiarity, dependence and involvement are as asymmetrical as authority, though in the opposite direction. In general Blacks have greater knowledge of the intimate details of White living arrangements than vice versa. Whites do not prepare the food of Black children, wash the underclothes of Black women or put drunken Black men to bed. As Preston-Whyte (1976) suggests, the key to this paradox lies in 'the very clear acceptance by both parties of the inferior position of the employee. Master and servant by definition can never be regarded as equals'.

Several Whites in Izolo said that they found it hard to believe that White people in Britain and elsewhere were as capable as Blacks of the kind of hard and tedious manual labour which they require their workers to perform for them. Indeed, they look upon their own manifest inferiority to Blacks in this respect as no less convincing evidence of their own innate superiority as an ethnic group than their conviction that South African Blacks are inherently incapable of performing skilled tasks without imitation or supervision, of showing initiative or originality in any creative activity, or even of doing sustained work of any kind unless induced to do so by some combination of stick and carrot. They largely ignore such evidence to the contrary as is provided by the industriousness of some Blacks when they are about their home avocations, looking after their own houses and gardens or tending their own livestock. Whites do not regard such activities by Blacks as work, since it is done out of hours and for no wages. As for themselves, however, they claim — as do their colleagues in East Anglia described by Newby and his colleagues (Newby *et al.* 1978) — that farmers are continuously on the job and that their working week constitutes virtually all their waking hours. Like academics, even when playing they say they are thinking and therefore working. Where sport and leisure activities are crucial factors in defining membership of a local community and also provide a setting for the informal exchange of ideas and information, farming as a way of life involves no clear separation between non-work and work.

Appendix

BLACK POPULATION OF MIDDELDAAL

1. Age groups

| | Approximate age in years | | | | | | | | | |
	0–4	5–14	15–24	25–34	35–44	45–54	55–64	65–74	75+	Total
Males	26	35	27	16	6	2	7	8	2	129
Females	10	46	28	20	6	4	5	2	4	125
Total	36	81	55	36	12	6	12	10	6	254

2. Category of worker

	Regular full-time workers	Regular part-time workers	Occasional and casual workers	Children not employed	Pensioners
Males	43	11	8	55	7
Females	33	13	18	57	9
Total	76	24	26	112	16

3. Place of birth

	Middeldaal	Other farm in Izolo	Elsewhere in District	Outside District	Not known
Males	99	10	6	6	8
Females	73	26	4	5	17
Total	172	36	10 11	11	25

The main figures for the Black population are given below. A sharp eye may deduce that a number of "children" under the age of 14 are in fact in some kind of employment.

As will be seen from these figures, there are relatively few members of both sexes between the ages of 35 and 64. Since there is no evidence that the number of Blacks on the farm showed a dramatic fall at any time, the presumed movement off the farm of males born between 1914 and 1943, together with their wives and families, must have been compensated for by a small number of outsiders coming to the farm and by the children born to those who remained. Females of the same age range are likely to have left the farm in any case in view of the virilocal residence rule applying at marriage; but in recent years, as mentioned in the text, a small number of un-attached adult females have settled on the farm.

Notes

1. This version of an earlier draft was revised in the light of discussions at the A.S.A. conference at the University of York. I am also particularly grateful for comments by the following individuals: A. Akeroyd, L. Brydon, A. Cohen, T. Crump, N. Klein, L. Mars, C. Murray, I. Schapera, S. Wallman and R. Werbner.
2. Izolo is a pseudonym; certain details are lightly scrambled in order to protect informants. I first got to know the locality when I lived and worked in the district as a medical practitioner from 1950 to 1952. I also paid a brief visit in 1976. Grateful acknowledgement is made to the Social Science Research Council for the award of a research grant which enabled me to carry out further fieldwork in 1977—78. For other accounts of work in the area see Loudon 1956, 1959, 1965, 1970, 1979.
3. The word 'Black' denotes those variously described in South African Government publications as 'Natives', 'Africans' or 'Bantu', while the word 'White' denotes those classified as 'Europeans'.
4. The new, second and re-titled edition (Hammond-Tooke 1974) of a standard work (Schapera 1937) has no chapter corresponding to Hunter's

contribution on 'The Bantu on European-owned farms' in the latter. Indeed, no more than six lines out of 480 pages of text deal with what the new editor refers to as "farm people . . . . . an important class" who "while not living under chiefs . . . . . tend to be strongly conservative". It is by no means clear what that blanket adjective means in relation to a category of people comprising some millions of men, women and children existing under a variety of conditions in different parts of South Africa.

5. Malinowski's remark about "smugness" and "unreality" arose from his polemical and (probably) wilful refusal to appreciate the realistic approach advocated by Schapera (1938) regarding the study of "culture contact" in "a specifically South African culture, shared in by both Black and White, and presenting certain peculiarities based directly upon the fact of their juxtaposition".

6. The census definition of 'urban' includes very small but non-agricultural communities; therefore it is mainly the non-farming White population which is classified as urban. In 1936 there were about 95,000 English-speaking Whites in rural areas; the average decline per annum since then has been about 0.3 per cent. In 1974 it was estimated that a total of about 280,000 Afrikaans-speakers remained in rural areas, that is to say about twelve per cent of the total of 2,332,000 White Afrikaans-speaking South Africans. This represents an average decline in the Afrikaans-speaking White rural population of 1.4 per cent since 1936 (Union of South Africa 1960; Watts 1976).

7. These three categories of farm workers are distinguished as follows in the Republic of South Africa's Department of Statistics' Agricultural Censuses: 'regular workers' are those normally engaged in farm work in agriculture, forestry and sugar-cane plantations; 'casual workers' are seasonal and occasional workers, excluding those employed by contractors; 'domestic workers' are those mainly or exclusively engaged in work in the households of their employers.

8. Statistics on which these figures are based derive from Keppel-Jones (1949) and from Republic of South Africa (1973).

9. The most vivid systematic account of this period in the history of Natal remains that by Hattersley (1950) where details of the daily life and personal backgrounds of many settlers may be found.

10. Perhaps one should not be surprised to find that about twenty per cent of marriages among members of the kinship and friendship networks of local farmers in the second half of the twentieth century involve couples both of whom can trace descent from people who were neighbours (and sometimes kindred) in the second half of the nineteenth century.

11. A theologically sophisticated inquisitor would be needed if the extent to which local White Anglicanism is shot through with threads of fundamentalism, pentecostalism and Christian Science were to be disentangled.

12. In all cases Izolo farmers have had at least eleven years schooling, followed in most cases by one or two years at an agricultural college. None so far have been to a university, though the sons of some local farmers are

currently reading for degrees in agriculture or agricultural economics at the Universities of Natal and Stellenbosch and intend to be farmers. In general, therefore, Izolo farmers are not typical of Whites in agriculture in South Africa, of whom only 30 per cent in 1970 had had more than eight years schooling and 35 per cent had had eight years or less (Republic of South Africa 1973).

13. When it seems necessary or helpful to give the sterling equivalents of the sums shown in South African currency, I have used the exchange rate operating at the time of my residence there in 1977–78. This was approximately £1 = R1.68. Although most Izolo farmers and workers still think of the Rand as being equivalent to ten shillings, it is in fact worth about 60 new pence.

14. MacCrone (1949) reported that 'very fond of sport' ranked first among the qualities comprising the English-speaking White South African group stereotype. The corresponding quality for Jewish South Africans was 'shrewd at business', while for Afrikaans-speaking Whites 'hospitable' and 'very religious' tied for first place.

15. This is most obviously expressed in well-worn jokes and 'van der Merwe' stories, involving a stereotypical Afrikaner and the derisive mimicry of English spoken with a lower-class Afrikaans accent. Asian accents are also sometimes imitated likewise, as are the 'plummy' tones of British vivistors like myself. On the other hand, some Izolo Whites are very sensitive about their own pronunciation of English and may be heard trying to correct their children's solecisms. Curiously, I do not recall having heard a White imitating English as spoken by South African Blacks. On the subject of South African English as a mother-tongue, see Branford (1976).

16. Improved communications, among other things, have resulted in making the present generation of White children in Izolo the first to have any direct contact with Afrikaans-speaking children. There are now two government schools in town, one each for the two languages. Before going to boarding schools, White farm children used to be taught at home by governesses; nowadays they go to the English-language school in town. I heard several anecdotes from them in which their accounts of open conflict with their opposite numbers were expressed in terms of a mixture of ethnicity and social class.

17. Some White farmers, when faced with the possibility of being alone in a car journey to town, invariably take with them at least one congenial male Black worker as a companion. But this is always presented as part of the work situation, since the Black passenger's ostensible function is to load up the boot of the car with goods or to be available to help to deal with emergencies, such as a puncture or breakdown.

18. The main figures for the Black population of Middeldaal may be found in the Appendix.

19. Conifers are of two main kinds, the patula pine (from Mexico) and the cluster pine (originating from the Mediterranean). Blue gums and black wattles are from Australia, both having been introduced into South Africa in the 19th century. Commercial wattle growing on a large scale in Izolo

started in the 1930s. The reasons for the present decline in demand for the timber of conifers and blue gums lies outside the scope of this paper.

20. I was told that on a few farms elsewhere Black women workers were beginning to be employed as tractor drivers, especially in plantation work where the wear and tear on tyres is very great because of tree stumps and other obstacles. It was said that this change had materially reduced expenditure on spares and servicing, since women tractor drivers are more careful and less prone to drive recklessly to prove their skill and courage. I do not know if female tractor drivers are paid the same wages as their male counterparts; but I think it highly unlikely.

21. In her study of race attitudes and behaviour among White employers of Black servants in two contrasted areas of Durban, Preston-Whyte (1976) appears to have forgotten about the situation on some farms in Natal when she writes that 'it is now only in domestic employment' in South Africa 'that individual members of the White and Black groups are in continual and intimate face-to-face contact and, despite segregatory legislation, can live near each other and interact without undue control or interference'.

22. This section of my discussion owes a great deal to stimuli from C. Murray, R. Werbner and S. Wallman, but they are in no way responsible for the tenor of the response.

References

Branford, W. 1976. A dictionary of South African English as a reflex of the English-speaking cultures of South Africa. In *English-speaking South Africa today*, A. De Villiers (ed.). Cape Town: Oxford University Press.

Hammond-Tooke, W.D. 1974 (ed.). *The Bantu-speaking peoples of Southern Africa.* London: Routledge and Kegan Paul.

Hattersley, A.H. 1950. *The British settlement of Natal.* Cambridge: University Press.

Hunter, M. 1936 and 1961. *Reaction to conquest.* London: Oxford University Press.

——— 1937. The Bantu on European-owned farms. In Schapera (1937) *q.v.*

Keppel-Jones, A.M. 1949. Land and agriculture outside the reserves. In *Handbook on race relations in South Africa*, E. Hellmann (ed.). Cape Town: Oxford University Press.

Lipton, M. 1977. South Africa: two agricultures? In Wilson *et al.* (1977) *q.v.*

Loudon, J.B. 1956. Social structure and health concepts among the Zulu. *Health Education Journal* XV (2), 90–8.

——— 1959. Psychogenic disorder and social conflict among the Zulu. In *Culture and mental health*, M.K. Opler (ed.). New York: Macmillan.

——— 1965. Social aspects of ideas about treatment. In *Transcultural psychiatry*, A.V.S. De Reuck and R. Porter (eds.). London: Churchill.

——— 1970. *White farmers and Black labour-tenants.* Cambridge and Leiden: African Studies Centre.

———1979. *Illness and social change in a rural community in Natal.* Report

134   *J.B. Loudon*

to SSRC on project HR5378/1.

MacCrone, I.D. 1949. Race attitudes: an analysis and interpretation. In *Handbook on race relations in South Africa*, E. Hellmann (ed.). Cape Town: Oxford University Press.

Malinowski, B. 1938. Introductory essay on the anthropology of changing African cultures. *Methods of study of culture contact in Africa*. International Institute of African Languages and Cultures Memorandum XV.

Newby, H., Bell, C., Rose, D. and Saunders, P. 1978. *Property, paternalism and power: class and control in rural England.* London: Hutchinson.

Preston-Whyte, E. 1976. Race attitudes and behaviour: the case of domestic employment in White South African homes. *African Studies* **XXXV** (2), 71–89.

Republic of South Africa 1973. *Department of Statistics, Agricultural censuses for 1973 and earlier years.* Pretoria: Government Printer.

Roberts, M. 1958. *Labour in the farm economy.* Johannesburg: South African Institute of Race Relations.

Schapera, I. (ed.) 1937. *The Bantu-speaking tribes of South Africa.* London: Routledge and Kegan Paul.

——— 1938. Contact between European and Native in South Africa: 2. in Bechuanaland. *Methods of study of culture contact in Africa.* International Institute of African Languages and Cultures Memorandum XV.

Union of South Africa 1960. *Bureau of Census and Statistics Union statistics for fifty years: Jubilee issue 1910–1960.* Pretoria: Government Printer.

Watts, H.L. 1976. A social and demographic portrait of English-speaking White South Africans. In *English-speaking South Africa today*, A. De Villiers (ed.). Cape Town: Oxford University Press.

Wilson, F. 1977. Reflections on farm labour in South Africa. In Wilson *et al.* (1977) *q.v.*

Wilson, F., Kooy, A. and Hendrie, D. (eds.) 1977 *Farm labour in South Africa.* Cape Town: David Philip.

Wilson, M. 1977. Villages for farm workers? In Wilson *et al.* (1977) *q.v.*

THE STIGMA CYCLE:

Values and Politics in a Dockland Union

GERALD MARS

The Structure and Organization of Dock Work

This paper will examine the implications of a division of values within
one union. Such a division provided the dynamic for union political
activity at different levels but it also affected the ordering of industrial
relations — that is the relations between the union and employers.
The union is the Longshoremans Protective Union of St. Johns in
Newfoundland, Canada (the L.S.P.U.). It was studied as part of a
wider anthropological study[1] of longshoreman (Mars 1972) and
supplemented by the examination of union records which allowed
detailed aspects of its political life to be reconstructed over a ten
year period. The union at the time of fieldwork and until 1968 was
unaffiliated to any other labour organization and comprised no
other locals.[2]

Dockwork is noted for the solidarity it develops amongst its
workers and members of the L.S.P.U. were no exception. Longshoremen constantly emphasized to outsiders that "all longshoremen are
brothers" and this solidarity was reinforced by their overall 'pariah'
status in the wider community. Unions, of course, tend to over-
emphasize the identity of interests of their members — as the very
word 'union' implies. There are occasions during strikes or lockouts
when a heightened consciousness of this identity is indeed strongly
affirmed and when divisions over policies, perceptions and interests
are minimised. But structural divisions in the L.S.P.U. were real,
nonetheless, and though these might be papered over during periods
of opposition to employers, they were evident most of the time.

This paper therefore looks at two problems. The first is: how is
political life organized in a union when its structure not only
segments its members but also insulates these segments from each
other? The second problem is concerned with more specific questions
to do with process. In particular: why was the union's political life —
both in its internal and its external relations — marked by periods of
calm interspersed with extreme turbulence? Why should some

elections pass by "on the nod" whilst others were bitterly contested; and why should some contracts be re-negotiated with ease whilst others involved violent disruptions to the normal pattern of industrial relations?

Structural divisions in this union were threefold. All three limited both perceived identity of interests and physical interaction. Firstly, members were divided by tenure: the principal division was between members of regular gangs and "outside men" – the one-in-three casuals who filled vacancies as and when they could. The second division was occupationally based; the union covered the whole range of job holders from foremen and shed checkers through all the specialized roles in the dock work gang – holdsmen, stowers, signallers winchmen, fork lift drivers, slingsmen and gang checker. The membership was also divided by wharf affiliation – most regular men taking their earnings from only one of the two main wharfs. Wharf affiliation was important too because it linked with physical residence – regular men tending to live near their wharf. A third division was based on religion. Approximately fifty per cent of the membership were Catholic and fifty per cent Protestant. And Protestants were further divided into two major segments and a number of minor sects. Religion however, was even further divisive since much of the town's social, educational, and political activities were based on religious groupings.

These divisions were manifest within Union Executives. In particular, the significance of workplace becomes apparent when Executive members are considered.

Of the approximately 620 active workforce, some 330 worked regularly at the two main wharfs. A further 60 worked mostly regularly, at various smaller premises, the majority being employed at the C.N.R. dock, whilst approximately 170 were outside men without regular affiliation to any particular wharf. But of the members of four Executives (1958, 1960, 1962, 1964) *none* worked outside two main wharves: employees of the smaller firms were not represented on the Executive, and neither were outside men – the former because they lacked the opportunity to exploit any large network of support; the latter because they were peripheral to any network. And though Executive Committees comprised nine positions, the total pool of men in these four Executives numbered only fifteen. By religion twelve were Catholics and three Protestants.

One further division, that between the literate and the illiterate, affected the size of the pool of men available for Executive office. Members of the Executive all thought that about half the members were illiterate. But all but two of the fifteen men who had served or were serving on the Executive were literate, and this had been an important factor in their selection. When men were asked whether they had ever stood for election they often replied that they lacked education by which they meant the ability to read, write and talk well.

Large segments of the membership were thus precluded from executive office, and those elected came from a narrow base. An illiterate outside man who was Protestant stood a negligible chance, whereas an educated Catholic, regularly employed as a stower at one of the two large premises, had a multiplicity of influences from which to launch a campaign. It is only within this minority — that is within some 20% of the total union membership — that personal charisma could be significant.

The primary problem for political activists was to exert influence on the Executive or move on to it themselves by mobilizing sufficient support to cross-cut these divisions. Firstly, they had to overcome occupational divisions which reduced identity of interests and indeed in some cases interests which were opposed. With a shortage of work and an absence of any scheme of work rotation for instance, the work that went to regular gang members was seen as at the expense of outside men. Yet activists needed support from both regular and outside men even though their main interests were in direct opposition. But for the most part, interests based on occupation were not so much opposed as lacking any basis for the perception of a common policy. Even regular men on different wharves found it difficult to coalesce. They rarely shared an interest with fellow regulars on other wharves, whilst support for a policy might be given or withheld solely because of its advocates' religion. Thus a section of the union's membership which might act together to further a policy should not on that account be thought of as necessarily structurally specific: the bases of recruitment to factions, as Firth (1957) has observed, can rest on specific interest or associational ties, or on a combination of several of these.

Because of the high number of social and occupational divisions within the union, factions which have been effective in influencing policy have always been based on combinations. Such factions were essentially loosely ordered and informally organized and the memberships of different factions were not consistent on different occasions. And, as I shall show, even within the union hierarchy which tended to social and occupational homogeneity, I found that structural aspects of union organization acted divisively.

The second problem facing activists was to overcome limits on the opportunities for association. Here distinctions of work task, wharf affiliation, residence and religion all limited the physical contacts of members and therefore reduced communication that could lead to concerted action (Raphael 1965).

Political process in this union can be understood as a series of shifts between two aspects of structure: on the one hand, the recurrent mobilization by activists of the union's membership which periodically overcame all its occupational and associational divisions: on the other, the reassertion of segmentary forces. For most of the ten year period studied, political action was quiescent since segmentary forces were too dominant to be overcome. But when they *were* overcome the floodgates of political action opened. And it was the manipulation of values by union activists that were vital in this process.

Political process flowed around two sets of events normally thought of as unconnected. These were union elections held in May every second year, and union/management contract negotiations which began in the closing months of the dying contract. All contracts in this period were scheduled to end on December 31st, except for one ending in April. Since contracts had a life of one, two or three years, contract negotiations were essentially erratic when compared to the more regular elections. In this ten year period seven contracts were negotiated; five were effected harmoniously whilst two involved serious lockouts, one lasting six weeks, the other nearly a year. In the same period there were six elections; four involved little disruption and two involved the turnover of a majority of each Executive. It is this transposition of harmony and turbulence that offers the clue to understanding political process in this union. But as we shall see, turbulence can be manifest in different forms: there appears a distinct linkage in the union's affairs between the incidence of *either* internal turbulence, manifest as changes on the Executive *or* internal turbulence manifest as a strike or lockout. This linkage becomes clearer when we come to chart the incidence of both elections and contract renewals and relate them to political turbulence.

Divisions Within the Union Hierarchy

The union contained an Executive of eight working longshoremen and one full-time President. Besides the President, who in 1963 received $5,000 a year, the union employed two other full-time officials — a Delegate who spent his time on the waterfront and who received $4,600, and a Union Janitor who received $3,000. Both latter positions were secure for incumbents once appointed and though either could be replaced by majority vote of the membership, this had never occurred or been at issue. A President, on the other hand, was liable to the insecurity of elections which, as we shall see, involved him in considerable role strain. Not only did elections place his own position at risk, they also threatened the position of his supporters on the Executive.

A President's role is only vaguely defined in the union constitution. It merely states that "the President shall preside at all meetings of the Union, conserve order and see that the constitution and bye-laws are carried out. He shall also superintend the general affairs of the Union". This description makes no mention of his main day-to-day activities; of his role as the union's figurehead in the town or his periodic role as principal negotiator of contracts with the employers. Nor does it mention his personal vulnerability to action for breaches of the management/union contract under the terms of the Trades Disputes and Investigation Act of 1948.

Members expected their President to be available daily in the union office, to wear a 'business suit' during office hours and to be able to answer queries that often had little to do with the waterfront. He was expected, for instance, to advise on relations with welfare agencies and on payment of local taxes, matters which often cause difficulty to men with a low standard of literacy. In these contacts with the men he was in many ways seen as a welfare officer. Day-to-day unionism on the other hand was understood both by management and men to be in the hands of the Delegate. As one manager expressed it nodding towards the Delegate's departing figure — "There goes the *real* power on this waterfront".

The Delegate's job was to act as a full-time union representative on the waterfront and he was formally subject to the authority of the Executive. It involved "policing" the agreement on the union's behalf and this required his constant presence on all the wharves of the waterfront. It is understandable, therefore, that the Delegate should often have been referred to as the man who knew more about the waterfront than anyone else. As such, of course, he was in a better position than the President, who was chairbound, and the Executive, who were individually restricted to one wharf, both in having information about particular events and in his control of communication. This control was two-way — extending both downwards to the men and upwards to the President and Executive. His position is central to an understanding of political processes within the union.

A Delegate's duties and the limits to his authority are also undefined in the union's constitution which merely states that "his powers and duties shall be defined by the Executive". Though this description allows for ambiguities, a Delegate's duties were well understood. As stated, it is his job "to police the agreement", a definition he always emphasized and one in which the President and various super-intendents concurred. The men's view of the Delegate's job often reflected a bitterness towards management — as a stower said, it is "to see the employers don't pull a fast one". Most of a Delegate's time was accordingly spent in ensuring that agreed limits of working capacities were not exceeded, that men were paid extra for dirty or dangerous cargo and that work ceased in heavy rain — a frequent cause of disputes in St. Johns with its annual rainfall of over 50 inches a year.[3]

The ambiguity and therefore potential conflict inherent in the Delegate's role come not from dispute over duties, but from debate about the limits of authority. These limits were perceived differently by the men, the President and the employers. All agreed that a watchdog function was legitimately part of a Delegate's job. But the decision he was expected to take if disagreement occurred about the weight of a sling load, for instance, or whether rain was too heavy for men to work, could not be arrived at through the use of an unambiguous formula — and further it had to be made on the spot. Ambiguity allied to the need for decisive action often led to conflict and reflected a situation found in other ports. A British Government White Paper investigating troubles in the London docks, records that:

> In the first place, there are certain inescapable features of dock work which create almost constant opportunities for disputes to occur, in a way which probably does not arise in any other industry. It is not suggested that the nature of dock work is such that frequent disputes and stoppages are inevitable; indeed, given goodwill and mutual trust, there is ample joint machinery for settling all differences without interruption of work. The fact remains, however, that there are greater opportunities for disputes to occur and for the activities of deliberate trouble-makers than in most other industries.

and

> ... in factory production there is not the same variety of circumstances nor the same range of materials to be handled. Moreover the workers employed on any one job in the docks seldom constitute a stable group as they would in factory employment. They do not continue to do the same kind of work in the same place for long periods, as normally happens in a factory. The precise circumstances of a particular job may never recur, and once it is finished, the men concerned will often be dispersed among other kinds of work and other employers. They are naturally anxious to see a settlement of any dispute about payments

before the job is finished, and therefore often slow up or stop work in order to enforce a settlement as favourable as possible to themselves. As, in so many cases, [where] the men are not in regular employment with the employer concerned, the trust which might otherwise exist is often lacking. (Great Britain. Docks 1951, paras. 15 and 18.)

Because a Delegate was on the spot when crucial decisions had to be made he often had to act alone. If such a decision was acceptable to all parties on the waterfront then, *ipso facto*, it was a 'good' decision from the viewpoint of the President. The same decision in slightly different circumstances could, however, fail to resolve or could even exacerbate a conflict. Then a President found himself called to a situation already pre-empted and which might have serious legal implications. An extract from the minutes of the Executive meeting on August 19th 1957 records a presidential rebuke:

After hearing the facts of the case the executive found the Delegate wrong in giving this decision. The Delegate was given a severe reprimand by the President in which he stated that the Delegate sometimes by his decision causes trouble amongst the men and the executive has to rectify his mistakes. In the future he must check more often with the President so he will know what's going on on the waterfront and won't be always in the dark. Also the President stated that the executive will back the Delegate, but they must know what his decisions are so they will know if they are right or wrong. If he has a difficult decision he must check with the President first otherwise he will not get any support . . . This stems from a decision of the Delegate . . . The decision almost caused the union to pay the *Blue Peter Steamship Co.* 23 hours wages for a single gang. Fortunately the union did not have to, but by treating the ship like any other ship this would not arise again.

Both Delegate and President often complained about the other's actions. One of the first act of a new President on taking office in 1949 was to invoke a disciplinary charge against the Delegate "for bringing disgrace on the union by his dirty and untidy appearance on the waterfront". There were men nearly fifteen years later who, because of this charge, still 'jokingly' referred to the Delegate as "Dirty Jack". It was generally understood that the President's action served "to show who was boss of the union" rather than to reflect a specific interest in grooming as such.

Because of this structural friction, Presidents found themselves at a double disadvantage in any dispute with management. Not only was it rare for a President to deal with a crisis from the beginning, unlike managers or Superintendents; but he needed also to depend upon the Delegate for a reliable account of what had happened. It was however, by no means certain that the account he received would be reliable, since some unsuccessful action would have been taken by the Delegate prior to the President's intervention. A President therefore faced in extreme form the common dilemma of supervisors in any bureaucracy: that information about problems tends not to be passed up by subordinates until a problem becomes a crisis.

A second strain was inherent in the President's role. As the political and administrative head of a democratic organization he faced election every two years. This meant he had to try to maintain contact with his rank and file at the same time that his job isolated him from them. But as a direct result of this physical and social isolation, a President was normally in no position to make any approach to sizeable segments of the membership. It was only at general meetings held to acquaint the membership with the state of negotiations with employers that large attendances were found. Attendance on these occasions could amount to ninety per cent. But these were essentially unusual events. This is why the President, much more than the Delegate, was concerned about poor attendance at the routine quarterly meetings when it was difficult to raise even a quorum of twenty members. The President constantly complained of union apathy as reflected in poor attendances, but the Delegate, from his different position, was quite positive that the membership was by no means apathetic — indeed he complained that there was too much to do: his every day was spent at the focal point of membership/management activity.

A third and perhaps the greatest strain facing a President came from his attempts to reconcile the political and legal aspects of his role. As we saw, a political head subject to election needs widespread support. At the same time, as a union executive vulnerable to the law he often had to make unpopular decisions which affected sizeable segments of his membership. Thus, after the 1958 lockout, managements were allowed by terms of a new contract to enjoy "the free and unrestricted use of mechanical equipment". The management of one wharf accordingly felt free to introduce fork lift trucks. This action was bitterly resented by the men and all on that wharf — numbering 150 — walked off against the terms of the contract and with the Delegate's tacit support. The President charged all those involved and the Executive convicted and fined them — after which all returned to work. This case (which is un-recorded in the minutes) was often referred to as an example of the management orientation of the President. Men who talked of it — as they still did five years later — neither denied the rights of

management nor failed to understand the President's legal interpretation of the contract. They argued instead from a view of what
they perceived as morally right — and to them moral values had
precedence over legal ones. As one man expressed it when I put
the legal position concerning management/union contracts, "I don't
care what the law says. It is not right for them to grab even more
money and put men out of work".

I term "moral values" those which justify arguments from a base
of what is projected as natural justice. Moral values are also concerned
with equity and comparability with outside groups. (Never with
internal comparability which is by definition divisive.) They were
promulgated by men out of the centres of power who were either
seeking election to the executive, or attempting to consolidate their
positions on it.

"Legal values" on the other hand were held by the President and
his close and experienced officers. These were people negotiating
with employers, aware of the main provisions of the various acts
and aware of their liability for breaches of the contract. But a
division of values as discussed here does not imply a lack of
acceptance of the alternative value apparently foregone. Though
values are graded, both sets in a division may be accepted (Firth 1964:
Ch. IX).

A President therefore, unlike a Delegate, found himself in a
situation comparable to but more intense than that of many first
level supervisors: his role involved the strain of attempting to
reconcile two sets of contradictory values both of which he could
accept but which he had to rate differently. Men, concerned with
moral questions of right and wrong, expected their elected
president to follow their interests as they perceived them: they may
be said to have been "locally" and "morally" oriented. The President
as he saw it however, had to follow "cosmopolitan"[4] and "legal"
values. He was often perceived therefore to be acting in ways in-
distinguishable from a boss.

One of the few ways a President could deal with these opposing
sets of values was by simple avoidance. When a new crisis broke on
the waterfront he could, and frequently did, make himself difficult
to locate. A common grumble by managers was that the President
could never be found when a problem had to be referred to him.
"He's impossible to contact when a decision is needed", was a
common cry.

A frequent source of dispute between management and the union
— in the person of the Delegate — involved wet weather working. If
it begins to rain when a vessel has only a few hours work prior to

sailing, management are naturally keen to continue work so the vessel may depart. But there are no limits of acceptable rainfall that can be written into a contract, and disputes often occurred over whether men should stop work or not. Men expressed their view in essentially moral terms and reinforced this by pointing to managerial criteria for stopping work which, they said, depended solely on whether cargo would be damaged by being unloaded in rain — irrespective of whether it was "right" that men should work in bad conditions. Men observed that managements required the unloading of cars or barrels for instance, to continue in what has been described as "near blizzard conditions", whereas when dealing with foodstuffs — which were packed in light cardboard — they would stop unloading in even a light shower. "They think more of their fucking beans than they do of us" was how one bitter skidsman expressed a widespread view.

It was management's complaint that in cases of disagreement between the Delegate and Superintendent (which were common), a dispute should, following the contract, be taken to higher level — that of wharf manager and union President — where the President could be made subject to legalistic arguments. Invariably, however, this kind of situation, typical of dock work where on the spot decisions are needed, would always founder because of the President's absence — or so management said.

The division of values, termed here legal and moral, and on which focussed so much presidential role strain, was also found within the Executive. During fieldwork the legalists — in the persons of the President, Treasurer, and Secretary — were referred to among the membership as "The Big Three" and the remainder of the Executive as "The Little Six". Members of the union, as well as of the Executive's two sections, confirmed that the Executive always contained two camps, though often known by different names. One of *The Big Three*, a member of different executives for over six years, said "There's always an opposition on the executive — they try to force the pace until they learn some sense". It was his experience that divisions went along the lines of experience — "they don't know the limits and are hotheaded at first". It appears that segmentation along these lines was an institutionalized characteristic of L.S.P.U. Executive Committees.

I noticed that divisions within the Executive were reinforced by the physical arrangement and use of office accommodation (see diagram). Members of *The Big Three* frequently locked the two doors A and B, and thus secure in Office Number 2, would discuss policy and tactics, while *The Little Six* were isolated in Office

Number 1. Within the locked security of their office the three also drank together, which further emphasized their solidarity and the isolation of the six — especially since alcohol is formally forbidden on union premises. This activity served too to bind the two legalists more closely to the President since he always paid for the drink and, as patron, distributed it.

Fig. 1. The layout of office accommodation within the L.S.P. union hall.

As well as these conflicts and the dilemmas inseparable from a President's role, further problems arose from his control and allocation of patronage. Working members of the L.S.P.U. Executive enjoyed few perquisites of office — though in the barren economic climate of St. John's these were jealously watched since even small benefits represented relatively important additions to incomes that rarely exceeded $2,500. Patronage offered to legalists was seen as reinforcing *The Big Three* at the expense of the moralistic *Outer Six*. As an example, two legalists were annually selected by the President, on no criteria other than his personal choice, to superintend the annual issue of 'union buttons'. These were membership badges certifying paid up status, and their issue took place in a fortnight during the winter months. Thus, the chosen two received about 90 hours pay at longshore rates — about $200 — during the time of year when work was slackest.

A more serious division arose within the Executive prior to contract renewals. The President had power to choose two Executive members to work with him and form the union's negotiating committee. He chose legalists and they were paid for their time at full longshore rates. During difficult negotiations payments could amount to several hundred dollars. But a second distinction arose from their position as negotiators which involved high prestige as being at the centre of affairs and through their possession of important knowledge about the state of negotiations.

Political Process in the L.S.P.U.

So far I have largely emphasized structural constraints which inhibited political activity. But the union's political life was dynamic and these constraints could be, and in certain circumstances were, removed. To understand the *processes* which governed their removal we must now consider two electoral conventions. Neither were formalized, but each operated without exception. They involved firstly, limiting candidates to standing for only one post and second, acceptance of the idea of public executive solidarity. Both conventions increased political activity prior to elections.

In most unions people may stand for one or several officerships and also for undifferentiated seats on an executive committee. By this means they can multiply their chances of possible election. The L.S.P.U., however, had no undifferentiated seats on its executive; all nine positions had distinctive titles, all post holders were officers and each, in theory, had a function. And because union tradition allowed a contender to stand for only one post, it followed he had only one chance of getting on the Executive. It also follows, that a man with a body of support he felt too small to secure his own election would be less inclined to risk his all on a single throw. Nevertheless, he possessed a valuable political asset. If two or more such men combined their support groups they could forward the campaign of one or both of them. The convention of one man being allowed to stand for only one post therefore encouraged the development of alliances and factionalism. It reinforced the need for alliances derived from the essentially limited bases from which insulated contenders for office had to launch their campaigns.

The resultant political manoeuvring necessarily extended beyond regular gang members on large wharves to all categories of the membership. A successful campaign for office had to be based not only upon a core from a man's own wharf, but had to extend to wider segments of the membership on all wharves.

The second convention encouraging political activity was the traditional solidarity of the Executive. It is normal practice in unions for an executive member who wishes to dissociate himself at a general meeting from the policy of his colleagues, to step down from the top table and speak as an individual against official policy. The L.S.P.U. had always operated the convention that such dissident voices must be publicly quiet. No Executive member had ever overtly disagreed with Executive policies at any general meeting. Such overt consensus allowed dissidents both to plot in secret, and to enjoy the valued prestige of office.

One effect of this conventional solidarity was to create alliances between seekers after office and dissident members of the Executive. The dissidents, who were prominantly moralists, often had access to information which could embarrass their legalist colleagues on the Executive. The tradition of public quiet however, meant that the information could not be publicly used. Office seekers, on the other hand, had ability to speak at general meetings but lacked access to information. An alliance between a dissident Executive member and an office seeker, could, therefore prove useful to both. It could lead the way to successful election for an office seeker whilst cleansing the moral reputation of an executive dissident if executive policies were to prove unpopular.

Because office seekers had to obtain support beyond their own wharf and occupational group, I have said they must arrange their campaign around an issue that made a maximum impact. Only one situation provided issues of such magnitude: contract renewal negotiations involved the reconsideration of all substantive and procedural rules which governed work and conditions of the whole membership.

An office-seeker, therefore, would aim to widen his support base by advocating popular policies for the union to pursue in negotiations with employers and by criticizing the negotiating committee's handling of negotiations. He would do this on the only occasions that provided an adequate audience — at general meetings. A similar situation has been observed in at least one other union (Lipset *et al.* 1956).

It thus occurred that the main division within Executives occurred during the crucial periods of contract renewal. With the President's selection of two legalists to form the negotiating committee, a battle for information then occurred between the Executive's two sides; legalists aiming to keep information from moralists; moralists seeking to gain it.

This control of information was justified by *The Big Three* on grounds of security. "They'll blab their mouths off", "Everything will be back with the bosses in an hour". Conversations with *The Big Three* showed that the desire to control information was concerned less with security and more with the aim to stop potential linkages between Executive moralists and membership activists. Opposition cannot easily be mounted if details of negotiations are not fully understood: attempts to withhold information aimed to limit the manoeuvrability of moralists and activists in electoral skirmishes. At the same time the prestige of an Executive member was largely maintained by his ability to give out 'scarce' information when asked for it by members. By restricting and in effect cornering the supply of information members of *The Big Three* were in position to reduce the prestige of *The Little Six* whilst simultaneously increasing their own.

Not surprisingly, *The Little Six* resented their lack of access to information, and especially was this evident during early negotiations with the employers in 1964. When one of the *Little Six* "had liquor in him" he knocked soundly on the inner door of Office 2, and when it was opened he swore at *The Big Three* within. "Why don't you tell us anything?" he shouted, "This is an Executive of nine, not an Executive of three." As negotiations proceeded the relationship between *Big Three* and *Little Six* became more and more strained until negotiations finally broke down when a lockout united all members of the union behind *The Big Three*.

A Faction Organizes: The Case for Time-and-a-Half

We can now appreciate some events which occurred in 1956 that illustrate the themes discussed and which were to have a marked effect on the union's subsequent history. Events focussed around a factional claim for time and a half pay for work after six o'clock in the evening and they involved the manipulation of both legal and moral values.

With confederation as Canada's tenth province in 1949, the way was open for Canadian labour practices to appear on the Newfoundland scene. By the early 1950s, many St. John's unions, unlike the L.S.P.U., had affiliated with labour organizations on the mainland. One result was that unions in St. John's tended to look for national comparisons when making a claim, whereas before confederation their horizons had been limited to the local scene. The main effect of the availability of wider comparisons and access to centralized services and personnel which affiliation permitted was that most unions in St. John's had, by 1954, succeeded in winning time and a half pay for overtime. This was bound to affect the city's longshoremen. During the relatively busy summer of 1954, the argument for comparability with other city unions was first raised amongst regular men at the Furness Withy Wharf — one of the largest in the port with a more regular basis of association than other wharves since much of its cargo came from the U.K. and was unaffected by winter closure of the St. Lawrence. Like other workers in the city who had succeeded in their claims, they too argued that work after 6 p.m. should also be paid at time and a half.

A differential of 20 cents was already paid for work after 7 p.m. and a successful claim would have meant an additional 47 cents an hour.

Pressure for the time and a half mounted during 1954 and 1955. By early 1956 and with an election due in May it was one of the most discussed topics on the waterfront. It was a unifying objective since a gain for one group was seen as not being at the expense of others. It appeared, however, wellnigh impossible to achieve in a situation of declining work without the union giving up considerable concessions. It was known that managements were adamant in their resistance and that the Executive, and particularly the President, were against such a claim, whilst the Delegate supported it. He had been useful to the faction by canvassing support on all wharves during his normal work. As early as 1955, the prerequisites for effective factional action against the Executive were already present. Firstly, a factional core existed with a grievance; second, this grievance was held in common by other groups and third, one of the most important prerequisites for factional action − winning the Delegate's support − had already been accomplished. Only the final requirement − an overcoming of the physical separation of men divided by affiliation to their wharves − had to be overcome. It was not however until the end of April 1956 that the contract was due for renewal which would catapult such a grievance into the political arena and provide opportunies for the membership to meet collectively.

An important concern of factions was always to have a moralistic voice on the union negotiating committee − the actual caucus which meets with employers. Since suspicion surrounded the legalistic President, it was ideal from a faction's view if they could use the moralistic Delegate as a countervailing force. Early factional manoeuvring had often focussed on ensuring this balance of power.

The normal form of a union negotiating committee comprised three members of the Executive, plus the President and Delegate. The 1955 minutes record a neat tactic by the President which allowed him to exclude the Delegate. In 1955 the minutes show that at a general meeting, "The chairman (i.e. the President) asked per- mission that the same procedure re the selecting of a negotiating committee as done in the year previous be given, that is, that the Executive be given the power to select three (3) members of the Executive to work in conjunction with the President as a Negotiation Committee (one of the three members to be the Recording Secretary)". Thus the President, by suggesting that "the same *procedure* . . . as done in the year previous", but without specifying the same *officers*, obtained authority from the body to pick a negotiating committee which excluded the Delegate.

In April 1956 with pressure mounting more strongly for time and a half after six o'clock, the contract, a one-year one, again fell due for renewal. At the first general meeting faction leaders who had planned the tactic beforehand this time sought to ensure that the Delegate became a member of the negotiating committee. The minutes record that the very first item raised from the body, a motion proposed and seconded by regular men from Furness Withy was: "That a Negotiation Committee consisting of the union President, *Delegate* (my emphasis), and Recording Secretary, plus two Executive members appointed by the Executive, be empowered to negotiate a working contract."

With the Delegate now on the negotiating committee the faction expected him to pursue their demand for time-and-a-half in opposition to the President. The President and other legalists, however, now isolated the Delegate from access to information about the negotiations. Before each confrontation with the employers, tactics were talked over between the legalists on the Negotiation Committee, with the Delegate being excluded from these informal and unofficial meetings. When the Negotiation Committee met the employers, he was in a weak position to make any positive contribution since he was unaware of his side's policy and tactics and could not speak out in case he revealed a split in union ranks.

Though the Delegate was to some extent made redundant by this tactic, he was not alone in resenting the aura of esotericism created. Moralist members of the Executive were similarly restricted in their access to information and similarly resented their impotency. The legalists were able further to restrict criticism of their tactics by simply not calling general meetings during the first months of negotiation.

Pressure from the body was eventually successful, however, and a general meeting was called on 8 May 1956, at which the President explained the state of negotiations. In return for time and a half, the employers required a reduction in the size of gangs, the introduction and use of mechanical equipment (specifically the use of fork lift trucks), and an increase in the weight of cargo that derricks were allowed to hoist on a sling load. These proposals were regarded as imposing such a strong encroachment on conditions of work that they were unanimously rejected.[5] It was decided to put the case to a conciliation board and the President of the Halifax longshoreman's union was chosen as the union's representative. At this meeting one of the faction leaders proposed a ban on work after 6 o'clock in an effort to press the case for time-and-a-half. The

President said such action would be illegal; "Under the Federal Labour Laws if an eight-hour day was instituted by a union, an injunction could be placed against the union". However, feeling among regular men, especially at Furness Withy, was so strong that in defiance of both President and employers the Furness Withy men refused to work after 6.00 p.m.

This was the situation when the Halifax President arrived a week later to address the membership. The minutes record: "Mr. Campbell . . . said, 'My advice to you is that you give your negotiating committee full powers to effect a settlement, including a reduction in manpower and increasing of sling-loads.' " In what seemed a surprising about-turn, two faction leaders from Furness Withy then proposed "that the union negotiating committee go back and get the best they can, bearing in mind the getting of time-and-one-half". This was also carried unanimously.

As a result of this motion the negotiating committee, in discussion with the executive, decided to satisfy most of the employers' demands in return for time and a half. Two moralist members at this executive meeting mentioned "that several members had made it clear that in their, the members', opinion the agreement could not be concluded by the negotiating committee until it was ratified by the body of the union at a special meeting". This view was discussed and, the minutes record, unanimously discounted. The ngeotiating committee then met the employers and signed an agreement which obtained time and a half in return for most of the employers' demands.

What followed is subject to various interpretations. The facts are that at the general meeting called to give the membership details of the new agreement, opposition to its terms was widespread. One faction leader said, "It's a bad mistake, we have taken a cut" (i.e. a reduction in gang size). Another remarked, "The contentious point with me is the two men lost". The minutes record that another of the Furness Withy faction then claimed, "that express permission was not given either to sign or not to sign". Two of these speakers were the proposer and seconder of the motion offered to the executive on advice of the Halifax President. The chairman insisted that the agreement *was* legally binding and its non-ratification "could develop into an act that would not stand up if an injunction was placed against the union and the issue brought to the Supreme Court by the employers". It was finally decided to hold a ballot. When this was counted 481 men rejected the new agreement in favour of the old, whereas 69 preferred the new. These 69, it was constantly suggested to me, were mostly shed checkers whose situation was hardly altered by the new agreement but who always stood to lose by any work stoppage. It should be noted that in the absence of any clear basis for determining redundancies the loss of two men from each gang made for insecurity among *all* the twenty eight members of every gang.

The Executive accepted the vote of rejection as a vote of no confidence and seven of nine members, including the President, resigned. The remaining two, who were those who had spoken out at the executive meeting, became the new President and first vice-president whilst the rest of the new Executive comprised men mostly from Furness Withy wharf who had acted as faction spokesmen from the floor.

This new Executive then met the employers who, despite divisions within their ranks, agreed to rescind the new agreement and to operate as before under the terms of the previous contract. The coup was a triumph for the moralists − they were however, during their time on the executive to become "contaminated" − and to pass in their turn into stigmatized obscurity.

Contract Renewals and Elections 1956−1968

With this background of structure and one detailed example of process we now come briefly to consider the L.S.P.U.'s subsequent history and the place within it of the crises caused by union elections and negotiations for contract renewal. In 1957 the contract again expired but elections were not due until the following year. The new contract, hardly different from the old, was signed with a minimum of negotiation and without pressure from factions in the membership for time and a half or indeed for any revision of conditions of work.

The contract again fell due for renewal in the following year, 1958, and negotiations continued to May when the Executive once more faced re-election. Pressure from factions for time and a half pay mounted again and the Executive in their turn pressurized the employers. The employers closed ranks, called a lockout, and after six weeks the union had to sue for terms. The new contract, in the words of the local Labour Relations Officer, "wiped the floor with the union". It scheduled dramatic cuts in gang size, did not grant time and a half pay for work after 6 o'clock and was, exceptionally, drawn up for a period of three years, i.e. until the end of December 1961.

1959 was marked by both internal and external calm. The contract was not due for renewal, no elections were held and both the political life of the union and relationships with employers were relatively uneventful. The previous contract was still valid in 1960, and though an election was held in that year this excited little interest, seven of the nine incumbents being re-elected without opposition.

In 1961 the previous contract was, again, still valid, no election was held, and the political life of the union, like relations with employers remained untouched by turbulence.

At the end of 1961 the three year contract signed after the lockout in 1958 expired. Negotiations for the new contract extended to the period prior to the May election of 1962. Turbulence in the membership was again manifest. Eight out of nine Executive positions were contested, including, for the first time, the Presidency. Although the President retained his seat, he found himself with a minority Executive since five of his supporters failed to be returned. The five new members conducted their election campaign by claiming they would press for that old chestnut: time-and-a-half pay after six o'clock.

1963 was a year between elections in which again the contract expired and needed to be renewed. Despite the professed policy aims of the new majority on the Executive, no pressure for time-and-a-half was evident, and the new contract was signed in terms hardly different from the old.

In the following year, 1964, both elections and contract renewal once more coincided. Pressure from the membership mounted for complete revision of the terms and conditions of work, including, for the first time, claims for abolition of the casual hiring system and its replacement by a rotationary scheme.

The President well realized that the union was in little position to satisfy these claims. Pressed as he was between obdurate employers on the one hand and militant and widely supported factions on the other, he expressed his position to me by saying "There's a knife grinding on the inside and a knife grinding on the outside".

In an attempt to buttress his fading electoral chances the President became known as "soft for a handout": to secure votes in the forthcoming election he dispensed loans to longshoremen who asked for them. These loans were found to have been embezzled from union funds, and the President one day disappeared, leaving the Vice-president in charge of negotiations. Pressure on the Executive continued and, as before, left no room for flexibility in dealings with the employers. As in 1958, the employers again presented a united front and declared a lockout. This lockout lasted for a year and resulted in a contract which, as in 1958, had a scheduled life of over three years.

The three years following the lockout, 1965—6—7, were marked by both internal and external calm. The contract was not due for renewal until 1968 and the election held in 1966 excited little interest. Two new members made an appearance on the Executive, but the majority of posts were uncontested.

TABLE I

Contract renewals and union elections 1956–68 and the incidence of internal or external turbulence

Year	Election	Contract renewal		Turbulence Internal	External
1956	x	x	7 out of 9 executive members resign	x	
1957		x			
1958	x	x	6 weeks lockout		x
1959					
1960	x				
1961		x			
1962	x	x	8 out of 9 seats contested. 5 executive members removed.	x	
1963		x			
1964	x	x	1 year lockout		x
1965					
1966	x				
1967					

The period (see chart above) reveals four peaks of turbulence; in 1956, 1958, 1962 and 1964. The intervening years, 1957, 1959, 1960, 1961, 1963, 1965, 1966 and 1967 were, in comparison, relatively pacific.

Turbulence is used here to define two types of phenomena. Firstly, there is pressure from within the union with implications for the Executive. In 1956, most Executive members resigned because they found demands on them impossible to accept. In 1962 the Executive again reflected pressures from the membership when five out of nine members lost their seats in the elections. A second type of turbulence again emerges from pressures of membership opinion, but is directed through the Executive and onto the employers. It was the hard and intransigent bargaining by the negotiating committee whose advice has been ignored, but who acted in response to militant and morally based membership mandate, that led to the lockouts of 1958 and 1964.

It is evident that some connections exists between 'internal' turbulence focussed on the Executive, and 'external' turbulence focussed on employers. Examination of the chart reveals the common denominators of these two types of activity. Thus, either internal *or* external turbulence is evident when two events coincide. This coincidence involved both elections and contract negotiations occurring in the same period. When this happened — as it did in each of the four years of crisis — then conditions existed for turbulence of one sort or the other.

When either one of these events were absent, political process was marked by calm. Thus 1957, 1961 and 1963 were all years when contracts required renewal and no elections were held. Each contract was renewed without difficulty. Similarly, 1960 and 1966 were both years when contracts were not renewable, but elections were held. Each of these elections attracted little interest or opposition, and the majority of existing post-holders were returned without difficulty.

A brief examination of the recent history of the L.S.P.U. can be said therefore, to have revealed connections between two sets of events.

1) Internal political disturbance in the union and acrimonious relationships with employers are not only related, they substitute for each other.

2) Such turbulence, whether internally *or* externally directed, required the coincidental occurrence of two events in the same period. These events, both representing crises for the union, are contract negotiations and the imminence of union elections.

The Union Career Cycle

These events show that a 'career' of union activist existed in the sense of a recognizable progression through well marked stages. Men started their 'career' on the 'shop floor' of the dock and obtained support over a period by speaking out for policies that cross cut the structural divisions within the membership. They extended their support base when contract renewals and elections coincided and they argued from a basis of moralistic values — of right and wrong. These arguments were promulgated at general meetings called to discuss the contract which were used as platforms to project candidature in the forthcoming elections.

In promulgating their populist policies they argued against the legalist oriented members of the Executive who in their policies were constrained by the weights of office and of experience. They then succeeded to office on the Executive and eventually — after discrediting their opponents — they too moved into its legalist section — *The Big Three*. In their turn however, they too become discredited and replaced by new activists who followed an identical career path.

What we have here then is a cycle — a cycle of stigmatization that ranged from moral activist to discredited legalist. It is a cycle that depended on a constant supply of new moralists arising from the shop floor if — as was the case — a discredited legalist is never reinstated. But this new supply of moralists was not available to the L.S.P.U. Because of a steady reduction in the number of ships and tonnages into the Port of St. Johns the union in 1956 decided to limit recruitment.

The result was an aging labour force and a shortage of new moral activists. This meant that by 1972 — on my last visit — political activity had processed every one of the limited field of eligible executive material and all of them had been discredited. As a result there were only two uncontaminated moral leaders left in the body of the membership, both Catholics and both illiterate stowers from the two largest wharves. Being illiterate, they had never been able to proceed onto the Executive and therefore, through the full career cycle. They had therefore retained their credibility. They had agreed in the last electoral crisis on a common candidate for the vacant Presidency and for the first time in over 60 years this post — as a result of their nomination — had gone to a Protestant. But by 1972 their problem was compounded by the continuing process of discrediting legalists and the absence of new moralists to replace them. In discussions with me they expressed dissatisfaction with the reigning President and, in obvious desperation for someone to play the role of "outsider", they offered me the post!

It is ironic that managements (whose power had increased with the deadline of shipping to the port after the mid fifties), should always have aimed for contracts to end at the end of December. By this means they believed they would be renegotiating their new contracts from strength because winter months were the slackest time for work. They failed to realize however, that by having contracts that ended in December they were likely to project negotiations into the pre-election period between December and May. When contracts coincided with elections they therefore faced intransigence from the Executive and popular support for militance from a united membership. If the removal of barriers to communication means an increase in democracy, then in this union at least it meant that the periodic emergence of democracy always led to turbulence.

As Martin points out (1968), union democracy — the response of union leadership to membership aspirations — is best shown by the existence of faction since the very presence of faction demonstrates a limit to leadership oligarchy. What is singular about this union however, is the marked contrast between the leadership's lack of responsiveness on the one hand and its periodically excessive responsiveness on the other. It is a distinction that emphasizes the importance of both structure *and* process. It shows that the periodic extinction of faction need not mean that the structure is necessarily undemocratic. It does not however mean that "periodic" or "latent" democracy is necessarily functional in serving membership aspirations.

Notes

1. Fieldwork extended for 18 months during 1962–4 and for 2 months in -1972.
2. The period 1956–1966 was chosen because it began and ended with two 'watershed' years whilst the intervening period was relatively stable. In 1956 the balance of power decisively shifted to the employers when declining tonnage to the port caused them to combine for the first time in opposing union demands. The period can be thought of as ending in 1968 when the union reduced the size of its executive and affiliated to the I.L.A.
3. St. John's has an annual moisture precipitation of 56 inches (compared to London's 25).
4. The terms *'local'* and *'cosmopolitan'* are taken from Gouldner, A. (1957–8).
5. 'Unanimous' as used in this union — and perhaps elsewhere in Newfoundland — has a singular meaning: it means 'overwhelming'.

References

Firth, Raymond 1964. *Essays on social organisation and values.* L.S.E. Monographs on Social Anthropology No. 28. London: Athlone Press.
—— 1957. Introduction to factions in Indian and overseas Indian societies. *British Journal of Sociology* 8, 291–295.

Gouldner, A. 1957–8. Cosmopolitans and locals. *Admin. Science Quarterly* 2, 281–306.

Great Britain. Docks. Reports of Commissioners 1951. *Unofficial stoppages in the London docks 1950–51.* Report of a Committee of Enquiry [Leggett]. Cmd. 8236. London: HMSO.

Lipset, S.M., Trow, M. and Coleman, J. 1956. *Union democracy: the inside politics of the international typographical union.* New York: The Free Press.

Mars, G. 1972. *An anthropological study of longshoremen and of industrial relations in the Port of St. Johns, Newfoundland, Canada.* Unpublished Ph.D. thesis. University of London.

Martin, R. 1968. Union democracy: an explanatory framework. *Sociology* **2**,
.205–220.
Raphael, E. 1965. Power structure and membership dispersion in unions. *Amer.
J. Sociology* **71**, 3 Nov., 274–284.

HOW SWEDEN WORKS:
A Case from the Bureaucracy

MORRIS A. FRED

The Swedish Context

Austin (1968) begins his analysis of Swedish society by accentuating
the inseparability of an individual and his function in society. He notes
that a perusal of the Stockholm telephone directory with job titles
after almost all of the names symbolizes the crucial connection
between the individual and the job he does. He goes on to point out
that because of this, any professional criticism of an individual has
grave implications, challenging the very essence of his identity and
thus his security in society, That identity remains intact as long as
there is a clear understanding of each individual's role and
respective area of competence. Swedish society functions on the basis
of differentiation of expertise, and communication patterns in work
reflect and tend to support this requirement for clear distinction of
role.

Portraying both Swedish society and the Swedish conception of
the individual in a Leonardian bubble, the individual organism can
be seen as divided up into problem areas — alcoholism, employment,
education, parent-child relations, etc. — each represented by a
corresponding group of technical experts situated in their respective
bureaucratic agencies. While such a process of social and political life
— identifying a problem and finding the necessary experts to handle
it — might be seen as a natural outcome of bureaucratic specialization,
the combination of such role specialization with the above-mentioned
attitudes towards work identity provides a basis for the formulation
of Swedish work patterns.

Furthermore, not to be underestimated in explaining work
organization in Sweden is the particular ideological framework
which guides its development. For some time Sweden has been
treated as a sounding board for the discussion of future economic
and political developments within Western democratic nations.
While from one standpoint its size belies strict comparison, it can
at the same time offer ample opportunity for viewing certain

structural and ideological contradictions faced to some degree by all
nations. These contradictions may be summarized under the rubric
of the democratic-bureaucratic paradox noted by Blau (1955:
264—5) in which the demands for hierarchical decision-making in
bureaucracy may come into conflict with the simultaneous effort
towards equality. In Sweden this dilemma is critical, for not only
has there been for the past fifty years a conscious striving for greater
economic equality among its inhabitants, but most recently (1977)
there has been instituted a law for creating greater distribution of
decision-making authority among employers and employees both
in the public and private sectors.

The problem this paper will confront is the effect of such
ideological and structural features on work organization within
the bureaucratic apparatus whose prime responsibility is the
application of Swedish immigration policy.[1] Viewing work
organization within the framework of immigration policy is particularly interesting in two respects. In the first place, as the field-
worker is most often concerned with contact situations between
Swedes and immigrants, the conflicts and contrasts brought to the
forefront illustrate a variety of Swedish attitudes and norms
regarding work. Secondly, the attempts at integrating the immigrants
into Swedish society and the problems raised by such a task tend
to highlight many aspects of the bureaucratic-democratic dilemma
faced by Swedish society in general.

The particular case to be examined is that of a newly-formed
group of social workers whose task it is to help immigrants adjust
to Swedish society. Their problem — the one to be analyzed in this
paper — is the means by which they attempt to define their
emerging occupational roles within the context of the professional
setting of Swedish bureaucracy. Barth has noted that, to understand
the institutionalized behavior that emerges in roles, one must
examine "the external constraints in those contexts where behavior
takes place and the role is consummated" (1971: 89). This provides
a framework for discussion. I shall treat the group in question as
undertaking the task of developing an occupational culture with
particular values and norms whose elaboration is constrained by
the bureaucratic structure within which the group functions.

Following a short summary of Swedish immigration policy, I shall
proceed to describe the attempts by these social workers to
formulate their roles by means of a national organization, placing
emphasis on the dilemmas caused by their ambiguous position
within the Swedish bureaucracy. In the following sections evidence
from their contacts with local authorities will be used to examine

the reasons for the difficulties they face in the process of role
clarification. I will argue that while the social workers must clarify
their job roles in order to forge communication links with others
in the bureaucracy, this tends to hinder the realization of the
longer-range goals of Swedish immigration policy.

Immigration Policy[2]

Resulting from both an economic recession and a steep rise in
immigration from Southern Europe and Finland in the middle sixties,
there has been a rising concern for controlling immigration and
developing means for the effective adaptation of foreigners to
Swedish society. Rejecting the *Gastarbeiter* policy of other
European countries, Swedish policy goals reflect an overall desire
to prevent immigrants from becoming second-class citizens and
endangering the continued development of the welfare state. Set
forth in a Parliamentary Bill in 1975, these goals, summarized
below, have become slogans for those involved in working with
immigrants and the immigrants themselves, and provide a basis for
the practical demands of both:

1) *Equality:* immigrants shall have the same opportunities,
social standards, responsibilities and duties as the rest of the
Swedish population.

2) *Freedom of Choice:* immigrants must be allowed to choose the
degree to which they will retain and develop their original cultural
identity and the degree to which they will assume a Swedish cultural
identity.

3) *Cooperation:* there should be established a mutual and com-
prehensive basis for collaboration between immigrant groups and
the majority population.

From the standpoint of realizing these goals, it should further
be noted that it is considered the responsibility of each state and
local authority — within the goals outlined above — to meet the
needs of immigrants within their functional realms and to develop
programmes for facilitating the immigrants' utilization of their
services. To assist in this task, both the State Immigration Board
and the local immigrant bureaux are to provide the initial links
between the authorities and the immigrants by informing the first
of the latter's needs and the immigrants about the machinations
of Swedish society. It may be said that what these specific
immigrant agencies are involved in is the production and distribution
of information that can be utilized by both immigrants and
authorities alike for facilitating the former's integration into a highly
organized Swedish society.

Family Pedagogues[3]

The subsequent discussion will concern one group of social workers whose prime responsibility is to serve as such links by helping certain refugee groups to adjust to Swedish society. While the distinction between immigrant and refugee has certain legal and economic implications (in terms of particular proffered aid) for our discussion, it will suffice to treat "refugees" as a sub-category of immigrants distinguished by the fact that they have been given asylum in Sweden as a result of political or religious oppression in their homelands. Moreover, while the social workers — called *family pedagogues* — represent merely one level of the official Swedish contact with immigrants, the problems raised in their case reveal notions about work role and organization observed throughout the bureaucratic hierarchy.

The seeds for family pedagogue work were planted in 1972 when it was proposed that there was a need to establish a new social work role with an entire minority group as the reference point. At that time work was begun among gypsies from outside the Nordic countries; today it mainly entails work with two additional groups: Assyrian/Syrian Christians[4] from Turkey, Lebanon, Syria, and Iraq; and Latin Americans.[5] Those people hired as family pedagogues were to serve as bridge-builders between the particular minority group with which they worked and the Swedish society.

Family pedagogues work in particular localities whose authorities have requested their appointment from the refugee section of the State Welfare Board (*Socialstyrelsen*). This Board has the responsibility for the health needs (both physical and psychological) of refugees throughout Sweden. While officially hired by the municipalities and placed within the structure of the local social welfare boards, the family pedagogues' salaries are reimbursed to the latter by the State Welfare Board.

From the outset, family pedagogues' work was seen as both experimental and temporary with respect to the ultimate goal that each authority would take over responsibility for dealing with immigrants. Here it is useful to summarize the goals of their work as set forth by the State Welfare Board (1977: 30–2):

> Family pedagogues, it may be said, are bridge-builders between minorities and the majority culture. They can, by spreading knowledge about the minority culture, seek to increase an understanding of its values, traditions and needs. They can even provide the minority group with information on Swedish society . . . The family pedagogue should be a communication instrument between cultures [so as] to prevent destructiveness in cultural confrontations.

The description goes on to delineate the various components of the family pedagogues' work:

1) *Fixing:* providing help in getting settled in the community. This includes such activities as filling in forms, applying for social welfare when needed, gaining entrance into job training classes, arranging doctors' appointments. The welfare board's description notes that it is unavoidable that initially the work will concern itself most with such activities.

2) *Informing:* serving as knowledge-mediators by providing information both to immigrants and Swedes about each other's cultural values and norms.

3) *Supporting Function:* providing support for immigrants in their daily contacts with Swedes. For example, should immigrants desire to participate in parent-teacher meetings, the family pedagogue can attend such meetings and encourage immigrants to express themselves.

4) *Arena-building:* seeking ways for immigrants and Swedes to meet so that immigrant-Swedish contacts are not limited to those of an instrumental nature, e.g. social worker-client, doctor-patient.

Finally, it is noted that family pedagogue work is a complement to other efforts, a complement that is brought about by the special situation of a minority group in a new and strange environment.

The Family Pedagogues' Association

In May 1978, the family pedagogues from throughout Sweden met in Stockholm to finalize plans for the establishment of an "interest organization" (hereafter referred to by its initials RFFA) whose purpose was to provide support to their members in dealing with various authorities. The preliminary discussion concerning the organization, held in the spring of that year, provide a glimpse into the problems they face in carrying out their professional functions.

Here we may begin with the job title itself. The name family pedagogue represents an attempt to avoid the connotations of other types of social work, particularly that of family therapist, which imply a certain illness (which in this case would be cultural background) on the part of individuals to be treated. The "pedagogic" appellation was suggested as a means to stress that the goal of the job is to prevent destructive culture conflicts by informing (and teaching) both Swedes and immigrants about the other's culture (Westin 1975). Nonetheless, the "family" part of the job title has often been viewed as both confusing and misleading. While much of their work may take place in contact with immigrant families, such a title is disorienting in a society where there exist such social work titles as "family therapist" and "family assistant".

Thus, despite the use of the term by the State Welfare Board, there was not an explicit title "family pedagogue" in most of the communities where they worked. They were placed within the local social welfare boards and functioned as special "social assistants" whose main distinction from the others was that they worked with a particular minority group and did not handle the distribution of monetary resources. At the outset of their work, other local authorities were often ignorant of their precise function.

Moreover, due to the organizational ambiguity in which the State Welfare Board reimbursed their salaries while the family pedagogues were officially hired by the municipalities, the latter often placed different demands and restraints on the family pedagogues. While their function had been laid down in general directives from the State Welfare Board, the separation between state and local decision-making in Sweden precluded the former from steering local activities. Thus, the specific activities that they were to undertake were left primarily to the family pedagogues themselves. While in the beginning their broadly defined tasks provided them with a certain flexibility in tackling problems particular to the communities in which they worked, the lack of clear work specifications came to be seen as hampering their relations with other authorities. Such specifications had been written by family pedagogues in several municipalities but it was felt that there was a need for delineating a unified set of standards for all family pedagogues, especially as a guide for those starting their work.

That a national interest organization was seen as one means for strengthening the family pedagogue position is hardly surprising: "Among modern societies, only the other Scandinavian countries approach Sweden in the development of organizational life . . . their society is *'genomorganiserad'*, . . . saturated with organizations." (Tomasson 1970: 242). To be taken seriously and hence heard within such a highly organized social order, individuals must organize into an interest group. Equally important, I would maintain that the effect of establishing such an interest group serves as *a priori* evidence within Swedish society of the existence of an occupational category or role called the family pedagogue, thus giving others a necessary reference point for communication.

In Search of a Role

I noted in the introduction that I considered it helpful to view the process of role clarification among the family pedagogues in terms of the emergence of an occupational culture. From my first contacts with the family pedagogues, it was apparent that they were involved in attempts to provide themselves with both a language for discussing their work and with values and norms for its evaluation. In courses set up for the family pedagogues by the State Welfare Board, social anthropologists were brought in as conference leaders and lecturers and terms such as "cultural relativity", "ethnicity", "double-bind", "role conflict" slowly became part and parcel of a common language for use within the group, and as key phrases in explaining problems to other authorities. After one such lecture arranged by a group of family pedagogues, I found an outline of the anthropologist's major points hanging in their office with significant terms written in bold face. As time went by, these terms have been incorporated into the everyday language of the group.

During the year, the Welfare Board also arranges three-day courses for the family pedagogues. In these they discuss and analyze specific problems and attempt to formulate common norms for dealing with them. Moreover, to the extent that Swedish society functions on the basis of expert specialization supported by credentials, the knowledge gained from these courses and the certificates awarded at their completion can be seen as providing an aura of expertise necessary for giving their opinions weight in discussion with local authorities.

The importance of educational qualifications for jobs came into focus during the process of discussing the establishment of RFFA. At that time one of the first matters raised concerned the question of qualifications for membership. This reflected the lack of clarity in their role, for due to the novelty of the form of work, job prerequisites had been left unstated by the State Welfare Board. It was felt that in order to accomplish their task as cultural mediators, their role should be clear to those with whom they must communicate and their position fortified by requirements denoting their expertise, a rational basis on which they could justify their views.

While in terms of training there was a lack of homogeneity among Swedes working as family pedagogues, the initial suggestion to require education prerequisites as a basis for being called a family pedagogue was even more problematic in those communities where Syrian Christians and Swedes worked as equal colleagues. Because of the experimental nature of the work, both Swedes and Syrian Christians had been hired in order to complement each other's knowledge of the two cultures between which they were to build bridges. However, once the desire for role clarification was presented in terms of educational prerequisites, the fact that few of the Syrian Christians had more than five years formal education became a point of conflict. For although educational requirements might bolster the family pedagogues' position in the eyes of other Swedes with whom they must work, such demands would exclude most of the Syrian Christians from the position, despite the fact that they provided a necessary element for accomplishing the work.

The Syrian Christians interpreted such discussion as an under-evaluation of their contributions — despite continuous claims to the contrary on the part of the Swedes. Ultimately, after lengthy discussion, it was decided that all individuals hired as family pedagogues would be included as members of the interest organization. Henceforth, one of the main tasks of the interest organization would be to provide a framework for elaborating what the job entails.

Phasing Out[6]

The following sections will deal with the various difficulties facing the family pedagogues attempting to provide themselves with a concise role definition. To understand these, one must consider their job within the framework of another critical issue raised during the procedures of forming RFFA: the phasing out of their work. In a press release issued immediately following the first meeting of RFFA, it was stated that the interest organization would strive to anchor the family pedagogues' work with the respective local authorities and political bodies so that the latter would take responsibility for immigrant and minority questions.

In one community where family pedagogue work among Gypsies has continued for four years, it was felt that the time had come to prepare other local authorities for the family pedagogues' eventual disappearance. These family pedagogues set up meetings with social workers from various parts of the city in order to formulate their position and evaluate the responses. While reactions were mixed, many of the comments revealed the problems that the diffuse roles of the family pedagogues had caused. One social worker asked if such plans for phasing out did not in fact show that the family pedagogues were tired of their jobs and thus wanted to leave. Others spoke of their own heavy workloads and noted that they had little knowledge of Gypsy culture and of how to meet Gypsy needs. The family pedagogues had come to be seen as experts on Gypsy culture and as such, best qualified to deal with the group's problems. These sessions also reflected that the social workers had not understood the temporary nature of the family pedagogues' jobs. Moreover, when in later meetings the family pedagogues raised the issue with the head of the city's welfare bureau, his response was unequivocal: there were still many problems among the Gypsies and to end family pedagogue work in the near future would be premature.

These early attempts to set the stage for phasing out their jobs provides a background for understanding the present frustrations and demands of the family pedagogues, represented in a recently published issue of the RFFA *Newsletter* (Nilsson 1979). Summarized below, these comments will serve to introduce the discussion of the effect that the loose definition of their family pedagogue role has on attempts to work within established bureaucratic communication channels:

1) Despite the fact that family pedagogue work has been going on since 1972 and has been evaluated periodically, many family pedagogues begin their work without a clear understanding of their goals.

2) The State Welfare Board has a general description of goals which do little to guide either the municipalities or the family pedagogues. Work whose goal is as unclear as that of the family pedagogue can be dangerous to all those concerned.

3) Because the municipalities receive funds from the State for family pedagogue work, this may mean that from the former's standpoint the need to plan is less important here than with regard to other work in the municipalities for which they bear the financial burden.

4) The result can be that problems of Gypsy or Syrian Christian families are expected to be dealt with by the family pedagogues alone and there is little need for the other authorities to understand these groups.

5) The family pedagogues should not go in and take over the roles of other authorities. When family pedagogue work begins, the process of phasing out should be considered from the outset. This will prevent the family pedagogues from being sucked into the role as fixers.

6) There is a need for secure employment so that the family pedagogues do not fear unemployment at the end of their work. Hence, they will be able to work more consciously for the phasing out of their jobs.

Expectations and Results

In his discussion of organizational roles, Hall distinguishes between the conditions of role overload and role ambiguity. The former refers to the state in which an individual finds it "impossible to complete all of his assigned tasks", while the latter describes a situation in which there is "insufficient information sent to a person on how he is to perform his role" (Hall 1974: 194). In the family pedagogues' case, both conditions are present. The dissatisfaction and stress so often mentioned by them can be seen as resulting from a combination of demands that often require incompatible forms of behavior on the part of the individual. In this and the following section, this role ambiguity and overload will be examined.

The importance of job security, reflected in recent legislation, has become a general feature of Swedish working life. While its economic implications are obvious, the demands in the RFFA *Newsletter* suggest a broader meaning of what such security entails. As a basis for self-esteem, this security includes the need of the individual for a clear understanding of what is expected of him, of how he is to carry out his work role. The lack of specific goals towards which they should strive leaves the family pedagogues often at a loss in terms of evaluating their work by concrete results. Often entering their jobs with high expectations regarding the cooperation of both authorities and immigrants, the family pedagogues are eventually faced with a situation in which they come to interpret the continual presence of such conflicts as personal failures. The request for direction from the State Welfare Board is hence an attempt to rationalize the demands placed on them and thus provide a clear basis for evaluating their successes and failures, and for adjusting their tactics accordingly.

Goal ambiguity also has an effect on interpersonal relations among the family pedagogues. Because the responsibility for designing their work rests for the most part within each group, they are faced with an added stress of choosing among a wide range of priorities. Because the context for such a choice is one in which a group of equals must reach unanimity, in those cases where opinions differ, the result is often that work patterns develop on an individual basis. This has grave implications for inter-organizational relations (to be discussed next). The danger of different patterns of work is that the role of the family pedagogue, already unclear in the eyes of many of the authorities, will become further confused, affecting their ability to transfer responsibility to the local bureaux and politicians.

In the Bureaucracy

The family pedagogues' difficulties in communicating with other organizations is due in part to their middleman position between the local authorities and immigrant groups. They are often placed in ambiguous positions regarding their loyalty, particularly in situations where interpretations of regulations by the authorities and immigrants do not coincide. While this dilemma reflects certain contradictions in the general policy goal of freedom of choice (where the implications of what is meant by "culture" are not carefully considered), its effect is to impair their ability to create the trust within both groups necessary for providing the linkages between the two.

With regard to communication within the bureaucracy, that trust is grounded on a clear perception of each individual's role, most often explicitly formulated in a set of responsibilities and means for carrying them out. In various contact situations between members of the bureaucracy, these role specifications are reinforced in cumulative interactions whereby predictability and trust are generated.

Lacking such clear role specifications, the family pedagogues' relationship with other local authorities is dependent on their developing a behavioral repertoire for their contacts with the latter. Past descriptions of the work of the family pedagogues, including that by the State Welfare Board have, in merely listing the various components of their job, failed to take into account the implications of the process involved in each activity which can lead to contradictory perceptions of what the role is. Most of the Swedish family pedagogues begin their work with little or no knowledge about the groups with whom they are to work. In order to provide themselves with a basis for being conduits of information, they must first familiarize themselves with these groups. In addition, as noted by the Welfare Board, many of the families in the first stage have problems which must be dealt with immediately. The family pedagogue here serves as a "fixer", helping individuals adjust to the community in which they live as well as providing support in their attempts to find employment, study Swedish, etc. Direct contact with both authorities and immigrants as well as active participation in contact situations between the two, enables the family pedagogues to develop a certain expertise regarding the problems faced by the immigrants in adjusting to Swedish society. During this time they are of course also acting as "informants", but it is important to recognize that the latter is taking place within the confines of the family pedagogues' obligation to "fix" individual cases.

After familiarizing themselves with their work environment, the family pedagogues seek to develop more regular contacts with those authorities by setting up meetings with respective agency personnel in order to discuss the various problems faced by the immigrants. Here the family pedagogues often begin by establishing priorities for projects, determining in which agency they shall concentrate their efforts. They attempt to divest themselves of the role as "fixers" and create the necessary arenas for immigrant integration into the existing organizational framework. It is in confronting the more general problems in society, illustrated in the following example with school authorities, that the family pedagogues face the major dilemma resulting from their diffuse roles.

With the Immigrants

Before proceeding with this particular example, I would like to note that, while within the confines of this paper I have chosen to concentrate on the family pedagogues' relationship with other elements in the bureaucratic apparatus, any expanded analysis of their role perception must take into account their relationships with the immigrants themselves. The latter's demands and expectations add an important dimension to role definition and its practical application. In seeking to transfer responsibilities to the other authorities, the family pedagogues often find themselves planning and participating in an increased number of meetings and conferences. In the community where I observed their work, these activities culminated in a letter from the Syrian Christian association to the family pedagogues. The Syrian Christians complained that the family pedagogues were not conducting their jobs properly, absenting themselves too frequently from the office. One family pedagogue noted that the immigrants seemed to perceive themselves as "employers" (cf. Wadel's discussion of *clients*, this volume) thus demanding greater concern for the particular needs of individuals and families in the group. The family pedagogues came to realize that not only had the authorities been unclear as to the goals of their work, but that so were the immigrants themselves. The result was that the family pedagogues had been caught between demands for "fixing" from both sides, which they saw as hampering direct communication between the two and ultimately their ability to phase out their jobs.

A Case in Point: The Schools

In the community studied, the family pedagogues working with Syrian Christians ascertained a need to deal with a problem in one lower secondary school (grades 7—9), where almost all the Syrian Christian children had been placed together in a single homogeneous class. In addition, due to a lack of resources, these children were given fewer hours instruction than the Swedish children. The family pedagogues had mentioned their concern about this matter to the teacher in charge, pointing out that segregating the Syrian Christian children from Swedes in school might have deleterious effects in socializing them into Swedish society. One of the family pedagogues set up a meeting with the school's principal and vice-principal and the assistant director of the local school system in order to discuss the problem. At the outset of the meeting, the school officials expressed hostility towards the family pedagogue, accusing the latter of being aggressive in criticizing the school's attempts to do what was deemed best for the children. The attack was demoralizing for the family pedagogue who then felt at a loss in continuing to discuss the problem.

Before the event, it had already been decided by the family pedagogues to call a meeting of a larger number of school officials in the community for the purpose of setting up a conference where problems of immigrants in schools could be discussed. An invitation was sent out by the group in which it was noted that the discussion should center around the problem of segregation/integration in school classrooms. The family pedagogues were nervous about the meeting as those working with Syrian Christians and with Gypsies had both had serious confrontations with certain of the officials who were to be present.

Before the arrival of the officials and teachers, coffee and cakes were placed on a central table around which chairs were arranged in a circle. As each person came in, he or she went around shaking hands with those present, introducing himself when necessary. After the coffee was served, the meeting was opened with reference to the hope that the discussion could lead to a future conference where school matters could be treated in depth. As planned, the family pedagogues were careful not to antagonize any of those present by referring to any specific complaint. But the atmosphere was filled with tension, reflected in the countenances of several officials and their initial unwillingness to discuss any problems facing Gypsies or Syrian Christians in their schools. During the meeting, the assistant director of the local school system involved in the previous confrontation noted that she had been angry with the family pedagogues and was glad that they would now try to approach the situation with less antagonism.

Once the meeting ended and the guests departed, the family pedagogues admitted frustration in their being forced to sit and listen to school officials deny any major problems, despite the fact that the family pedagogues perceived school conditions to be far from satisfactory and wanted to take practical measures for dealing with the situation.

This case represents the difficulties faced by the family pedagogues in moving from their role as "fixers" in individual cases to that of confronting what they view as essential problems relating to long-term goals. When the family pedagogue group sought to take the initiative in defining a problem – in this case the existence of segregated classrooms – their action was viewed as an aggressive infringement on the territory of another institution and a challenge to the legitimacy of its expertise. The knowledge that the family pedagogues had gained in the initial stages of their work had allowed them to develop an understanding of both the needs of the immigrants and the structure of various elements of Swedish society. Hence, they found themselves in a position to identify problems, an activity that was at once perceived as criticism of work within the schools.

This situation with school officials represents some of the difficulties faced by the family pedagogues in moving from one part of their work role to the other. The instrumental nature of their role as "fixer" had allowed them to gauge the success of their activities by concrete results. Because of their need for an evaluative basis for determining success, their behaviour continued to show qualities of both "fixer" and "informant". The result was that they came to suggest to other authorities how to effect changes so that cultural conflict could be minimized.

Moreover, the job of family pedagogue – both as "fixer" and "informant" – is complicated by the fact that contact with other authorities takes place within the realm of horizontal inter-organizational settings, in which there is an understood equality among participants that is reinforced by role specialization. Because the family pedagogues' role is defined generally and comes to be based upon information about both Swedish society and the immigrant groups, they are faced with problems in supplying information without transgressing the requirements for communication among equals.

Here Blau's comments on exchange can help to understand the dilemma they face. He notes that:

some individuals can supply important services to others for which the latter cannot appropriately reciprocate, and the unilateral transactions that consequently take place give rise to differentiation of status (Blau 1964: 328).

I would suggest that in the initial stages of their work, the family pedagogues as "fixers" are involved in reciprocal rather than unilateral exchanges with the authorities. As they provide information to the local authorities regarding individual cases, those authorities elucidate the regulations within which they must work and reciprocate indirectly to the family pedagogues by supplying necessary services to the latter's client groups.

However, as the family pedagogues come to understand the situations in various Swedish institutions and familiarize themselves with the rules involved, they become less dependent on these authorities for information. Here, in attempting to transfer their knowledge to other authorities who are seen as ultimately responsible for the immigrants' well-being, the activities of the family pedagogues carry with them the potential for unilateral communication. Their behavior often takes on the qualities of fixer-informant, in which they suggest to other authorities how immigrant needs can be — or should be — met. In such information-giving instances, they become role-senders to these authorities, asserting a status which is not explicitly formulated in their roles or in their structural position in the bureaucracy.

Conclusion

In understanding work patterns within the Swedish bureaucracy in general, the family pedagogues' job is instructive: it has been formulated on principles that are in sharp contrast to the basis on which communication takes place and decisions are made in the wider bureaucratic structure. Brittan notes that "organic solidarity creates an interdependence of parts, while at the same time separating and encapsulating those same parts" (Brittan 1973: 178–9). In Swedish bureaucracy the means for maintaining such organic solidarity is by first encapsulating its parts into specified roles and by then providing a mechanism for communication among them.

One of the most striking features of Swedish bureaucratic life is the vast amount of time consumed in intra- and interorganizational meetings. These meetings are organized most often around a previously determined theme which both symbolizes and creates an atmosphere of organic solidarity. The pattern for discussion is based on an examination of the problem at hand by individuals, each of whom has a clear notion of both his and others' roles and areas of competence. The fact that few clear-cut decisions are reached in such meetings reflects the limitations of interorganizational communication. In terms of immigrant policy, the traditional division of powers between ministries and boards on the one hand and state and local authorities on the other requires that its application take place for the most part along horizontal cross-organizational channels. Lacking power to impose one's viewpoint on those in another agency, one can only hope that through continual meetings organized around a key theme, the importance of that issue will be incorporated into the other organizations' future plans.

With regard to the family pedagogues' job, the danger of their being sucked into a permanent role as fixers for individual immigrant cases is one that develops from the need for the authorities to clarify and limit the functional realm within which the family pedagogue is to work, thus allowing communication between them to proceed. At the same time this hinders the family pedagogues' attempts to relinquish such activities and turn them over to responsible local authorities. They are today faced with the paradox of needing to formalize their role in order to provide a basis for its elimination. For in trying to maintain the integrity of their transience, they must continually struggle against the pull of the authorities to incorporate them into a structure which can lead to their permanent existence.

Finally, while Swedish immigration policy aims to create a pluralistic society in which each immigrant can choose the degree to which he maintains his cultural identity, the structural realities of Swedish bureaucracy may lead to quite opposite results. As both family pedagogues and others in the immigrant bureaucracy are drawn into roles as experts concerned with treating a particular problem, the effect is to identify the category "immigrant" as the problem in itself and to render it permanent in the eyes of both Swedish authorities and Swedes in general.

Notes

1. This paper is drawn from an ongoing project (1978–9) funded by the Swedish Ministry of Labor under the rubric of the Swedish Commission on Immigration Research (EIFO). I am indebted to the family pedagogues with whom I have been associated for allowing me to become one of their "team". I would also like to thank Ulf Hannerz, Camilla Hollander, and Björn Ranung for their helpful comments on an earlier draft.
2. An historical perspective of Swedish immigration policy may be found in

Widgren (1979). Following the 1975 census he notes: "The figure of one million is the total foreign citizens resident in Sweden, plus Swedish citizens born abroad, plus an estimated 300,000 children and grandchildren of postwar immigrants born in Sweden." (1979: 30). Figures from the State Immigration Board (January 1979) note that there are approximately 425,000 foreign citizens residing in Sweden, of whom about 45% are from Finland.

3. Problems similar to those raised in this paper are noted in an evaluation of "family pedagogue" work among gypsies (outside the Nordic countries) carried out by a team of social anthropologists from Stockholm University (Lithman (ed.) 1976).

4. Among this group of refugees there is disagreement over the name they wish to be called. The *family pedagogues*, in order to maintain a neutral stance, most often refer to the group as Assyrian/Syrian. For reasons of simplicity, and because it is the preferred form in the community in which I have studied, I have used "Syrian Christians" in all subsequent references to the whole group now living in Sweden.

5. There are also family pedagogues working with Swedish and Finnish gypsies as well as several working with Kurdish and Palestinian refugees. According to figures from the State Welfare Board, in November 1978 there were 157 family pedagogues in 42 localities.

6. While the following examples are taken from the community where research has been conducted, contact with family pedagogues throughout Sweden has suggested that the problems raised are general ones despite demographic and political differences among the various localities.

References

Austin, Paul Britten. 1968. *On being Swedish.* Coral Gables, Florida: University of Miami Press.

Barth, Fredrik. 1971. Role dilemmas and father-son dominance in Middle Eastern kinship systems. In *Kinship and culture*, F.L.K. Hsu (ed.). Chicago: Aldine, 87–95.

Blau, Peter M. 1955. *The dynamics of bureaucracy.* Chicago: The University of Chicago Press.

——— 1964. *Exchange and power in social life.* New York: John Wiley and Sons, Inc.

Brittan, Arthur. 1973. *Meanings and situations.* London: Routledge and Kegan Paul.

Hall, Richard H. 1974. *Organizations: structure and process.* London: Prentice/Hall International, Inc.

Lithman, Yngve (ed.) 1976. *Ideal och Praxis.* Stockholm: Socialstyrelsen.

Nilsson, M. 1979. Avveckling av vad? *Newsletter* of *Riksförening för Familjepedagogisk Arbete.*

Tomasson, Richard F. 1970. *Sweden: prototype of modern society.* New York: Random House.

Westin, Charles, 1975. Familjepedagogik för Zigenska Flyktingar. In

Invandrar-problem, Anna Greta Heyman *et al.* (eds.). Stockholm: Norstedts.
Widgren, Jonas. 1979. Sweden. In *International labor migration in Europe*,
R. Crane (ed.). New York: Praeger Publishers, 19—44.

WORK AND VALUE:

Reflections on Ideas of Karl Marx

RAYMOND FIRTH

Introduction

The sociological significance of Karl Marx's ideas has been a matter
of debate now for about a century. One of the keystones in Marx's
construction of a critical theory explaining the capitalist mode of
production was his assertion that work is the basis of value, leading
to "the law of value" as it has been commonly called. Anthropologists
have shown understandable reluctance to face the questions involved
in this conception of value, though a few of them, such as C.S.
Belshaw, R.F. Salisbury and Maurice Godelier have considered the
notion of labour-time as providing a plausible measure of comparative worth in exchange.[1] I have thought it of interest to examine
Marx's ideas about value further, with special reference to their
possible significance for economic anthropology. First I outline his
general views on the subject; then I explore the implication of some
of the terms used, since they have often been accepted uncritically.
After a brief glance at some economists' commentary on Marx's
propositions in this field I then look at what may be the relevance
of these propositions for the kind of non-monetary economy with
which anthropologists have often had to deal.

Marx himself recognized that dealing with the concept of value
prsented some difficulty, though characteristically he saw this as
a problem for the reader rather than the writer. The essence of his
view was that in the whole process of production and distribution
it was work alone that gave title to the product. A view often put
forward in less systematic form, it was expressed by Marx with
such analytical keenness, flair for categorization, battery of
argument, and intolerance if not sheer brutality towards demurring
opinion that its impact was immense.[2]

Outline of the Law of Value

In outline what Marx himself wrote in the first volume of *Capital*
is fairly clear. He distinguished between exchange-value, use-value,

and what he called "value" without qualification but which sometimes appears as the "substance of value". Descriptively, each of these can be identified without much trouble. Exchange value or price is what an object produced for exchange, a "commodity", will fetch in the market. Use-value is the consumer's estimation of the object as ful- filling the technical function for which it was produced — as a table has use-value for standing things on. "Value", unqualified, is defined neither in money terms as exchange value is, nor in utility terms as use-value is, but in labour terms: the substance of value is labour; and the measure of value — its "magnitude" — is the labour time socially necessary to produce the object, its labour cost to the producer. Marx regarded his "law of value" as applying only to developed commodity production. In simple commodity production (and pre- sumably in less well developed economic conditions) where things are produced to fill wants and are exchanged only to meet further wants, the standards of value invoked are those of use-value. Only in developed commodity production, where things are made specifically in order to sell them, are use-value standards replaced by exchange-value standards. But "value" is still there as the amount of materialized, objectified or "congealed" labour embodied in the thing produced.

The "law of value" fell into three major propositions. The first was that the value of an object produced was the labour time socially necessary to produce it. The second was that in a capitalist society with a wage structure, the labourer receives not the whole of the value he produces, but only a portion of it. He is paid not for his labour in producing a thing but only for his "labour power" (a concept to which Marx attached great importance) — his capacity to work, which is maintained in effect at a subsistence level for himself and his family (the source of future labour power). The third proposition was that having acquired in exchange the whole value of the product and paid to the worker only a maintenance allowance, the capitalist absorbs a substantial part of the value — a part which has been generally translated in English as Surplus Value.

In discussing Marx's labour cost theory of value one must remember that he wrote in German, and that handling his writings in translation can easily involve subtle divergencies from his own original meaning. His statements used as basis for the present dis- cussion refer to *Arbeit* and to *Wert*. The multiple roots of our terminology allow us to render *Arbeit* either as WORK or as LABOUR. The connotation of "work" is of direct activity, applied to an object. The emphasis is on expenditure of energy — linked with use of it for measurement purposes in physics. But it also implies, in a more personal sense, that the energy expenditure does not give complete satisfaction in itself — as recreation may be thought to do — but is in pursuit of some further end — if only the acquisition of further energy. The connotation of "labour", though similar, tends to carry the notion of more protracted activity, with emphasis on the more negative aspects of energy expenditure. One may speak of the satisfactions to be gained from work, but not so easily of satisfactions to be gained from labour. The distinctions are vague, but it is significant that in English "labourer" is a low-status occupation of little skill, whereas to describe someone as a "worker" can imply a positive contribution. So the labelling of Marx's theory in English as the "labour-cost theory of value", not the "work-cost theory" carries an implication of pain and sacrifice which would seem to be in accord with Marx's concept. Marx's term *Wert* can similarly be translated into English more colloquially or more abstractly, as either WORTH or as VALUE. "Value" seems adequate, but to have translated his *Mehr-Wert*, literally "More-Worth" as Surplus Value seems to give the concept a twist not implied in Marx's term, for which Added Value or Additional Value might have seemed more appropriate. But though superficially to read of Surplus Value may give a false idea of Marx's concept, the term does conform to Marx's insistence on the production of increment or surplus on capital as the supreme driving force in capitalist production, and need not stop merely at the idea of some part of value just "left over".

Marx was careful to specify that labour operated within certain parameters. Labour was the source of value, not of wealth. He castigated the formulation of the Gotha Programme which began "Labour is the source of all wealth" by commenting

> Labour is *not the source* of all wealth. *Nature* is just as much the source of use values (and it is surely of such that material wealth consists) as labour, which is in itself only the manifestation of a force of nature, human labour power. (1968: 315; also 1976: 134.)

Labour is purposeful, resulting in products, and the products are not only the results but also the essential conditions of labour, and so on. But what Marx consistently implied also was that labour was the source of relationship, between persons as well as between persons and things.

Critical Significance of Human Energy

It is this notion of a relationship created by labour that, it seems to me, is in part responsible for the logical jump that Marx makes right at the start of his exposition. He stated that if we disregard the use-value of commodities, only one property remains in them, that of being products of labour. Even if not quite accurate, since presumably properties of dimension and specific gravity still remain, this is acceptable in the analytical context of socio-economic discourse. Marx held that the commodities can be regarded as congealed quantities of homogenous human labour power. But when he proceeded "As crystals of this social substance (human labour) which is common to them all, they are values — commodity values" he made a statement of a different order. The transition from *labour* to *value* is simply an asserted identification, which Marx nowhere attempted to justify. Further, he appeared to involve himself in some literal contradiction. In the same section of his enquiry he argued

> Nothing can be a value without being an object of utility. If the thing is useless, so is the labour contained in it; the labour does not count as labour, and therefore creates no value. (1976: 128, 131, cf. 179. The German text — MEW 1972: 23 : 52, 55 — is to the same effect.)

This looks like a complete give-away. If it is necessary for an object to have utility in order to have value, then value cannot be determined by labour alone, and the "law of value" seems to be imperilled. In the light of such contrasts, one can see why books have been written with titles such as *What Marx Really Said* (Acton 1967) and *What Marx Really Meant* (Cole 1934).

When Marx asserted that the value of a commodity is measured by the labour necessary for its production, he was intent on distinguishing this labour-value from its use-value on the one hand and its exchange-value on the other. He was thus ruling out the estimations of the utility of the commodity by would-be purchasers, and the immediate price paid for the item in the marketplace. But what he was left with as *value* was a shadowy and elusive concept in its own right. His description of it in labour-time terms seems to leave it without any independent conceptual status.

It seems to me that what Marx was really arguing was the case for recognition of the primal role in human experience of the application of human energy to things. Nothing in nature is relevant to the purposes of man unless human energy has been applied to it. But the result of application of energy to things is *change*. And the change takes place in the human being applying the energy as well as in the thing to which it is applied. This Marx expressed in various ways, such as "what on the side of the worker appeared in the form of unrest now appears, on the side of the product, in the form of being, as a fixed, immobile characteristic" (1976: 287. The German text contrasts directly "unrest" [*Unruhe*] with "unmoving character-istic" [*ruhende Eigenschaft*] — MEW 1972: 23: 195). But in all his discussion of the labour process and its relation to the valorization process he just assumed that labour creates useful things. He saw change as of primary significance, and gave it the name of value. More than that, he sometimes used the term value without qualification when it seems clear that he meant it with a qualification, usually exchange-value.[3] Looking forward to Marx's pronouncements about "surplus value", what he was saying about work and value could be put in another way: Things are useful to man only when they have been changed by human effort; this change is the one fundamental process that has happened to them from a human point of view; and therefore irrespective of any subsequent relation-ships, the person who made the change should get the benefit.

From this point of view the fact that things are "owned" by people is irrelevant. Their differential ownership in no way changes the fundamental quality of the things; only human energy applied to the things does this. So from Marx's position as a sort of cosmic observer — which is what he seemed to see himself as — all rules for ownership are just so much froth stirred up by society on the surface of the deep-flowing waters of human progress. Hence Marx's objections to the institution of private property. From this too came the inference that any claim to the product of energy application on the ground of "ownership" of things was sheer impudence. So also the virtue of capital, that stock of equipment which enabled production to be undertaken with greater efficiency, lay in its being a store of accumulated labour.

All this is an intelligible, if one-sided, way of looking at the productive process. Though not new, the thesis has a certain compelling force. But it does leave out of account the fact that some kinds of change due to human endeavour have repercussive effects of a negative order, e.g. destruction of the environment. Here some concept of "usefulness" is needed to give meaning to any simple association of value with labour. Also, if value standing alone is reduced to an alternative label for human energy-change it is deprived of the precision needed to allow it to be compared closely with other variables in the economic system. The ambiguity and amorphous character of the concept of "value" have led to much difficulty in interpreting Marx's ideas.

But it is plausible to conclude that what Marx was aiming at was not any very logical examination of the concept of value as such, but at the establishment of an entity capable of fairly simple figurative expression. He was seeking as the "substance" of value some quality (labour) which was both "contained in" a commodity and yet distinguishable from it, which could be generalized away from the particular use-qualities of the commodity and which could be capable of expression in quantitative terms. And his ultimate aim was a political, not simply an economic expression. It is very relevant here to note that in Marx's thinking, so it appears, his concept of surplus value was not derived from this theory of value, but the reverse (Meek 1973: 126). The "manifest existence of surplus value in the real world" led to a labour theory of value to explain it. The concept of value as embodied, crystallized labour, as Meek has emphasized, in effect expressed Marx's view that the economic process should be analyzed in terms of the social relations between men in the production of commodities. His idea of the formal requirements of a theory of value was subordinate to his wish to demonstrate the principles governing exchange ratios, in particular the ratio between the prices given to a worker for the use of his working capacity and the price received for the worker's product in the marketplace.

> For Marx . . . the task of showing 'how the law of value operates' was virtually identical with the task of showing how relations of production determined relations of exchange. (Meek 1973: 156, 164.)

And in the forefront of the relations of production Marx placed the institution of private property and the economic power which this gave to the capitalist entrepreneur.

If one focusses on the main trend of Marx's argument rather than on his precise formulations, there are several points of interest to note.

Marx and the Mediaeval Canonists

The labour theory of value in its most general form was not invented by Marx but, as has often been pointed out, had a long history in economic and social thought. He himself makes it quite clear that his formulations owed much to the classical economists, especially to Adam Smith and Ricardo. His long traverse of their theories[4] accepts their exposition of the basic role of labour in the creation of values, and focusses critically on the defects, from his point of view, in their perception of the role of other factors in production, and of the nature of the distributive process resulting in rent, interest and profits. But as Hannah Sewall showed long ago (1901) in a study of the theory of value before Adam Smith (she was not concerned with Marx), a fundamental conception of the mediaeval canonists was that the true or real value of anything was the social estimation of the sacrifice needed to produce it. The emphasis was on the amount of labour expended upon the creation of the thing rather than on the satisfaction to be derived from using it. This was essentially a labour-cost theory of value rather than a utility theory, and was associated among much else with the scriptural text that "the labourer is worthy of his hire". Indeed, Albertus Magnus argued further, that there was a social necessity for the labourer to be paid his price, otherwise the product of his toil would not continue to be supplied to the community (Sewall 1901: 12–15, 121). Moreover, running through much of the mediaeval exposition was the idea that whereas "natural" exchange of things to meet the needs of life was a proper activity, gainful exchange by trading a thing for more than one paid for it was in some sense dishonourable. The mediaeval concept of the just price came to be overborne by what appeared as the impersonal forces of the market but the notion of value as related primarily to producer's cost persisted as an ethical as well as an economic theme. It is clear that Karl Marx's labour-cost theory of value was in line with a tradition of the great ecclesiastical moralists from the 13th century onwards. Marx, unlike the mediaeval thinkers, was not concerned with criteria for the establishment of a just price, but he believed as they did in the idea of a true value for things, and of this being based ultimately on the worker's effort in the making of the things.

Marx's concept of the "substance" of value or absolute value as embodied or materialized labour involves several assumptions about the character of work which he himself took for granted and did not examine. One such is a production assumption — that labour in itself is somehow a worthy, or worth-creating activity. This view Marx himself would probably have denied, claiming that recognition of the creation of value by labour arose from perception of historical process and involved no moral preconceptions at all.[5] Yet throughout the argument of *Capital* runs the theme that while it is part of the historical development of commodity production that the capitalist entrepreneur should absorb part of the fruits of the labourer's effort, such absorption is a matter for disapproval, indeed of fierce criticism. An obvious question here is: what happens to the analysis if this normative assumption be qualified or rejected? Should it be conceded that not all labour is worthy activity, or not all labour is equally worthy, then how does the value theory fare? This is the point

at which some discrepancy between individual and social understanding of the meaning of "work" can emerge. The mediaevalists
met the problem in a pragmatic way by introducing the element of
community estimation as the basis of just price. (Market conditions,
they thought, could be trusted to yield a just price, but this could
only be ascertained by experts capable of interpreting the community's estimation — which suggests an analogy with modern
central planning conditions!) They also argued that a fair compensation to the producer of a good should depend on the quality of
living customary in the class to which the producer belonged — A
a concept which is reminiscent of distributive schemes over a wide
range of socio-economic systems. Marx ignored such notions. He
disposed of one common norm of evaluation in the notion of
"productive" labour by defining it simply in terms of capitalist's
profit expectations. In the capitalist system productive labour is
simply that type of work which yields the capitalist a surplus value
which he can absorb. But Marx did make some concession to
possible challenge to his normative assumption by introducing a set
of qualifications — or refinements as Meek terms them — to his
concept of the way labour relates to value.

Conceptual Difficulties in the Theory

He had to meet two obvious problems — about difference between
skilled and unskilled workers, and between fast and slow or even
lazy workers. So he was concerned, he argued, with homogeneous
human labour, abstract labour, and not with the variation of innumerable individual units of labour. And the production of an
article in normal technical conditions was conceived in terms of
average labour time, socially necessary labour time. While these
qualifications were represented or implied by Marx to be manifest
in the historical process itself, they were really logical rather
than empirical insertions into his notion of labour as a factor of
production. Insofar as they did have an empirical referent they also
indicated the existence of a social component of judgement by
comparison which could not be completely eliminated if the
historical dimension was to retain any meaning. When Marx was
arguing that his notion of abstract labour was justified by a
reduction of skilled to unskilled labour he put forward the view
that more complex labour counts only as simple labour intensified,
or rather, as multiplied simple labour, a given quantity of skilled
labour being considered equal to a greater quantity of simple
labour. "*Simple average labour*, it is true, varies in character in
different countries and at different times, *but in a particular society*

it is given" (1976: 135 — my italics for last clause; cf. Meek 1973: 169). By this analytical reduction of skilled to unskilled work, however necessary for the logic of this argument, Marx robbed the concept of work of a very important criterion, the *quality* of the activity. Involved in this is not merely the possible satisfaction in creative activity which can arise even in relatively simple technical manipulations, but also the pervasive identification of job accomplishment with personal status. Even in the simplest tasks in our industrial economy, the notion of doing them well or badly still tends to be bound up with notions of personal evaluation. Marx appealed to experience to show that the reduction of skilled to unskilled labour was constantly being made. A commodity may be the product of the most skilled labour, he argued, but its value, by equating it to the product of simple unskilled labour, represents a definite quantity of the latter labour alone. And by this value, Marx expressly stated, he meant not the labourer's wage but the value of the commodity in which that labour time is materialized. But if "experience" be appealed to, then an anthropologist can justifiably comment that in a "given society" the "value" of a commodity produced by skilled labour is *not* equated to the product of simple unskilled labour. In some societies this is manifested in differential spheres or circuits of exchange. A Tikopia canoe, requiring the work of skilled craftsmen to build, cannot be equated with any quantity of food produced by the labour of relatively unskilled people. Canoes and food lie in different circuits of exchange, and their "value" as products of labour alone is not directly commensurable. When therefore Marx has stated "The various proportions in which different kinds of labour are reduced to simple labour as their unit of measurement are established by a social process that goes on behind the backs of the producers; these proportions therefore appear to the producers to have been handed down by tradition", an anthropologist can reply that in some societies which have come into his own experience, tradition has debarred such reduction in certain major types of production.[6] It can of course be argued that Marx was writing only of commodity production, and only of goods brought to the bar of exchange, and that societies such as Tikopia fall outside this category. While this can be agreed, there is a question as to how far some presentations of goods in exchange in a pre-commodity phase of production may not show the same principles of value determination as in simple commodity exchange conditions.[7] But more to the point, perhaps, if a commodity is defined in terms of its social qualities, the social function which it performs (cf. Kautsky 1925: 2), if it is wanted at all for its use-value, then any estimation of its "value" in labour terms may well incorporate elements of regard for skill as well as for quantities of abstract labour-time.

There are still further difficulties about this "value as congealed labour" concept. At the same time as Marx stressed the significance of *abstract* labour as the element of common reference in value he also argued that commodities had an objective character as values only insofar as they were all comparable expressions of an identical *social* substance, human labour, and their objective character as values was therefore "purely social" (1976: 138–139). From this it follows "self-evidently" that this value character can appear only in the "social relation" between commodity and commodity. In Marx's argument "social" (*gesellschaftlich*) was conceived in a very austere if not even impoverished sense as response to the existence and pressure of others in inequality under capitalism rather than to a broader more positive set of rules and obligations. But to an anthropologist this recognition of the social criterion at the heart of the value concept would seem to open the door to admission of elements other than simple abstract labour as a value determinant.

Marx's argument about comparability was very ponderous. In explaining his notion of how the values of commodities can be arrived at he not only distinguished the object which is being valued from its measure in exchange by the terms relative value and equivalent value, he also retained the concept of a "value" which is different from either of these. So he conceived of "real changes" in the magnitude of value as being manifest in variation of "relative value" of a commodity although its "value" remains constant; of variation in the "value" of a commodity though its "relative value" remains constant; and finally of simultaneous variations in "the magnitude of its value and in the relative expression of that magnitude" (1976: 140–46). In more ordinary language what he seems to have envisaged were distinguishable changes in price and in the amounts of labour needed to make the article. And what he considered to be a change in the "real values" of commodities would be apparently an increase or decrease in their quantity for a constant labour-time in manufacture. Marx was also concerned with the relation of form to content, and of general to specific (or of species to individual), but the language in which he expressed this concern was by no means clear. Notions of the activation of properties of a thing by its relations, and of conditions of reflection in relationship (1976: 148–50; MEW 1972: 72) can be interpreted and may be suggestive, but tend to be obscure where they are not banal.

Marx was concerned with important distinctions, but his way of conceptualizing them was cumbrous and didactic, and his insistence on the "mystery" of forms of value which he alone was able to solve smacked of arrogance. One can see then why economists of various shades of thought have found the labour theory of value unsatisfactory. G.D.H. Cole called it a dogma, and said that Marx's idea of value was purely and simply objectified use-value, an attempt like the classical economists to find some objective validity underlying the subjective valuations of the market. Joan Robinson, one of the most distinguished commentators on Marx's economics and not unsympathetic to his theories, has praised Marx's penetrating analysis of exploitation but criticized the labour theory of value as a misleading oversimplification of the economic situation in any industrial economy. She holds that it is awkward, obscuring Marx's position, and indeed any of the important ideas which he expressed in those terms could have been better expressed without it. The labour theory of value, Robinson argues, merely provides the "incantations" in which Marx clothed his bitter penetrating analysis of capitalism and hatred of oppression (Robinson 1966: 10–22). In the course of a rigorous mathematical examination of the labour theory of value, Morishima, another sophisticated commentator, has demurred at the position taken by most orthodox economists, that Marxian values were not operationally meaningful, i.e. did not have any measurable counterparts of analytical interest. He has considered Marxian labour values to be of direct operational importance as employment multipliers, as measures of the rate of exploitation in the economy, and as giving stable weights in problems of aggregation of industries. But he regards Marx's theory of value as inadequate as a guide to production conditions, since admission of the heterogeneity of labour leads to implications which contradict Marx's own theory of exploitation and the simple two-class view of the capitalist economy. Morishima suggests to Marxian economists that they ought to revise radically their attitude to the labour theory of value, though he seems to think this unlikely because of the inspiring ideological rationale it provides for the workers in their struggle against bourgeois régimes (Morishima 1973: 18, 190–4; cf. von Weiszäcker 1973).

These are views which are strenuously opposed by most Marxist writers. They are inclined to argue, as Meek has done, that while the concept of value could not be "proved" in any very formal sense (Meek 1973: 164) the logical abstractions of Marx in regard to values have been borne out by historical experience. Or, like Pilling (1972), they argue that prices are the appearances which conceal values.

But while historical experience can be claimed in various ways to support or illustrate Marx's more general analysis, it has proved rather embarrassing when applied to the concept of value. This has proved particularly so in the problem of how Marxian "values" are related to prices. In the first volume of *Capital* (the only volume actually produced by Marx himself) Marx stated that exchange value is nothing more than a specific social way of expressing the labour that has been applied to a thing. "Price is the money-name of the labour objectified in a commodity." (1976: 195). He held that there is no complete coincidence — the possibility that price might diverge from the magnitude of value is inherent in the price-form itself. But he did not attempt any precise formulation of the relation between price and value, i.e. between money-exchange equivalent and labour-time equivalent. (If he had, he might have been forced to admit that the incongruity lay not simply in the nature of the "price-form" but in the weakness of the labour theory itself.) The statements in volume III of *Capital* (which was edited by Engels from an incomplete first draft and published in 1894 after Marx's death) seem both to Marxists and to their critics to provide a price theory which is more realistic than the value theory of volume I. But they also raise the problem of how far this price theory can be seen to emerge from the earlier value theory or to be completely independent of it — in short had Marx revised himself? Argument on this issue has been highly technical, not within my proper competence, and not particularly relevant to this present paper. But it is of interest in its bearing upon the general problem of the role of work in an economy. Briefly, the line that western economists have taken is that Marx's value theory was too rigid in its assumptions to be of much use in the interpretation of actual economic processes and situations. Modern economists are much concerned with output concepts such as level of capital employed, level of real wages etc., and to use Marx's "value" in the sense of labour-time as a guide is "to measure with a piece of elastic" as Joan Robinson put it, since with technical progress and capital accumulation output per man-hour tends to rise and the "value" of commodities to fall. Prices could be proportional to values, i.e. labour-time expended, if capital per unit of labour were the same everywhere , and profits were uniform. But for technical reasons more capital tends to be employed in some industries than in others, and profits relative to wages tend to be high where the ratio of capital to labour is high. In practice, competition tends to establish a uniform rate of profit on capital, not a uniform ratio of profit to wages. So prices do not correspond to values. Again, a distinction of great significance for Marx was that he drew between variable capital (used to pay wages) and constant capital (used for investment in equipment and materials). When he wrote of the "organic composition of capital" he was concerned with the proportion between the labour-time currently employed and the labour-time expanded in the past to build up the stock of capital goods. But for simplification Marx made some basic assumptions, notably that capital is always used to capacity, and that this capacity is determined by technical conditions. But economists are very familiar with changes in employment of capital in response to changes in estimation of the state of trade. So, as Joan Robinson comments, even for Marx himself the concept of value has had to be strained a good deal for him to maintain the value-price broad correspondence (Robinson 1966, 1968; Samuelson 1971).

A clue to understanding some of this argument, and the defence of Marx's expressions by Marxist apologists, can be found in a remark summarizing the essence of Marx's view in 1865, in a compilation on *Value, Price and Profit*, edited by Marx's daughter, Eleanor Marx Aveling:

> to explain the *general nature of profits*, you must start from the theorem that, on an average commodities are *sold at their real values*, and that *profits are derived from selling them at their values* ... If you cannot explain profit upon this supposition, you cannot explain it at all. (Aveling 1899: 53–54 – orig. ital.; Marx 1968: 206).

From this point of view then, the labour theory of value was a necessary assumption for Marx in his interpretation of capitalism. Not that he had any particularly mystical view about the nobility or sanctity of labour. Despite some background in the Romantic period he had no specially romantic view of the labouring process. But what was essential for him in the development of his argument was to assume that there was, if not identity, at least a close correspondence between prices and *labour* contribution, in order to be able to eliminate profit as a contribution in its own right. His basic position was, not so much that value is the result of labour as that relative prices express more or less directly *relative labour input* and *nothing else*. (This assumes that return to "constant capital" in equipment is also a return to earlier labour input.) As with some other features of his exposition (see Firth 1972), Marx in effect wrote his argument backwards. Hence since the labour contribution can be divided into a subsistence portion and a "surplus" portion, it must be from the latter that any returns to capital, land etc. can come. In a sense, as some commentators have noted, the *value* concept is irrelevant for Marx. Commodities, he held, are basically exchanged against their proportionate components in labour-time alone, but the labourer gets only a fraction of what his product fetches.

Labour Values and Prices

In this sense, one can understand Joan Robinson's point that the value concept in Marx is only a matter of words, of definition of amounts of labour. And Samuelson's point too is intelligible — that the famous "transformation-problem" is no problem at all: price = value because it is necessary for the argument that price shall be completely taken up by the labour component, leaving no space for profit as return to any other factor contributing effectively to the product.

Uncertainties about Marx's "law of value" have been more acute in socialist countries, because actual production decisions have often had to try to interpret and resolve them. Some of the issues have been: did the "law of value" indeed apply to socialist economies; should labour-time cost (with or without depreciation) be primary in production decisions, or should scarcity of other factors such as investment resources be taken into calculation; should marginality be recognized as a principle in the face of Marx's insistence on average labour cost? For a period the argument was protracted and fierce, but as it proceeded the tendency grew to forsake crude dogmatic insistence on the primacy of the labour factor in value determination in allocation of resources, in favour of more pragmatic considerations of relative scarcity, marginal productivity and strength of demand. The Soviet position was crystallized at one point by J.B. Stalin, who roundly argued that the law of value of course still continued to operate under socialism because of the persistence of commodity production and the exchange relations between agriculture and industry. He denied that it had been transformed — as some Soviet writers had postulated — by socialist planning controls. But he was rather guarded, ascribing to it the function of a "regulator" in the personal consumption field only, and in the production field as an "influence" only, through the way in which the consumer goods were needed to compensate the labour power expended in the process of production. Stalin pointed out that value, like the law of value, was a historical

category connected with the existence of commodity production.
With the disappearance of commodity production, value and its
forms and the law of value would also disappear, and the amount of
labour expended on the production of goods would be measured
directly and immediately by the number of hours worked. The
allocation of labour and production generally would be regulated
by "the requirements of society" in the growth of society's demand
for goods. In socialist countries outside the Soviet Union there has
been more open questioning of the validity of the law of value itself.
Alfred Zauberman (1960) and Wlodzimierz Brus (1964), for instance,
wrote of uncertainties, enigmatic statements and confusion in the
attempt to follow Marx's theory, and by 1965 Oskar Lange was able
to write that instead of using average costs as Marxian orthodoxy
would have it, most Polish economists favoured using marginal cost
as a basis for price formation, as allowing planners more rational
choise of inputs.[8]

The upshot of the economists' argument seems to be that in a
marxist interpretation the "law of value" is a valid statement of a
very general kind in regard to developed commodity production
though in practice its operation is qualified by other factors than
labour cost. By a non-marxist reading, the qualifications are so
serious that the theory as expressed in Marx's terms has very little
significance. But it seems to be agreed that Marx's theory was
devised to explain production in a capitalist economy alone. What
then of its relevance for a pre-capitalist economy, especially an
economy where commodity production has not developed? On a
literal marxist interpretation the labour theory of value cannot
apply to such conditions, but I think it is of interest to enquire if
some of Marx's general ideas on value and value determination
cannot be used as points of stimulus for anthropological analysis.
Though it be labelled as historically specific, the labour theory of
value embodies categories of economic process which can be used
negatively as well as positively to illumine a great range of economic
conditions.

Work in a Pre-capitalist Economy

First, take the concept of labour, or work itself. There is an idea
that "work", as a concept for energy expenditure to acquire new
energy at some sacrifice of comfort, is the development of an
industrial type of society concerned with commodity production
and the isolation of individual human energy as a marketable item.
I think this is an inadequate, unduly restrictive view. In traditional
Tikopia society, for instance, the marketing of individual human

energy in a competitive sense did not occur. But there was a concept of work, described by the term *fekau*, used to indicate expenditure of energy for accomplishment of ends, at some sacrifice of comfort or leisure. And there was overt consideration of work in terms of scarcity, of *fekau* in terms of competing uses of energy resources of men (and women). Marx made great play with the notion of external labour, labour in which man alienates himself with self-sacrifice, does not feel content but unhappy, does not develop freely his physical and mental energy but mortifies his body and ruins his mind. He envisaged the labour as not belonging to the worker's essential being, as being not voluntary but coerced, and therefore meaning that the worker does not affirm himself but denies himself. If the product of labour does not belong to the worker, if it confronts him as an alien power, he argued, this can only be because it belongs to some other man than the worker. But while this was meant as a characterization of the industrial worker, and came from Marx's early thinking on the subject, it suggests by contrast a kind of naïve view of pre-industrial labour which is anthropologically unacceptable. Tikopia work involved burdens and disabilities; was often a matter for discontent, discomfort and bodily pain, was coercive and not simply at voluntary choice, and often resulted in a product held in the possession or control of other than the worker himself (Firth 1939: 110). The Tikopia worker was certainly not alienated in the Marxian sense, but he was no happy communal primitive enjoying simply the product of his own energy output, with labour as its own reward. The ethnographic situation is more complex than Marx by inference postulated, and his own concepts can become more widely applicable than he himself envisaged.

In the light of Marx's concepts of abstract labour, average labour and socially necessary labour-time it is pertinent for anthropologists to enquire more systematically into indigenous definitions of work, into contrast between work and alternative occupation, into concepts of skill and creative invention in work, and into what kind of relation is postulated in any particular society between skilled and unskilled work. How far, for example, is it thought that skilled work can be equated with or compensated by any amounts of unskilled work?

Some problems arising from Marx's exposition of his notions of value can be of particular interest to anthropologists. One is the linkage Marx made between the labour contribution to production, the distributive system of the economy and the socio-political structure of the society. How far, in a relatively simple technological situation, with production primarily for use rather than for exchange, can any equivalent to surplus value be recognized? And if surplus value can be isolated as a category, is it accompanied by or manifest in what may be termed exploitation? Then what is the nature of the ideas that people of a society have about the character of their economic system? How far can anything resembling a "fetishism" of goods entering into exchange be identified? Can there be said to be a "mystification" of the relations of production in a traditional economy such that the productive forces of the workers are made to appear in their view as generated by other elements in the economic system? Commodity production, an elaborate system of private property, a developed class structure linking economy and society are not found in most African and Oceanic societies. Yet the main problems of Marx's exposition — the identification of the economic basis of power, and the relation of the dominant mode of production to the social, legal and political institutions of the society, are still relevant.

Superficially, even in a small-scale technically undeveloped society such as Tikopia, some critical points of comparison appear. As a measure of the comparative worth of many objects, both when held as group property and when used in exchange trans-actions, their labour cost appears as a prime element in the relative estimation. A pandanus mat, taking many days of plaiting to com-plete, is esteemed more in exchange than a barkcloth sheet, taking hours rather than days to prepare. As bedding, the mat underneath and the sheet on top have parallel use-values. The mat tends to be used more often, and with its more coherent fibres, to last longer, but the labour cost is the outstanding differential for exchange ranking. In this relatively undifferentiated field of women's crafts special skill is recognized. A Tikopia man's small waist mat or kilt, made of fine pandanus strips and ornamented with a geometrical pattern of red-dyed fibre, is a product particularly associated with skills of women from Anuta. These mats have been traditionally related as a commodity to the Tikopia field of exchange in two ways. They have entered into transactions parallel to those in which bedmats and barkcloth figured, though they have been transferred only rarely and by "something extra" being given in exchange for the waistmat. Again, waistmats have sometimes been "contracted for" by Tikopia men with Anuta women in the occasional visits between people of the two communities, and have so been brought into the general exchange field. But the article against which a waist-man has been contracted for production has often been a cylinder of turmeric, one of the items of top evaluation in the Tikopia scheme. What is represented here for the Tikopia is not any amount of abstract labour or socially necessary labour time, but two sets of labour inputs of very different duration, given quality by two very different sets of skills demanding precise handling — of female plaiting on the one hand and male turmeric extraction expertise on the other — compounded by scarcity of those skills. The relative value of the waistmat and the turmeric cylinder have been com-pounded by another type of scarcity — of turmeric raw material, which is entirely lacking in Anuta (the pandanus grows in both islands). Now Marx's concept of abstract labour, and of "value" embodying this, were so hedged in by qualification in terms of commodity production, separation of individual workers and general exchange that they cannot be applied within Marx's scheme to any Tikopia phenomena of the kind described. But in his endeavour to secure historical specificity and explain the capitalist form of production Marx confines the scope of his terms unduly. He states "It is only by being exchanged that the products of labour acquire a socially uniform objectivity as values, which is distinct from their sensuously varied objectivity as articles of utility." (1976: 166). This is unexceptionable: when priced in exchange goods have comparable value which they lack when considered only as satisfying wants. But what about the qualification — this division "appears in practice only when exchange has already acquired a sufficient extension and importance to allow useful things to be produced for the purpose of being exchanged, so that their character as values has already to be taken into consideration during production" (ibid.). Again, lacking a generalized market, not every article will be produced for exchange, and complete comparability cannot be achieved. But what of partial com-parability? Many systems of exchange in Oceanic communities are so elaborate that it seems unduly restrictive to deny the operation of a concept of "value" in them, and the need to have some formulation to express the relation between the labour inputs they represent and the exchange-equivalents they generate. In other words, what I am arguing is that anthropologists should refuse to accept the limitations of definition Marx has placed on concepts of labour and of value, but be prepared to use them outside the economic boundaries he laid down, while at the same time recognizing the importance of the ideas he has stimulated.

I would argue further, for instance, that Marx's "fetishism of commodities", which he regarded as a hallmark of capitalism and money exchange, is not the prerogative of a capitalist economy alone. It is a special case of a more general phenomenon of symbolism of social actions and social conceptions by using material goods. Marx

concentrated his notion of definite social relations between human
beings assuming the semblance of a relation between things, on
where useful things are produced expressly for exchange. But such
commodity fetishism seems to operate more widely, in any form
of exchange where a relation between groups or persons is expressed
by the transaction. In a conventional Tikopia exchange, I would say
that thoughtful Tikopia seem quite aware of the "semblance" aspect
of the transaction — but they also behave as if the transfers
represented a real exchange of use-values, and the social relation
between men assumes the "fantastic form" of a relation between
things. Marx uses religion as an analogy, but the analogy is perhaps
closer than he thought — as Godelier has pointed out (Marx 1976:
165; Godelier 1977: 163—4).[9]

Surplus Value and Exploitation?

Marx's concept of surplus value seems less applicable to the conditions of non-commodity production — though he himself remarked
that capital did not invent surplus labour. In the traditional Tikopia
economy it would be hard to identify an extra gain obtained by an
entrepreneur who was able to mobilize the labour of others and
reap an advantage by exchange of the product against other items
or services. Where an element of surplus value in exchange may be
looked for more plausibly is in modern conditions, where Tikopia
sell items of traditional culture, made by themselves or by others,
for money, either to occasional tourists or to other Tikopia in
settlements away from the home island where traditional goods are
harder to come by. Very recently, I gather, at Waimasi, a Tikopia
settlement on San Cristobal, traditional items of barkcloth, mats
and bowls have become scarce, and still being wanted for institutional
transactions, are sought at substantial prices: 50 cents to $1 for a
barkcloth girdle, $5 for a barkcloth sheet, $10 for a wooden bowl,
$10 to $20 for a pandanus mat. Price varies according to quality,
scarcity of the goods and of money to pay for them, and kinship
relations sometimes modify the amount of money that changes
hands. But these ratios, which broadly correspond to the amount
of labour and skill incorporated in them, do exemplify traditional
Tikopia evaluations of the goods (Firth 1939: 337—44; cf. 1959:
144—45, 150). Theoretically, then, a Tikopia man who acted as an
intermediary between an Anutan or Tikopia woman waistmat maker
and a Tikopia or westerner abroad could extract a margin of value
over and above the initial payment to the mat maker. But this would
not be surplus value in Marx's sense. The situation still does not have
enough generality, and the craftswoman's subsistence does not

depend, even nowadays, upon payments initially or subsequently made to her by the intermediary. Even nowadays too, such purchase often has a distinct utility aim.

But if surplus value cannot be identified, what about exploitation? This question is complicated by the structural factors of chieftainship and rank of members of chiefly families. Both concepts are value-laden, but whereas the position of chiefs is empirically defined, the existence of exploitation must be inferential. Undoubtedly, in contemporary socio-economic conditions as well as traditionally, Tikopia have contributed to the support of their chiefs what may be termed a production surplus. They work occasionally in a chief's taro gardens, they take baskets of food and fine fish to his house, and in modern times they give him presents of money. The form of support varies according to circumstances, e.g. whether he is living on or off Tikopia, but no chief yet is simply living off his own personal resources. There is evidence,too that such contributions are at times resented by some Tikopia, and linked with the power exercised by chiefs in major policy decisions for the community as a whole. Occasionally, though usually fairly muted, criticism of undue privilege is voiced.

Any judgement as to the existence of exploitation of people by their chiefs involves certain assumptions as to the nature and validity of the processes of selection of those leaders, and of the immaterial assets and services they represent and render to the community. If it be thought that the Tikopia chiefs obtain their living and build up their wealth from the contributions of their people, with no return to the latter, then one could correctly speak of exploitation. If Tikopia chiefs, instead of always living among their people, were to behave like absentee landlords and live away from other Tikopia upon the proceeds of the work of the community, the case would be clear. Even if while living among other Tikopia, chiefs and their families worked manually in their cultivations and engaged in various forms of craft manufacture — as they do — their relationship could still be judged as exploitation if they creamed off the energies and superior products of their people to their own benefit. But this is not so. Tikopia chiefs and their families do not live as a class off Tikopia ordinary people. Elements of such exploitation, and the potential for its development can be detected in both traditional and modern Tikopia society, but they have been held in check by a complex combination of relations of production: the holding of land in relatively small, scattered parcels; a strong conceptualization of kin-group rights to land and other major property; the absence of alternative markets for products of labour; and what may be

termed the ideology of reciprocity. For the material transactions
are certainly not only one way. Food supplies sent in to the chief
are disbursed by him substantially to other, non-chiefly households;
chiefs reciprocate in exchange and engage like commoners in
provision of services demanded by kin obligation. All this is very
familiar to anthropologists.

The most controversial issue, however, is estimation of the
significance of *immaterial* assets and services. From the material
side, Tikopia chiefs may be regarded as "appropriators of surplus
value" in a way reminiscent of Marx's conception of the role of
guild-masters (1976: 423, 1029–30; cf. Kautsky 1925: 117). But
Marx's insistence on the social parameters of labour ought to draw
attention to such immaterial elements in the socio-economic process.
Here it is clear, from Tikopia recent history that almost all if not
all Tikopia regard their chiefs as essential components of their
society. They speak of the chiefs as contributing much to the
public recognition of Tikopia in the contemporary Solomon islands
social and political scene, they accept the decisions of their chiefs
on major political issues — though they may not always agree with
those decisions — and they go out of their way to welcome and
show respect to the chiefs whenever they appear in settlements of
Tikopia abroad, and use them as foci for general assembly. An
obvious inference is that the chiefs help to give to all Tikopia that
element of unique identity as a society and culture which is very
relevant to preservation of the integrity of a people (cf. Firth
1969).

Marxists are fond of reiterating that in capitalism, power relationships are not transparent — as if by contrast they have been transparent in other forms of society! I would not find it easy to argue
that power relations have been transparent between chiefs and
people in Tikopia society. But I think there is a difference
between lack of transparency, and the "mystification" syndrome
in Marx's diagnosis, where the true nature of exploitation is concealed by representing it as reciprocal service.[10] It would be arrogant,
though, in the line of Marx's own exposition, for an anthropologist
to claim that he had revealed the "mystery" of Tikopia power
relations. I doubt if these can be considered a mystery to the Tikopia.
They do contain substantial non-rational elements, such as a belief,
even in modern conditions, in some aspects of the sanctity (*tapu*)
and special powers (*manu*) of Tikopia chiefs. But Tikopia can
discuss these beliefs objectively, can speculate how far they may be
validated in actual cases, and have been known both to criticize
chiefs for some of their actions and approve the institution of

chieftainship for the values it represents to the Tikopia. So while the issues are complex, to the Tikopia as to an anthropologist, a considerable degree of rational judgement and argument is exercised by Tikopia upon them.

The question of possible exploitation is bound up with that of freedom of choice by the parties concerned. Here the opinion of a Marxist economist is of interest. E. Wolfstetter of the University of Dortmund has pointed out that in almost every society we can distinguish between one part of the net product which serves as subsistence for those who do the work and another part which serves for general social purposes. Accordingly, we can divide the total labour-time expended into two respective parts: necessary labour and surplus labour. The latter is the work spent in order to provide for maintenance of equipment and future growth — or capital-building in non-Marxist terms. When the production decisions eventuate from an egalitarian decision process "nobody could consider this surplus labour as an index of exploitation". So while surplus value in its phenomenal form of profits represents a capitalist form of production, "positive surplus labour" as result of a free decision by the owners of the means of production is "not a sufficient condition for establishing that there is exploitation" (Wolfstetter 1973: 799). Now this, which could well be an apologia for a socialist form of production, clearly involves assumptions about the nature of "free" decision and of "ownership" of the means of production in the particular social economy under consideration. But as a general statement it can be taken as applicable to the Tikopia situation, in its traditional setting.

Over the last twenty-five years, however, the question of exploitation in the Tikopia economy has taken a new turn. The work situation of many Tikopia, mainly men and children, but also some women, has changed radically. Those living on Tikopia itself — perhaps about half of the total population — and many of those living off Tikopia in settlements in the Russell islands, of San Cristobal and elsewhere still engage in cultivation of the soil and fishing for themselves and their kin. But a high proportion of those off the island are also workers in a modern industrial structure, of coconut plantations, government service or other wage or salaried employment. And most of the children, both on and off Tikopia, now go regularly to school. A labour-cost theory of value with a concomitant of exploitation is not easy to apply to such service areas as school, hospital, police or welfare organization employment. But in the plantation labour area, application of such theory can follow a more well-worn path. What should be noted, though, is that any surplus value realized from a Tikopia wage-worker's production is of a different kind from any which may be categorized from his gift to his chief. The gift to a chief is an excess from production: it represents more food or other goods than is wanted by the family of the producer, or items of superior quality which can be foregone without great loss. The profit from plantation labour is an excess from exchange — of money-wages for labour power and of money-price for copra. The traditional Tikopia type of surplus has been dependent upon the vagaries of nature, but there has been no alternative market for it. The modern plantation product has been dependent not only upon the vagaries of nature but also upon the vagaries of the market. Tikopia traditional circumstances saw a relatively constant demand; modern industrial circumstances see variable demand, with prospect of unforeseen losses or windfall gains, with the ingenuity of the entrepreneur as bargainer as a contributory factor to the amount of the surplus. In the traditional Tikopia situation the amount of "surplus" accruing to a chief has not been dependent on his manipulative skills. The structure of the modern production situation then, with its more remote and more impersonal economic and social relationships has more potential for exploitation of the Tikopia worker.

Now I want to return more directly to the value problem. But first a note about exchange. Marx had some odd ideas about exchange in a non-market economy. He held that in primitive societies property was controlled in common. There was no "reciprocal independence" of men as individuals. He seemed to think that individual exchange corresponds to a definite mode of production which itself corresponds to class antagonism. And he asserted that only when things have fully become commodities is it that "custom stamps them with definite magnitudes" (or "fixes their values" 1976: 182). Such statements can be interpreted in a special sense, but in ordinary ethnographic terms Marx was wrong about this. He was so preoccupied with his ideas about the historical development of value as a category and its relation to the development of the idea of labour as a commodity that he constructed an over-simplified scheme of development of exchange. Certainly, in the traditional Tikopia economy, there were individual exchanges, and not just in class terms; and the care taken in matching items in exchange showed a clear conception of relative magnitude. There was no general price system, no money medium to distort the relationships, but the transactions were not simply transfers of use-values.

The Nature of Marx's Contribution

That Marx's model is too simple can be seen by considering the value of turmeric in the traditional Tikopia economy. Turmeric is a crimson pigment of high esteem, used in decoration of the person on recreational and especially ritual occasions. In the form of bark-cloth-wrapped cylinders of pigment it was treated as a most prized possession, to be transferred only against goods such as a decorated waist mat, a bonito hook or a canoe, or to be sacrificed in ritual destruction at the burial of a chief or other man of rank. It was not a commodity in Marx's sense since it was not produced primarily for exchange. Did it have value in any economic sense — or at best only use-value?

Involved in turmeric production is a substantial labour input, of both skilled and unskilled labour (Firth 1939: 137—38, 276—77, 289—91). The process of production is carefully measured in days of work, but the skilled labour is recognized as being of special quality, not reducible to terms of unskilled labour. The initial technical processes of digging, grating and filtration of the turmeric are relatively simple and the outcome is predictable. But the later processes of decantation, of baking the pigment and withdrawing it as a cylinder from its wooden oven need expert direction and considerable judgement and manual dexterity. They involve considerable anxiety, and uncertainty is a definite component in the calculation of yield. The technical means of production — troughs, bowls, filters etc. — are contributed by households and are pooled for the duration of the production. The raw materials, the turmeric roots, however, are owned by domestic groups on a sub-lineage basis, with ownership expressed in terms of rights of senior men. So the product of pigment is carefully kept itemized on this basis, and the operations are carried on with a series of turmeric batches held separately. Considerable allocations of food resources are needed to maintain the workers, and a turmeric owner must be able to afford that item in the cost of production of the pigment. As a joint product an edible flour is also produced along-side the pigment. And as immaterial benefits, prestige accrues to a successful turmeric manufacturer, while traditionally it was regarded as fulfillment of a religious obligation to a premier god.

In such a description, a model with a number of interrelated variables, the value of turmeric is dependent upon: scarcity of supplies and of skilled and unskilled labour; alternative uses of such factors — say for canoe building or feast-giving, which occasionally compete with demand for turmeric manufacture; a significant joint product (of edible flour); a considerable degree of uncertainty about the outcome of the enterprise; and a set of power considerations involved in mobilization of labour. Measurement of all these factors is hard, but some idea can be given of the relative magnitudes of most of them. Value is then the resultant of a complex set of variables of which labour power in the forms of abstract or average labour can be only one. All this can be fitted into conventional supply and demand analysis if institutional factors are built in and allowance made for change.

I think it is no accident that with the objects that are ranked together in the highest category of traditional Tikopia esteem, the element of uncertainty appears strongly in the technical outcome. In turmeric extraction and canoe-building the quality of the product can vary greatly, and in fishing with bonito hooks the chances of non-success are high. And while turmeric, canoes and bonito hooks are produced or associated partly with food, they are markedly dissociated from food in the evaluation list, and tend to be associated with rank and office. In other words, these things hold their significance not just as simple use-values, but as objects of normative estimation, normative claims and symbolic status. I would argue then that these normative elements serve in part as a diffuse prototype of effective demand in the economist's sense — i.e. wants backed by action — and so help to regulate resource allocation. If one wished to argue that in such a non-market economy labour is "the substance and immanent measure" of value, it must pass through a screen of normative estimations before being incorporated into the value schedule. Transactions whereby goods or services pass from one person or group to another in such conditions are not just an exchange of labour.

Conclusion

To conclude, I think that as positive theoretical expressions, Marx's "law of value" and the labour cost theory of value generally, are inadequate. They express important truths, but only part of the truth. And in wrestling with problems of analysis, of abstraction, of generalization, Marx allowed himself an exaggeration of language which at times he seems to have mistaken for argument. His elaborate descriptions of economic process in terms of mystery, metamorphosis, social metabolism, were forms of figuration which may be conceptually attractive and can fit a quick conspectus. But they need to be carefully examined in detailed presentation before being incorporated into a theoretical interpretation. His analysis of commodities and money was rich in metaphor — commodities are in love with money; they must divest themselves of their natural

physical body when they enter into exchange; and they do so un-
gilded and unsweetened . . . (1976: 197, 199, 202 — the German
expressions are parallel) which could not be taken literally. For
much of his argument in *Capital*, I suggest, one can regard Karl
Marx's handling of his subject as a kind of secular parallel to John
Bunyan's handling of *Pilgrim's Progress*. Scepticism and irony have
replaced simple faith, and Marx took a more personal interest in
the slaying of the dragons he identified.[11] But there was a similar
distrust of the world of appearances, a similar exhortation to
awareness of damage done to the spirit of man by acceptance
of the world's standards, and a similar belief in the ability of man
in the long run to attain a state of freedom — though Marx substituted the law of history for Bunyan's reliance on the grace of
God. But underneath all this figuration Marx's treatment has been
very fertile for theoretical development. In particular, he gave a
new dimension to the concept of work by relating it in an elaborate
historical framework to the development of relations of power,
and to the clothing of these relations in conceptual form which
can obscure their essential character.

Notes

1. "No item may be chosen with exact significance as a standard element
   symbolizing real cost. Perhaps the nearest measure in Melanesian conditions
   would be use of the elasticity of demand for time" (Belshaw 1954: 149–
   50). Theoretical and practical difficulties of this approach were considered
   by Belshaw in an appendix to his original Ph.D. thesis in social anthropology
   in the University of London. Some of the difficulties emerge in the pains-
   taking effort R.F. Salisbury made to use labour-time as a comparative
   measure of activity and of capital accumulation among the Siane. His
   results reveal the great diversity in individual behaviour and the very broad
   assumptions that had to be made in order to get comparable data. For
   example, his estimate that work with stone axes took three times as long
   as similar work with steel axes is a conservative figure based on a remark
   by his most reliable informant; but consensus of other Siane opinion was
   that "stone axes took between three and four times as long". But
   Salisbury points out that if he had taken a multiple of four times instead
   of three, his calculations about the use of capital relative to labour
   would have been markedly different (1962: 146–8, 216–20; cf. Godelier
   1977: 126–51. For more general references to recent studies of labour
   time see Van Arsdale 1978.).
2. A brief index to his attitude is his reference to "the most violent, sordid
   and malignant passions of the human breast, the Furies of private interest"
   among the enemies to free scientific enquiry, in the Preface to the first
   edition of *Capital* (1976: 92).
3. For example: "Our capitalist has two objectives: in the first place, he wants

to produce a use-value which has exchange-value, i.e. an article destined to be sold, a commodity; and secondly he wants to produce a commodity greater in value than the sum of the values of the commodities used to produce it, namely, the means of production and the labour-power he purchased with his good money on the open market. His aim is to produce not only a use-value, but a commodity; not only use-value, but value; and not just value, but also surplus-value" (1976: 293). When "value" is used above for the first time without qualification it cannot mean labour-cost but exchange value.

4. In his preface to vol. I of *Capital*, published 1867, Marx wrote of further projected volumes, including a Book IV, "the history of the theory". In his preface to vol. II Engels notes that a section had been written by Marx between 1861 and 1863 on the theory of surplus value. This was completed (after Engels's death in 1895) by Karl Kautsky between 1905 and 1910 and published not as Book IV of *Capital*, but as *Theories of Surplus Value* (*Theorien über den Mehrwert*) in a German edition of three volumes. Various subsequent editions and translations have been published in Moscow, and Berlin. A selection from the volumes, translated by G.A. Bonner and Emile Burns was published (by Lawrence & Wishart) in London in 1951, and a full edition in 1969, from a translation by Renate Simpson. A very substantial part of Meek's book (1973) on the labour theory of value is devoted to an historical analysis.

5. It has been strenuously denied for Marx, e.g. by Croce, and by Meek in criticism of Lindsay's argument, that the labour theory of value is primarily a theory of natural right rather than a theory of prices (Meek 1973: 215—225). But to my mind this is taking Marx too much at face value and crediting him with a neutralist position which is really foreign to his basic stance.

6. Some translations have "custom" – the German is *das Herkommen* (1976: 135; 1972: 59. Cf. Firth 1939: 340–2; Nadel 1951: 149–52).

7. In some types of exchange in non-monetary economy the goods transferred may be given and sought as much for their character as status-markers, as for their capacity to satisfy material wants. Here Marx's formula of C-M-C for simple commodity exchange can be replaced by an expression such as S-C-S, which has some analogy with M-C-M of capitalist exchange, but where S stands for status instead of money.

8. In November 1951 a conference of Soviet economists and other Marxists was held to consider a preliminary draft of a textbook on political economy. Materials from this conference were submitted to Joseph Stalin, who was associated with the project from the outset. His comments and his replies to several participants were published in the Soviet press in October 1952, and an English translation emerged the same year (Stalin 1952). In 1943 Oskar Lange, one of the most considerable Polish economists, had reviewed Sweezy's *Theory of Capitalist Development* (*J. Philosophy*, **40**: 378–84) and argued for the introduction of demand and of marginal analysis explicitly into Marxian analysis. Lange modified his expressions somewhat after his return to Poland later, but his *Theory of Reproduction and*

Accumulation (trans. J. Stadler and edited by P.F. Knightsfield from a Polish edition of 1965, Oxford: Pergamon, 1969) was still critical of aspects of Marxian theory. He pointed out that according to Marx's assumption, e.g. means of consumption cannot serve as means of production, whereas in practice different situations arise, as with grain in agriculture. At various times economists of the Polish Planning Commission called for rational application of the "law of value" to planning, and for more serious discussion of Lange's views on the significance of demand factors in price determination. See also J.M. Letiche, Soviet Views on Keynes, *J. Economic Literature* IX, 1971: 442–58; Alexander Bajt (of Ljubljana), Investment Cycles in European Socialist Economics: A Review Article. *J. Economic Literature* IX, 1971: 53–63. See also discussion by Meek (1973: 256–84) and Montias (1960).

9. The subtle and stimulating treatment of Marx's ideas by Maurice Godelier (see especially 1970, 1977) has done much to improve dispassionate appreciation of Marx's work by anthropologists.

10. As Alvin Gouldner has pointed out (*For Sociology*, 1973: 222n.) it was Marx's concern for reciprocity in economic relations that formed the basis of his notion of exploitation, though he was interested mainly in its negative aspects.

11. Marx took money and labour as examples of simple abstract concepts. But his own experience of them may have given him a distorted view of the industrial process. Labour he knew personally only as a writer, and he championed the cause of the manual workers at some remove. Money gained from his writings was never great, and for years he was subsidised by Engels. It would be absurd to try and explain the essentials of Marx's massive analysis in terms of his admiration for the manual work he never did and his hatred for the money of which he never had enough. But his resentment against bourgeois society (as shown in his letters) for trying to turn him into a "money-making machine", and against money as the symbol of his "really nauseating poverty" is, I suggest, a factor of relevance if one is to understand the images in which he expressed much of his analysis.

References

Acton, H.B. 1967. *What Marx really said.* London: Macdonald.

Aveling, Eleanor Marx. 1899. *Value, price and profit.* Chicago: Kerr.

Belshaw, Cyril S. 1954. *Changing Melanesia.* Melbourne: OUP.

Brus, Wlodzimierz. 1964. The law of value and the market mechanism practice in a socialist economy. In *Problems of economic theory and practice in Poland: studies on the theory of reproduction and prices*, Alex Nove and Alfred Zauberman (eds.). Warsaw: Polish Scientific Publishers, 299–335.

Cole, G.D.H. 1934. *What Marx really meant.* London: Gollancz.

Dobb, Maurice. 1955. *On economic theory and socialism: collected papers.* London: R.K.P.

Firth, Raymond. 1939. *Primitive Polynesian economy.* London: Routledge.

—— 1959. *Social Change in Tikopia.* London: Allen and Unwin.

—— 1969. Extraterritoriality and the Tikopia chiefs. *Man.* 4, 354—78.
—— 1972. The sceptical anthropologist social anthropology and Marxist views on society. *Proc. British Academy* 58, 177—213.
Godelier, M. 1970. Preface II. *La Pensée de Marx et d'Engels aujourdhui et les recherches de demain sur les sociétés précapitalistes: textes choisis de Marx, Engels, Lénine.* Paris: Editions Sociales, 106—42.
—— 1977. *Perspectives in Marxist anthropology.* Cambridge: CUP. (Trans. in major part of Godelier, M. 1973, *Horizon, trajets marxistes en anthropologie.* Paris: Maspero.)
Kautsky, Karl. 1925. *The economic doctrines of Karl Marx.* Trans. H.J. Stenning. London: A and C Black.
Lange, Oskar. 1969. *Theory of reproduction and accumulation.* Trans. J. Stadler; P.F. Knightsfield (ed.) (from Polish ed. 1965). Oxford: Pergamon.
Marx, Karl. 1968. *Karl Marx and Frederick Engels: selected works.* London: Lawrence and Wishart.
—— 1972. *Das Kapital: Kritik der politischen Ökonomie. Erster Band. Karl Marx-Friedrich Engels Werke* (MEW) 23. Berlin: Dietz.
—— 1976. *Capital: A critique of Political Economy Volume One.* Introd. Ernest Mandel; Trans. Ben Fowkes. Harmondsworth: Penguin.
Meek, Ronald L. 1973. *Studies in the labour theory of value.* 2nd edn. London: Lawrence and Wishart.
Montias, J.M. 1960. Producer prices in a centrally planned economy: the Polish discussion. In *Value and plan: economic calculation and organization in eastern Europe,* Gregory Grossman (ed.). Berkeley: U.Calif. Press, 47—65.
Morishima, Michio. 1973. *Marx's economics, a dual theory of value and growth.* Cambridge: CUP.
Nadel, S.F. 1951. Work in early societies. *Question* 3, 139—60.
Pilling, Geoffrey. 1972. The law of value in Ricardo and Marx. *Economy and Society* I, 281—307.
Robinson, Joan. 1966. *An essay on Marxian economics.* 2nd edn. London: Macmillan.
—— 1968. Marx and Keynes (1948). In *Marx and modern economics,* David Horowitz (ed.). London: MacGibbon and Kee, 103—16.
Salisbury, R.F. 1962. *From stone to steel.* Melbourne: University Press.
Samuelson, Paul A. 1971. Understanding the Marxian notion of exploitation: a summary of the so-called transformation problem between Marxian values and competitive prices. *J. Economic Literature* IX, 399—431.
Sewall, Hannah R. 1901. *The theory of value before Adam Smith.* New York: Macmillan.
Stalin, Joseph. 1952. *Economic problems of socialism in the U.S.S.R.* New York: International Publishers.
Van Arsdale, Peter W. 1978. Activity patterns of Asmat hunter-gatherers: a time budget analysis. *Mankind* 11, 453—60.
Weiszäcker, C.C. von. 1973. Morishima on Marx. *Economic Journal* 83, 1245—54.
Wolfstetter, E. 1973. Surplus labour, synchronised labour costs and Marx's labour theory of value. *Economic Journal* 83, 787—809.

Zauberman, Alfred. 1960. The Soviet debate on the law of value and price formation. In *Value and plan: economic calculation and organization in Eastern Europe*, G. Grossman (ed.). Berkeley: U. California Press, 17–35.

THE ESTIMATION OF WORK:

Labour and Value Among Paez Farmers

SUTTI ORTIZ

Introduction

When talking about work, most anthropologists have focused their
attention on the incentives that move people to action, to accept
wage labor offers, or to increase their productive output. Others have
focused on labor as a potential unit to measure flows and outputs. It
is only recently, thanks to the polemical writings of Marxist anthropologists, that we are reminded that work is a complex creative
activity like any other human activity. Work should be examined in all
its complexity as the transformation of seeds and nature into food
and tools. To that purpose I shall forget that one can conceive of
work as a problem faced by all of us when we have to allocate
resources. I shall also disregard the equally interesting Ricardian
contention, initially introduced into anthropology by Salisbury
(1962) and recently revived by Gudeman (1978a) that the concept
of work can be used as a unit of measurement to help the analyst
understand the dynamics of production and distribution. Instead,
I examine what does work engender besides tools, food, and
commodities.

Although one can pretend to hold a fresh analytical vision, I
shall turn to the framework already provided by Marx and, in
particular, by his labor theory of value. My reasons are rather
pragmatic. Marx's theory of value is certainly suggestive and
pregnant with questions for future research. I feel, however, that
before we spend too much energy arguing about "transformation"
of labor into values, wages, and prices, we should re-examine what
type of transformations are in fact involved in the working of the
soil and the chipping of a stone. Social relations are indeed
created or transformed when a woman, as wife, becomes a farmhand,
or ceases to be the tender of food crops. Meillassoux, Terray, and
many others have already examined this aspect at length; for this
reason I shall leave it out of my discussion. Instead, I want to focus
on the suggestive proposition that work not only engenders social

relations but that it also engenders values. I shall let my Paez peasant farmers bear the burden and, to some extent, the responsibility of my comments. In the second part of this paper, I describe how they talk about work and calculate work, labor, or energy inputs. I use their sayings to comment on the notion that work gives value and may sometimes be used to measure the value of what it creates. But first I must briefly summarize what Marx and anthropologists have said on the subject.

Marx and the Labor Theory of Value

It was left to Marx to add life and history to Ricardo's labor theory of the value. Ricardo was concerned with the illusory essentials of economic systems. He believed that these rarefied models could be better understood by using labor time to measure value and evaluate relations. Whereas for Ricardo, labor time measured value; for Marx, labor assigned value.

Marx was a political economist concerned with historical trends and social relations. Although his theory can and has been used to examine resource flows, the relation of inputs and outputs and equilibrating forces in the fluctuations of prices, his major concerns lay elsewhere. He was concerned with how and when do commodities acquire certain values and what are the consequences of a multiple system of valuation on relations of production and class relations. He answered his own questions philosophically by looking into the possible meanings that commodities may have for individual and when is each meaning likely to come to the fore.

The most obvious meaning that commodities could have to the social beings who peopled Marx's illusory world is their *use value*. But use value is always relative. A commodity, for example, may be of greater use value to a social being other than its producer, in which case the producer will exchange it. This new act, the act of exchange, gives a new value to the commodity: an *exchange value*.

> . . . the use value of objects is realized without exchange, by means of a direct relation between the object and man, while, on the other hand, their value is realized only by exchange, that is by means of a social process. (Marx 1921: 95–96.)

Marx confronts us with the dilemma that the use value quality of commodities eventually will lead to their being exchanged which, in turn, will add new meanings to the commodities. Furthermore, the act of exchange implies a disparity between use value and exchange values. He felt compelled to resolve this disparity by assuming that commodities must contain some other quality that can be used to measure the relative value of each, thus facilitating their exchange.

That other something was, for Marx, the *labor* entailed in producing it.

> In the direct barter of products, each commodity is directly a means of exchange to its owner, and to all other persons an equivalent but that only insofar as it has use-value, of the individual needs of the exchanger. The necessity for a value-form grows with the increasing number and variety of commodities exchanged. The problem and the means of solution arise simultaneously. (Marx 1921: 100.)

As Marx was not concerned at this point in his argument with real people and real societies, he remarked that it did not matter if one person used up more energy or more work time than another person to produce the same commodity. He was referring, he insisted, to human labor in the abstract.

> We see then that that which determines the magnitude of the value of any article is the amount of labor socially necessary, or the labor-time socially necessary for its production. Each individual commodity, in its connection, is to be considered as an average sample of its class. Commodities, therefore, in which equal quantities of labor are embodied, or which can be produced in the same time, have the same value. (Marx 1921: 46.)

By socially necessary labor, Marx meant not the actual amount of labor time but a fixed quantity of human labor considered by all as necessary to produce it. He may have meant the average required, which is the usual interpretation, or he may have meant a judgment of what people think is the average required. The two, although often confused, are quite distinct; the objective average and the socially agreed-upon estimates may in fact be quite different, and the difference is of great significance in the valuation of commodities, as I shall let the Paez farmer explain later in this paper.

Furthermore, Marx qualified his equation, value = socially necessary labor, with the warning that this would only hold true for a particular type of economy. It would be true only in the case of economies characterized by simple commodity production (that is where laborers are in control of means of production and exchange what they produce), or in capitalist economies characterized by industries with same value composition of capital. These two types are ideal types which do not correspond exactly to any historical or contemporaneous economic system. For most other societies, labor value could not be expected to be the *determinant* of the exchange value.[1]

Whatever is the final form, scope, or intent of Marx's labor theory of value, his arguments are rooted initially in his writings about alienation.[2] In *Economic and Philosophical Manuscripts*, he talks about the "product of labor is labor which has been embodied in an object, which has become material: it is the objectification of labor" (Marx 1975: 272). Furthermore, it is through the product of his labor that man proves himself to be a species-being. Twenty-three years later, Marx wrote in *Capital*:

> While the laborer is at work, his labor constantly undergoes a transformation: from being motion, it becomes an object without motion; from being the laborer working, it becomes the thing produced. At the end of one hour's spinning, that act is represented by a definite quantity of yarn; in other words, a definite quantity of labor, namely that of one hour, has become embodied in the cotton . . . but the product, the yarn, is now nothing more than the labor absorbed by the cotton. (Marx 1921: 211.)

It is in man's relation to nature that the earth, air, fruits, and tools acquire value.

> Thus Nature becomes one of the organs of his activity, one that he annexes to his own bodily organs adding stature to himself in spite of the Bible. As the earth is his original larder, so too it is his tool house. (Marx 1921: 199.)

By transforming the objects of his environment, man not only satisfies his needs and gives them value, but he also separates the objects and makes them his own. The transformation of objects into possessions is through labor. So it is through labor that man defines himself. Through labor he shows his capacity and establishes a claim. He cannot, however, establish a claim to what Marx calls the natural conditions of production. He may establish a claim to the wheat he has planted and reaped, but not to the land he used in the process. The natural conditions of production are the prerequisites to his own existence

> Membership of a *naturally evolved society*, a tribe, etc., is a natural condition of production for the living individual, Such membership is, e.g., already a condition of his language, etc. His own productive existence is only possible under this condition . . . Property therefore means *belonging to a tribe* (community) (to have one's subjective/objective existence within it), and by means of the relationship of this community to the land, to the earth as its inorganic body, there occurs the relationship of the individual to the land, to the external primary condition of production. (Marx 1964: 90–91.)

When man loses control over the means of production, he must then also sell his labor. Henceforth, the products of his labor are no longer his. Such changes lead to the alienation of individuals from himself and others.

Marx now faces another problem. Granted that labor may have served as the yardstick to relate the value of one commodity to another, how is now the value of labor to be measured? He suggested that the guiding criterion must be "the value of the means of subsistence that are physically indispensable". Work is used as a yardstick, yet it contains value: the value of subsistence. At best, on its technical level, this argument is circular: value equals required labor, which equals a given quantity of subsistence goods, which, in turn, equals a given amount of labor. The difficulty is that subsistence can never be a static, agreed-upon measure.

Marx's argument has thus raised two technical problems: the transformation of labor value into exchange value or prices, and the transformation of means of subsistence into wages. He then proceeded to resolve them. Although his solutions are interesting and controversial, they are beyond the scope of this paper which is to examine the value-rendering qualities of labor, as well as the problems involved in the measurement of labor value.

It has often been remarked that there is a sharp stylistic difference, on the one hand, in Marx's writing about alienation or labor as the essence of value and, on the other hand, about how labor time may render some relations intelligible. The stylistic contrasts mirrors the fundamental differences in the nature of the arguments he was developing. One argument is about the profound relation of self and product, the meaning of work; the other is a technical argument about the dynamics' of economic systems. His two arguments are linked; in fact they are necessary, to follow his discussions on exploitation and social relations. There are, nevertheless, two quite different problems and he argues each one from a very different stance. I shall replicate his manner of thinking and separately discuss: the meaning of work and commodities for the Paez; the measurements of socially necessary labor time.

Economic Anthroplogy and the Labor Theory of Value

A decade ago, Godelier entered the battlefield of economic anthropology with yet another set of arguments that led to even more confusion amongst the so-called substantivist and formalist camps. In one of his many arguments, he reminded us of what Marx had said: "the common property that makes them [commodities] exchangeable is 'the fact that they are products of labor' " (Godelier 1972: 204). He lucidly describes how Marx arrived at his explanation of labor value: by letting himself be carried by the analysis of the object's structure towards the origin of such a structure; the origin in this case is labor, so the exchange-value must be congealed labor.

Godelier's exposition should have intrigued economic anthropologists into a more careful examination of value-rendering processes. However, most of us were still limiting ourselves to the exploration of the range of equivalences, or the discontinuities in the system of relative valuation (e.g., spheres of exchange), or the fluctuations in prices in response to supply and demand. With reference to this last point, Godelier also reminded us of Marx's warning that when price comes into being, the real value of commodities, instead of becoming more apparent, is obscured by the equivalence expressed in the price.

> The "equivalent form" of a commodity therefore *masks* the value's essence which is that of being a social reality and an expenditure of social, therefore, abstract labor; it makes this value a feature of things, thus creating the enigmatic and fetish nature of commodities. (Godelier 1977: 169.)

In order to examine whether in a trading primitive economy exchange value still closely reflects congealed labor or whether the medium of exchange used (even if it is not true money) manages already to confound the true value of commodities, Godelier studied production and circulation of salt bars among the Baruya of New Guinea. In this society, many commodities are exchanged for salt; hence, salt bars are an equivalent that can be used to measure the value of other commodities. However, there are still many other items that cannot be exchanged for salt. Godelier concludes that salt bars are not money in our sense of the word; they are, nevertheless, a primitive form of money. "Baruya salt is therefore a primitive form of money and precisely because it is 'primitive' this money offers us an exceptional opportunity to explore the mysteries of the theory of value" (Godelier 1971: 66).

Godelier proceeds, strangely enough, with Marx's more technical aspect of his argument, rather than exploring how the Baruya view the relation of work to commodity or what values may be embodied by the salt bars in the process of producing them. Instead, he calculates the labor "congealed" in the salt bars in terms of the days required to cut and burn the grass as well as produce the bars. It is not clear from either his tables (ibid.: 56–57) or his description how he arrived at his estimates of socially required labor time; that is, whether the figures are averages derived from his own observations or statements about labor requirements in salt production. Furthermore, he disregards the labor required for initially preparing the irrigated field and subsequent maintenance to ensure continuous production at a same level of output. Nor does he consider whether second and third harvests will yield as much salt and hence, whether they would require larger labor inputs for the same output. Labor time for tool replacement is also ignored. Although the very general and unqualified nature of his data mars the validity of his specific conclusion about prices and their equivalences, his argument on the nature of equivalence or of primitive money cannot be questioned.

It is regrettable, however, that Godelier did not come to terms with the process of production of salt as a step in a sequence of labor transformations. This is one of the more intriguing, yet technically difficult parts of Marx's argument. Whey he did avoid it will become clear when I examine how Paez farmers estimate labor requirements.

As explained, according to Marx, the means of production transfers value to the new product

> Suppose that in spinning cotton, the waste for every 115 lbs used amounts to 15 lbs which is converted, not into yarn but into "devil's dust". Now, although this 15 lbs never becomes a constituent element of the yarn, yet assuming this amount of waste to be normal and inevitable under average conditions of spinning, its value is just as surely transferred to the value of the yarn, as is the value of the 100 lbs that forms the substance of the yarn. (Marx 1921: 228.)

From the above we can see that Godelier's calculations do not reflect Marx's concern and cannot be an accurate way of determining whether there is or is not a labor equivalence in the exchange rate of bark capes for salt. Nor can we arrive at a conclusion on the basis of his figures regarding potential exploitation in intertribal relations.

Although Godelier's calculations prove to be spurious, he gives other information which is very relevant to our argument about value acknowledgement

> When a Baruya is asked the reason why he exchanges one salt for five or six bark capes and not for one or two, on the one hand, or more improbably for eighteen or twenty on the other, the answer is generally given in two parts which in no way exclude each other. He will first of all emphasize that he does not exchange for himself alone but for his wife (wives), his children, his brother's children, etc.; that is to say, he refers to the importance of the collective need. At other times, however, he will refer explicitly to the long and difficult work involved in the production of salt. From our own observations, he will, during a trading session, use the first type of argument in order to play on his partner's emotions: "My children have nothing left to cover their backs with . . . etc." Later, if the partner remains unmoved, he will bring work "in consideration". An informant told us one day, "When we are bargaining work is the last motive put forwards." Work is something belonging to the past and almost forgotten. It is only remembered if the partner is exaggerating his demands. (Godelier 1971: 66.)

In this passage, Godelier is, of course, concerned with exchange value which is distinct and may differ from labor value. He concludes that the rate of exchange in Baruya is primarily regulated by the volume of social necessity. His conclusion does not help us clarify the genesis of labor value in Baruya society, but two points in this quote bear on our subject: first, that work is the last motive put forward,[3] and secondly, that if one receives a satisfactory reward (not an equivalent), work is something belonging to the past and is forgotten.

In the above paragraph, Godelier, perhaps unwittingly, questions the advisability of the unqualified use of the "labor value" concept. It is often a difficult category with which to deal. Furthermore, I believe that at times the notion is only an illusory measure that may obfuscate exploitation. I return to this point later.

Rowlands, in a paper presented at the last ASA Meeting, commenting on Godelier's paper, warns us also that we must be careful not to equate different types of labor. Salt is made by men; bark capes, by women. Female labor may have a different exchange value than male labor or, as Rowlands says, a man may be willing to exchange bark cloaks embodying two or three times the amount of wives' labor in exchange for salt that would require his labor if it were produced locally. In other words, Rowlands implicitly reminds us that labor should not be considered an homogeneous commodity if we want to make use of Marx's insightful analysis of the relevance of the natural conditions of production. Simply stated, labor accounting, without also considering modes of production, will get us nowhere.

Scott Cook is one of the few anthropologists who has attempted to integrate supply-demand analysis (Cook 1970) with labor-value analysis:

> ... value is a property of commodities or that is something that attaches itself to them like "utility" and is reflected in their market price or in the socially necessary labor-time they embody." (Cook 1976: 421.)

These values are realized only through a sequence of marketplace exchanges. The *metateros* (manufacturers of grinding stones) emphasize that a primary consideration is an adequate compensation for their labor, a compensation which was calculated at the ongoing wage rate. The actual price of a *metate* at sale time may be higher or lower than the *metateros'* labor value, as they are keen in exploiting the possibility of higher profits while also aware that when demand is low, they will not easily find a buyer willing to pay the "appropriate" rate. Cook (1970) demonstrates that although the price of *metates* varies in response to supply and demand, it also hovers around the labor value of the commodity. By labor value, he means the required quantity of work expressed in monetary terms; he makes the conversion by multiplying labor time by the ongoing local wage rate. After some careful observations and accounting, Cook is able to demonstrate a relatively good fit between *average price* of *metates* and the *average social labor* required to produce them. He excludes from his estimates some cost of production and some labor inputs: tool maintenance and replacement, powder and fuse, pumping of water from the quarry, marketing transport, marketplace surcharge, as well as the cost of paint. Although such costs are not entered in Cook's table, he adds them later to arrive at good equivalence. He cautions the reader that his estimates are sensible, average estimates but that they are not exact. In fact, he warns us that given sharp monthly and seasonal market fluctuation, the exchange rate in the short run is best explained with supply-demand analysis (Cook 1976: 414).

Cook is careful as well to point out that although producers do consider the act of transforming the stone into *metate* as a claim of ownership over something of value (i.e. containing use and labor values), no thorough accounting of labor inputs is made to arrive at a proper value estimate of what they own and will exchange. As with the Baruya, past labor is forgotten.

Despite all warning of possible inaccuracy of estimates, Cook's analysis is technically more successful than that of Godelier. Leaving aside differences due to the care taken by Cook, his greater success could be attributed to the nature of the case he examines. The *metates* are correctly described as commodities. In Oaxaca, the division of labor and production for exchange is much more extensive than that found among the Baruya. Furthermore, *metateros* own their means of production. Cook's example comes closer to the ideal type of simple commodity production considered by Marx. The adequacy of the examples begs the question already raised by Meek (1956: 305ff), as to whether a "value-epoch" (when labor values approximate exchange ratios) had historical reality. Meek answered his own question by acknowledging that historically it may not be identifiable, yet the ideal type is a useful concept as long as factor mobility is added as another characteristic of simple commodity systems (1956: 199).

Morishima thinks yet another condition is important: mobility of labor must not be impeded sociologically or geographically, so that income is equalized throughout the society (a condition he derives from Marx's internal logic). It is hard to imagine that any one historical society could ever have approximated the Marxist abstraction with all the conditions now added to the definition of simple commodity production. In fact, Morishima argues the "commodity production develops fully only under capitalism and only when the capitalist mode of production has conquered all sectors of the economy, agriculture included" (Morishima and Catephores 1975: 313). Baruya, Oaxaca, or Paez peasant economy could not be expected to fit Morishima's refined definition. The cases analyzed by anthropologists therefore cannot be used as test cases. In fact, the Paez example, as we shall see, tends to support Morishima on a basis other than the ones he discusses in his joint article with Catephores. The hint is not a proof; we should not be discouraged to examine further cases. The authors, after all, acknowledge that regardless of how logical their arguments may be, it would "turn out to be irrelevant if it could be shown on the basis of factual historical evidence that individual exchange-ratios in pre-capitalist economies did approximate the labor-determined value of goods" (ibid.: 313). They could find nothing but comfort from Godelier's findings.

From a different perspective, that of Ricardo and Sraffra, Gudeman (1978a) wants to make a case of the use of labor input accountancy to interrelate all production processes. Although some may argue (Meek's Introduction to his second edition of *Studies in the Labor Theory of Value*) that there are many parallels as well as some added advantages to Sraffra's approach, there is at least one basic difference with the arguments by Marx which I have chosen to summarize in this paper. For Sraffra, it may be convenient to reduce value to labor, but unlike Marx he does not argue that labor generates value. Despite the difference, some of the difficulties I describe in using labor as measurements may also impinge in Gudeman's attempts to analyze the dynamics of distribution systems for some — but not necessarily all — peasant economies. Regardless of whether one is able to make a case against the use of Marx's labor accountancy to examine the dynamics of production or distribution or exploitation, one still could make a case for labor as a value-generating activity. In the next section I discuss each argument separately.

The Work of Paez Peasants

A Paez farmer[4] with sufficient land to grow more than enough food for the subsistence of his family will produce as well one of the several local cash crops: coffee, sugar cane, wheat, potatoes, beans. He may produce more than one of these crops for sale, choosing those best suited to his land resources. Manioc, arracacha, plantains, maize, and some varieties of beans and vegetables are grown basically to feed his family. If some of the food crops are sold, it is either in a small amount when there is a need for a bit of cash and there is no other way to obtain it, or it is when friends or kin, having lost their harvest, come to request it (the sale price in this case is fixed and below market price). The land used by a farmer is the patrimony of the community; he has a right to a share of the community's land as long as he maintains it under production and remains in residence. But a right to a share will only be acknowledged if the farmer is the head of a household; it is the household then, rather than the individual, that controls the land. Labor resources of the household are pooled and used by the family on their farm. The husband (or mother, when she is single or widowed) serves as the administrator and controller of the resources; all other members have a right to receive, in the form of food, clothing, shelter, and amenities, a share of the proceeds of their labor. However, the household head, as administrator, manages to appropriate a larger share of return, which he will then use to entertain friends with beer, to buy himself a horse, or to buy more elegant clothing. In principle, he is not to receive any more than the others, nor is he to make decisions without consulting his wife and older children; in practice, he often abuses the privileges of his status.

For a Paez man or woman who has land, farming, spinning, and weaving will yield the satisfaction of eating well, of feasting friends, and of keeping warm. After the cash crops are sold, purchases can be made. But cash and bodily comforts are not the only returns to one's labor; a nicely woven *ruana*, a beautifully decorated woven bag brings prestige to the woman who wove it or knotted it; a well-tended field brings respect and prestige to the head of the household. Not every Paez is considered to be equal to others. Some are thought to be more clever, more competent; their unusual capabilities are expected to be acknowledged in monetary terms when they sell a field of manioc or a piece of woven cloth. No distinction is made in wage labor received.

When Do Paez "Work"?

When you ask a Paez what he did the day before, he may reply that he went to "work" in his field up the mountain. If he is talking in his own language, he uses the word *mahin*, which they translate into Spanish as *trabajar* and which I translate into English as *work*. *Mahin* is used, as well, to refer to wage labor and to day-exchange labor with friends or kin. It is not used to describe the act of washing, cooking, selling food or cash crops, marketing, or of walking to far-off fields to give salt to their animals. A Paez *visits* his animals; no mention is made of the effort to walk up the mountain, only to the cost of the salt. Likewise, there is no mention of the effort to get to the market. The focus is on the act of selling. If a woman wants to tell you that she spent the day cooking, she will use words which describe the food rather than the act of preparation. A farmer may also use a very specific word to describe some farming activities such as weeding, planting, harvesting, without telling you that he *worked*. But the point is that he can describe all such acts either specifically or with the category *mahin*, whereas he will never use that category to describe marketing, taking salt to his animals, or any domestic activity.

There is another important qualification to the use of the word *mahin* which relates to the social context in which the work is performed. The word is appropriately used if the work efforts yields food from the field, labor (in the case of arranged labor exchanges), or cash (in the case of wage labor). *Mahin* will not be used when he the effort is used to discharge a social or communal obligation. When a Paez spends the day clearing the field of a friend or of kinsmen and joins in the usual festivities at the end of the day's work, he will come home and tell you that he spent the day helping in a *minga* or *minka*. The person whom he helped will, in turn, explain that he had *invited* some people to come to his *minga*. The word is of Quechua origin and may well have been introduced into the area during colonial times; it means a gathering of people to perform a task. The *cabildo*, or community council, may also *invite* member households to a *minga* to repair any of the local roads or community property or to initiate a community project. It is unfortunate that the word *invite* to a *minga* does convey a large degree of freedom to comply when, in fact, a person or household so invited should attend. There is often resentment of so-called invitations to *cabildo mingas*, partly because the *cabildo* has not often acted in the best interest of member families and partly due to the fact that the projects are often forced onto the *cabildo* by higher government offices. There is a better attendance and no resentment of an invitation by kin or by a friend. Participants know that they will receive food and drink at the end of the day (none is given during a *cabildo minga*); they know they will celebrate and that the hosts will, in turn, attend their *mingas*. Attendance, however, is not meant to yield food or return labor; in fact, the guests may never or may rarely become hosts themselves. Attendance is meant to generate a social bond. Those farmers who never invite their kin to *mingas* or to drinking parties, or who never attend either, are neglected when in need.

The Paez, of course, are not naïve. They are deeply aware that whether invited to come to a *minga*, or hired to work as *peon*, requested to *work* in exchange, ready to weed their own fields, weave a *ruana*, or to cook a meal, energy is spent and something is created (food, money, or social bond). Yet, the distinction is relevant and fits closely to what is included and what is left out from labor accounting, as we shall see in the last section of this paper.

In summary, the concept of *mahin* or *work* implies the energy spent by men, women, and children in the provision of food or cash and in the manufacture of commodities. I limit myself to activities so labeled only because they come closest to the activities encompassed by the concept of labor as used by Marx, Godelier, and Cook. I do not intend to imply that other energy expenditures are irrelevant or insignificant. Quite to the contrary, the resources engendered and distributed through *mingas* or domestic activities are important and significant and should not be neglected in the study of the production and distribution of resources and outputs. My first reservation to an unqualified use of the labor-theory framework is that it would tend to exclude much of the energy spent or outputs engendered as spin-off from activities other than those labelled as *work*.

In Marx's illusory society of simple commodity production, the work of a man engenders a commodity. His energy transforms nature and yields something which he values because he can use it, share it, or he can trade it. Not only does he create a useful commodity, but he also vests it with a characteristic which he recognizes as relevant; the energy spent in producing it. Commodities can be evaluated by their characteristics (use, energy contained); man's capacity, by the value of the commodity he creates. Marx focused on labor as the only quality that can be used to evaluate commodities traded.

When a Paez *works*, he also creates a commodity which is his, by virtue of his creation. Labor creates something to which he has a claim. Clearing a patch of land transforms *monte* (scrubland) into *roza*. The *roza* is his to use until he lets it go wild again. By the same token, he has a right to the crops he plants in his *roza*. But the Paez are members of a real society, hence, more complicated than an ideal case. A Paez farmer is seldom acting on his own. Instead, his labor represents the labor of the family. In other words, his children and his wife have an equal claim to the food in the field even though they may not have spent any time weeding or harvesting. It would almost be more appropriate to say that the household engenders commodities and establishes a claim over them. By the same token, when working for wages, the earnings belong, at least in theory, to the household and are administered by its head.

Work transforms nature not only into commodities but also into things of quality: well-tended fields, smooth and delicious cubes of sugar. Some farmers are known for detecting the right point at which cane sap will crystallize and yet retain an amber color and a light flavor. Others are renowned for their ability to process coffee in such a way as to enhance the quality of the bean. Products and labor are not homogenous units in the mind of the Paez. The quality of a product is given recognition: prestige or more money is received by the producer of a quality product. Labor creates prestige as well as commodities. Prestige belongs to the person; commodity, to the entity the laborer represents.

Hence, Paez recognize several meaningful characteristics of commodities which can be used to evaluate them: usefulness, quality and quantity of labor. The first characteristic can be used as a guide to trade but not to arrive at an exchange rate. The second can be used to rank commodities and individuals, hence, it could be used to determine the proportionate share received by each member of a producing unit. The third characteristic can also be used to rank commodities and, theoretically, can be used to determine rate of exchange.

Joint labor contributed by the family is used to transform nature and make the products their own. But the labor serves only to establish a claim to be shared and not an identification with the product. Furthermore, only unpaid labor (*mahin*) or domestic activities gives a person a right to a share of what is produced; *minga* work gives only the right for an eventual return of a service. I think it is also important to keep in mind that the joint claim that members of a producing unit gain over nature is in competition to potential claims of other producing units. With their joint labor, they withdraw resources from the communal pool. Labor brings together members of a household in an alliance which, at any rate, is riddled with questions that separates them from others. The fact that the products of labor are rarely shared with other producing units adds to the separation. Conditions of production are such that labor energy does not serve for men or family to prove themselves. It is the quality of labor which, in Marx's words, gives stature to man. It is thus important not to reduce all labor to a homogeneous labor in a peasant society similar to that of the Paez.

Recapitulating what has been said from a different perspective, the products of labor (except *minga*) embody three evaluative characteristics: their use, their quality, and the labor embodied in their production. A Paez farmer would add another characteristic of great relevance to them: the quantity of cash or scarce resources embodied in them.[5] A *ruana* with stripes is more valuable because wool has to be tinted with anilines and one cannot just tint the exact amount of wool, nor buy only the aniline one will need for a single *ruana*. Crops that require outlay of cash are more valuable than those which can be reproduced with last harvest's seeds. Marx addressed himself to this problem when he talked of the various values which are transferred in the process of production: the necessary raw materials including the wasted material. All such costs should and can be included if we express them by labor quantities required to produce them, then adding such estimates to the labor required in the transformation of the final commodity. In other words, one would have to add the labor required to acquire and tint all of the yarn used or wasted; in the case of seeds, the labor required to generate the cash to buy the seeds. Such computations, however, are often disregarded,[6] as they are hard to estimate. Yet, by so doing, we are minimizing the labor value of commodities. In an economy like the Paez, the essential value of a sack of coffee, of a yarn of cloth, is then much more than the labor entailed in its final phase of production.

Estimates of Socially Required Labor

When asked about the work required to produce coffee, a Paez farmer answers with an average number of days required to weed the plantation, adding as well the number of days required to harvest an average yield, or estimating the average weight that a person can harvest per day. Sometimes the estimates are based upon personal experiences that take into account the slope of his fields, the age of his trees, and the yields he remembers as the most frequent ones for his plantation. The Paez who must now till slopes scarred by erosion are deeply aware that the amount of labor required to transform nature into food depends on the quality of resources available. "*El trabajo no rinde*" (work does not yield) is a frequent complaint. In contrast with theoreticians, peasant farmers must constantly come to terms with the sad reality that labor only sometimes engenders a product to claim and to use socially and symbolically. Their own personal experience provides them with a guide as to the range of the productivity of labor. The norm is based upon requirements for a stereotypic, local farm. When the estimates are based upon their own farm, they vary from peasant to peasant; when estimates are based upon stereotypic farms, there is a considerable degree of agreement. This second instance, I think, comes close to what Marx meant by the socially necessary labor time.

There is, however, a serious discrepancy between their concep-

tualization of socially necessary labor time and Marx's conceptualization of labor value. Marx included all labor required directly or indirectly in the manufacture of the commodity. The Paez consider
only the labor required in some of the stages of production. They
exclude from their calculations of coffee production: clearing of
the land, purchasing or transporting the seedlings, planting the
seedlings, weedings required before the trees begin to produce,
replanting of trees which die or cease to produce, processing the
beans (washing, soaking, pulping), drying and selecting the beans,
making or purchasing the storage sacks, marketing the dry product,
or replacement of tools. If asked a specific question about labor
times spent in any of the above-listed activities, one is likely to
get answers from those who have one hectare, or more, planted
in coffee. But even then it is impossible to get estimates for
acquisition and transportation of seedlings, replanting of trees, or
drying the beans and marketing. These activities are never performed
by hired labor and, although arduous, do not require continuous
attention.

Labor-input estimates for growing sugar cane and producing
panela (uncentrifuged sugar cubes) follow a similar pattern; activities
which are not continuous are excluded: amassing firewood, wrapping
of sugar cubes, acquiring cane for planting, marketing of the sugar
cubes. Other activities are excluded because no standard measures
are used. For example, when the cane is cut, irregular bunches are tied
to a horse to bring to the sugar press; when all the canes are processed,
a few more trips to the field are made. It is almost impossible for
them to average out how much time had been spent transporting
the cane to the mill.

The above observations are in keeping with Cook's experiences in
labor accounting in Oaxaca. Unlike the *metateros*, however, Paez
farmers have no general knowledge of labor requirements in the
manufacture of a significant number of commodities regionally
produced (Cook 1976: 424); only those farmers who plant cane
can estimate labor inputs required by the crop; only those who
plant a field with beans for sale can give planting and harvesting
estimates.

It is an entirely different matter to elicit average labor requirements for subsistence crops. When estimates are solicited, Paez
farmers answer with stereotypic estimates (rather than averages)
of time required to clear about a hectare of land and plant a mixed
field. They will also tell you the number of days required to clear
such a field. All farmers agree in their stereotypic judgments, but
many often add, "of course, it depends on the farm". Yet they are

not able to summarize their past experiences at planting mixed fields except with the very general rule of thumb or stereotypic judgment.

Most farmers have, as well, fields where only corn, manioc or potatoes are planted. Thus, for these three subsistence crops, farmers will upon request also give estimates of time required to plant so many pounds of maize or so many manioc stems, the number of days required to weed each field, and when fertilizers and insecticides are used, the labor required to apply them. Those farmers who must fence their fields can also calculate labor time required to erect fences. There are, however, many minor and major activities which are excluded from their computation of labor requirements in subsistence farming. The most serious lapse is the exclusion of estimates required to harvest the crop.[7] As the estimates for single crop subsistence fields are derived from experiences in their own fields, they vary greatly from informant ot informant. Time required for planting corn varied from fifty days to twelve days per unit of land; for weeding, from ten to twenty-five days. Variations in soil condition and terrain account for the disparity. Farmers are quite aware that the single answers or the range of answers do represent experiences rather than true averages: it depends with the field, they say.

Calculations of labor time input rest also on yield estimates,[8] which are hard to arrive at when the field is used as a storage bin and the crop is only harvested when it is needed for the stew pot. Farmers could tell me the number of cobs likely to grow on a corn stem, but each cob yields a different weight in grain. The same is true for potatoes or manioc. Cash crops, on the other hand, are harvested at once and sold by weight. Furthermore, even small differences in yield are of great importance to the farmer, hence, effort is made to retain sufficient information to arrive at a range of expected yield and expected returns.

Conclusion

Labor input calculations gained from farmers may either be stereotypic judgments, or experienced requirements for a stereotypic farm, or experienced requirements in their own farms. The first type of estimate is more likely to be their answers to questions about subsistence farming; the last two estimates are more likely to be their answers for fields planted with cash crops. There is often great divergence between the answers, hence, they are not quantitatively comparable.[9] Each one represents a different reality. The stereotypic judgment is an evaluation of past experiences and expectations; it is a judgment about a crop, local farms, or an economic strategy to be used as a general guideline, or as a justification for farming decisions. It is not meant to reveal comparable labor accounting. The labor required for each crop in a stereotypic farm comes closer to what Marx may have meant by "socially necessary" labor, but only when farmers are able to estimate average labor inputs or at least believe their estimates to be average ones. These labor estimates can be and are used for comparable labor accounting. Furthermore, because they represent standard measures, they are used to argue about their collective economic position *vis-à-vis* other classes or population sectors. Labour estimates experienced in their own farms are taken to reflect the farmer's own economic position, his own reality, his own efficiency or the farm's efficiency. When such information has been mentally collated, it is the one used in decision making; as we shall see, average labor requirements for their own farms are not always kept in mind, in which case farmers have to rely on more general rules of thumb. The important point to remember is that we cannot use one type of estimate and argue about a different reality. The only time when the various types of estimates can be brought together is when analyzing farmers' decisions, and then if, and only if, the farmers themselves compare stereotypic judgments about labor required in subsistence with more detailed average estimates for other crops.

Average estimates are abstractions from real experience. To arrive at such estimates, the number of days worked at a given task must be noted and remembered. The precise nature of what is recalled depends on how it is structured in memory (see Ortiz 1979 for a description of retention and processing of information). Some of the details perceived are merged with other data in an initial systematizing process: time spent taking in and putting out the beans to dry merge with the time spent in other concurrent domestic activities. Some categories are, at times, subsumed under more encompassing categories: when the days worked as wage laborers are numerous, the amount of time thus spent is expressed in terms of months; twenty days may become a month. Data are often fitted into qualitative rather than quantitative categories and retained in that form: the time to harvest a given weight of roots or grain is expressed as the amount of time spent when the harvest is "good" and "barely good enough". As the process of categorization and systemization proceeds, the information becomes fuzzier and more difficult to use for precise estimations; one is consequently more likely to get an accurate and quantitative answer about labor input in sugar cane production just after the fact, rather than months later when the experiences of sugar processing from first and second cuttings are subsumed under one generalized estimate. How precise is the information retained depends on how important it is to retain it; in other words, it depends on the concerns of the farmer at the time of observation. For this reason, labor estimates for cash crops, or for activities where wage labor is used, are likely to be expressed in more precise, quantitative terms than labor estimates for subsistence crops. For example, estimates for labor required in maintaining and harvesting coffee are given in number of days, whereas the same farmer, if he plants beans only for subsistence, will simply explain that it takes much more work to grow beans than to produce manioc.

Quantitative estimates of labor inputs are more likely to be accurate when the labor itself is a commodity used to produce a cash crop. Marx's warning, as to the limited applicability of his equation of labor with value, is of greater significance than may appear at first.

Morishima's extension of conditions seems relevant. The power of Marx's suggestion rests on the assumption that there must be some consciousness of the labor value of the commodity. Only when labor requirements are met to some extent with wage labor, or at least when the product is a commodity regularly sold in the market, is such awareness likely to be expressed in a form which can be used to comparatively evaluate commodities. It is for this reason that Cook was more successful than Godelier. The labor value of subsistence goods or of goods occasionally bartered is likely to be remembered as a vague qualitative statement which may be used, at most, to rank goods or to compare roughly whether something is twice the value of another; it cannot be used for finer comparisons or to assign value.

Inaccuracies of labor estimates lead to an over- or under-evaluation of labor requirements of commodities. In peasant economies where many of the activities are excluded from final accounting, the error would be to under-evaluate one's own effort in production. A "just" retribution for his labor is not "just" to the *metate* maker or to the coffee grower. A commodity embodies labor, but the labor it embodies is not the labor described by the peasant as the socially necessary labor, just as the price of the commodity does not represent the labor embodied in it. By assuming that the two are identical, we are colluding with the peasant in obscuring the extent of his exploitation, an exploitation for which he himself is initially responsible. It is only later, when labor becomes a generalized commodity, that producers are more likely to become aware of the extent to which they are exploited and, in turn, will exploit their own dependents. It is easy to fall into the same trap that Marx pointed out to us: the use of illusory categories which falsely reveal one's material activities.

Notes

1. The applicability of labor theory, as well as conditional requirements, is discussed in the next section of this paper. See also Morishima (1973) for a discussion of conditions to the applicability of labor theory to capitalist systems (pp. 36–39).
2. Meek (1975: xi) argues that *Capital* could in fact be viewed as a book about alienation.
3. Firth examined exchanged equivalences and noticed that for the Tikopia value in exchange there is no relation to amount of work entailed in production. He suggested that among other things, it relates to the scarcity of means of production, to durability, and to the social significance of the object manufactured. The Tikopians in practice never relate a canoe to a bonito hook in terms of the labor required by each (Firth 1965: 332–344).
4. Paez are peasant Indians who live in a *resguardo* in the southern highlands of Colombia. They form a small nucleus of 200–300 families, represented by their own political authority and exploiting a depleted ecological niche in competition with neighboring Colombian peasants. They grow all of their subsistence crops and produce coffee, potatoes, wheat, or beans for the national market. For a detailed description of their farming activities, see Ortiz (1973).
5. Firth had already alerted us to this characteristic.
6. This is exactly my criticism of Godelier. Gudeman (1978b: 132–37) acknowledges similar difficulties for sugar-cane estimates.
7. Most subsistence crops are not harvested at once. Manioc and arracacha keep better if covered by soil, hence, they are stored in the field. Corn is used before it is fully mature; the remainder is allowed to dry on the stalks. Only what is left is harvested at once, when dry. Plantains and bananas do not mature at once. Only small patches of potatoes and beans are likely to be harvested when ready.
8. Godelier fails to tell us how yields of salt-bearing ashes vary with climatic oscillations or with subsequent cuttings. The average socially required labor should be based upon labor inputs over a number of years.
9. Gudeman (1978b: 76–90) makes a distinction between the "socially expected" and the "actual" labor estimates. The first represents the traditional standards of expectations that peasants have about their basic subsistence work. The actual labor estimates were derived from a questionnaire and I assume (as Gudeman himself does not make it clear) that they represent the farmer's recollection of experienced labor inputs in their farms. Both sets of figures are useful. The problem arises only when he combines both sets of figures to estimate socially expected costs

and determine conversion ratios, value created per labor day, profit and surplus. If Gudeman is interested in determining who receives which goods and in what proportion, as he states on page 3 of his book, then he must rely on objective labor input requirements. On the other hand, if he is interested in elucidating *what* determines the distribution between the subsistence level and surplus, he must examine as well (but independently) the socially necessary labor required and the actual labor required as conceptualized by the peasants.

References

Cook, Scott. 1970. Price and output variability in a peasant-artisan stone-working industry in Oaxaca, Mexico: an analytical essay in economic anthropology. *American Anthropologist* 72, 776–801.

—— 1976. Value, price and simple commodity production: Zapotec stoneworkers. *The Journal of Peasant Studies* 3, 395–428.

Firth, Raymond. 1965. *Primitive Polynesian economy.* London: Routledge and Kegan Paul.

Godelier, Maurice. 1971. Salt currency and the circulation of commodities among the Baruya of New Guinea. In *Studies in economic anthropology*, G. Dalton (ed.). Anthropological Studies No. 7. Washington, D.C.: American Anthropological Association.

—— 1972. *Rationality and irrationality in economics.* New York: Monthly Review Press.

—— 1977. *Perspectives in Marxist anthropology.* Cambridge: Cambridge University Press.

Gudeman, Stephen. 1978a. Anthropological economics: the question of distribution. In *Annual review of anthropology*, B. Siegel (ed.). Palo Alto: Annual Review Press.

—— 1978b. *The demise of a rural economy.* London: Routledge and Kegan Paul.

Marx, Karl. 1921. *Capital*, Vol. 50. Chicago: Charles Kerr & Company.

Marx, Karl and Friedrich Engels. 1939. *The German Ideology.* New York: International Publishers.

—— 1975. Economic and philosophical manuscripts. In *Collected works*, Marx and Engels (eds.), Vol. 3. New York: International Publishers.

Meek, R.L. 1956. *Studies in the labour theory of value.* London: Lawrence and Wishart.

—— 1975. *Studies in the labor theory of value*, 2nd edn. New York: Monthly Review Press.

Morishima, Michio. 1973. *Marx's economics: a dual theory of value and growth.* Cambridge: Cambridge University Press.

Morishima, Michio and Catephores, G. 1975. Is there an "historical transformation problem?" *The Economic Journal* 85, 309–328.

Ortiz, Sutti. 1973. *Uncertainties in peasant farming.* London School of Economics Monographs in Social Anthropology, 46. London: Athlone Press.

Ortiz, Sutti. 1979. Expectations and forecasts in the face of uncertainties. *Man* 14, 64–80.

Rowlands, M.J. 1978. *Specialization, exchange and the consumption of wealth on the Bamenda Plateau, West Cameroon.* Unpublished paper presented to the Annual Conference of the ASA, Cambridge, April 1978.

Salisbury, R.F. 1962. *From stone to steel.* Melbourne: Melbourne University Press.

MAPPING MEANS

STEPHEN GUDEMAN

Managing Information

With any productive technique are associated certain information
requirements. Shifting agriculture is no exception to this rule. In
this form of production the worker constantly changes the siting of
his effort expenditures; indeed, failure to do so results in diminished
agricultural yields. But in order that he may move continuously,
the laborer must have information, about work sites. The incessant
movement of the worker in shifting agriculture poses a need to have
and store information about the land.[1]

Managing, having a way to organize such information, may be
accomplished by use of a map, or at least this was the case for a
group of shifting cultivators in central Panama. Actually, these
swidden agriculturalists held several shared maps of the land they
worked, but their home-made maps were rather different from the
more formal varieties.

Within Western society commonly encountered maps are those
of roadways and political divisions, although physical representations
of the earth's surface are constructed for other purposes as well:
geological, demographic, even to locate the spread of diseases. By
contrast to these formal uses, geographers have begun to develop
new kinds of maps, such as how a populace defines its neighbor-
hoods and landmarks, or what value it places on different locations
(Downs and Stea 1973, 1977; Gould and White 1974). Certainly,
these mental representations are well removed from classic
Mercator projections, yet they too are not equivalent to cultural
maps. The parameters of such "mental maps" are set in advance
by the investigator and the map is then constructed by eliciting
responses from a population; the methodology has its basis in
social psychology. A home-made map, by contrast, has neither
written form nor visual semblance, and it has been evolved
and is used by a people (Bohannan 1960).

Formal or folk, written or not, a map generally consists of a set of

terms or signifiers which refer to space. These units have an arrangement or pattern; such is the map's structure. The fact that a home-
made map has a structure bears testimony to the classifying capacity
of a people, but this is not in itself the map's meaning. The existence
of a cultural map poses the dual task of understanding its structure
and the meaning of its form.[2]

Access to a cultural expression, such as a map, is sometimes best
gained in a time of transition, for then the old and the new become
luminous by juxtaposition. When a map changes over time, when
the structure of communication about locales is transformed, an
unusual opportunity is afforded for gaining an understanding of
mapping principles. Such was the case with the Panamanian
shifting cultivators. In the space of thirty years their work maps
underwent two transitions. The traditional plan, or Map I, originated
in the distant past and lasted through the late 1960s. Map II began
to come into existence sometime in the late 1940s and endured
until the 1970s. Map III, encountered in the mid-1970s, followed
upon a radical change induced by the government. Each of the
maps was used to provide spatial directions to work sites but
under differing conditions of production.[3]

For these shifting cultivators map form was closely tied to work
process. But the puzzle to be here untangled can be stated more
precisely. Shifting agriculture is possessed of the unusual feature
that the principal means of work, the land, serves also as the locale
of work. The materials on which the laborer performs his activity
constitute the siting of that activity. Therefore, information con-
veyed about work sites is information transmitted about the
principal work means. An information guide to the one will serve
as guide to the other. What impact, then, has this correspondence,
of means of work and site of work upon the pattern of the
information system? Or, to pose the same question differently, in
what manner is the form of that structure, a people's map,
determined by land use and possession? The unusual characteristics
and requirements of shifting agriculture first invite and then
oblige us to relate the form of a people's land map to its socio-
economic underpinnings.

Map I — A Natural Image

The first map obtained in an economy which had endured for
several hundred years and was still in existence in the 1960s.
Encountered throughout Panama and particularly in the Province
of Veraguas, this economy was founded upon autonomous domestic
units. In the village of Los Boquerones, as elsewhere, the household

was occupied usually by a nuclear family and constituted the unit of production and consumption (Gudeman 1976, 1978). Traditionally, only sporadic material exchanges prevailed between households, but each unit always sold some of its produced objects to outsiders in order to obtain commodities such as clothing and salt.

The productive system was based upon shifting agriculture, although some animals were also held. Among the many crops raised, the principals were rice and maize. The productive pattern exhibited variation, but the usual practice was to farm a plot for two years in succession and then allow it to regenerate for eight to ten years. The machete and the digging stick were the primary tools used, while the seed stock was accumulated from year to year. A key technological practice was the use of fire, for combustion helped greatly to clear the land of the downed forest and released some of the accumulated nutrients to the soil. To obtain sufficient product, each household utilized $1-1\frac{1}{2}$ hectares of land; but even if a household harbored sufficient labor to work such an area, it often secured the services of outside persons during the course of the year. The motivation for obtaining such aid varied from the desire for conviviality to the need for rapidly harvesting a ripened crop. The work itself was repaid by labor, in kind or by cash.

These practices set the broad requirements for the system of information concerning work sites. Aside from the general need to communicate where one intended to work, directions to sites often had to be given to laborers who were from without the household. But not only did the work site of a household change every several years, in any single year a group usually worked more than one plot. A man would farm several pieces of land simultaneously, for by selecting plots with varying characteristics he would have some insurance against the uncertainties of the environment. These farming practices meant that there had to exist an information system about work sites which was highly shared, was capable of directing people to rather small plots of land, and "allowed" for human mobility or impermanence in the use of the land.

The home-made map used in the village, and most of the rural area, consisted of designation by natural features. In the people's terms these were names of "workplaces".[4] The land surface, including house locales, was divided conceptually into irregular patches, almost all of which bore the names of unchanging, non-man-made, natural features. All areas were included, there were no empty spaces, and each was of equivalent importance, whether house or work site. The map had no valuation component within itself. As one person stated, "All the places have names, names are equal in this respect".

The various designated, real, sites had no physical boundaries; by mental image also the topography was continuous, and one patch shaded into another. The name of each land piece was taken — or was said to have been taken — from a natural feature found in the area. One region, for example, was termed "Dark Shrub", after a large shrub found in the general domain. "Vantage Point" referred to a locality surrounding a hill where a vision of the entire community could be had. Not all areas bore the name of a natural feature — Antonina was one exception — but the majority did, as illustrated in Appendix One.

The community extends for 2800 hectares, and with approximately 26 topographic names, including that of the village itself, each region designated on average more than one hundred hectares. The meaning of the mean, however, is here deceptive, for residential areas as well as some of the less usable land were not finely differentiated. A named work locale might cover only 60 hectares (about 775 meters square) and this was an area within which sight and sound could be used to pinpoint a worksite. Orientation was provided by combining the label for an area with a cardinal direction; one man might say to another, "I am working to the north of Deep Spring". Work sites were designated in terms of their proximity to the direction from or within a geographic feature or space.

This mapping system was not confined to the village, for it is still found throughout the rural area, nor was it entirely unrecognized by the state; indeed, nearly all the names of the land areas are also the names of villages and larger settlement groupings in Panama. The same stock of names is used for communities as for land plots within communities. In the 1960 census, for example, of the 8595 listed community names, six are Green tree, while 28 are some variant of tree (*Censos Nacionales de 1960*).

Because a linkage exists between land names and settlement names, an indication of the range and types of names used for the land, beyond those recorded for a single community, can be gained by examining the various censuses.[5] Some years ago Angel Rubio (1950: 106–8) used the 1940 census to classify village names. The total recorded population of 622,000 persons lived in 4687 recognized settlements. Of these settlement names, 2430 were used two or more times. Focusing upon the repeated names, which he saw as "a reflection of the rural mentality", Rubio sorted them into the categories displayed in Table 1. Based on the actual names in the categories and not the descriptive category labels, it may be concluded that at least 86% of the repeated names are one or another "natural" term. Although these names are the repeated ones only, and they are from human settlements, not the land itself, they do provide an indication of the natural character of the geographic names. In fact, my own experience suggests that the land names are even more consistently natural than the names of settlements, where historical factors have often impinged upon the naming process.

TABLE I

Categories of settlement names

Names related to topographical relief*	638
Names related to vegetation*	580
Names related to hydrography and coasts*	475
Names related to religion and other beliefs	244
Names related to fauna, cattle and fish*	174
Names related to the nature of the land*	137
Names related to routes and transport	38
Names related to agriculture*	38
Names related to travel or colors*	36
Names related to living areas and domestic utensils	28
Names related to aspects of government or domination	20
Names related to mining*	15
Names related to climate*	7
	2430

*Designates a "natural" category.

These observations speak to the extent but not the basis of the naming system. Within the community the land names were a natural terminology not only because they referred to natural features but also because they possessed no social history and were deemed to have always existed. No one knew when the labels originated nor who conferred them upon areas. The names were there, it was said, when the village founders arrived. Given to society apart from individual volition, the system's sources were — for the people — outside culture.

Must it be argued, then, that this map system was offered up by nature in respect of being an immediate product of human sensation? Of course, there exists no necessary relation between a sound pattern and its concept; they have no intrinsic connection. The concepts themselves, however, appear to be non-arbitrary in that they refer to and were taken from real world features. Did perceptual features from the land serve as the differentiating characteristics of the map because they "preceded" the concepts?

Have we encountered an instance in which "pure sensation" alone can be seen as evoking or giving rise to the socially shared category? Before the anthropological perspective is abandoned, the ethnographic facts require a closer appraisal. Actually, a few of the labels were non-natural, and many had no real topographic referent in the village, no direct graphic correlate in the landscape. At certain points only did the meanings of the labels coincide with the visible features of the land patches, as if the map were a canvas tacked down here and there by a stake or two. The singular point of importance was that difference – within sameness – be signaled, and this was recognized by the peasants themselves. As one individual explained,

> People put on the names to distinguish them, to call your attention, so you know where to go to work. Like a dog needs a name; if you say "dog", any dog may come.

The special feature of the map, then, was not that particular labels and regions "coincided" in meaning but that the terms were drawn from one general domain or category, that of "natural" names. Thus, if it was not the phenomenal world which "forced" the individual labels to be selected, what was the impulse behind selection of the encompassing category?

The source of this mapping system was, I maintain, the way in which the work means were used and possessed. Throughout Veraguas Province, land was held in various ways, but predominantly it was owned by absentee landlords (Figueroa Navarro 1978). Most used their land to raise cattle and to maintain an almost symbiotic relation with the local farming populace. In the area of Los Boquerones the land originally was owned by a general of the army who helped lead a revolution against Colombia in the 19th century. His descendants, who inherited the land, used it for grazing their herd but also permitted peasants to live on and to farm it. Upon securing permission, the peasants would cut down a forest area for use in the agricultural cycle. Following the burning of the land, the people would construct wooden fences about the plots to keep out the wandering cattle. After the normal two years of use, the fences would be demolished so that the cattle might forage in the cleared area while the shrub and brush grew back. Thus, one benefit the landowners received was pasture clearance and maintenance. In addition, for the right of usufruct the peasants paid either $1.00 or a day of labor per year, regardless of field size or land quality. But this use right was itself limited. The peasants were never allowed to seed a crop that was a perennial,

nor could they construct permanent houses — all were of the stick
and thatch variety. The landowners explicitly prohibited the populace
from holding or retaining a permanent investment in the land,
whether in the form of crops, land improvement or housing. "In
the old times one was owner only of what he planted or worked. In
those times only Fábregas were owners." The local population
operated under stringent constraints concerning the use of the
work means.

This ultimate appropriation and control of the work means had a
direct impact on the technology which the peasants were able to
deploy. In agriculture, labor, tools, seed and soil are used as the
means for obtaining a harvest, itself an enlarged quantity of the
seed. But the proportions by which the several inputs are combined
can vary enormously. In rural Panama the constraints imposed by
outside control of the land meant that labor as roundabout work
was of little use. There existed, on the one hand, no reason for the
peasants to impact their own labor in the land, to work to improve
or preserve the fertility of a plot for future use. The use of delayed
labor as equipment, on the other hand, was not possible due to
reasons of access, cost, and the fact that such equipment is usually
operated on the premise of amortizing an initial use over time.
Consequently, for the peasants, the land alone, the land as unimproved resource, had to constitute a high proportion of the inputs,
as compared to other farming systems. The terms of the social
control dictated that technologically the land had to be the central
means, and this in turn meant that shifting agriculture had to be
practised, for an unimproved resource rapidly degenerates. The
form of production, the technological system, was an externality,
a condition the peasants had to accept if they wanted to live and
work in the area.

The production process of the peasants was, therefore,
decisively shaped by the external context. In moving from this
context to the local community, however, we encounter an inversion.
Outside possession of the land meant that access to it and how it
might be used were determined by forces impervious to peasant
influence. Nonetheless this external control made the land a free
good within the community. Through the first half of this century
the forest was in plentiful supply, and little competition actually
existed for the use of particular pieces. More important, among the
peasants access to the forest was always unrestricted in that no one
had superior claims; all persons were equal at the onset of the year,
with no one holding past rights to work sites. Village rights were
secured on a yearly basis by erecting crosses about the area one

wished to work. It was as if there were a communal reallocation of rights to resources every year. In consequence, there existed the moral assertion that a peson should be allowed to work wherever there was available forest. This local land ideology, or theory of allocative equity, was the logical outcome of the externally imposed conditions, but it also contradicted these same facts. The everyday life of the peasants presented to them the unreconciled experiences that the means were freely accessible yet outside their ultimate control.

This encounter with the work means had its repercussions upon the local axioms about production, the theory about the factors or forces making for a successful conversion of inputs to outputs. In actual fact the limiting factor on production was a household's labor supply and output desires, and indeed the importance of labor was always recognized. The work process was understood to add value. Never was it held, however, that work created something beyond its brute powers, or that humans have a special capacity to coax from the means more than they, the humans, consume in the process of doing so. By contrast, the forest and the land were imputed, at least unconsciously, to have powers which could be drawn upon in production. Land needed to be "rested", and good land was said to have "strength" or "force", it would "give" a good crop. Particular areas "lent" themselves for certain crops. Such expressions do not mean that the peasants lacked a technological sense of the possible; to the contrary, all the expressions were used in the context of evaluating and assessing the land and forest for particular farming uses. There was a technological truth in the fact that a farmed area had to "return to nature" to get new force if it was to be used again. Still, the expressions indicated a conception in which the land was seen to be almost animate, an agent rather than an object in production. Conceptually, then, labor was seen to be "passive" in that it transported and added but did not create new value; by contrast, the land was thought to possess some extra powers.

This production theory was laid atop the social relations. It was their own labor which the peasants commanded while the land was outside their social control. In their theory, however, the land not only came to represent, it became endowed with a "thought of" potency, while labor, being limpid to their view, remained a passive agent. Theory inverted social experience.

Given this context we may decisively reject any suggestion that the map was only another example of the science of the concrete, a cognitively patterned organization of perception. Rather, the map was a determined ideological system which brought the concrete into the service of the social. In the perspective of the actual social order of the countryside, the map was a denial or masking of reality. Of course, the peasants were aware and could articulate that outsiders owned the land, that their own economy was formed on the edge of a greater one, but treating the final reality as if it were nature was a way of shutting out this awareness from everyday life. Behind the facade of the "naturally given" the map concealed that outsiders had real control of the means. At the same time, the natural map suggested that within the community itself the land was freely available. The means were "possessed" in nature, outside society. The map expressed that the land was "of a piece" and not bounded by a local social grid; it was the land, being impermeable to human history, to human intervention, to human control, which remained forever constant whilst people moved. But the map also represented the social comprehension that the land was a special force. It was the uncontrolled, the power outside social command, that formed the sensate materials of which the map was composed. The map was constituted of the concrete precisely because the concrete had a significance; and this significance was determined by the social locale of the command over the productive means.

Map II — Private Labor, Private Property

Beginning in the 1940s several changes combined to make the usable land more scarce and into an improved means. These transitions, in turn, had a critical impact on the work process and mapping system.

This period witnessed, first, a shift in the control of the means. Throughout the decade the landowners allowed their herd to decline in size, and eventually in the early 1950s they took the first steps toward selling the land to another cattle grazier. To this proposed action the peasants objected violently and after intense squabbling the government, through its land reform agency, purchased the land in 1963. The intention was to apportion the land in some fashion to the users. Even so, the future of the area remained uncertain, and the people were unsure about what rights, if any, they would hold to the land they worked.

In this same interval the population density of the area increased, due both to a slackening in infant mortality and a predominance of in-migration over out-migration. In addition, as the cattle were removed, the forage grasses began to dominate, and the bush which previously had grown back rather rapidly now began to be regenerated more slowly. Both absolutely and per household, usable forest land was decreasing.

Finally, in the late 1950s — primarily as a consequence of improved roads — two sugar cane mills began to introduce the growing of sugar cane as a cash crop. Cane had always been raised, but only in small amounts for home consumption. Sugar cane is a perennial, which, as raised in Panama, produces a profitable harvest for some five years. But a sugar cane field never ceases to produce a little (unless ploughed), the cane wears out the soil, and where it is planted only slowly does the forest grow back.

In parallel to these ecological transitions, during the late 1940s the people began to construct wire fences in the fields. Barbed wire, because of its ease in use, had already begun to replace wooden fences, but in the 1940s the fences changed in purpose and became permanent. They were erected not to keep cattle from damaging crops but to stake visible claims, claims to forest land, and later to sugar cane. Each man began to have "his" own piece or pieces of land in subsistence crops, forest and sugar cane. No longer did an individual jump each year from one strip of land to another. Thus, by the late 1960s nearly all the land was fenced, and the economy was roughly "balanced" between subsistence farming and cash-cropping.

Under these conditions a new method of mapping the land arose among the people. The land was conceived as being divided into parcels, each of which was demarcated precisely by physical boundaries. Personal names were used to designate the fenced pieces of land, and a plot, regardless of size, was known by the first name of the person who had fenced and claimed it. The map enshrined land claims. But it also was used for providing spatial directions. To have effective communication, however, everyone had to possess a greater quantity of social information than formerly, for the map terms emanated from society. In the first system a person had to possess information about the topography, but in the second he had to have information about the people of the community, about plots and about the interrelation of the two. Thus, in cases of lack of information the second map might be supplemented by use of the first which was still in existence: "I shall meet you on Juan's land." "Where?" "Near Green Tree."

In terms of its historical constancy, the second map differed markedly from the first. Land areas in Map II were linked to specific individuals but rights to plots could be, and were, sold; and plots themselves were split and joined in fresh ways. As these property rights shifted, the land map was transformed in that its boundaries and labels had to be changed. Unlike the first map, this was a truly historical map, a map encompassing change, a social map linked to living people.

How are we to understand the causes for the change from the one map to the other? Which factors in the work process determined that there would be a transition in the mode of presenting spatial information? Map II was based on a system of private property, but what was the essence of this private property? Was it private land or private labor, the work means or the work, which the map was encoding?

The rationale for the shift in maps actually had two facets. In the first place, the availability of the non-produced resources, the land and forest, had changed dramatically. The land remained nearly costless, but it no longer was "free", for it ceased to possess an extensive margin. This was one cause for the local enclosure movement; as the people said, putting up a fence gave them a right to the land. Scarcity of the work means was an impetus for the change in spatial representation. The people were attempting to appropriate the land's powers for personal or exclusive use.

There was, in addition, a second source of the map change, one intensely individualistic and rather close to Locke's notions about property. The land or means began to "contain" personal work. People claimed the right to use a plot of land not only because they had fenced it but also because they had worked it — "the work that I have done", as one said. There existed the idea that labor improved the land or added something to it. Thus, when in this interval plots were sold, the people asserted that they sold not the real land itself, but the right to use it plus the right to the work performed on or the value of the improvements made to it, such as the "cut" of the forest, the fencing, and land preparation. This conception had the flavor of Locke:

> Whatsoever then he removes out of the state that nature hath provided, and left it in, he hath mixed his labour with, and joined to it something that is his own, and thereby makes it his property. (Locke 1963: 354.)

This second form of claim was not based on the idea of raising future productivity through labor; it was rather that an individual had "mixed" his work with the means. He had advanced the means along the stages of production and therefore created property.

Both these impulses for the change in the treatment and mapping of the land were linked by the idea of scarcity. The land's powers were becoming scarce relative to the desires of the occupying group, and it became an arena of competitive claims. The labor of an an individual is always scarce in that it represents an allocation of a limited lifetime, an allocation of the existential self to the means.

In spite of these transitions, this era did not witness a full-scale change in the axioms of production. The land was still conceived to have powers, and though labor was valuable, it was still not thought to create new value. That the peasants' conception of the value of work did not change may have been closely linked to the new market relations in which they were engaging. The people conceived themselves to be selling a commodity, sugar cane, to the mills. Actually, the cane was raised on (what was for them) costless land and was totally financed — from seed to fertilizer to weeding and the harvest — by the mills. The mills also controlled the supply price of the seed and the selling price of the produced cane. In one or another form they had command over the productive means. Peasant proprietors did no more than add their labor in the agricultural process. In theory the people were petty producers selling a commodity on the market; effectively, they had become wage laborers, although compared to industrial workers they had a degree of independence. The peasants had become rather like piece-rate workers; as laborers the only time controls they faced were to provide the mill with cut cane on a certain date. Of crucial importance, however, this real change to wage laboring passed unrecognized by the people. They expressed dissatisfaction with the mills but continued to conceive that they were independent and to throw attention on the inanimate means of work; after all, to become a wage laborer *qua* petty producer, a man first had to have permanent access to work land.

Map II, then, reflected the critical importance of the land as means in the productive process. Signalling exclusive control of the means by individuals as against others, the map was based upon permanent rights to work on objects as well as rights to the work already in objects.

Map III — Product Distribution

Following the 1968 elections in Panama, a revolution occurred and a new government assumed power. Led by a general who had been born in the rural area, this government took a fresh interest in the countryside. As part of its development programme in Veraguas Province, it prevailed upon the peasants who lived within one 10,000 hectare area, a region including the village of Los Boquerones, to raise only sugar cane. By 1973, the government had constructed a modern sugar cane mill to service the area, and in this year the mill began grinding cane.

Planned as a people's cooperative, the mill actually has been administered by government appointees. Its power has been immense and the changes it has instituted have been far-reaching. At the outset it acquired the terrain of Los Boquerones from the land reform agency. The mill recorded approximately how many encircled hectares each person held and shortly after it converted the entire area to the growing of sugar cane. All the old fences were torn asunder, new roads were cut through the region, a few hills were levelled, and the raising of subsistence crops was prohibited. Now, almost all the men work directly for the mill — some in the fields, some on heavy equipment, some in the factory — and receive cash wages. Each "land holder" also collects a fee for the area of land ($70.00 per hectare) he has under sugar cane cultivation. Eventually some of the return flowing to the usufruct holders will be used to pay for the land so that it may be passed completely to them. The people, in sum, have been converted from being subsistence farmers and cash croppers to being a rural proletariat and rentiers.

Physically, the land is now divided into large rectangular blocks of densely growing sugar cane. The unplanted spaces between the blocks are used for access, for irrigation and as firebreaks. The new land plan has a technical rationale. With respect to any parcel, therefore, several people may hold proportionate rights, while any one individual may have rights in more than one block. Individual owners, however, have no control over their land. The mill organizes the entire enterprise and transports workers to the fields, where they work block by block. Work areas and ownership areas do not coincide, and only by happenstance would a person actually work on his land. In fact, because an owner receives a set fee for land use, the real output from his means is of no concern to him.

In this new context the older mapping systems have little use. Most of the physical landmarks have been obliterated, and the new ones, such as roads and land parcels, physically resemble one another. More pointedly, there is little need to give directions outside the settlement area, which itself has been concentrated at the urging of the mill. The older mapping systems are still recalled and used, rather vaguely, at times amongst the villagers; but with the new mill and new techniques, most of the land is being worked by hired laborers who come from distant areas, and they have neither the background information nor the need to understand and use the older maps. Moreover, each land parcel bears a plaque with a number, and thus in the infrequent conversation concerning land — among villagers or between villagers and outsider — it is the number which is used to designate a work site: "Today, the mill is working parcel 62." When a personal name now is used it usually refers to a house and house site alone.

This third system offers, of course, some marked contrasts to the two prior ones. As in Map II, this map refers to bounded and enduring physical areas. But spatial difference is here signaled by numerical variation, and neither the blocks nor the numbers correspond to the parcels and names of the second system.

Like the first map, the third map also has an immunity to social history, although it may change with advances in the technology of production. This historical cauterization owes itself to the fact that the map by itself conveys no information about social possession of the work means. The people retain proportionate shares in a physical parcel, but the map encodes only the parcels of land. To derive the social information a second transformation of parcels to personal shares must be made, and this information is stored separately by the mill.

Actually, the epoch in which Map III is encountered sees the completion of changes begun earlier. Prior to the advent of the government mill, the peasants were selling a commodity, although their own production contribution was limited to the offering of labor. After the institution of the government mill, the peasants become unambiguous wage workers; to receive their pay, they have to provide a certain amount of labor per day as measured by a set (and long) time interval.

In this final context, also, it seems an illusion for the peasants to maintain that they are landowners who receive a "rent" for the use of their land. Individual land quality makes no difference to the size of the return and, more important, no one can specify which is his piece. Land ownership has disappeared, having been swallowed up by the mill and converted into a fractional share of the assets of the enterprise. The peasants have neither right of use nor control over "their" land, anymore than a shareholder of a corporation may appropriate a piece of equipment from "his" company. What the peasant proprietors receive is not a rent but a set share of the sugar mill profits, rather like a "preferred dividend" paid for each stock share. Unlike most owners, however, the peasants have obtained their capital shares on "margin". With the generated returns they may hope to pay off their accounts due.

As laborers and possessors the peasants have lost command over the means and their work efforts, being separated from them by a layer of government administrators. Not inappropriately, therefore, does Map III use impersonal integers — themselves imposed by the mill — to signal spatial location. The map has a technical origin, reflecting only an organization of the means for óptimal production, nature reformed for human purposes. The map represents land unrelated to the people who use and "possess" it. On the other hand, the land is the entity through which proportional claims to the output are registered. When the land parcels encoded in Map III are transformed to personal shares, the map does detail the distribution of the final product. For the villagers, although the map no longer signals access to the means, it does suggest and register their access to the ends.

Classification and Meaning

These three maps actually constitute a remarkable example of social transition, for they represent change that is not piece-meal but from one structure to another. Change did not entail a partial or simple substitution of terms — Juan for Green Tree, Parcel 62 for Juan — rather, one entire system of commensurate terms, one total way of formulating the work environment, replaced another. And this was a 'change that was recognized but not consciously formulated by the people involved.

Given that the terms within each system were and are commensurate in order to signal difference, what differences were they in fact signaling? At the broadest level, the maps represented the way in which a society comprehended nature. But this was a nature that was put to use, and for each map the terms signaled how the means of work and the work itself were socially organized. The first map, based upon natural signals, was an expression of the fact that the peasant worked upon but had only a transitory relation to the means which yielded his livelihood; the second map, encoded on jural persons, reflected a permanent relation between "natural" means and worker, where the worker also exercised some command and right of disposition over these means; the third, utilizing numerical terms to signal technologically formed divisions, reflects an impersonal and impermanent relation between workers, possessors and the objects used.

The first transition from natural to social coding was brought about by a change in the command over the means of production which in turn had an effect upon their form of use. The second, from names to numerals, was motivated primarily by a technological shift in the use of the means, from small-scale farming to large-scale cropping, although again this transition was dependent upon prior control of the means. Changing control of the work means and their deployment lay behind the two map shifts.

Most familiar to us is Map II, for it bears the illusion of all personal property, that there is an immanent relation between an individual and an object, whether the object is a means or an end of production. The temporal succession of the maps, however, underlines that such a property image is only a derivative relation, a secondary result brought about by the association, on the one hand, of a series of different work sites and, on the other, of a set of human laborers. The designation, Juan's land – this objectification of the person – occurred only when the person and the site were each differentially distinguished within, respectively, a system of persons and a system of sites. There exists, then, a similarity between Map II, the personal property map, and what has been termed the totemic illusion.

Lévi-Strauss (1962) has argued that totemism represents only one instance of a more general tendency to classify, being a precipitate of, or a deduction sometimes drawn from, two systems of categories which have been placed in an analogical relation. Given the comparison (clan) A : (animal) X :: (clan) B : (animal) Y, it is sometimes inferred that clan A thinks itself to be animal X, while clan B thinks itself to be animal Y. But this is usually an illusion of the observer or, at most, a real but secondary formation. The primary connection remains between the two overall levels of classification. For this reason totemism as substantialism is not a valid analytical concept. Nonetheless, the idea was in vogue some time ago, and in considering why the notion took such a grip on the mentality of an earlier generation, why it became "seen" or "visible" when in fact the data did not suggest it, Lévi-Strauss likened it to hysteria and suggested that the totemism concept was an intellectual mechanism used by Westerners to differentiate the others from us and to reassert the Western contrast between natural and cultural objects. Seeing totemism in the ethnographic material not only made "them" different but of lower capacity.

Of all possible forms, however, why was totemism used to draw this barrier? Why did totemism, as an explanation, appeal to the Westerner? Given the prior analysis I suggest that the concept of totemism was motivated by our own private property image. As a transference of person-thing relations from the economic to the mythic and ritual domain, totemism was a reflection of our own practical experience. The theory of totemism may have represented an attempt to assert a difference between the savage and the modern, to invent his strangeness; but it was also a method that coped with real strangeness by assimilation to the understood. To comprehend, to tame, and to differentiate we invented what was in the savage, seeing in him a hidden and transformed — from the practical to the mythic — version of ourselves. The irony is that to make him different we made him like us; then, we reproved in him that which was from us. All the while we refused to learn from him something about the oddity of a conception which would treat as natural and as having an immanent basis the pairing off of individual humans and discrete things.

But this makes my point rather obliquely; let me try it more directly. One aspect of the structuralist assertion is that the world really exists, out there, but it becomes understandable only when a classification is thrown across it. This grid is a kind of "mediation" between the "raw stuff" and the human actor. Meaning itself emerges only in the context of classification, of discontinuities. I have here argued that a home-made map of the land is one such classification; when such a mental representation changes it does so as a totality, for it is not the terms but the pattern itself which is undergoing transition. But this is not the end of my argument. To suggest that the map classifications were only the result of a material attraction to objects of use in the environment — the rumblings of the stomach — is, of course, insufficient as explanation. But the maps represented more than a people's desire for a cognitive order of the concrete. After all, the mind — like the body — can be satisfied in diverse ways. What is it that determines which set of discontinuities will be selected? Here is where a purely structuralist argument sometimes falters. The maps as classification forms were produced, I hold, not simply in response to urgings of "the human mind" but more immediately to the social relationships delineating the allocation and use of the means for human work. Directing the organizing capacity was a socio-economic pattern. The meaning of the maps derives from the mapping of the means onto social bonds. This, if one wishes, provides a socio-economic foundation to a structuralist view of the maps.

Appendix 1

LAND NAMES

"Natural" Referents	"Supernatural" Referents	"Social" Referents
El Alto Laia – Large Flat Stone*	*El Duende* – Goblin	*Antonina* – Diminutive of. personal name
Los Cagajones – Dungheap		*Ciriaca* – Personal name
Cerca de Piedra – Stone Fence		*Juarez* – Family name
Cerro de Carmen – Carmen's Hill		
Cerro de Guavita – Guavita Hill		
Cienegon – Marsh, Bog		
Coiba – Name of island in Pacific Ocean, south of Province		
La Coloma – (The cemetery) Heaped up, Overflowing		
La Cucha – Lagoon		
Charco El Tronco – Log pond		
Guayabal – Grove of Guava Trees		
Mataprieta – Dark Shrub		
Mirador – Vantage Point		
Palo Verde – Green Tree		
Picorales – Place of Sharp, Pungent Taste or Things		
Pinto – Spotted		
La Playa Prieta – Dark Beach		
Pozohondo – Deep Pool		
Pozolindo – Pretty Pool		
La Sementera – Sown Land		
Sitio Campo – Campo (name) Site**		

*"This word, of Galicia – Portuguese origin, is frequent in Panamanian vocabulary and is not uncommon in toponymy" (Robe 1960: 22).

**This was the name of a house and farm site, taken from the person who "first" worked the area. The individual and family no longer exist in the area, and the name is here used in a de-personalized manner.

Notes

1. I am most grateful to Antonio Barros de Castro and Roxane Gudeman for helpful commentaries. This paper was written while in residence at the institute for Advanced Study, Princeton.
2. Two cartographers have recently defined a map as a graphic representation of the milieu. It is "a space in which marks that have been assigned meanings are placed in positions relative to one another in such a way that not only the marks, but also the positions and the spatial relationships among the elements, have meanings" (Robinson and Petchenik 1976: 16). As these authors point out, research into the combined area of mapping — cognition — meaning has only begun.
3. The work maps were not the only representations the people deployed; others concerned the location of saints' shrines and political centers. The ones evincing change, however, were employed only in the context of agriculture.
4. The term used was *"trabajadero"* which is an interesting neologism made up of the word "work" (*trabajo*) and the suffix "place of" (*-adero*).
5. The 1960 census provides a summary or alphabetical list of all settlement names, unfortunately the comparable 1970 census (*Censos Nacionales de 1970*) does not.

References

Bohannan, P. 1960. Africa's Land. *The Centennial review* IV (4), 439—49.
Censos Nactionales de 1960, vol. I. *Lugares Poblados de La Republica*. Panamá: Dirección de Estadistíca y Censo.
Censos Nacionales de 1970, vol. I. *Lugares Poblados de la Republica*. Panamá: Dirección de Estadistíca y Censo.
Downs, R.M. and Stea, D. 1973. *Image and environment*. Chicago: Aldine.
———— 1977. *Maps in minds*. New York: Harper and Row.
Figueroa Navarro, A. 1978. *Dominio y Sociedad en el Panamá Colobiano (1821—1903)*. Panamá: Impresora Panamá.
Gould, P. and White, R. 1974. *Mental maps*. Harmondsworth: Penguin.
Gudeman, S. 1976. *Relationships, residence and the individual*. London: Routledge and Kegan Paul.
———— 1978. *The demise of a rural economy*. London: Routledge and Kegan Paul.
Lévi-Strauss, C. 1962. *Totemism* (trans. by R. Needham). Boston: Beacon Press.
Locke, J. 1963. *The works of John Locke*, vol. V. (Reprint of 1823 edition.) Germany: Scientia Verlag Aalen.
Robe, S. 1960. *The Spanish of rural Panama*. Berkeley: University of California Press.
Robinson, A. and Petchenik, B. 1976. *The nature of maps*. Chicago: University of Chicago Press.
Rubio, A. 1950. *La vivienda rural Panameña*. Panamá: Banco de Urbanización y Rehabilitación.

THE WHALSAY CROFT:

Traditional Work and Customary Identity in Modern Times

ANTHONY P. COHEN

Crossings of net and ploughshare, Fishbone and crust. (George Mackay Brown)

Introduction

Whatever else it may accomplish, it seems reasonable to assume that the publication of this volume will further undermine the axiomatic restriction of the concept 'work' to economic activity. The *analytic* division of society into discrete institutional and function areas has been pretty thoroughly discredited (e.g. on 'economy', Sahlins 1965), and the conventional *empirical* boundaries of 'economy' have been blurred by, for example, the debate about the 'economic' status of domestic labour. By extension then, we have already recognized that 'work' is not merely synonymous with 'economic activity' nor with the production of subsistence. Rather than pursue definition here I report an ethnographic case which suggests the need for a good deal of elasticity in our concept of work which would allow it to go further beyond the realms of economy, occupation and sub-sistence to accommodate also symbolic social processes through which ethos and identity are maintained. Presumably, most work has some symbolic significance. My argument here is that the work I describe means more now as symbolism than as 'economic' activity informed by a cost-benefit calculus; and that such 'work' might be seen as a model for the culture in which it inheres.

Based- on data from the Shetland island of Whalsay, my case deals with the local activity of crofting whose economic character and significance has changed to a point at which it seems clear that its description as primarily economic process would be highly partial. I will argue that although it still wears the guise of economic or subsistence enterprise it would now be more fully understood as symbolic labour. The case meets Firth's suggestion that the anthropological study of symbolism should focus on behaviour in which there is

a gap between the overt, superficial statement of action and its underlying meaning. On the surface, a person is saying or doing something
which our observations or inferences tell us should not be simply
taken at face value — it stands for something else, of greater significance
to him. (1973: 26.)

My argument in this paper will be that crofting has been transformed by changes in other aspects of the island's economy from
work which had a primarily economic rationale to work which has a
primarily symbolic rationale — the maintenance of a valued
collective identity. I contend that from the analyst's point of
view it does not cease to be 'work' merely because it has ceased to
be economic. The imputation of symbolic significance to crofting
is underpinned by the rather special use in Whalsay of the word
"work" which has emerged as a discriminative term as an apparent
consequence of this economic change, and which now generally
refers to specialized paid employment.

The tendency to specialized occupation is a relatively recent
phenomenon, and has become established only during the last
twenty years. Whalsay households customarily pursued multiple
economic activities which could not have been adequately described
by the gross category 'work'. The accuracy of their designation is
an important matter, for the plurality of skills and of forms of
adaptation was and remains an explicit value. The component
activities of the household economy were therefore designated in
specific terms and, indeed, each gross activity — fishing, crofting,
cutting peats — would itself have been broken down into myriad
elements each of which would again be designated specifically. The
ideological values of such skilled versatility and self-sufficiency
are still expressed in calling somebody "a hard worker", but this is
an evaluation of a person's character and is not restricted to any
particular activity, nor to judgements about a person's material
achievements: it expresses proximity to a symbolic ideal rather than
an actual record of effort. Further, a person might refer to his
use of any materials in any task as "working with" them. But it is
usually only his job — that is, activity which is unambiguously
economic — which would be called simply "his work". This
semantic descrimination echoes Parkin's discussion of the use of
the word *kazi* (work) among Giriama fishermen (this volume).

My task here, then, is to account for the symbolic significance of
croft work in Whalsay, and to suggest that the viability of a comparative concept of work requires that it should include labour

whose primary rationale is symbolic. The argument is prompted by the fact that, although crofting now has an increasingly marginal significance for the Whalsay economy and, indeed, may actually involve financially unrequited costs in time and money to the active crofter, it does not survive merely as a traditionalistic relic, but as a central element in everyday ideology. I present crofting as the symbolic medium through which Whalsay men locate themselves in their cultural tradition; and as work which, in directing them to the central values of their culture, provides them with a 'cultural model' in the sense which Geertz's analyses expound so powerfully (e.g. 1975: *passim*, but esp. 412–453). Finally, I speculate on the implications of this case for an anthropology of work.

The Context

Whalsay is an island community of approximately eleven hundred people lying 2 miles off the north-east coast of Mainland, the largest island in the Shetland archipelago. After the cession of Shetland to the Scottish crown by Denmark in 1472, the entire island of Whalsay gradually came into the ownership of one of the lines of the clan Bruce, another of which owned land in various parts of Shetland. It remained in the possession of Bruce lairds until 1903 when the nearly bankrupt Estate was broken up into crofts, some of which were sold and some let to local residents. Prior to this, Whalsay land has been divided among tenanted crofts, a tenanted farm and the Estate farm. Successive reforms in crofting legislation have reinforced the udal legal tradition of pre-Scottish Shetland, and guarantee the right of continued tenancy to a working incumbent of a croft. More recent legislation (e.g. 1976) has been intended partly to encourage tenants to purchase their own crofts. There are presently in Whalsay one hundred and thirty crofts though a somewhat smaller number of crofting units since households may own or work conjointly more than one croft. Whilst a croft is usually registered in the name of one owner or tenant, it may in fact be worked by two or more householeds related cognatically or affinally to the legal incumbent.

It follows that most Whalsay households (total in 1973–74, approx. 495) participate to some degree in croft work and have access to croft produce, but only a minority of households actually own or rent crofts. A model might be as follows: A father with N children is titular incumbent of a croft. If the first child to marry does not thereby gain affinal access to a croft, the father may give him a piece of the croft land to be "de-crofted" and used as a house site. In due course, this child will become titular

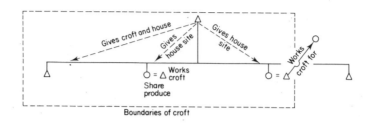

Boundaries of croft

Case 1. Eldest son, unmarried, who lives with his parents, inherits croft and house. His two sisters are given house sites. His eldest sister's husband does most of the croft work and this household shares in the produce. His younger sister's husband does relatively little of the croft work and works his own mother's croft, but also shares some produce.

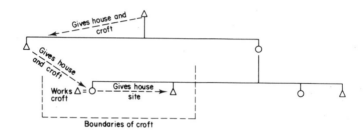

Boundaries of croft

Case 2. Crofter bequeathes croft to his son who has already bought his own croft and house. He, in turn, passes his inherited croft to his sister's eldest daughter on her marriage. Some years later, a further portion of the land is de-crofted to provide a house site for the new incumbent's eldest brother.

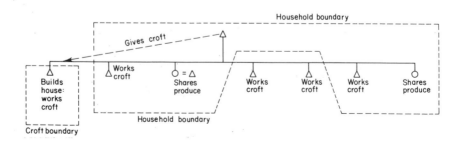

Case 3. Father gives crofting unit (two crofts) to eldest son, who requires a house site. This son works the croft with four brothers, though produce is shared by the entire family.

incumbent of the croft, although his siblings (and their spouses) may also share in the labour and produce and, indeed, may also eventually get house sites, particularly if they also do not gain access to a croft through marriage. Three exemplary cases are reported opposite.

The produce referred to here in all cases is mutton, lamb, wool and potatoes. Most decrofted house sites will contain sufficient land to provide each household with its other staple vegetables. House sites also carry entitlement to peat banks. In case 1, the crofter and his eldest sister's husband cut their own adjacent banks, but help each other to cure and bring home the peat. In case 2, no peat is cut. In case 3, the brothers all cut the same banks and divide the peat among the entire family according to the needs of each household.

Although only a minority of adults own or rent crofts, most are associated in some way with a croft, whether as resident, co-worker or recipient of its produce. The economic significance of this association is virtually impossible to quantify. Official policy on crofting has always stipulated that the croft should only supplement income which the crofter would receive from other means of employment; crofting was not to be a full-time occupation (see Collier 1953; Hunter 1976; Mewett 1977). Nevertheless, the contribution of crofting to the household economy of the pre-War Whalsay family would have been considerable, for it would have been the central element in the multiple economic activity of the household. It provided dairy produce, poultry, pork and staple vegetables. It provided access to the peat bank, a source of free fuel. It provided a stable basis for subsistence against the unpredictable summer herring fishery. It provided a focal point for the establishment of the households of married children or siblings and, thereby, the pool of labour which was necessary for households and their extensions, the crofting township, to pursue their plural economic adaptation. Thus, a father might have come home from some years at sea to croft and participate in the summer herring fishery. Of his sons, one might work with one or two cows, and help out on other people's crofts; another might be a year-round fisherman; another might work away for some time either at sea or as a labourer, possibly remitting some cash to the family; a fourth might be primarily responsible for the arable crop, the few sheep, and go to the herring in the summer. The mother and daughters would be responsible for manufacturing butter and *blaand* (buttermilk) and for the poultry, would bait lines for the fisherman son, and help with cultivation. One or more daughters might go away 'into service' for some time. After the men had cut the peat, the women would cure it. All might help with *rooing* (plucking) the sheep, and women would spin the fleeces into yarn. Father and sons would make *rivlins* (cowhide moccasins) and dungarees, and the women would knit the universal sweaters and socks, and sew underclothing. It was a system built upon the possibility of sharing labour whilst allocating primary responsibility for the diverse tasks among several people. The crofting township was thus able to sustain a considerable degree of self-sufficiency. But the economic centrality of crofting in Whalsay diminished after the Second War, and especially during the last twenty years as economic activity and labour became increasingly specialized.

The Decreasing Economic Significance of the Croft

Before the Second War the modernization of the Whalsay fishing fleet had been very slight. The most important fishery remained drift-netting for herring during the summer season. The winter fisher (for white fish) was still based mainly on small boats, long-lines and baited hand lines, and the seine net had made little impact on the community. But after the war, a number of the recently de-mobilized men bought larger second-hand vessels from the Scots coast, and thus gave their unique knowledge of the prolific Shetland waters a practical technological base. These were multi-purpose vessels which could be used throughout the year, rigged for drift-netting in the summer and for seine-netting in the winter and spring. They had larger and more reliable engines than the earlier "haddock boats" and could be taken both to fishing grounds further offshore and to the Scottish north-east coast markets at which prices were higher than those available in Lerwick. As a result, full-time fishing became a financially practicable enterprise and, moreover, one which could generate a much larger cash income than the croft could produce.

During the 1950s, the general economic circumstances of Shetland were bleak. Out-migration continued at a steady rate, and unemployment was high. But in Whalsay men were learning to fish with the new technologies and, indeed, were fishing successfully. Often, the younger men would get some experience on mainland trawlers, and would then return home with expertise and cash to invest in their own vessels. The late 1950s saw the first custom-built vessels delivered to Whalsay owners, and the general spread of radio, radar and echo-sounders through the fleet, making the fishery far more efficient. During the 1960s, increasing numbers of men took their 'skipper tickets', qualifying them for command of larger boats and, from then on, boats over 70 feet became the norm rather than the exception. At the same time, electronic navigation devices were installed, again opening up the possibility of new grounds further off-shore. Landing prices for fish rose substantially. Large numbers of Whalsay men began ordering new boats. Thirteen of the twenty first-class boats now fishing out of Whalsay were built since 1969. Eleven of these were custom-built for their Whalsay crews. The commercial fleet in Whalsay now (1979) comprises:

a) Six purse-seiners. These vessels fish for herring and mackerel, and can also trawl for white fish and fishmeal species. The two latest vessels in this category were designed to fish at the 200 fathom line for blue whiting and cost, respectively, £1.3m and £1.8m.[2]

b) Fifteen seiner-trawlers, which can fish with either seine-net or trawl for white fish and fishmeal species and which, in a recent innovation (1978) can also fish with the purse-seiners for the lucrative herring and mackerel.

c) Two shell-fish and lobster boats, which can also tow light trawls and long-lines. These boats have recently halved in number, partly because of the closure of rich scallop grounds which lie in the tanker channels to the oil terminal at Sullom Voe.

The fleet engages an annual average of 150 men (which may rise to 160 during the summer), nearly all of whom are co-owners in their vessels. It presently has a minimum capital value in boats and gear in excess of £8m. Ownership is entirely within the hands of the Whalsaymen who crew the boats: there are no 'shore-owners'. Further, Whalsay has a new fish-freezing and filleting plant, in which forty fishermen are minority shareholders, which employs an annual minimum of thirty full-time men and women workers. There are also three men engaged full-time in the manufacture and repair of fishing nets. In sum, the vast majority of the community's capital resources and some 70% of its able-bodied male population of working age is engaged full time in the fishing industry. What is left for crofting?

The transition to full-time, year round fishing activity meant that the practice of crofting agriculture had to undergo fundamental change. It was no longer possible for the fisherman-crofter to commit himself to daily activity on the croft. It thereby became virtually impossible for cows to be kept. Now only did the *kye* involve daily attendance for milking, but also required substantial areas of the croft to be cultivated for feed. Whilst this might have been un-economic, given the cost of freight on fertiliser and seed, it was the 'dis-economy' of time and labour which has brought the tending of *kye* to an end within the last twenty years.[3]

Indeed, the burden of freight charges has really precluded the

intensive working of croft land. It is only during the last twenty-five
years or so that households have ceased to be self-sufficient in
vegetables and animal feed. Arable cultivation would now only be
a viable proposition with the cooperative bulk purchasing of
fertiliser and seed. Even if a marketable surplus could be produced,
the costs of exporting produce would be very substantial. During
the last eighteen months, forty of the more active crofters have
formed an association for the cooperative purchase of veterinary
supplies, pesticides and herbicides, and for the construction
and administration of permanent pens for the annual sheep sale.
But it seems doubtful that it will make the further developments
into the purchase of machinery, chemical fertiliser, seed and stock
which would be required to put crofting on a financially profitable
basis. The financial objective of the Whalsay crofter is to break
even — but to do so and to work the croft successfully, he has to
inject into the croft cash which he has earned from his other
employment (cf. Ennew 1977).

In this era of specialization, intensive crofting has also suffered
from the decreased birthrate. There is no longer the labour available
to maintain the traditionally plural economic activities of the household. The men are at the fishing, the unmarried women are in paid
jobs, and the married women do not engage so actively in the daily
labour of the croft as they once did. They may help with hay-
making, sowing and weeding and with the poultry, but their
collaboration in the heavy labour of cultivation, livestock husbandry
and general maintenance would seem now to be a thing of the past.
Moreover, in order to service the heavy loans which they have taken
out for boats and gear, the fishermen have to spend ever longer at
sea. For example, one new seiner-trawler, delivered in 1975, spent six
and a half days weekly at sea during its first working year. Before
quota restrictions became general for all commercial fish species
in 1977–78, none of the boats fished for less than five days
weekly. Further, the purse-seiner crews would be away for three or
four weeks at a time during the winter herring fishery in the Minch,
and now at the Cornwall mackerel fishery. As a consequence the
time available for crofting was very limited. Presently, many boats
make a practice of leaving one man ashore each week but this
means, in effect, that a man has no more than one week in eight to
attend to all the crofting labour, as well as to the maintenance of
his house, the latter being a continuous chore in the severe
Shetland climate. A crofter-fisherman might come ashore on Friday
evening or Saturday mid-day and have to plunge almost immediately
into his croft work before going to sea again on Sunday evening. At

best he might have a week in which to look to his sheep and, depending on the time of year, cut peat and hay, plough and sow his vegetable plot, maintain his fences and ditches, slaughter and prepare the winter mutton, paint and repair his house, and so on. Even with the two or three breaks which the boats take each year for refit and repair, Xmas and the summer Regatta, the pressure of work on a fisherman who wishes to croft conscientiously is formidable.

The calendar of croft and related work runs approximately as follows. Spring (*voar*) in Shetland does not really begin until April, when there is sufficient sunlight to allow growth. In April the vegetable plots (*rigs*) are ploughed and sewn with potatoes and other root crops, brassicas and salad vegetables and, possibly, "corn" (Shetland oats). Sowing and planting goes on throughout the latter half of April and into May. In May, the banks are usually sufficiently dry for peat cutting to begin in earnest. This is also lambing time in Whalsay, and flocks have to be checked at least twice daily for ewes who may be having difficulty in labour; and for lambs who may have fallen into drainage ditches or who may have suffered from marauding crows and gulls. The long June days, when there is little darkness at all, are ideal for intensive outside labour. Thus, men will be at work erecting new fences, building, painting, cutting peats. Also there are the routine jobs to do: lambs to be tended, crops to be weeded, peat to be cured. In July, hay making gets under way. This can be a frustrating, tedious and long drawn out job in Shetland, because of the poor weather and lack of mechanization. Nowadays, most Whalsay crofters will hire a man and his tractor to cut the hay, or will use a multi-purpose cultivator, though some still cut by scythe. But it has then to be cured by manual spreading and turning. The frequency of rain or even of sea fret means that a nearly dry crop can be drenched in minutes, and then the whole process has to be restarted. At this time too peat is still being cured, bagged and transported home, all of which activity is very time-consuming. In August, the last of the hay is cured and stacked (*biggèd*), peat brought home and stacked, corn cut and dried, and the shearing gets under way. As the pure bred Shetland sheep have diminished in number, the plucking of wool (*rooing*) has virtually died out, and hand shears are now used.[4] Shearing also requires all the hill sheep to be called in — again, a time-consuming job involving the cooperation of various members of a common grazings. The fleeces have then to be rolled, bagged and shipped to the mainland mills where they will be exchanged for half their weight in spun yarn. There are also the fences and dips of the three common grazings to be maintained. In September, the crops have to be lifted and stored. The sheep will be called in to select some for the annual sale, held in the middle of the month, and some to be slaughtered and frozen for home consumption. In the late autumn, sheep will be dipped, and cultivated fields may be ploughed, if they are not already too wet, in order to take advantage of the winter frosts. In early winter a ram is put to the ewes. Throughout the winter, the sheep have to be fed on hay and various supplements daily and a vigilant watch kept on the flock for disease and accident.

These constant demands actually constitute the *least* intensive agriculture which has been practised in Whalsay, and must some-how be fitted in to the little time left over from the full-time occupation.

One final contextual feature should be mentioned. Because of the economic, domestic and occupational circumstances described above, the nature of crofting agriculture in Whalsay has changed considerably. The croft is now used primarily to support sheep Depending on breed and quality, these will be sold either as store-lambs (cross-bred Cheviots and Suffolks) or kept primarily for wool (Shetland). Most crofters slaughter several lambs each year to deep-freeze for their own winter use, and would also kill one or two ewes for *reested mutton*, a traditional cured meat which is a great favourite on Xmas and New Year sprees and as a staple during the winter.

Crofting land is itself divided in ways which have direct implications for strategic sheep husbandry. The *inbye* land, that is land within the croft boundaries, is used to graze the bigger breeds, like the Cheviots and Suffolks. The Crofter's Commission offers grants for the improve-ment of this grazing through re-seeding, drainage and so on. Crofters may also apply to the Commission for an "apportionment" of the common land, which they will then reclaim through drainage, re-seeding and other improvement, for quality grazing. But all crofters also have rights to the *scattald*, or common grazing. This is spread over the peaty and heather-clad *hill*. It is, therefore, poor quality grazing and is really most suitable for the support of the small and hardy Shetland or Shetland-crossed sheep. There are now relatively few pure-bred Shetland sheep left on the island. They are too small to be useful for mutton; the poor wool price — a consequence of Shetland's exclusion from the Wool Marketing Board — and small yield means that their fleeces also are not economic products. The main financial value of hill sheep to a crofter is the government subsidy of £3.70 per head,[5] though this is now under threat from the EEC. A good many Whalsay crofters graze other breeds on the hill with rather poor results. With the exception of a handful of men, they are not skilled shepherds. One or two men are called upon constantly for help at lambing time and for the diagnosis of illness. Only four or five are really skilled with hand shears.

The Whalsay croft, therefore, is now used for an agriculture in which local skills are somewhat scarce and in which many crofters do not feel the confidence born of sure competence.

The Mystery of Crofting

The foregoing account might then be summarized as follows. The real economic income generated by the croft is increasingly marginal. The labour supply has diminished; the productive capacity of the croft has diminished. The croft is a burden on a man's cash income and, as he spends longer at sea, it is also a severe imposition on his time. Traditional crofting agriculture is no longer viable, and crofters are now forced to engage in a type of crofting adaptation — sheep husbandry — in which few are skilled, and which produces hardly any cash benefit at all. And yet, there is a constant demand for crofts and an enduring, even vibrant interest in crofting and crofting performance. How might we account for this?

A Crofting Culture

Shetlanders from other islands are often surprised to learn that crofting is so widespread in Whalsay, because the island is known in Shetland for its fishery. Indeed, it is portrayed as a community of untypical affluence, and is crudely caricatured as the island whose road gets clogged on Sundays when every family exercises its two cars.[6] The caricature predates the oil-related developments and is a bitter comment on the emergence of a successful fishery in Whalsay, with consequent full employment on the island, which would seem to have originated in areas of Shetland which were far more dependent on crofting. By comparison with those of mainland Shetland, Whalsay crofts are rather small. Yet crofting remains a central and crucial feature of Whalsay life and there is a sense in which Whalsay's might be described as 'crofting culture'. Documents dating back to the early 17th century show that there has been a remarkable stability in domiciliary locality on Whalsay: families are still resident in the areas of the isle in which their ancestors lived three hundred years ago. It is clear that this stability is largely explained by the croft. "Home", then, is not merely where one lives or was born, but is lineage territory and, as such, is a fundamental referent of identity.[7]

For all their customary association with the sea (see Cohen 1978a: 458) Whalsaymen are also significantly identified by each other with their shore 'place' — their crofts. This is reflected in one of the principal forms of nicknaming which associates a person with the croft of his birth, his father's birth or his past residence. It is apparent also in the nature of the crofting township as a kinship locality and in the incidence during the recent past of "neighbours" combining with groups of agnates and/or affines to form fishing crews. Neither boats nor crews are such stable referents of a Whalsayman's social identity: he may change both, and many men do so. But croft or place seems to be *permanently* associated with a person in the minds of others, even though he may actually move his domicile to another part of the island (see Cohen 1978a: 464—5).

The croft is then a focus for the residential organization of kinship. As such a locality, it may also provide the basis for other forms of association such as friendship (neighbouring) and co-membership of fishing crew. It is also a stable referent in the communally-allocated identity of the Whalsayman.

Two other features of Whalsay life may serve to amplify my description of it as a 'crofting culture'. Social life on the island is characterized by intensive visiting, especially during the winter. Visiting relationships are usually bounded by kinship and neighbourhood, but often extend also to previous neighbours who have moved to other parts of the island, and to present or past crewmates or their spouses. Although all of these basic forms of a association may have their logical origins in shared locality, they may now actually be dispersed through the isle — though invariably with particular spatial concentrations of kin around its core crofting township. But although "neighbourhood" may therefore be spatially amorphous, it remains one of the two bases of fundamental social association (the other being kinship with which it frequently coincides) within the community. The very intangibility of the modern 'neighbourhood' perhaps requires that it be expressed in some more concrete way than through the structure of mutual support and obligation which comprises the ideology of neighbouring. Hence "neighbours" — even though they may no longer live close to each other — will tend also to *spree* together, that is, to go out together on the peripatetic parties which cross the isle on the great social occasions like Xmas and New Year, Regatta and weddings (see Cohen 1978b: 15—16). They also indulge to a considerable extent in exchanging gifts of produce. Most fishermen regularly bring fish ashore at the end of the week for non-fishing households within their "neighbourhoods", and these households will reciprocate at some point with produce to which they have access. But these transactions cannot be wholly explained in terms of either material value nor the discharge of obligations. Frequently, the exchange is materially redundant because the receiving party himself produces a surplus of the same product. Frequently also it may be akin to "comparing notes" on the relative success of crops grown on different crofts, or of experimenting with seed potatoes grown on the other's croft. But it is also the case that such gifts often do not have these utilitarian rationales — and often, also, that the utilitarian rationalisation may be retrospective rather than motive for the gift. Gifts of potatoes or of mutton to people who already have both are surely to be regarded as *gifts* rather than as material transactions, even if they are informed by an ideology of reciprocation (cf. Firth 1973: 376).

Of course, this kind of phenomenon is well-known elsewhere. But its significance for our present purposes is that it requires the produce of a croft. Such informal gift exchange never involves the transaction of consumer goods apart, perhaps, from wool, which is reserved to formal gift-giving as at Xmas, birthdays and weddings. Neither does it involve the gifting of money, except from adult to child, which is reserved to a more formal transfer of property or to loans or gifts towards cash deposits on new fishing vessels. Thus, the croft might be regarded as providing a currency for social interaction rather than for economic exchange.

The traditional[8] organization of life and work in Whalsay was characterized, as we have seen, by a plurality of sources of subsistence, a multiplicity of subsistence tasks and an extraordinary versatility of skills. Although the exigencies of modern economics and technology have led to an increasing specialization of labour, this is masked to a substantial extent by the retention of the traditional scenario in Whalsay ideology. The skipper of the massively capitalized and sophisticated purser-trawler, who brings home earnings of £15,000 or £20,000 in a year, will also be seen hauling his peats in his ancient and rackety tractor, turning his acre of hay with wooden handrake, *caa'in* his few hill sheep for dipping, or painting and repairing his house. He may also be seen walking the stormy shore looking out for drift or wreck-wood or carrying home some coarse salt to cure a bucket of herring for the winter. He will be seen in his small motor boat on the Sound fishing for a few haddock or *piltocks* (young saithe) with his hand-line, or ferrying some sheep to summer grazing on a holm. This versatility speaks of a real egalitarianism. But it also indicates the importance of self-sufficiency, of manifold competence, in the ideal of the Whalsayman. Of course, there are very few people who are highly skilled in all of these activities. But there are many who would attempt all of them. To be known as *handless* — having to rely on the manual skills of other people — is to be viewed with some contempt. To be known as failing to exploit all of the available resources is to be seen possibly as lazy or feckless as "uninterested" or merely to have deserted the cherished ideal.

Crofting is one of the facets of the versatility which Whalsaymen value. As such, it is not an *alternative* adaptation or occupation. It is, rather, a fundamental dimension of 'being a Whalsayman'. . Those few people who are not themselves crofters and who lack any association with or access to a croft might equally be thought of as lacking structural connections to the community as such. Despite its very different economic circumstances, Fox's *Tory Island* offers an instructive parallel:

> To be without land is a disaster. Without at least a cow's grass, one has no stake in the island, no place in the social scheme of things . . . (1978: 85.)

Crofting as a Symbolic Medium

My contention is, then, that crofting has retained its salience and appeal in modern economic and technological circumstances largely because it is *not* regarded as merely economic activity. Rather, it is part of what one does in "being a Whalsayman", in pursuing the ideological charter which is implicit in Whalsay identity. Indeed, it could well be that the very depth and pace of change in Whalsay during the last few years has itself *increased* the salience of crofting in this respect. Modern economic activity cannot be located within the customary orthodoxies which enshroud the performance of routine manual tasks. The enormity of modern financial commitments cannot be encompassed within customary scales. The geographical insularity and cultural integrity of Whalsay as a community have been breached and threatened by the imperialism of television and the convenience of the new inter-island ferry service. In the face of such a massive disruption of the established order it is hardly surprising that people seek some symbolic means of stabilizing their identity — that is, of associating themselves with the cherished heritage of the symbolic past and precedent. Crofting provides just such a syncretic celebration of received tradition. It is a way both of masking the cultural distance which has been travelled, and of reinforcing commitment to the ideals of the community. This latter is important since the more integrated with the metropolitan political economy the community becomes, the more inconvenient and costly becomes its peripherality.

I would suggest that this largely explains the incongruity of the contemporary economic circumstances of Whalsay with the present clamour for crofts. It is not, of course, the total explanation. When fishermen talk of wanting crofts so that they have something to retire to, or because "it's fine to be able to walk over your own land", they voice genuine sentiments. But in the light of the circumstances which make it an uneconomic activity, such sentiments still beg the question of "why crofting?". Crofting provides an ideal symbolic medium since nearly all Whalsay people do have access of some kind to a croft. Moreover, it is activity whose past is still available, both physically and through lore. Croft boundaries have remained fairly stable over the years and old boundary divisions, such as turf walls, are still to be seen. The *crubs* (circular stone enclosures within which seedling plants were grown) of traditional cultivation are still dotted all over the island, though few of them are still in use. There still remain old croft houses, many now considerably enlarged and renovated. Parts of crofts are still known by their associations of generations ago — "Annie's toon", "Eppie's yard", "the whaley midden dyke". Thus, the 'cultural map' (to borrow Gudeman's term, this volume) or the crofting community has not changed, as houses, crofts, parts of crofts, rocks, dykes, hills, inlets, holms and skerries are still designated by names whose origins lie far back in the mists of time. There is, thereby, a tangible sense that the same paths have been trodden, the same ditches cleared, the same boundaries maintained for generations past. Moreover, the croft evokes the natural calendar, which itself sustains the customarily plural adaptation of the Whalsay household, and thereby masks the transition to modern techno-time with its specialization of work and castration of skilled versatility. It also recalls a lost commonality, when time could be taken to collaborate in tasks or, at least, to discuss them and much else over the *ferthingmaet* (working snack) in a way which allowed orthodoxies to emerge and thus constitute the distinctive practices of the community. The croft is the repository of that valued tradition in which resides the idea of community.

Crofting and Work

I would suggest that it is instructive to note that in Whalsay the tasks of crofting are not referred to generically as "work", as a job would be. In this respect, work *qua* economic activity is conceptually distinguished from crofting as a characteristic activity of "being a Whalsayman". This may be purely fortuitous for the ethnographer's present argument, but its occurrence in the very different crofting culture of Lewis (Mewett: personal communication) seems to indicate that it is not mere coincidence.

Crofting activities are almost always designated in particular terms. Thus, a man would not say, "I'm going to the croft to work today", but "I'm going to turn the hay", "dip the sheep", "*dell* (dig) da tatties", and so forth. "Work" is not merely economic activity; it is also a word which fails to discriminate among different activities, and it is the very plurality of activities and the richness of their diversity which are such important values in Whalsay ideology. Hence, "work" is used in Whalsay less to refer to particular activities than to the application a person brings to them. To be "a hard worker" — accolade, indeed — is not merely to work hard at one's job, but to apply oneself diligently to everything. By extrapolation we may conclude that for the Whalsayman "work" does not designate a discrete set of processes and structures (i.e. the 'economic', as opposed to everything else) in life. It is so conceptualized that it cannot be distinguished in this way, and this is congruent with the more general perception of the community as an holism in which everything bears upon everything else. It is, in fact, an ethnographic model for Wadel's heuristic concept of work (1977) which depicts all relationships and values as requiring 'maintenance labour'. The ideology of Whalsay, its valued distinctiveness and self-conscious collective identity, requires such deliberate maintenance work, and crofting is to be seen as an integral part of that work effort. That it is not referred to by Whalsaymen as "work" is entirely consistent with the view that its functions and significance are symbolic rather than merely economic. This is not to suggest anything so simple-minded as the proposition that the man who breaks his back in his *toon* from morning until night aspires to symbolic virtuosity. He wants to produce a bountiful vegetable crop and fat lambs. But in doing so, he is conscious always of his cultural context, of the orthodoxies of practice which it imposes, and of a certain anomaly between his labour and the prevailing economic circumstances.

The case validates Wadel's contention (this volume) that, by the very nature of the term, the anthropologist must go beyond the emic category — though taking full account of it; and, more important, must recognize as *work* the processes through which cultural and ideological values are achieved and maintained. The Whalsay crofter grows his own potatoes, not merely because it is cheaper to do so but because that is the proper thing for a Whalsay man to do. Indeed, even the ways in which particular varieties of potato are evaluated is provided for by local idiom to the extent that the introduction of some new criterion in the course of a conversation would be recounted widely with wry smirks and much weary head-shaking. The ways in which the crops are cultivated, the sheep shorn, the grass cut and cured, the ditches maintained, the peats cast and stacked are all viewed and judged not as matters of economic performance but for their conformity to established factional practices to which aesthetic values are attributed by their followers. I will risk exaggerating my case to say that in modern Whalsay, the economic significance of croft produce is treated almost as if it was incidental. Croft work is one of the ways in which a Whalsayman makes himself recognizable both to himself and to others *as* a Whalsayman and as belonging to a particular structural nexus in Whalsay. It is in this regard that I follow Geertz's usage and talk of 'work as a cultural model'.

There would seem to be two general and rather obvious implications of this argument. The first is that a social anthropology of work faces the problem of dealing with a concept of activity which we may expect to vary widely from one culture to another. The word 'work' does not carry intrinsically unambiguous referents and boundaries of meaning, any more than does 'kinship', 'politics' or 'religion'. This is not to make the gratuitous point that 'work' as an emic concept is culture-bound. It is, rather, to suggest that an anthropology of work must be catholic in the definition of its subject matter and that it must not treat work axiomatically as a discrete aspect of social life whether in functional, processual or structural terms.

The second implication is, therefore, that as an *analytic* term, 'work' must accommodate topics broader than those of the production of economic life, occupation and so forth. It must also embrace labour whose primary rationale lies in symbolic terms, such as the propitiatory rites which Murray (this volume) calls 'the work of custom'. It must include performance which is not measurable in economic terms at all. I do not wish to argue that these things should be regarded *only* as work. My case is, rather, that work accomplishes more than economic ends; and, secondly, that like crofting in Whalsay, these processes would be misunderstood if their explanation was to be couched solely within their own particular terms. They are to be seen as expressions — though not as definitive and reductionist statements — of the cultures in which they inhere and which they thereby illuminate.

Notes

1. This paper is based on research conducted under SSRC grant HR 2987. I

gratefully acknowledge the helpful comments of participants in the A.S.A. Conference, and those of Isobel Emmett and Patrick Hanrahan who kindly read an earlier draft.
2. At the time of writing, two of these six crews have placed orders for new vessels, one of them — at 140 feet — to be the largest by far in the entire Shetland fleet.
3. Cows are now kept by only four crofters, all of whom work ashore fulltime, two as dairymen, one in heavy construction and one as postmaster.
4. In 1977 and 1978 demonstrations were given with electric shears, but few if any men seem likely to adopt these in the near future.
5. This figure includes the additional "islands supplement".
6. This caricature is even bought by visiting social scientists, who should know better (see e.g. Mageean 1979: 160).
7. In his recent discussion of ethnicity, Epstein also comments on the association between collective identity and the continued occupation of a piece of land (1978: 122).
8. I use this term not to denote any particular historical period, but to refer to the apocryphal and customary past which Whalsay folk refer to simply as "the aald days".

References

Brown, George Mackay. 1974. Black Furrow, Grey Furrow. In *Fishermen with ploughs*. London: The Hogarth Press.
Cohen, A.P. 1978a. "The same — but different!" The allocation of identity in Whalsay, Shetland. *Sociological Review* 26 (3).
——— 1978b. Ethnographic method in the real community. *Sociologia Ruralis* 18 (1).
Collier, A. 1953. *The crofting problem.* Cambridge: University Press.
Ennew, J. 1977. The changing croft. *New Society* 40 (767), 16th June, 546–48.
Epstein, A.L. 1978. *Ethos and identity: three studies in ethnicity.* London: Tavistock.
Firth, R. 1973. *Symbols: public and private.* London: Allen and Unwin.
Fox, J.R. 1978. *The Tory islanders: a people of the Celtic fringe.* Cambridge: University Press.
Geertz, C. 1975. *The interpretation of cultures.* London: Hutchinson.
Gudeman, S. 1979. Mapping means. This volume.
Hunter, J. 1976. *The making of the crofting community.* Edinburgh: John Donald.
Mageean, D. 1979. Oil and development in Shetland: social structure and change. In *The promise and the reality: large scale developments in marginal regions*, J. Sewel (ed.). Aberdeen: ISSPA.
Mewett, P.G. 1977. Occupational pluralism in crofting: the influence of non-croft work on the patterns of crofting agriculture in the isle of Lewis since about 1850. *Scottish Journal of Sociology* 2 (1).
Murray, C. 1979. The work of men, women and the ancestors: social

reproduction in the periphery of Southern Africa. This volume.

Parkin, D.J. 1979. The categorisation of work: cases from coastal Kenya. This volume.

Sahlins, M.D. 1965. On the sociology of primitive exchange. In *The relevance of models for social anthropology*, A.S.A. Monograph 1, M. Banton (ed.). London: Tavistock.

Wadel, Cato. 1977. Hva er arbeid? Noen refleksjoner om arbeid som activitet og Begrep, *Tidsskrift for Samfunnsforskning* 18, 387–411.

—— 1979. The hidden work of everyday life. This volume.

THE POLLUTED IDENTITY OF WORK

A Study of Benares Sweepers

MARY SEARLE-CHATTERJEE

Introduction

This paper is concerned with a particular group of "Untouchables" in a large, pre-industrial city — Benares, the holy city of North India. The people that I studied are mostly employed by the municipal authority to sweep the streets and clean the public lavatories. Their work requires regular contact with substances considered to be polluting although they are not responsible for moving and handling animal carcasses or corpses. First, I describe the organization of their work and the interactions in which it involves them; then I discuss the fact that the identity given by it is one which is debased in the eyes of the larger society and polluting.

Benares, or Varanasi, as it is now called, is a very ancient city characterized by cottage industry. It has a settled population of about half a million, apart from the floating population of pilgrims. Sweepers usually live in close-knit localities separate from other castes. The particular group studied are first and second generation migrants from the rural areas of Kanpur, nearly 200 miles further west. In the villages they are engaged in earth work and agricultural labour as well as being Drummers. Sweeping, being a primarily urban activity, is of hardly any importance.

The Concept of Work

It is useful to begin by asking how far the Sweepers conceptualize their experience in the same way that the Anglo-Saxons do when speaking of "work". Sweepers use a general word for "work", *kaam*, denoting, on the one hand, activity which is purposeful and, on the other hand, activity which cannot be avoided. It can, then, be applied to the performance of ritual and social obligations as well as to earning of a livelihood, housework etc. (cf. Wadel, this volume). Work is doing (*karna*) and the deeds of "work" one does both cause and constitute one's fate, *karma*. It is in the nature of things that men and women should work and the word *kaam* is is generally, though not always, used positively. Sweepers' concepts are not so very different from English ones where there are two main categories contrasted with ",work". One is "rest" or "leisure", the other is "play". Similarly in India, common phrases make the same contrasts: *kaam* versus *aaraam* (ease, relaxation and nowadays at least, "leisure"); and *kaam* versus *khel* (play), the former referring to the absence of activity and the latter to activity which is non-purposeful. Here we find a distinctive aspect of Indian thought. All *kaam* is purposeful, but insofar as purpose rather than inevitability is the meaning in the forefront of a speaker's mind, *kaam* suggests involvement, instrumentality and self-interestedness, even desire (*kaami aadmi*, a lustful man). In this sense, *kaam* can be avoided because deeds can be performed without attachment. I suggest that when Sweepers use the word of themselves they are thinking of the inevitability of their deeds; but when they use it of the high castes, they are referring more to the instrumentality of actions. For the high caste philosophers *kaam* was to be transformed, by a change of perspective and hence attitude, to its opposite, play, *khel* (in literary language, *lila*). So the contrast of work and play for them existed only at one level of thought. The possibility of such transformations are generally remote from the thought of Sweepers, though not totally absent. It is my impression that the variations in the way that different castes in India use the word *kaam* are not so great however, as those in the usage of the word "work" by different occupational groups in Britain. Other words used by Sweepers are *naukari*, referring to their status as employees of other people and the English words, "service", again with bureaucratic, employee reference and "duty", with its reminder of a more colonial era. Work is distinguished from holidays, *chutthi* (previously meaning holy day).

For the purposes of this paper I shall use the word "work" in the sense of earning a livelihood. In fact, Sweepers are engaged in a variety of income earning activities of an informal kind, quite apart from their sweeping. They keep pigs and scavenge dung for fuel as well as rags and odd bits of wood etc. Some of them earn money from drumming in marriage processions or make and sell baskets. Within the locality a few earn money by selling various items, by letting out a bicycle or by occasional performance of ritual duties. This paper is concerned only with the work of sweeping since this is by far the most important.

Systems of Sweeping

Sweepers in Benares are involved in two quite distinct work systems, each with its characteristic ideology. One is based on municipal organization, itself partly determined by statutory regulation. In this, Sweeper men and women, known as "class IV employees", are paid monthly and receive fixed holidays, maternity leave and so on. There is a clear structure of authority and demarcation of work areas. In the other system, Sweepers are employed by private house-holders and receive payments in kind as well as in cash. They enjoy certain traditional rights to clothing, food remaining after feasts etc. Although neither Sweepers nor householders refer to this as a *jajmani* relationship, it clearly has hereditary familial aspects characteristic of what anthropologists often describe as rural *jajmani* system (Lewis 1958).

The contrast between the two systems is reminiscent of Weber's distinction between a bureaucratic framework and "traditional", more patrimonial and personal patterns said to be characteristic of most non-industrial societies (Weber 1964). It has, of course, become a commonplace that the Weberian model was oversimplified, as, indeed, all models are. Studies of work places both in Europe and the USA as well as in areas traditionally studied by anthropologists have revealed the interplay between informal, personal and, in Weber's sense "non-rational", patterns and bureaucratic ones (Roethlisberger and Dickson 1964; Sheth 1968; Shih Kuo-heng 1944). At first, and even as late as 1962, this was interpreted as due to the survival of older, inappropriate forms (Kerr 1962). More recently, it has even been argued that the appearance of such non-bureaucratic elements, apart from being inevitable, may even on occasion be conducive to greater efficiency (Blau 1955: 148). In the case of the Sweepers, however, the pattern of organization of work cannot simply be classified as a mixed case any more than it can be described in terms of one or other of Weber's models: it comprises two distinct systems — i.e. both of Weber's types but in spatial and temporal separation.

I shall describe first the bureaucratic sphere — the municipal organization of street sweeping — since in terms of hours and remuneration it is the more important. This order of presentation may be surprising: it is natural for a European to assume that the household system is the older one from which municipal sweeping evolved or on to which municipal sweeping was imposed. In fact, however, there have been systems of municipal government and hence of municipal sweeping in various periods of Indian history, in very ancient times as well as under the Moghuls and, more recently, since at least the 1914 Town Area Committee Act. It appears that at other times too, urban street sweeping has been organized bureaucratically, if not by a municipal council, by the administrative office of the local *nawab* or *raja*. In times of crisis it could be organized by the locality councils which received regular income from fines and sometimes from fixed contributions made by householders (Den Hollander 1956; Lynch 1967). Occasionally, such councils owned land, the rent or produce from which was used for a variety of purposes. In the mediaeval period there are occasional references to kings setting aside land to pay for the regular cleaning of tanks. It is likely, however, that cleaners of sacred tanks were of somewhat higher caste then Sweepers.

However, there are today urban areas in South Asia which do not organize regular street sweeping on a totally municipal basis. In some of the small town-like settlements in the hills and even in Khatmandu, a capital city, garbage is either eaten by animals (as, indeed, much of it is in Benares); or remains in large mounds only very occasionally shifted. Even areas as large as Karachi do not have all areas swept by municipal organization, some being sub-contracted out or dealt with privately (Streefland 1977).

Although in India all municipal areas organize the cleaning of streets by means of paid civil servants, there are variations in the way that the system operates. An official report (Government of India 1974: 178) points out that in some towns municipal authorities have been able to insulate themselves almost entirely from state directives relating to the working conditions of Sweepers by increasing the number of temporary and hence less protected employees. Sometimes these are mainly women. In some areas sweeping has even become the preserve of women, men being found in a variety of other unskilled jobs. Clearly, too, the situation is different in towns whose population is not expanding (Streefland op. cit.).

In Benares, at least, there is no shortage of sweeping work. The city has doubled its size in the last 50 years. The expanding city needed more Sweepers and this increasing demand was not simply in proportion to the population increase. Open land was progressively brought into use and garbage could no longer be left to be absorbed into the soil. At the same time Sweepers were not increasing at the same rate as other groups. The infant mortality rate is 2 out of 5 as compared with a national rate (1961) of 1.4 (i.e. 140 per thousand). Additional Sweepers were required by the expansion of the hotel business, although the main demand is not in the private sector of the economy, but in large Government and public offices, as would be expected in a country where the expansion of the bureaucracy speeds apace. Although I shall restrict

myself to the Municipality, what I say applies more or less equally
to the hospitals, Railways, Insurance, Banking (in which demand
has increased several hundred fold since nationalization in 1969),
the Power House, the Police Service, University and other educational
institutions, as well as the larger private factories, except that
Sweepers in many of these earn considerably more, rising to Rs.200
per month in the Banks.

Sweepers in the Municipal Bureaucracy

The Corporation is a large organization employing 2305 Sweepers,
under the jurisdiction of the Health Officer. Conditions of work are
governed by written regulation broad guidelines for which are laid
down by the State Government and in the Public Health Manual
and, even more generally, by the Central Government, for whom
the Commissioner for Scheduled Castes acts as a watchdog in his
annual reports.

The formal system is as follows: Sweepers work from 5–7 on
summer mornings and from 7–11 in the winter and again for
three hours in the afternoon. Each individual is attached to a sub-
office in a particular ward and within that district is allocated a
particular area of 1200 sq. ft. which is to be swept and have its
drains and public lavatories cleaned. The rate of pay for this at
the time of study (1972) was 103 rupees (£1 equalled Rs.21) per
month rising by annual increments of one rupee per year for
seven years. There are three other types of cleaning work with
which I shall not deal as they are generally handled by persons of
other castes, i.e. underground work in the sewers, removing
corpses or animal carcasses (*Doms*) and watering the gutters in
the early morning (Muslims known as *Bhistis*).

Work areas are allocated to individuals, but Sweepers working in
neighbouring streets may assist one another; one may push a cart
and another shovel rubbish into it but there is no fixed demarcation
of tasks. Unlike Sweepers in many other cities in India they do not
have to remove excrement from dry latrines since these are non-
existent here. This does not, however, greatly affect the nature of
their work as the streets are used as latrines in the early morning
by most of the poorer people. The rubbish thrown out by house-
holders is swept up into heaps and shovelled into head baskets and
then into handcarts which take the garbage from four Sweepers
and are assigned to every fourth one. These are pulled along to
more central places where they are unloaded into buffalo carts
which in turn carry rubbish to the trucks which take it outside
the city. Truck and bullock cart drivers receive an extra Rs.2 per

month. Sweepers are officially supplied monthly with bristles and sticks and have to trim them and make their brooms themselves. They are also supplied with baskets and they shape their own "shovels" from the scrap iron supplied. Tools, then, are controlled by the individuals who use them, many taking their own home at night although they are supposed to leave them in the depot.

There is a fixed hierarchy of roles relating to the work of each ward sub-office. The ordinary Sweeper, *mehter*, is under the general supervision of a *jemadar* (a word which is sometimes used honorifically for all sweepers), who, in only a couple of cases, has been promoted from the Sweeper ranks. There are only five of these in each sub-office. They are paid Rs.150 per month and ride around on bicycles, scolding and swearing at the 20–25 Sweepers in their charge. In each ward there is one *daroga* or *havildar* (earning Rs.250) who supervise the work at the office. No Sweepers have, as yet, been promoted to this position.

The last three of these terms resemble occupational titles in the police service and it is for this reason that children in Benares sometimes shout "bumpolice" as Sweepers go by. Even the word *mehter* was originally an honorific title with courtly and military connotations (Russel 1975 reprint). This is, perhaps, related to the fact that sweeping has had a longer association with bureaucratic organization than most other occupations, and that it is – after police and military service – the supreme bureaucratic occupation.

I have already referred to the rates of pay and to the fact that remuneration is not only in cash. Sweepers receive clothing supplies every winter officially worth Rs.75 and in summer to the value of Rs.36; as well as 14 days "casual" leave, one month "privilege" leave, two weekly half days, 12 months sickness leave in a lifetime (though not more than 1½ months at a time) and 42 days maternity leave for up to three children. Cheap accommodation is supplied or else a housing allowance per person per month. In addition, interest-free loans of up to Rs.400 are available from the Municipality Co-operative Society. Repayment is then deducted in monthly instalments. These forms of remuneration are, of course, more resistant to inflation than simple cash payments. However, as can be seen from the list of complaints published by the Sanitation Workers Union in 1972, they are not always given on time. Weekly holidays, too, are often cancelled when important political figures are expected. Moreover many Sweepers (about one fifth), admittedly mainly teenagers, are temporary employees and hence not entitled to all these benefits. Apart from the remunerations laid down in the regulations it is also customary that the people living in houses fronting the streets that a Sweeper cleans should give small sums of cash on special festival days. The municipal sphere of work, then, cannot simply be seen in impersonal bureaucratic terms nor in terms of the cash nexus.

Recruitment to sweeping, although in one sense governed simply by the universalistic requirement that an employee be willing to handle excrement, is at the same time governed by particularistic factors: in general only persons of certain castes are prepared to satisfy this requirement. Recruitment is also affected by an unwritten law (which Sweepers are trying to get written into the regulations) requiring that when a Sweeper dies or retires, preference in the allocation of the vacancy should be given to members of his family, either male or female, who are not yet employed. Municipal housing, too, is inherited, usually by the youngest son. If there is no close relative in need, another Sweeper may, by paying something to the family of the deceased man or woman, be allowed to pretend to be a relative and hence secure either the flat or the post, but this would be a rare case. For highly coveted sweeping posts such as those in the Railways or Banks, a sum of about Rs.500 could be exchanged. In most cases, however, there are family members at hand who fill the vacancy.

Again in the actual organization of the work of sweeping there is a great deal of flexibility and fluidity. Knowledge of the regulations alone gives little idea of what happens in the streets. Sweepers often unofficially stand in for one another. Payment of a small bribe to the *jemadar* enables a considerable number to be absent at any one time. Although the Municipality does not in theory employ Sweepers under the age of 15, children often stand in for their parents or help them with their work. Family members also try to exchange their areas to be closer to one another. Sweepers, like most lower level employees, are expected to be available for additional forms of unpaid work such as cleaning lavatories in the homes of their supervisors. When they work in wealthier organizations like Banks or the University, they may have to clean the drains in inner courtyards or sweep garden paths or clean roofs for their superiors.

Identity and Demeanour in the Municipal Work Sphere

A Sweeper need never fear that brooms or barrows left around will be stolen by other castes. While going about his work he may stop for tea but he will drink it in an earthen cup to be thrown away afterwards, or in a separate one reserved for his use, and he will sit or stand on the ground, not on the bench provided. Only when he is without his broom and in other parts of the city can he mingle unknown in the crowd, eating and worshipping wherever he pleases. While going about his work, in a narrow lane, a Sweeper will be circumspect in his movements. In the alleys with many temples near the holy river Ganges, Sweepers call out as they move along, warning worshippers to avoid them, for if someone accidentally touches a Sweeper or his broom he will not be able to worship without a purificatory bath. Many Sweepers in fact avoid the riverside area in the early morning to avoid contact with newly purified bathers. Brooms, when not in use, are carried high over the shoulder, partly for the same reason.

In broad streets, however, Sweepers walk boldly, and confidently, even contemptuously, knowing how people fear their touch. Similarly, in their dealings with municipal officials at the Health Office they are forthright and unabashed. They deal, after all, only with low level officials, themselves not of much higher caste, and they have the strength of numbers.

Change

Changes in the organization of municipal sweeping come partly from above in the form of technical innovation thought to be in the interests of public cleanliness as when tractors and trucks were introduced to supplement the work of bullock carts. Changes in ideas about what is acceptable or desirable also affect the rules. There is now in official circles a general feeling that carrying of garbage and excrement in head baskets should come to an end and State Governments have been asked by the Commissioner for Scheduled (or untouchable) Castes to work towards elimination of the custom. It is for this reason that the New Provincial Constitution of 1970 laid down that, on Municipality Co-operative Society Executive Committees, eleven members (i.e. about one third) must be Sweepers.

Change also arises from the awareness of political leaders of the importance of the votes of the lowest castes. This awareness is kept alive by activities from below, by the militancy and energy of the Sanitation Workers' Union. By playing indirectly on political fears and, more directly, on the threat of strike with the consequent likelihood of epidemic conditions developing, it has been able to secure very considerable economic gains. Sweepers are now among the best paid of the Scheduled castes: a combined household income may amount to as much as the earnings of a University lecturer. State Governments have also allocated a considerable sum to housing such groups. The pre-Independence activities of Gandhi and

Ambedkar, the Untouchable leader, have made the Congress
Janata leadership very sensitive to the hardship suffered by Sweepers
as well as to the inexpediency of having such a large group alienated
from the Hindu majority.[1] Since Partition, the Government has
redoubled its efforts to solve the problem of the Untouchables,
with the Sweepers being the best known and most dramatic example
of the category. Today they are potential supporters of more radical
parties.

Sweeping of Private Households

Now to turn to the other system of sweeping — the daily morning
cleaning of lavatories for rich or high caste households. This may
be an alternative form of employment to municipal sweeping but is
more commonly an unofficial supplement to it. The work is not
absolutely delimited. Sweepers may clean drains in the garden or
inner courtyard or do certain kinds of garden work. They do not
in Benares sweep floors in the house, though they do in Delhi,
and they certainly do not clean sinks. Sweepers carry a brush, but
many housholds provide their own which they expect to be used
along with their cleaning powder. Many Sweepers work in 6–10
housholds in addition to doing municipal work, earning a few
rupees a month in each. They also receive "gifts" of cash or clothing
at major festivals and at important household ceremonies, as I
mentioned earlier. Old clothing is given occasionally, as is the food
remaining on plates after weddings and other feasts. Cooked food
that has been spilt or contaminated by insects may also be given.
On the *Kitcheree Sankranti* festival, Sweepers may receive the raw
ingredients for cooking kedgeree.

   Work for private householders also provides the possibility of
access to loans and of influential contacts which can provide openings
to jobs sweeping in better paid institutions, or even to other types
of work such as being a night watchman or artisan. The rates of
remuneration change more slowly than in the municipal sphere but,
because the payment in kind is often more important than the
cash payment, tend to be more immune to inflation. The right to
work in a private house is usually inherited by whichever son or
daughter is nearest at hand most in need, with priority being given
according to age rather than sex. Only in the case of exceptionally
rich or generous households might it be sold, but this is rare. House
Sweepers do not generally receive any fixed holidays but often do
remain at home on important festival days.

Identity and Demeanour in the Private Sphere

When a Sweeper cleans the lavatory in a private house the owner will
pour the water for him so that he will not touch the bucket or tap
himself. Many bathrooms, even in new flats, have an outer door to
enable the Sweeper to enter without passing through the rest of the
house. In older houses the lavatory is played in a corner of the
courtyard, well away from the main building. Modern houses are
sometimes built without a courtyard and older relatives may be
reluctant to stay when they find that the lavatory is incorporated
into the main building. In very orthodox homes the householder
may pour water on any areas where a Sweeper has walked, even on
an outer verandah. If by any chance the Sweeper requires water, he
may be given it in a separate glass, or it will be poured so that he
can cup it in his hands. The same practice is common among higher
castes — in their case to protect themselves as receivers from any
possible contamination from an unknown source.

The relationship between Sweeper and householder is usually
reserved and aloof on both sides. Sometimes Sweepers adopt a subservient and cringing manner when they enter a house, although
nowadays, in homes without a separate entrance, they often walk
proudly, even insolently, as they pass through the main part of
the house. Sometimes a chatty, even gossipy, friendship may
develop, with the housewife pumping her woman Sweeper for
information about the houses and behaviour of neighbours. Only
very rarely a woman Sweeper has sexual relations with the male
of the house when his wife and children are away. He will ask her
to bathe before she does so and will give her a couple of rupees
in payment. But these relations are not easy to arrange: Sweepers
normally only remain for a few minutes a day and the neighbours
will soon notice any deviation from normal custom which will be
more reprehensible if it involves an untouchable than any other
caste. High caste men certainly like talking to Sweeper women
in private, but they do not, in public, like to be seen taking
much interest in them. In the obscene pamphlets published during
the Saturnalian Festival of *Holi*, lewd poems refer to all low caste
women except for Sweepers.

The Power of the Polluted

There are many resemblances between the two systems of work. My
initial account of them has magnified the differences for analytic
purposes. Threat of withdrawal of labour as a means of securing
·compliance is one of the most important features common to
both systems. Municipal Sweepers all belong to the Sanitation

Workers' Union which has several times been able to get wages raised by petitioning the Local Authority. In Benares, they have twice in living memory been on strike. The most notable of these occasions was in 1960. The Authorities called in Sweepers from outside, from Kanpur, in an attempt to break the strike. Fights broke out between the outside Kanpuris and the Benares Kanpuris as well as others, and several informants spoke of having been sent to prison for several days along with other family members. Wages were, however, raised. In 1972, the Union had a three month programme of weekly processions through the city in support of 17 points. A strike was threatened if the grievances and demands were not attended to. It is interesting to note that many of the demands are for implementation of provisions already granted on paper, but not given in reality. They were as follows:

1. Pension or Provident Fund.
2. Wages should be paid on time.
3. Interim help should be given as laid down by the State Government.
4. The Board has not implemented its decision to give Rs.10 to all labourers.
5. Benares must no longer pay less than the Municipalities of Agra, Kanpur, Allahabad and Lucknow.
6. Brooms and baskets should be given regularly every month.
7. When extra work is required on holidays the full amount of pay should be given as laid down in the regulations.
8. Clothing to the value specified in the rules should in fact be be given.
9. Sweepers should not be required to work on weekly holidays.
10. When vacancies for *jemadar* and *daroga* occur they should be filled by educated Sweepers.
11. When a worker retires, preference for temporary or permanent work should be given to members of his family.
12. Existing homes should be repaired and new ones built.
13. Those who come from afar to work in the city should be given city allowances.
14. The requirements of the Public Health Manual Act should be in force, i.e. the full number of Sweepers, buffalo carts and trucks should be utilized.
15. Handcarts should not be used for long distances which are supposed to be covered by trucks.
16. Holidays should be given as required by law.
17. Money raised from fines for absenteeism should be spent on free education, books and medical treatment for their children.

Between 1972–4 there were large scale strikes by Sweepers in Delhi and Kanpur. Their demands were "ambitious" but were mostly acceded to because of the risk of epidemic conditions developing. Sweepers can make efficient use of Trade Unionism because few castes are prepared to challenge their monopoly of a low status yet socially indispensible occupation. They continue sweeping partly because they fear to move out of the security of the known world into an alien and unsympathetic one; other castes, on the other hand, fear to move into that lowly world through taking up the economically attractive work of sweeping. The very lowness of Sweepers in this sense gives them a certain amount of power. Sweepers can make further efficient use of Trade Unionism because their occupational and residential homogeneity, again partly due to their despised status, enable rapid mobilization. Of the nine localities surveyed, the vast majority of persons were employed in municipal sweeping. Even sweepers engaged in other kinds of work tend to remain in the same locality. Only a handful of Sweepers were found living outside Sweeper areas. If Uma Sankar Dube, the Brahmin Secretary of the Sanitation Workers' Union, wishes to publicize a meeting, all he has to do is to ask ten committee members each to inform ten committee members each to inform ten households to ensure that news reaches the whole caste.

Threat or implementation of strike action is not a new phenomenon. Strikes of Sweepers in municipal areas were reported in the nineteenth and early twentieth centuries (Crooke 1896; Blunt 1931: 242). Crooke referred to an attempt by a local authority to sell night soil. It was forced to abandon its proposal by striking Sweepers who considered that to be their prerogative. It is unlikely that this was something new even then, though I lack information about the period prior to the British Administration. It is not clear to what extent Sweeper "power" rested on governmental restraints on the use of overt violence against them. Even at the end of the eighteenth century, however, the Abbé Dubois noted that though "a pariah is not allowed to pass a Brahmin street in a village nobody can prevent his approaching or passing by a Brahmin's house *in towns.* The Pariahs, on their part, will under no circumstances allow a Brahmin to pass through their (collection of huts) as they firmly believe it will lead to their ruin (1973: 61).

Sweepers sometimes withdraw labour to force private house-holders to give them what they consider to be their due. In suburban villages of Benares it is customary for householders on certain festivals to give delicacies of cooked food to the municipal Sweepers who clean the drains fronting their homes. If due to illness, for

example, the householder forgets to present the appropriate items
he finds a stinking unswept drain facing him for two days.
References in the literature to special days when village Sweepers
beg from door to door are misleading. The verbal part of the Hindi
word for begging, *mangna*, also implies want and demand.

Apart from the fact that they have a work monopoly, Sweepers
are prepared to unite and use physical force if they feel that they
have been wronged. The utter lowness of their position makes them
unaffected by the inhibiting status concerns of higher groups. In the
normal context of private work Sweepers do not show much
solidarity. A householder who sacks a Sweeper will find a replacement fairly easily. But if a major conflict has arisen, Sweepers may
congregate noisily in the street or, if a charge has been made, outside
the police station. If a matter of honour is involved, Sweepers may
act with ferocious unity. On one occasion, outside the railway
station, a taxi driver, notorious for his rough behaviour, touched a
Sweeper woman's breasts and made obscene gestures and comments.
She swore vociferously at him but neither she nor other Sweepers in
the vicinity were able to retaliate in any other way because of the
fifty or more other taxi drivers at hand. The next day, by chance,
about six Sweeper women working on the other side of the railway
line met three taxi drivers, one of whom was recognized as the
offender. The women descended on them in fury, tucking up their
sarees and shouting abuse, beating them repeatedly with their long
iron-tipped brooms. The men were unable to defend themselves
When they eventually escaped, they were bleeding profusely from
the head and face.

Sometimes Sweepers take advantage of high caste fears of contamination. Until ten years ago, according to the Secretary of the
Sanitation Workers Union, Sweepers would mob any high caste
person entering their locality. They would amuse themselves by
seeing his discomfiture and would sometimes continue to touch him
until he gave them money to be rid of them. Sweepers do this
even now, though to a much lesser extent than formerly. I suspect
that in urban situations where Sweepers are found in large numbers
in compact groups, they have always had at least some advantage
over other low caste groups: their extreme lowliness makes persons
of higher caste likely to attempt violence only as a last resort
because of the degradation involved in touching, pulling or even
beating them.

Sweepers, then, are neither penniless or impotent, despite the
fact that they are quite without status. Their situation lends support
to Dumont's view that in India, economic and political values are

clearly disjunct from religious ones. What is more, one can say that power and prosperity, relative though they may be in this case, actually rest on degradation.

Sex and Sweeping

I have not yet mentioned the work of Sweeper women as distinct from that of men. Indeed, I have not needed to do so since they generally do the same work as men and earn as much — in some cases more, because of working in additional private households. There are only very minor differences in the work done by men and women. Men more often lift dirt out of underground drains; it is more common for women to unload into lorries the head baskets into which men have shovelled garbage; and truck drivers are all men. However, the bulk of the sweeping work is done by men or women interchangeably. Sweepers are in this respect quite unlike high caste groups among whom there is a marked sexual division of labour. Nor are Sweeper women fettered by purity and status concerns: it is not surprising that for society at large they are the lowest of all. But here again there is a paradox, for Sweeper women have a strength which no other category of women has. Their style of walking is, for example, distinctive: they stride along in a way unlike any others. When disputes break out in the street, it is the Sweeper men who have to restrain their women lest they outdo them in vehemence and vulgarity in defence both of their husband's honour and their own.

Caste and Identity

The identity that a Sweeper derives from his work is one which is considered debased and polluting. Work is a major determinant of self identity and status not merely in an industrial society: the identity given by caste membership is in many cases associated with a particular traditional occupation, even if that is not the main work of the group, but simply its distinctive activity. Very many caste names are, in fact, derived from occupations. The Sweepers whom I studied were by origin mainly of the *Nangarchi/Toraiha* group. The former name is derived from a word for a large drum, the latter from a wind instrument (Risley 1908). Although in the villages these groups were mainly engaged in agricultural labour (as are practically all castes), they provided music on those occasions when it was required. Work with either leather or bamboo, two of the most important materials in musical instruments, was considered polluting. So, consequently, were music makers — except for those playing brass cymbals or fibre-stringed instruments such as the *ektara* played by roving holy men. The other Sweepers were in origin *Dhanuks*, a term derived from grain and referring to their traditional work as grain cleaners, a "purer" occupation. Even the so-called tribal or non-functional castes, such as *Doms*, are widely known to be associated with a particular kind of work, in this case, basketry. The orthodox Hindu explanation of untouchability does, in fact, refer to the nature of the occupation.

The people described here have a new occupation in the city since sweeping is of negligible importance in the villages from which they come and in which their identity as musicians is far more important. In the city they refer to themselves by a new name, *Mehter* (a polite word for Sweeper) or as *Hela*, a term referring to a particular endogamous group of Sweepers of the Benares district. This is a group with whom they do not actually marry, but under whose rubric they see themselves to be recently classified.

I have already described some of the implications of the Hindu belief that sweeping is polluting. Sweepers are not only low themselves (the word *Balmiki*, meaning Sweeper, is one of the more common swear words), they can also pollute others; they have taken the dirt of society upon themselves and hence must be avoided. Others take a variety of precautions in self-protection. Despite the new laws, Sweepers are often not allowed to worship in local temples or shrines where they are known and people avoid touching them in the street — old ladies often quite ostentatiously.

It should be noted that only certain kinds of sweeping are considered polluting: every housewife uses brooms to sweep the rooms. But although the word, *jharu*, is the same, these brooms are very different from the heavy large brooms used for the streets. Street sweeping is different not simply because it involves serving others in public areas, but because it is associated with removal of other peoples' excreta, whether from the streets or public lavatories. Temple floors in Benares are generally washed with water and a cloth, not with a broom. It is interesting that the phrase *jhalaar hillaana* is of the same root but refers to the use of a very superior and lightweight dusting stick, used for sacred images and for keeping flies away from Maharajas, hence implying the paying of respect and even the worship of saints etc. Although the root implies something that is shaken or moved about and reappears in the word for flag, something much associated with temples and worship, it is not used for a fan (Apte 1963). Is this just a matter of chance or is there a common semantic element implying demarcation and clarification of space and hence worship as Turner found in the use of sweeping vocabulary among the Ndembu (1975: 70)? In Europe, too, witches sweep out the old year. Whatever may be the case, this kind of boundary-making activity is associated with the highest and the lowest groups, with the Sweeper and with the religious devotee or priest, as well as with the work of women.

Self Esteem and Alternative Definitions

How far do Sweepers internalize attitudes which others have towards the work of sweeping? Do they feel too that they are polluted by it or do they feel alienated from their work and hence uncontaminated by it? Do they in fact identify with it in any way?

Sweepers express different attitudes and feelings at different moments so it is not possible to give a clear answer to these questions. They all consider that sweeping is dirty and unpleasant. Many, however, say that they prefer to live in a city and sweep than to live in a village and work in the fields. They also say that sweeping is essential work and requires strength. My impression is that they consider sweeping to be physically dirty rather than polluting, and that in most cases they attribute their lowliness to the power rather than the superiority of others. Some, however, say that they are low because they are uneducated and drink excessively, and many of the older Sweepers will not enter the most sacred Visvanath temple, even though they are now allowed to do so. They feel that it would show a lack of respect.

When talking to persons of high caste, Sweepers may suppress mention of customs such as eating pork and drinking. But away from a multi-caste context they express no shame about either of these customs, or about their work as Sweepers. In the language of social esteem theorists (Coopersmith 1967), it is the "significant others" who who are important — in this case the caste itself. Sweepers make only half-hearted attempts to modify their behaviour to suit the tastes of the higher castes. They show no interest at all in the grooming of their children's hair or clothing, a matter closely related to the esteem of the urban higher caste mother. I believe that in this case this is not due to fear of the "evil eye" but to lack of involvement with higher caste concerns. Sweepers are perfectly conscious of high caste feelings; they simply do not share them.

Sweepers associate their work of sweeping with a toughness that they admire in both men and women; with drinking and eating of "hot" substances, meat and strong liquor. Linked with this is their belief that they are hot-blooded and highly-sexed. Both men and women lay great emphasis on "honour" and will in defence of it fight without much provocation. "It's a matter of honour" is a very common phrase. *Dom* sweepers lay particular emphasis on readiness to fight and frequently bring out long spears. Sweepers also admire those who are spirited and can outwit the authorities, and those who are physically strong: their children play with clay body-building weights.

The Sweepers' sense of identity and self esteem comes from their style of life rather than from their work, though they see both to be part of the same complex of toughness. It would be misleading, however, to over-emphasise their self esteem as Sweepers. Individuals within the group aquire status and respect from skills in basketry, music making, story telling, literacy and also from committee membership and riches acquired in the pig trade. The work of sweeping is the major, but not the only source of a Sweeper's identity, and the meanings he attributes to that work are different from those attributed to it by the larger society.

Notes

1. Sweepers use the word "hindu" to refer to the upper castes rather than to themselves.

References

Apte, V.S. 1963. *Sanskrit English dictionary.* Delhi: Motilal Banarsidass.

Blau, P. 1955. *The dynamics of bureaucracy.* Chicago: University Press.

Blunt, E. 1931. *The caste system of north India.* Oxford: O.U.P.

Coopersmith, S. 1967. *The antecedents of self esteem.* San Francisco: W.H. Freeman.

Crooke, E. 1896. *Tribes and castes of the north west provinces and Oudh.* Calcutta: Thacker.

Den Hollander, A.N. 1956. Changing social control in a Bengal city. In *Transactions of the third world congress of sociology.* Vol. 6.

Dubois, J.A. 1973. *Hindu manners, customs and ceremonies* (trans. H.K. Beauchamp). New Delhi: Mamta Publishers (Repr. pt. 1 and 2 of the 1897 edition, orig. publ. in French by L'Imprimerie Royale, Paris.)

Government of India. 1974. *Towards equality.* Report of the Committee on the Status of Women in India, Ministry of Education and Social Welfare.

Kerr, C. 1962. *Industrialism and industrial man.* London: Heinemann.

Lewis, O. 1958. *Village life in north India.* Urbana: University Illinois Press.

Lynch, O. 1967. Rural Cities in India. In *India and Ceylon: unity and diversity,* P. Mason (ed.). London: Oxford U.P. for the Institute of Race Relations.

Risley, H. 1908. *The people of India.* London: Thacker.

Roethlisberger, F.J. and Dickson, W.J. 1964. *Management and the worker.* Chichester: Wiley (first published in 1939).

Russell, R.V. (ed.). 1975. *The tribes and castes of the central provinces of India.*

Delhi: Cosmo Publ. (Repr. 1916 edition, London: Macmillan).

Sheth, N.R. 1968. *The social framework of an Indian factory.* Manchester: University Press.

Shih, K.-h. 1944. *China enters the machine age.* Harvard and Oxford.

Streefland, P. 1977. *Sanitation in developing countries today.* Oxfam.

Turner, V. 1975. Ritual as communication and potency. In *Symbols and society*, C. Hill (ed.). Athens: Southern Anthropological Society. (Distrib. by University of Georgia Press.

Weber, M. 1964. *The theory of social and economic organization.* New York: Free Press. (First published in 1925).

THE SELF AND THE PRODUCT:

Concepts of Work in Comparative Perspective

ERIK SCHWIMMER

Introduction[1]

The cross-cultural comparison of concepts is part of the anthropologist's trade. Whatever the concept, we find ourselves asking whether anything resembling it exists among the people we study. The concept presents itself very often in English: law, government, religion, friendship, reciprocity. A school of thought often arises which holds that the concept is not universal but confined to a limited set of cultures, inevitably including our own. Such a suggestion is usually opposed by others who propose definitions of the concepts so as to make them look universal. The concept of *work* is clearly of that type.

There are good reasons for thinking that this concept is a product of 18th century Europe and the industrial revolution. Work as a concept is based on the assumption that, from a certain viewpoint, all economically useful activities are fully comparable by a yardstick transcending their diversity, in other words, that labour has become a commodity and that the technical and administrative direction of that labour has become part of the same kind of commodity. This is a perspective with which we have become familiar through Mandeville, political economy and Marxism (Baudrillard 1973; Dumont 1977). On the other hand, it has been shown that the Ancient Greeks had no corresponding concept (Vernant 1965) and it is not difficult to show that the Melanesians did not have it either, until they came into contact with western capitalism. One of my Orokaiva informants was categorical on this point: "The people of olden times," he said, "did not take up work (*pure*) for it was only Jesus Christ who gave them work (*pure*) to take up."[2]

On the other hand, some very prominent authors have presented 'work' as a universal concept. One of them was Karl Marx to whom the concept 'work' was just as much a universal as man's supposedly perpetual 'transformation of nature to human ends'. In his theory all modes of production have their 'labour force'; what he opposes is that capitalism has turned this labour force into a 'commodity'. In that state of communism, work will become "le premier besoin vital" (Manuscrit de 44). As for Freud, when he was asked (according to an anecdote) what should be the main preoccupations of the normal healthy adult, he answered: "Lieben und Arbeiten". In this respect he appears to have taken the same view as Hesiod, in whose world view "la fécondité et le travail apparaissent comme deux fonctions opposées et complémentaires" (Vernant 1965: 188).

Faced with such complications, two possibilities are open to anthropologists. The solution most frequently adopted is to avoid the difficulty and to rely, instead, on concepts that are easier to define and operate. Thus economic anthropologists working in Melanesia have given up measuring labour force participation and concentrate instead on the concept of 'time allocation' as a measure of socio-economic relationships (Lawrence 1964), cost and value (Salisbury 1962; Belshaw 1949, Appendix IX) or price (Godelier 1973).[3] Another possible solution, which is beginning to find adherents in anthropology, is to subject the concept to what one might call comparative semiotic analysis.

This solution was, in fact, suggested by Sir Raymond Firth at the present conference when he said: "it is pertinent for anthropologists to enquire more systematically into indigenous definitions of work . . .". What would such an enquiry involve? As not all cultures have a concept of work, there are some cultures which, strictly speaking, could not be called upon to define it.

There are some simple, practical ways of coping with this problem. Michel Panoff, for instance, in a paper presenting concepts of work among the Maenge of New Britain (1977), suggested glossing the term 'work' by "des activités visant à la production de l'utile" (p. 7). Undoubtedly this provided an operational definition. On the other hand, as Panoff himself acknowledges, terms like 'production' and 'useful' raise problems of precisely the same order as a term like 'work'. Cultures which do not differentiate 'economics' as a category from political, social, religious etc. phenomena could not very well class together some of their activities (but not others) as 'production' and even less could they subdivide the category so obtained into useful and useless. Panoff counters: "On ne commencerait jamais s'il fallait, chaque fois, réinventer totalement le vocabulaire".

Needless to say, Panoff had to pay the price of his haste. Thus, he finds a Maenge equivalent for 'activities' in gardening (*kuma*) and tells us they take, on the average, four hours per day. Next, he proceeds to admit that his informants do not conceptually distinguish 'productive' from other activities (such as sleeping, eating, etc.). On the other hand, they do have a concept for 'toil' (*milali*). Evidently, they cannot say, in their language, whether they are 'working' but they are perfectly able to say whether they are 'toiling'. Moreover, in transactions with affines (p. 11) a man may sometimes claim compensation for *milali* he has done in an affine's garden, but he could never claim compensation for *kuma*. After all this, one wonders whether the latter word is fully covered by the gloss 'une dépense d'énergie' (p. 15).[4]

Panoff is correct in saying that it would be futile, every time a concept is explored, to reinvent the 'vocabulary'. I suppose he means by this the finding of an ingenious phrasing that gives an impression of universality. On the other hand, a semiotic investigation of a concept ought to tell us what ontological commitments are normally implied when members of the culture in question refer to the concept. Such implications may not become fully clear unless one knows the myths, rituals, ideology, behavioural norms of the culture in which the concept is embedded.

In other words, there is a corpus of information that must be presented before we can have even an approximately clear idea about what a Maenge means when he uses the concept *kuma*. No doubt such understanding will always be approximate and a 'full' investigation would be of infinite length. As in any ethnographic investigation, it would be professional practice to continue enlarging the corpus as long as this continues to add appreciably to our understanding of the concept and to end the investigation when a certain degree of clarity has been obtained and returns begin to diminish.

With regard to the concept of 'work', the first such investigation was not, to my knowledge, made by an anthropologist, but by a classical scholar, Jean-Pierre Vernant, in a series of papers brought together under the title *Le travail et la pensée technique* (Vernant 1965; 183–247). It will be useful briefly to review these papers both from a comparative and a methodological point of view.

Concepts of Work in Ancient Greece

Vernant's central interest lies not so much in agricultural work but in concepts of craftsmanship (TEXNH) and of what one might roughly call practical intelligence (MHTIΣ). To the latter topic he has recently devoted a book-length study (Detienne and Vernant 1974), with the special purpose of giving its due to a form of intelligence that our own culture has tended to grievously under-value in favour of theoretical and literary intelligence. This neglect appears to Vernant (a Marxist) like an aspect of class warfare in western society, though its ideological armoury was forged, without doubt, in Ancient Greece, more particularly by Plato.

Even though Vernant's central interest in the 1965 compilation lies in the concept TEXNH, he includes agricultural labour in – as one might say – his semiotic domain. It is for this reason that comparison of his analysis with Melanesian data (the focus of my present study) becomes highly relevant. Vernant nowhere explicitly defines his semiotic domain but from internal evidence I suggest it comes down to Prometheus' gift to man. Marxist though Vernant may be, he does not fall into the trap of defining his enquiry in other than Hellenic terms. Use-value, exchange-value and alienation are used as tools of analysis, not as boundaries of a semiotic domain. Though Prometheus, in Attica at least, was specifically the god of fire, pottery and metallurgy, and was specifically linked with the social category of artisans, the semiotic domain defined by Prometheus must include all the implications, as perceived by Ancient Greeks, of Prometheus' conflict with Zeus (1965: 186).

From this viewpoint, the Prometheus figure is as relevant to agriculturists as to artisans, a fact that is reflected in Hesiod's treatment of Prometheus in his *Theogony* as well as in *Works and Days*.[5] Hesiod, in fact, presented the deity mainly, in the latter work, as the god of the peasants and thus linked with Pandora, celebrated as goddess of fertility.

It is largely in Hesiod's terms that Vernant presents to us what we may call the Greek peasant's concept of work. While we may regret the paucity of informants, Hesiod's credentials are satisfactory: both he and his contentious brother are genuine peasants whose father had come to Boeotia destitute. The myths on which Hesiod's conceptual system rests are specifically those of his social class in a society where "every social class has myths of its own" (Jaeger 1946: 61).

In this, context, then, we are offered a definition of EPΓON and its related verb EPΓAZEΣΘAI.   The verb

> paraît spécialiser son emploi dans deux secteurs de la vie économique: l'activité agricole, les travaux des champs, TA EPΓA et, à l'autre pôle, l'activité financière . . .

It has some more general meanings besides, but cannot be substituted as in English for the notion of action (ΠPATTEIN) or the notion of manufacture (ΠOIEIN) (ibid. 198). These are matters of semantic detail: if we wish to grasp more deeply the meaning of a term such

as ΕΡΓΟΝ, it can emerge only from Hesiod's account of the myth of
the conflict between Zeus and Prometheus which explains both the
trouble and toil inseparable from human life and the origin of
culinary fire, source of man's nurture and survival. The concept of
toil (ΠΟΝΟΣ) is therefore traced directly to Prometheus.

The conflict between deities, as told in Hesiod's myth, ends in a
compact whereby the gods promise riches through labour and toil
and whereby those who labour become a thousand times
dearer to the immortals. Work (sweat of the brow) becomes a way
to virtue (APETH), a term which expresses not only a moral quality
but also (in Greek) welfare, success, repute.

Several other key concepts are likewise defined in this system,
in direct relation to the concept of work. For instance, strife
(ΕΡΙΣ) is defined in terms of the strife between Prometheus and
Zeus, and therefore as ambivalent — producing both good and
evil. Strife or struggle, in its positive aspect, is labour in the fields
whereas, in its negative aspect ΕΡΙΣ acts by violence, lies and
injustice. It is thus that the Prometheus myth becomes linked to
Hesiod's key concepts of ΔΙΚΗ, translated by Vernant as 'justice'
and ΥΒΡΙΣ (*démesure*). The argument appears to be that in view
of the primacy of strife, man faces the alternatives of settling by
submitting to arbitration and accepting compensation or
judgement; or of proudly rejecting such a settlement and thus
rejecting the intervention of the gods, relying on his own strength
instead (Vernant 1965: 39—40).[6]

It is by tracing connections of this kind that we begin to understand what 'agricultural activity' would connote in the mind of a
Greek peasant. 'Work' in such a culture implies a relationship with
woman, with fertility, with disease (ΠΑΝΔΟΡΑ), an experience of
toil, trouble, misfortune (ΠΟΝΟΣ), with culinary fire, with
contentions and litigations, and finally also, with a belief in moral
values and their material efficacy. Up to this point we may expect
to find rather similar concepts in Melanesia, even though their
cognitive organization is somewhat different.

Vernant shows that the cultivator's concept of work, briefly
sketched above, was in opposition to the artisan's concept of
making or creating (vb. ΠΟΙΕΙΝ noun ΠΟΙΗΣΙΣ). While the
peasant, as a strong man and toiler, could always take arms and turn
his APETH towards the defence of his own country, the artisan was
by his mode of life far removed from toil or danger. Agriculture,
to the Greeks, was no craft. Trades have secrets but the earth has
no secrets. All it demands is 'husbandry' (ΕΠΙΜΕΛΕΙΑ).

Vernant argues that this difference between tradesman and

peasant is due to the fact that "l'activité de l'artisan appartient à un domaine ou s'exerce en Grèce une pensée déjà positive" while agriculture remains integrated within a system of religious represent- ations. Farming is not considered as transformation of nature to human ends, but as participation in a supra-human order which is natural and divine at the same time (ibid. 204–205).

It is interesting that Vernant is nonetheless not presenting trades as fully secularized. The model he presents is highly relevant even in a study focussed on swidden cultivators where little specialization of work is found, because many of the characteristics here attributed exclusively to artisanship will be found structurally similar to concepts developed by these cultivators in a purely agricultural context. The model, very briefly summarized here, operates on two levels.

The first level is that of the artisan's customer who pays for the work and who, by commissioning it, causes it to be done. Thus, the practice of artisanship begins when the principal actor (who is of course the customer, not the craftsman) perceives a need (XPEIA) for the object. The next step is for the principal actor (again, not the craftsman) to decide upon the plan or design or templet of the object (ΕΙΔΟΣ), even though here the customer and prospective user has to respect the traditions and the limitations of the craft in formulating his commission. The customer's right to decision is justified ideologically by the fact that he alone will have the use (ΧΡΗΣΙΣ) of the object and will therefore know what requirements it has to satisfy; he will be the best judge of it.

Vernant demonstrates that throughout this transaction, it is the user who acts independently and freely on his own behalf (ΠΡΑΞΙΣ) and it is the craftsman who obeys. The technical function (ΠΟΙΗΣΙΣ) is thus in a subordinate position. This does not mean, however, that craft, in Greek ideology, was equated to a purely mechanical operation, as it is in the contemporary West. The category 'craftsman' (ΔΗΜΙΟΥΡΓΟΣ) comprises, apart from wood- and metal-workers, also diviners, heralds, healers, poets. Divine craftsmen, in Greek mythology, helped to create the world. They require not only specialized knowledge, apprenticeship, trade secrets, but also a particular power (ΔΥΝΑΜΙΣ) inherent in individuals as natural qualities (ibid. 212). By means of this special power, craftsmen may give material form to their 'model' (ΕΙΔΟΣ) of good health or of a house, but in the end the artifact is handed over totally to the person who commissioned it, so that the maker retains no connection with it: 'un ouvrage extérieur à l'artisan et étranger à l'activité qui l'a produite' (ibid.: 223).

Vernant reaches two conclusions: the Greek craftsman was producing use-values rather than exchange values;[7] he was 'alienated' from his labour in the sense of losing all control over it when finished. In this last respect he was evidently unlike the Greek peasant as well as unlike the "active man" who commissioned and used what the craftsman produced.

From the viewpoint of Marxist theory, the position of the Greek craftsman is certainly somewhat special. In a mode of production where labour is a generalized commodity and where the division of labour serves merely to improve efficiency in the production of exchange values, one may well predict 'alienation' of the labour force. But how can alienation occur when the creative power of each individual craftsman is freely acknowledged and when the full unfolding of this creativity is hampered by no managerial constraints? The fact that the product is intended to be used by some alter would not in itself cause alienation, or else no craftsman, in the wide sense intended by Vernant could even be free of it. Are all physicians alienated unless they heal themselves? Nor can we simply put the phenomenon down to relations between social classes because there would be no class difference between, for instance, a flute player and a maker of flutes.

It would be easier to believe that 'alienation' refers merely to a particular relation of production rather than to a relation between categories of persons, because, after all, a flute player is not only a user of flutes but also a professional in a musical craft. User and creator roles are normally combined in the same person.

Is there something, then, in the Greek concept of craftsmanship that is distinctive to Greece and causes alienation? This is a question raised but not answered in Vernant's essay of 1965. It is raised again and more nearly answered in the Detienne-Vernant study of 1974. Whatever the Greek data eventually yield about this question, it is plain that technical intelligence is still grossly undervalued today while abstract intelligence is overvalued. It is also plain that the undervaluing of technical intelligence became, somewhere along the road, part of the ideology of the western ruling classes.

However, this be, alienation can clearly not be identified with a particular mode of production or a particular criterion of value. Not only is alienation apt to arise in societies where exchange values are unknown but its opposite, identification, is by no means absent even in a capitalist mode of production.

Works of Art

To test this possibility,.let us consider a major subculture of
capitalism, namely that of literature, music and the arts. Here, work
is manifestly being converted into exchange rather than use values.
Works of art today, even if 'made for' or 'dedicated to' particular
persons, are not really made primarily for their use or personal
edification, but rather a kind of communication between the maker
and the world or universe. Unlike the craftsmen of Ancient Greece,
they do not (except reluctantly) produce work after a design imposed by their paymasters; they do not subscribe to any 'alienating'
reduction of their work to 'average labour'. Moreover, on the
juridical level, they have continuing rights in the product of their
labour even if they 'sell' it — rights that are codified and enforceable
in law. They live by the market value — the exchange value — of
this labour. Clearly we have here a system that combines exchange
value with identification.

This configuration: identification + exchange value is not, of
course, unproblematical. What is a fair price for a poem or
painting? In practice, this depends entirely on reputation. In other
words, it is normal to spend several years in a garret until one has
acquired sufficient,reputation to be able to claim a rate of
remuneration not less than, say, the basic wage for the 'socially
necessary labour time' that goes into one's poems or paintings.

There is a vast perceived difference between the various value
estimations: the exchange value (very low), the use value (very
high if the work is 'good') and the value based on socially
necessary labour time, i.e. what the poet or painter would receive
if he became a 'government artist' in a Marxist-controlled economy.

If the artist wishes to avoid starving in a garret, he can always
take a 'job', i.e. sell his labour not as an artist but as a teacher or
clerk or carpenter or whatever. This labour will in his estimation
have much less use value than his art, but it has far greater exchange
value. He will tend to feel alienated from his 'job' whatever it is
but identified with the art which is his 'real' work. Sedentarized
Indian hunters in Canada and urbanized Orokaiva taro-cultivators
see a rather similar relationship between their 'jobs' and their
'real work'[8] (cf. also Cohen, this volume).

Towards a Melanesian Definition of 'Work'

The present enquiry concentrates on the analysis of concepts of
work found in a specific society, the Orokaiva of the Northern
Province of Papua New Guinea. These concepts, described as an
indigenous semiotic system, are presented with reference to two

oppositions assumed to be universal or at least to be suitable for cross-cultural study.[9]

Vernant's study already implied such a double perspective: he developed the folk model upon a mythological frame while including ethical, ritual and organizational specifications. Next, he interpreted this model in terms of

a) the extent to which the yield of labour was a market commodity (an exchange value, EV) as opposed to serving specifically to satisfy the needs of a particular user (a use value, UV) (cf. Vernant 1965: 222);

b) the extent to which the maker was 'alienated' from the work he produced.

Vernant did not fail to note (ibid., footnote) that alienation, in the Marxist sense, is not supposed to come into being except in a mode of production where commodity production is the dominant category. He tried to overcome this difficulty by presenting the social formation of Ancient Greece as transitional between what one may call elliptically a UV and an EV formation. If, however, we consider a wider sample of societies than Vernant, we soon recognize that alienation existed in this world long before there were any Greek tradesmen, for it is present in the simplest social formations.

Likewise, the implied opposite of 'alienation', viz. identification between man and his work, is by no means confined to formations where the use value category predominates, as our example of the contemporary art world has demonstrated. The present paper proposes that it is useful to study work concepts not just with the aid of the one opposition UV/EV as Vernant has done, but with the aid of a second, independent opposition between identification and alienation (I/A).

This theoretical innovation requires, however, that we first redefine, for our purpose, the rather vague term 'identification'. Our starting point, in defining occupational identifications, is Lévi-Strauss' discussion of caste in *La pensée sauvage* (1962) after the analogy of totemism. Here the occupational identity of castes and sub-castes is signified by a set of rules and prohibitions setting up ideological boundaries between them while implying their interdependence. It comprises many levels of conceptualisation: social, culinary, moral, philosophical as well as occupational.

Two papers develop further our understanding of identity as arising out of the *karma* of occupational castes in India. Searle-Chatterjee's (this volume) analysis of polluted castes shows that occupational identity implies a pattern of collective ritual and psychological characteristics. Not only the work but also the worker are classified as polluted.[10] Parry's (1979) paper about polluted Brahman caste groups[11] presents their occupation as involving identification ("consubstantiality") with the deceased at funerals. The payment they receive for this act of autopollution is represented as gifts they undertake to transmit to the dead. Parry raises the question that these gifts to the Mahabrahmans are not followed by "counter-prestations" in the sense of Mauss (1924). Might not therefore their pollution result from their thus retaining riches they should have passed on or recompensed? This is an important suggestion which it will be convenient to develop a little further.

Let us first, however, return to Vernant's point that man's occupational identity is closely linked with his fertility and sexuality. It is therefore as normal to identify with the work one does as with the sexual activity one emits. In this respect, we would disagree with Baudrillard (1973) who believes that to identify with one's work is to espouse a "puritan ethic". Alienation would then occur if the self is somehow denied further contact with work done, whether this be in the occupational sphere or whether it concerns children, sexual partners etc. Alienation occurs when the yield of such "production" of the self is taken away by others who retain control over it and who return no equivalent gift.

The occupational task of the two caste groups referred to above is to take away productions of other people's selves. The musician sub-castes make and use exclusively passion-arousing music, thus taking away the equanimity of a man's soul; the Mahabrahmans take away with them the deceased they embody. Both groups are essentially abductors who are polluted because it is their occupational role to alienate.

Now, the question is if and how this concept of alienation, derived from Mauss by Parry, relates to Marx's own concept. Mauss (if we may rely somewhat on Sahlins' (1974) interpretation of his argument) represented exchange as involving three partners; a first donor (A), a first recipient (B) and a second recipient (C) who makes a return gift to B. In Mauss' and Sahlins' discussion, there is no suggestion that A is out to make a profit but only that he claims from B some part or all (it is not clear which) of the yield of his gift. If B makes no such return the original gift is 'alienated' from A. In a formal sense, then, the polluted caste groups are *ex officio* in the position of B.

But let us now consider[12] the position, if A is a worker, B an employer/entrepreneur and C a customer. If C pays a remarkably high price, then by the principle just put forward, A would feel entitled to part or all of this yield, but if B will pay nothing except the minimal wage needed to keep A alive, A will feel alienated. He is not kept informed of the true yield of his labour and is allowed no rights over it. Marx's concept of surplus value and Mauss' concept of yield (*hau*) appear therefore to be homomorphous, though bearing on different modes of production. It is for this reason that we believe that identification and alienation in the meanings used here are truly opposites.

What then is the relation between the two sets of oppositions we have developed here? It appears, in the first instance, to be a difference between types of economy and types of conceptualization. When we contrast formations where UV or EV are dominant, we are contrasting types of economy. When we contrast occupational identification/alienation, we contrast types of conceptualization. In the second instance, we may apply the same distinctions within a social formation having more than one mode of production. The Orokaiva social formation falls quite obviously into that category today. We may thus, within that society, distinguish four systems of work concepts, classifiable by the following properties:[13]

1. identification where UV dominant: congruence
2. alienation where EV dominant: congruence
3. alienation where UV dominant: incongruence
4. identification where EV dominant: incongruence.

Possibilities 1 (the 'traditional' system) and 2 (the 'cash income' sector) are congruent in the sense that the concepts of work they present fit ideologies well adapted to reproduce the respective modes of production. Possibilities 3 and 4 are incongruent in the sense that the concepts of work they present do not fit the ideologies serving to reproduce the respective modes of production, but appear to be part of variant or deviant ideologies. The latter two possibilities are often neglected in analysis, but need to be explored if we are to exhaust the logical possibilities or our semiotic domain. It is by envisaging these two possibilities that Orokaiva may be led to conceive of radical changes in patterns of social relations.

How can we test whether the four possibilities we have generated by purely logical processes have a real existence in the case of the Orokaiva social formation? If each possibility represents a system in the sense of Vernant's analysis, then we ought to be able to find in each one a mythological framework, an ethic, a body of ritual and organization. As we shall see, such a demonstration will meet with little difficulty in respect of possibility 1 (the traditional system, with its deities and myths), possibility 2 (where a dominant role has been allotted to Jesus Christ, as we saw above) or possibility 4 (supported from the outset by the vast Melanesian cargo cult literature). On the other hand, alienation where UV are dominant, is a possibility for which documentation is rare indeed. All we appear to have are sporadic cases of cruel exploitation by Melanesian managers.[14]

Yet, if we take a wider view, such exploitation is no isolated phenomenon. Even in societies lacking slavery, we may find instances of it among the defeated in warfare, and in groups of notable political weakness, ruthlessly exploitable by stronger neighbours. For irrevocably alienated individuals only one hope remains of restoring the balance, namely posthumous salvation which often involves vengeance by the ghost after death. While belief in vengeful ghosts is extremely widespread, there are few ideologies where ghostly vengeance constitutes the chief principle of interpretation of the laws of the universe. One such is the ideology of the Kutubu as presented in much detail by F.E. Williams (1976) where the chief myths, deities and religious practices concern disease caused by such vengeance. These facts do not suffice to set up possibility no. 3 as a system among Orokaiva, but they appear to justify some investigation in the framework of the present investigation of work concepts.[15]

It will be possible to define, for each of the four possibilities, distinctive work concepts, forms of management, fields of specialization in skills and crafts, forms of toil, notions of virtue, a principle of strife. Furthermore, for each possibility there is a separate corpus of knowledge, different operating models, techniques, supra-human powers.

The fact that we end up with four such categories (instead of, say three or five) has no special significance. The categories have been logically generated and provide a possible principle of data sorting. But data sorting has no virtue as such. Our categories have the advantage of showing how a culture reacts to the basic contradictions that exist within it. It forms, not only a plurality of ideologies, but of action systems as well each informed by its own ideology.

While there is no need for semiotic classifications to be binary, they do have to be logical rather than experiential. There is a connection between the contradictions that objectively exist and the concepts that are generated. The main point is that there is not only a traditional and a cash system (and on this everyone will at once agree), but there must also be two intermediary logical forms which come down to a cooperative and an exploitative system. These two systems are the traumas generated by the contradictions between the other two. Their existence is known, but some will not see their cognitive genesis. They tend to arise as they are logically implied by the two dominant ones; anyone who does not like 1 and 2 cannot help but think of 3 or 4 or both.

Identification in the Creation of Use Values

When Councillor Colin said that '*pure ari*' did not begin until Jesus Christ (i.e. people did not 'work' before that time) he ignored that *pure ari* in its primary meaning stands for 'to garden' and *pure* is a garden. From an empirical viewpoint we know exactly what goes on in a Sivepe garden, as Waddell has carefully measured it. The daily visit to the garden described by informants as *pure ali* takes a mean of 265 minutes of which 'main task' and 'ancillary tasks' take up in all 44.2% (Waddell and Krinks 1968: 113). The rest is devoted to travel, rest, meals, cooking, washing, other tasks. People always go to the *pure*; they do what they need to do. The amount of 'work' they have does not determine how long they stay. Sometimes they 'work' very hard, sometimes hardly at all.

The gardening tasks are done at a moderate pace which is pleasurable. Rushing and heavy burdens are avoided when possible, but when they are necessary they are classified as 'toil' (*pure gaiha*) and people rest later to make up for it. The only time measures used are: early morning, midday, afternoon (meaning: time to go home) and evening-night (meaning: after supper). Though gardens have a principal crop, mostly taro, the subsidiary crops, ornamental trees, garden house etc. are charmingly land-scaped so that the garden is in a sense an artistic creation (Malinowski 1935; F. Panoff 1969). Whether rows are regular and what is the general standard of husbandry are very much individual matters. It is said that by looking at a person's garden one can read his or her character. Among the Orokaiva the girls are said always to look at a boy's garden before marrying him. De Coppet (1976) reports the same for the Are'are of Malaita, except that it is the girls who are more under scrutiny. The criteria would partly be the style of the garden, showing a pattern of mind, but also and largely the size of the garden, the size and the health of the plants, the quality of the varieties.

One could keep on with such description for a long time without coming closer to defining garden work as a concept. Myths and rites prescribe details of the gardening cycle for each of the principal crops while at the same time establishing identification between grower and crop: taro is a mother; a mother Taro is invoked; married women think of their taro as their children. The

taro ancestress is usually described as discovering the taro in a lake
or other 'round water'. The demigod Totima comes closest to
providing a general model of the primeval world of the swidden
agriculturist and pig-raiser. Like Prometheus he is a sacrificial
figure.[16]

Totoima was at the origin of the feasting institution (though
there are other myths of the origin of feasting). It is here that
questions of moral values mostly arise as feasting (*ergo* peace
making) is the moral act *par excellence*. A direct connection is
laid between the virtue of settling conflict and of feasting on the
one hand and the fertility and yield of the garden on the other,
as enemies are thought to ensorcell the gardens. Another important
factor was the 'care' (*simbari*) (a general term covering magical as
well as technical aspects) taken of the garden. The eldest male of the
extended family, as father of the land, had a special duty as regards
simbari. Garden magic was, however, made by all married males;
they also made gifts to ancestors, who were thought to live in
gardens and be reborn from there.

The model of the virtuous man was he who shared out his produce
and made feasts (*hande embo*). Such a man would grow a surplus of
food in a feasting garden. His power (*ivo*) would be manifest in the
abundance of his pigs and taro. The model of the 'active man'
would be the organizer of feasts in which the whole village participated (*kiti jigari embo*). Subordinate to him, but still high in
reputation, would be experts at sorcery, healing, feather
decoration and various forms of hunting, as well as those excelling
in debate, rhetoric and diplomacy (*keari embo*).[17]

Identification occurred not only with crops, gods and ancestors,
but also with trees harbouring local spirits, plant emblems harbouring
lineage ancestors, animal guardians and plant doubles which were
kept in the garden (usually surrounded by medicinal herbs) and
contained the owner's life spirit, or perhaps name-spirit for the
man bore the plant's name. A more complex aspect of identification
with pigs and feast gardens is that such produce is destined to be
given away, i.e. the owner expects to lose control over it; yet the
donor remains identified with it and it calls for a return.[18] The
same is true for the range of manufactures (clothes, pots,
ornaments) that change hands at feasts.

The pattern described here is characteristic of what Sahlins
(1974) called the domestic mode of production. Such a system
produces, in his opinion, nothing but use values, even if they are
'exchanged' at feasts, for such 'exchange' is symbolically equivalent
to a temporary extension of commensality. Slightly more complex

is the contemporary case where money replaces traditional valuables. Is this money a 'use value'? Anthropologists have often analyzed it as such and not without some justification; the Orokaiva for instance present brideprice banknotes tied one by one to a tall sapling carried aloft by the donor and thus transported to the wifegiver. After presentation it is often stored in wait for other similar occasions. The fact is, however, that eventually this treasure is converted into exchange values. Furthermore, it owes its status as a valuable to its potential exchange value. It is therefore more easily accounted for in the preset four-system method of analysis as will appear later.

The same remark may be made in respect of labour assistance between households which is normally given without payments except for a meal at the end of the day. If, however, the service is given in connection with work for which the person assisted will eventually get paid, then the service falls within a different category and must be paid for. The same rule applies to the granting of land useholds for which no rent is ever demanded if the land produces (only) use values, but the situation changes when it produces exchange values. Use value is therefore a concept determining Orokaiva behaviour.

Finally, it is as true of the Orokaiva as of the ancient Greeks that conflict and war (*isoro*) did not have a necessarily negative connotation connotation. They might be bad or good according to circumstances. War, sorcery and other forms of negative reciprocity are part of this mode of production; they cannot be equated to 'alienation'. There is increasing evidence that Levi-Strauss (1943) was correct in viewing war in these societies as a modality of interdependence.

To sum up, the Orokaiva had a basic classification of *pure* as between subsistence and feasting. An inspection of the crop by the feast-giver was needed to let crops pass from the subsistence to the feasting category. (It was not done if the harvest was insufficient.) The term *pure ari*, whatever its customary translation into English, was never used to denote any kind of effectiveness in ensuring a food supply. In case of garden failure, people did not ascribe it to neglectful *pure ari* but rather to neglectful *simbari*. It is the demigods of the various crops and the ancestors who do the actual producing in the garden, and all that is expected of man is to clear, to plant and to protect against magical and technical dangers. Watchfulness is the key; toil is a consequence. A flawless garden testifies to watchfulness in the first instance; to physical prowess also, but only in the second instance. In this respect i.e. the technical as well as the magical watchfulness, *pure ari* is intermediate between the Greek concepts of EPΓON and TEXNH.

Time is therefore a highly inappropriate measure of useful activity in Orokaiva gardens. Whether *simbari* is effective or ineffective does not depend just on the time spent. It depends on the warding off of sorcery and hence on ensuring one has no dangerous enemies. It depends on harmony in the family. It depends on avoiding straying pigs, not just by building fences but by being the kind of person into whose garden one does not want one's pigs to stray. The anthropological observer notices a certain selectiveness in Orokaiva pigs . . .

A great man, or a manager, is not always a gardener. He may be a sorcerer. But if he is a gardener he is a great gardener. He accomplishes his garden as a craftsman accomplishes a model, an ΕΙΔΟΣ, or as Orokaiva say, an *ove*. His image of the world is not dark like that of Hesiod or of Adam's curse. An Orokaiva inform-ant once recorded for me on tape his version of the relevant portion of Genesis:

> "You will bear children, lift string bags, draw water; you will do all those things and be loaded down with sorrow, so He said; and then He spoke to her husband Adam thus: You will take the axe, cut the second growth, chop down the trees, lop off the branches. In the hot sun, in sorrow, with pain all over your body, you will labour hard." He said.
>
> He thereupon determined that Eve and Adam spoke thus: "This is the way we shall all wish to act on earth: our bodies will be painful from work; and the women as well as the men will be in pain and sorrow from hard work. And as our food will be prepared and ready we stay to eat. All right we did not know that God would not let us have what we had taken and eaten."
>
> Therefore God said to them: "Long will be the day of sorrow when you have sorrow, but when you have happy days you will be happy." So he said. Therefore we shall live in this way from now onwards . . . [19]

This interpretation is not, I believe, merely garbled. It is a clear message that the Orokaiva just will not understand why, after working hard in the sun, they should afterwards eat their bread or taro in sorrow. To them, this is not a mere question of how they would feel, but a moral matter. Whoever wrote the original of this text was obviously lacking in respect for bread or targo.

Daniel de Coppet (1976) rightly suggested gardening in Melanesia was a religious act, like a sacrament, as is also eating the produce. Whatever pain there may be is sacramentally transformed. Man feels his unity with the Taro goddess and also with the garden and the crop.

Alienation in the Creation of Exchange Value

In the Orokaiva village, exchange value may enter in four ways: through cash crops, outside gifts, labour and business. The two latter categories are recent. Whereas wages were an insignificant item in most villages during my 1966–67 study, a recent income survey (Newton 1978) in a typical village showed an overall income of about K675 per household, made up of coffee returns 35%, wages 37%, migrant gifts 12%.

We have no special studies of work concepts in this sector, but some general indications. It may seem surprising that Jesus Christ was nominated as the originating deity of monetary compensation for work, but New Guineans widely regard him as originator of European wealth and therefore also, not illogically, of the concept of money and exchange value. The idea of converting labour into money, in itself, greatly interests New Guineans. Thus Daniel de Coppet shows that in the Are'are social system there is but one traditional method of converting food and services into shell money, viz by acting as an undertaker. For this reason the office of undertaker was a highly valued one. Thus Councillor Colin might well genuinely revere a deity or culture hero who instituted the full convertibility of labour into money.

The term *pure ari* is appropriate to describe the white man's labour if for no other reason than that a 'job' just like the *pure* is a place where one spends the day. The new dispensation has, sure enough, its own conflict (*isoro*) and mode of conflict resolution. Councillor Colin brings this out by his example of the policeman who puts village men into handcuffs and takes them off to court. In such a case it was the task of the sorcerer to ensure that the men would escape conviction and be set free again.[20] Virtue, in such a system, is largely a matter of keeping out of trouble, but also it is a matter of not squandering the money but reserving some — ideally half — of it to serve the needs of kinsmen and fellow villagers: contributions to ceremonial payments, feasts, travel expenses etc. Briefly, wages tend to be converted into political power.

No great value was usually attached to conversion to western commodities, except where these became valued prestations. Thus, when transistor radios became valued prestations, they began to appear in large quantities in the villages and were mostly paid for by absentee workers.

The subsistence/feasting duality continues in this system in that some money is needed for the former but a labourer would have little status in his home village if he did not set aside something for the latter. Also, migrants normally leave behind a family member with the task of looking after the land (*simbari*) in a technical, magical and juridical sense. Often he also leaves behind a wife for whom he is saving brideprice but who meanwhile must be looked after by his relatives. Money sent home therefore covers not only feasting contributions but also the function of *simbari*. This is not because village people would not perform such services free of charge but because, when a man earns money, those who help him earn that money are entitled to their share.

If we look only at the relations of production migrants have in their jobs, they seem totally 'alienated' (cf. Parkin, this volume). Not only have they no control whatever over the product of their labour but this product lies entirely outside their conceptual universe. Yet these migrants avoid proletarianization in the full sense because they continue to have a stake in the village environment, which has its own economic, political and ideological base.

Our remarks above apply similarly to the village cash-crop sector. With the exception of coconuts, the use value Orokaiva see in European cash-crops is either very limited or non-existent. Coffee and cocoa are classified as non-foods, rubber latex as an unusable substance. Even the coconut, though an important food when fresh, represents no use value to Orokaiva when dried into copra.

This lack of perceived utility has not stopped cultivation of these crops on village land nor their processing by village-purchased machinery. Everyone irrespective of age is growing coffee. Those who are pressed for time tend to give priority to coffee and to partially replace their plantings of taro with 'German taro' — less valued but less laborious.[21]

Growing coffee is not considered pleasurable like growing taro. When suggesting to an informant that coffee trees have a sweet smell, I was firmly told: "*We* think the smell is dreadful". Such feelings go to show that the division between the spheres of use value and exchange value is not purely analytical but corresponds to a conceptual boundary between two models of life and work, and that Orokaiva try to keep this boundary clear. Coffee is grown because it takes far less time than it would to grow subsistence crops for the market, but the grower feels alienated from it while he feels identified with the subsistence crops. A small quantity of subsistence crops — surplus to requirements — is in fact sold in local markets for consumption by local people, but growers take the same care with them and regard them in the same way as the food they eat.

It is paradoxical that the work represented as introduced by Jesus

Christ does not, like traditional work, have a palpable virtue such that the good man will succeed at it while the bad man will fail. Anyone at all can succeed at New Guinea wage labour — *wok mani tasol* as it is called in Neo-Melanesian.[22] Yet this money, when it enters the village gift exchange circuit, will establish claims to status on an equal footing with wealth available only to cultivators with real traditional power (*ivo*).

It is this anomaly that appears to have been coped with by the New Guinea gambling system. The game called *laki* (lucky) is supposedly a game of pure chance but if chance is with you it shows that a powerful ancestor is supporting you. Your luck at the game shows your spiritual resources just as luck at gardening shows this. It is the people with weaker ancestors who lose. Medicines are also used to improve luck, but they are secondary. Evidence for supranatural intervention is that the results of the game, instead of being random as one would expect from the rules, always favour the same individuals. Whether these individuals play honestly I cannot tell, as the game goes on day and night and only a very weak lantern is used at night, my tilley lamp being considered unsuitable.

Laki is played by Orokaiva especially when the coffee proceeds have just been distributed and generally whenever a large number of community members receive money from non-traditional sources simultaneously. Play may continue for several days without interruption, until all the money is cleaned up by a single winner. This redistribution restores the traditional status pattern disturbed by the culture hero Jesus Christ.

Playing cards are outlawed in Papua New Guinea; nobody is allowed legally to possess them or to import them. Though this legislation was a response to popular pressure, it was in the churches that the pressure was in fact generated. It is thus hoped that New Guineans will eventually allocate status on the basis of the mere possession of money. The total inefficacy of this government legislation shows that New Guineans have great difficulty in accepting this secularized concept of work and status. Magico-religious tests have the function of hallowing money. They also assert the supremacy of traditional work concepts over modern ones.

Alienation in the Creation of Use Values

It is especially the French Marxist africanists such as Terray, Meillassoux, Auge,[23] who have alerted us to the prevalence of exploitation in tribal or lineage-societies where anthropologists tended to play down such a possibility. While the concept of exploitation is perhaps more directly relevant to Marxist theory than alienation, it has certain drawbacks that are now widely recognized. Where use-values are predominant it is common practice to set up not so much a division of labour (Vernant has rightly argued one cannot call it that) but rather an allocation of tasks to persons or social categories who are thought to have special competence for them. Thus, as the most common example, certain tasks are allocated on the basis of criteria like age and sex. Now, this is not in itself exploitation though obviously it may well lead to exploitation. We therefore need a criterion, other than that of the task allocation itself, to determine whether exploitation in fact occurs.

I shall press this point by citing one counter-instance. Among the Orokaiva only women are considered competent to harvest. Men never do it and claim that, if they did, the taro supply would be exhausted too soon. As an exception, they do harvest taro for feasts, and this exception only goes to confirm that they would be far too prodigal to act as daily harvesters. Is this just a story to exploit women? When crops are being marketed, the rule among Orokaiva is that the men carry the coffee and are paid for the coffee, but taro and other subsistence vegetables, when taken to market, are taken by women who also retain the money. Their right to the produce is maintained not only for the daily food supply but also when there is money to be earned. Their right to the product of their labour does not seem to be questioned. Thus, by the criteria we have been using, Orokaiva women are not an alienated labour force and it will be seen that *alienation* is more convenient in an operational sense than the concept of exploitation, which may be too broad.

While studies of alienation in Melanesia are rare, it is possible to give some indication of the patterns. M. Panoff, in his study of Maenge suicides (1970), did not question the generally accepted model of Melanesian society as governed by certain strong exchange and 'equivalence' principles. He points out, however, that there may well be a minority of marginal individuals who are somehow too weakly established to be within the range of those principles: they may at times press their rightful claims, but without success. Panoff shows that the male suicides among the Maenge occur as a general rule against this background of ruthless and unlimited exploitation. In fact it is only suicide that sets a limit to exploitation in such cases. The proportion of people Panoff places in that category appears to be of the order of 5% of male population.[24]

These people were alienated by the criterion we chose because they had been working for someone who refused them what they considered their proper reward — in other words, the right to the product of their labour. At the same time, we note that the phenomenon described by Panoff was marginal: the other 95% of the male population were not alienated.

It is my impression that there are still other alienated categories in Melanesia, especially among defeated groups or clans who lost their land after a war and are reduced to the status of wanderers or, again, who remained on their land but were constantly at the mercy of marauders. When I discussed such cases, I was told by several informants from different villages independently that there were certain weak groups with whom in olden times they practised no exchanges but had only relations of warfare. Such groups evidently possessed some valued resources — not only women but also feathers and other forest products, for instance, but they lay outside the circle where moral principles applied (cf. Williams 1930).[25]

The theoretical importance of such cases may be far greater than their statistical importance. These are, after all, the cases projected by Hobbes in his model of the stateless society. Anthropologists have been much concerned to prove Hobbes wrong, but this concern should not blind us to that minority of situations where he may well have been right. There is not, to my knowledge, any Melanesian ideology which validates and elaborates the Hobbesian model, nor the Nietzschian model[26] that gives full weight to the principle of reciprocity while condemning it as a weakness to be transcended. But is even a Melanesian Nietzsche completely inconceivable?

Identification in the Creation of Exchange Values

Our discussion of the culture hero Jesus Christ was necessarily incomplete. For he did not institute merely payment for labour — a real gift to man but, as we have seen, somewhat limited in scope, but he also gave to the white man all his immeasurable wealth and power. But this wealth and power did precisely not, in the New Guineans' estimation, come to the European by his own wage labour. It came by methods New Guineans did not at once understand. This whole cargo ideology is too well documented to need restatement here, but any study of Melanesian work would be quite incomplete unless it included the category of cargo work, i.e. work to obtain cargo.

Cargo deities are renewed for each movement; in all cases their return to earth would not only bring the wealth but also a new moral order. They would banish strife, indeed brotherhood between tribes is a condition of their return. This idea existed in the Northern Province of Papua New Guinea as early as the Taro movement of 1914 (Williams 1928). The work to be done is ritual work for which the design (*ove*) is laid down by the prophet of the cult. The form of *simbari* required here has to do with certain ritual places where the miraculous return might take place — among the Orokaiva, often graveyards. As for the cargo itself, the correct term is *hande*, i.e. generous sharing out of the treasure that has previously remained hidden from the New Guineans.

All these concepts will seem marginal until one sees their implications for everyday events. To this end, let us consider the position of money as *hande*. Most anthropologists have treated ceremonial money prestations as simply equivalent to traditional valuables. But is it really? First of all, it is common knowledge that traditional valuables are no longer acceptable as a substitute for money. This has sometimes been interpreted as a purely secular liking for money, which to a westerner seems so plausible that he does not see the need for explanation. If the money is presented as a money tree, this again can be explained away as substitution within a traditional idiom.

When I discussed savings societies, I expected to be given an explanation in terms of practical spending projects or other economic considerations but was given a political argument instead. It was to equal the power of the Europeans, so I was told. Again, a friend was presented with a dollar to be taken back with him to New Zealand. He should put it in the bank there, so he was told, and then it would multiply a thousandfold. On an apparently quite different topic, wages, I was told that the wealth created by them exceeded by far what they were given as pay.

It is for this reason that Orokaiva are exceedingly interested in 'business', both cooperative and individual. I have personally observed a copra cooperative and several trade store and truck projects, both cooperative and individual. Newton (1978), in a village close to the ones I know, describes in much detail six trade stores, four truck ventures and a cattle project, which represents a great deal of activity for one small village over a six-months period. Several of these projects were cooperative. All of them were failures. The fact that the ventures all fail does not stop people from repeating the experience year after year.

Let us now consider in detail one of the events described by

Newton. She points out that though, in general, people help each other without expecting payment in money, cash must be paid for activities where the employer expects to make a profit, i.e. where he is engaged in 'business'. There was a Youth Group who offered themselves for labour contracts but nobody "hired the group to build a house — a subsistence activity". Labour was "treated as a commodity" and used only to create exchange values.

Now, Newton suggests this was because such money-making "was seen as a corporate action and necessitated profit sharing". Thus, children were paid if they carried cash crops to market. They were, however, compensated according to age, rather than according to time and labour input. "Eldest sons and daughters received a large portion, as might senior shareholders in a family company."

Thus, people were doing exactly the same labour in the village as they were paid for outside. Outside, this labour was alienating because workers had no control over the product of their labour. In the village businesses, they did share control of the product. But, from the pay rates quoted by Newton, it is clear that the 'business' could never afford the rates allowed. Why this perpetual disproportion between the small yield and the large distribution to shareholders?

The common pattern in all the data I have quoted lies in the miraculous increase of which money is thought to be capable once it has been subjected to certain ritual practices which the Orokaiva call 'business'. These are rituals which work when practised on a taro shoot — it swells, it multiplies. Ever since the taro cult, taro is the model for multiplication.

But the problem thus posed is insoluble. How, indeed, could these businesses prosper? Only by paying the workers less, by giving no credit, by ensuring that one takes more money from the brothers in the village than they ever get back. Only, in fact, by their alienation. There are so few of them; they have so little — one must be greedy indeed to survive in those villages in business. But alienation is not part of their project. They want the businesses to succeed without alienation. It is in this that they are a religious rather than economic practice.

Thus it is not from ignorance that they fail. Furthermore, it is only the White observers and social scientists who see anything tragic in these failures. If the Orokaiva thought them tragic, they would stop setting them up again and again. Miss Newton rightly comments that you gain status even by, and especially by failing. Your business dies; its limbs or assets are spread among the multitude and increase exceedingly. It is a religious practice.[27]

Conclusion

This paper has been an exercise in semiotic anthropology. Semiotics has always been a part of anthropology (cf. Schwimmer 1977b), but we are becoming more conscious about it and borrowing some methods. We therefore set up a domain, consisting of two sets of oppositions (use value/exchange value; identification/alienation) which seemed to be in some need of clarification. We broke the domain down to its modalities and as a result, I hope, clarified a number of Orokaiva concepts of 'work' — all a little unexpected, probably, and certainly not clear to myself until I began analysis in the form described here. Moreover, the two oppositions that formed the frame have become a little clearer too.

Semiotic anthropology has a limited role, but this role is precisely what has been attempted here: clarifying concepts. I might have made up an abstract model from the modalities and the categories but refrained as it would have added little. I have tried to make the connections visible: semiotics does not compose master schemes, it decomposes them.

Notes

1. Fieldwork done in the Northern Province of Papua New Guinea (1966–67, 1970, 1973) and used as basis for the present discussion was supported by grants from the Canada Council.
2. This statement was made to me by Councillor Colin in a taped oration held in Torogota in 1966. His words: '*Iji aramiko ambo ainge eaora. Amina pure mo umbae. Amora pure re Keriso na ikena umbasi ea avo.*'
3. Melanesian time allocation studies have recently been the subject of a detailed economic analysis (Kirkpatrick 1977). It is of interest that the field studies of time allocation which were given the highest "subjective rating" (ibid. Table 6.1) were Waddell (1972) and Waddell and Krinks (1968). The latter study was conducted in the Orokaiva villages of Ionda and Sivepe, where I myself did intensive research some years later, on a different subject. As I have already published a detailed commentary on the Waddell and Krinks study (Schwimmer 1969: 144–152), I say little about it here. It is, however, highly relevant to a conceptual study such as the present one.
4. M. Panoff reports that *kuma*, in the sense of subsistence activities, took up an average of four hours per day among the Maenge. He mentions no cash crops. Kirkpatrick's statistics (1977, Table 6.3) show that the mean time spent per man on all agricultural tasks in nine Melanesian villages is about 22 hours per week. One may thus assume that Panoff's figure refers to all tasks making up agricultural activity in Melanesian time allocation studies. But what is here meant by 'activity'? As we show in the present article, it includes not only the main and ancillary agricultural

tasks but also travel, rest, meals and miscellaneous "other tasks" — the most mentionable of which are cooking and washing. The phrase "dépense d'énergie" must thus be taken very broadly.

5. The present author's knowledge of Greek antiquity is at undergraduate level. From an anthropological viewpoint, an interesting general discussion of Hesiod will be found in Jaeger (1946). But see also Vernant (1965: 19–47) and Detienne and Vernant (1974: 59–124).

6. The translation of ΔIKH as 'justice' obscures an interesting difference made in Greek between two kinds of justice. *Themis* (ΘEMIΣ) justice as dispensed by the early kinds and nobles whereas ΔIKH appears to be a system of dispute settlement by compensation payments to the injured party. The fundamental meaning of ΔIKH is 'due share' (Jaeger 1946: 103). YBPIΣ would then be to refuse compensation and seek justice by force.

7. Vernant's explanation (p. 222) of this classification is as follows: "Dans la perspective de la valeur d'usage, le produit n'est pas vu en fonction du travail humain qui l'a créé, comme travail cristallisé; c'est au contraire le travail qui est vu en fonction du produit, comme propre à satisfaire tel besoin de l'usager . . . Marx écrit, de façon frappante, qu'en qualité de valeur d'échange, la marchandise n'est plus envisagée au point de vue du service qu'elle rend mais du service qui lui a été rendu par cela qu'elle a été produite." (*Critique de l'Economie politique*, p. 32.)

8. It has been objected that a work of art differs from a taro in that the former is a statement about patterns in the universe while the latter is not. My own view of taros, however, is that in the sense of Hjelmslev, they ought to be regarded as sign as well as substance; as signs, which they are whenever handled ritually, they do contain statements about the universe. On the semiotic issues involved see Hjelmslev (1953), Schwimmer (1977a, 1977b).

9. For relevant ethnographic data on Orokaiva, see Williams (1928, 1930); Waddell and Krinks (1968); Schwimmer (1967, 1969, 1973, 1974a, 1979a). For specifically semiotic investigations on Orokaiva, see Schwimmer (1974b, 1977a, 1979a, 1979b.)

10. Searle-Chatterjee demonstrates that group identity among the polluted caste groups remains firm and positive. It appears to be threatened only by the attempted suppression of the notion of caste by the central government. If this should ever succeed, caste identity would be threatened, because public belief in its toughness, hotbloodedness, honour etc. would be lost.

11. While I have learnt a good deal from Parry's fascinating analysis of the Mahabrahmans, I wish to dissociate myself from Parry's comments on Louis Dumont, as it would not be very difficult to reconcile Parry's findings with Dumont's theory.

12. I wish to acknowledge a debt to Mr. Edwin Ardener who suggested this argument to me during conversation at the York conference. He is not responsible, of course, for what I did with it. A rather similar point is made by Dumont (1977: 118, 182).

13. This method of setting up semiotic domains for study is probably due to Lévi-Strauss, long before it became canonized as part of the science of semiotics (Eco 1972). See also Schwimmer (1977a), for an Orokaiva example.

14. The term 'manager' instead of the tedious 'big man' is due to Burridge (1969) and is heartily recommended to practitioners.

15. I briefly analyzed Williams' Kutubu study (Williams 1976), but missed the full implications of the myth cycle reported by Williams. A rea-reanalysis of that work, with full use of the myths, is overdue.

16. See for a first analysis Schwimmer (1973), later supplemented by Schwimmer (1974a) (coconut, areca and taro) and (1979a) (pigs).

17. A discussion of work specialization among Orokaiva (of which there is but little) will be found in Schwimmer (1967). An interesting type of specialist not so far described is the expert body decorator (Schwimmer 1973: 177, 185) to whom the ritual payment of a pig is due when he officiates, and who appears to officiate regularly at initiations.

18. For a full discussion of the concepts involved see Schwimmer (1979a).

19. The text: "*Umo meni ingesoa, eti atimbasoa, i umbasoa, umo timbasoa; donda deire tapa amo aisi oa eto tunga osaga umbasoa.' Ainge ena. Ainge ivu ta ena: 'Adam, umo ainge hogoro umbasoa, andage aisi oa eto i gaipi oa, pure jirembasi oa; iji vevere tunga osago hamo memega re tapa pure gaiha aisi oa.' Ainge ena. Ainge eto ikena avo embo Eave te Adam te ainge ena: 'Ainge dombo dago tapa endata emo ainge do aisi uje eagora: pure te deire amo tapa hamo memega te tunga osaga te tapa pamone ainge ga earora, dago embo ainge hamo memega te tunga osaga te tapa pure gaiha avo earora. Eto donda matu nunuga ena avo indie iraetera avo. Aravorate, ungo kiaekiae eto God na taekena avo umbuto india. Aravo embo eto avo God ena: 'Avo iji koso ami tunga osaga iji tunga osaga aisi ova, ainge tunga javatoho iji amo tunga javatoho aisi ova.' Ainge ena. Avo embo dago tapa emo oroho emite ue irora.*" Robert, Sivepe, 1966.

20. The text: "*Embo handa pirisi embo na punduto umbuto, sokova ari ke eto umbuto, Kokoda pambuo, koto ea, aramiko pure mo aravora.*" Councillor Colin, Tórogota, 1966. After describing a number of devices used by magicians and miracles they wrought, Colin continued: "*Avo da pirisi embo na samani eo pambuto re koto ea, amiko donda aravo porakau aravo pure puvuna.*" Translation: Police handcuffed village people and took them to Kokoda if they were believed to be telling lies. Court was held; then they would start work . . . When a summons was issued by the policeman, then those magic things would be put to work.

21. At the time the Waddell and Krinks study was done, only the younger men grew coffee; the authors therefore saw a correlation between age and coffee growing. During my restudy I found this correlation to be false, first because it did not apply to the clan omitted from the earlier authors' chosen sample, and secondly because the oldest men they studied began to grow coffee shortly after their departure. The sub-stitution of German taro (*xantosoma* sp.) for classical taro (*colocasia* sp.)

appears to be the standard response to lack of time, rather than foregoing coffee.

22. On New Guinea concepts of paid labour and the yield of such labour I learned a great deal from Cloutier (1975–1978).

23. Auge's material on the rich who were inevitably suspected of being zombie masters (1975) is a good illustration of our theme. But on this same phenomenon, see also Ardener (1970).

24. For a somewhat similar analysis of suicide, this time in Polynesia, see Firth (1967, Ch. 5) on suicide and risk taking in Tikopia.

25. For a further example of 'exploitation' of the defeated see Meggitt (1977: 25–26).

26. In *Zur Genealogie der Moral*, Nietzsche (1954: 761–900) offers a detailed discussion of the principle of reciprocity, concerning which he held views rather radically opposed to those of Marcel Mauss. He regarded it as a delusion to be eradicated. Orokaiva likewise regard it as a delusion if practised outside the 'security circle' (see Schwimmer 1979a).

27. This argument, and indeed this entire essay, is close in orientation to Dumont (1977) which can be read as an attempt to set limits on economism in anthropology and elsewhere. We do not question the importance of economics but the delimitation of economics as a separate domain.

References

Ardener, Edwin, 1970. Witchcraft economics and the continuity of belief. In *Witchcraft confessions and accusations*, Mary Douglas (ed.). A.S.A. Monographs 9. London: Tavistock Publ.

Auge, Marc. 1975. *Théorie des pouvoirs et idéologie*. Paris: Hermann.

Baudrillard, Jean. 1973. *Le miroir de la production*. Paris: Castermann.

Belshaw, Cyril S. 1949. *Economic aspects of culture contact in Eastern Melanesia*. Unpub. PhD thesis, University of London.

Burridge, K.O.L. 1969. *Tangu traditions*. Oxford University Press.

Cloutier, Guy. 1975–1978. Field reports on migration, urbanisation, authority patterns, economy, education, the supranatural, spirit beings, Christianity at Lae, Papua New Guinea. Manuscript.

De Coppet, Daniel, 1976. *Jardins de vie, jardins de mort en Mélanésie*, *Traverses* 5/6, 166–177.

Detienne, Marcel et Jean-Pierre Vernant. 1974. *Les ruses de l'intelligence. la métis des Grecs*. Paris: Flammarion.

Dumont, Louis. 1977. *Homo aequalis*. Paris: NRF.

Eco, Umberto. 1972. *La structure absente*. Paris: Mercure de France.

Firth, Raymond, 1967. *Tikopia ritual and belief*. London: Allen and Unwin.

Godelier, Maurice. 1973. *Horizon, trajets marxistes en anthropologie*. Paris: Maspero.

Hjelmslev, L. 1953. *Prolegomena to a theory of language*. Madison: University of Wisconsin Press.

Jaeger, Werner. 1946. *Paideia: the ideals of Greek culture*, vol. I. Oxford:

Basil Blackwell.

Kirkpatrick, G. 1977. *An analysis of time allocation and labour supply in the rural village sector of Melanesia*. London: Brunel University. Multigraph.

Lawrence, P. 1964. Work, employment and trade unionism in Papua and New Guinea. *The Journal of Industrial Relations* **6** (2), 23–40.

Lévi-Strauss, Claude. 1943. Guerre et commerce chez les Indiens de l'Amérique du Sud. *Renaissance* **I** (1–2), 122–139.

—— 1962. *La pensée sauvage*. Paris: Plon.

Malinowski, B. 1935. *Coral islands and their magic*. Vol. 1. London: Allen and Unwin.

Mauss, Marcel, 1924. Essai sur le don. *Année Sociologique*. 2e serie, t.I. Reprinted: *Sociologie et anthropologie*, 1950, 143–279.

Meggitt, Merwyn. 1977. *Blood is their argument*. Palo Alto: Mayfield Publishing Co.

Newton, Janice. 1978. *No bucks – an analysis of money in an Orokaiva village*. Melbourne: Monash University, Mimeo.

Nietzsche, F. 1954ff. *Werke*. Band II. München: Karl Hauser Verlag.

Panoff, Francoise. 1969. Some facets of Maenge horticulture. *Oceania* **XL**, 20–31.

Panoff, Michel. 1970. Du suicide comme moyen de gouvernement. *Les Temps Modernes* **288**, 109–130.

—— 1977. Energie et vertu: le travail et ses répresentations en Nouvelle-Bretagne. *L'Homme* **XVII** (2–3), 7–21.

Parry, J.P. 1979. Ghosts, greed and sin. Paper at ASA conf. 1979.

Sahlins, Marshall, 1974. *Stone age economics*. London: Tavistock.

Salisbury, R. 1962. *From stone to steel*. Melbourne: University Press.

Schwimmer, Erik G. 1967. Modern Orokaiva leadership. *Journal of the Papua New Guinea Society* **I** (2), 52–60.

—— 1969. *Cultural consequences of a volcanic eruption experienced by the Mount Lamington Orokaiva*. Eugene, Department of Anthropology, University of Oregon.

—— 1973. *Exchange in the social structure of the Orokaiva*. London: Hurst.

—— 1974a. Objects of mediation: myth and praxis. In *The unconscious in culture*, I. Rossi (ed.). New York: E.P. Dutton, 209–237.

—— 1974b. Friendship and kinship: an attempt to relate two anthropological concepts. In *The compact*, E. Leyton (ed.). Newfoundland: Memorial University I.S.E.R., 49–70.

—— 1977a. What did the eruption mean? In *Exiles and migrants in Oceania*, M.D. Lieber (ed.), ASAO Monograph 5. Honolulu: University Press of Hawaii, 296–341.

—— 1977b. Semiotics and culture. In *A perfusion of signs*, T.A. Sebeok (ed.). Bloomington: Indiana University Press, 153–179.

—— 1979a. Reciprocity and structure. *Man* **14**, (2), 271–285.

—— 1979b. Feasting and tourism. a comparison. *Semiotica*.

Vernant, Jean-Pierre. 1965. *Mythe et pensée chez les Grecs*. Paris: Maspero.

Waddell, E. 1972. *The mound builders*. University of Washington Press.
Waddell, E. and Krinks, P. 1968. The organisation of production and
  distribution among the Orokaiva. *New Guinea Research Bulletin* **24**.
Williams, F.E. 1928. *Orokaiva magic*. Oxford University Press.
—— 1930. *Orokaiva society*. Oxford University Press.
—— 1976. *The Vailala madness and other essays*. London: Hurst.

THE CATEGORIZATION OF WORK:

Cases from Coastal Kenya

DAVID PARKIN

Introduction: The Understanding of Work

My analytical interest is in how a folk-concept of 'work' becomes
distinguished from and opposed to concepts of non-work. It would
seem that when 'work' as a general concept and types of work themselves become subject to discrete and unambiguous classification,
then this entails a struggle for, and possibly a shift in, control of
the individual's productive capacity from him/herself to other
persons. We then get the development of the familiar etic view of
the producer's alienation from the products of his labour. That is
to say, discreteness of classification facilitates accurate measurement,
a neat emic separation of labour-time from leisure-time, and a
struggle between the consumer and the producer, usually *via* an
entrepreneur, as to how the producer's activities should be
defined as appropriate to each of these two categories. Historically,
this struggle can be seen most obviously in the movement from
pre-industrial to industrial society.

There is, however, also an ahistorically relevant level of
fundamental concept at which the basic opposition is between
productive tasks or activities which offer the individual control
over his own and his family's destiny and those that do not: the
controllable activities are classified as 'good' and the uncontrollable
ones as 'bad'. This concern with the moral basis of folk-definitions
of activities as either worthy or unworthy takes us below the
surface, ethnocentric concern with what we translate as 'work'. It
enables us to see the common logic underlying varying cultural
responses to, for example, the introduction of wage employment.
The logic is that of a constant re-definition of the best methods
of controlling forces external to humanity, whether these be
'material' or 'spiritual'.

The clearest historical example of the categorization of work
as a discrete notion, in opposition to that of leisure, can be found
in Victorian England, and is well documented by a number of

social historians (Bailey 1978; Lowerson and Myerscough 1977; and Malcolmson 1973). We are given by these historians a clear picture of English pre-industrial culture (i.e. before 1830) as having no clear-cut conceptual division between labour and leisure (Bailey 1978: 2). In rural areas festivals and holidays were tied in to the seasonal regularities of the agricultural cycle, sometimes reinforced by religious breaks, so that it was essentially nature which was seen, by the people themselves, to reduce or increase people's work-load or which demanded the "complementary sociability" (ibid.) that went with the collective endeavours of digging, planting, and harvesting. In towns "traditional craft practices laid down the ritual patterns of celebration and good fellowship". Intermediary between town and country, fairs combined trading with fun-making and leisure pursuits. The rural and urban ruling classes contributed happily to the rituals of licence which also accompanied the seasonal festivities and which, for one day only, reversed the roles of power and privilege. In all these ways, work and leisure were seen as shading into each other almost imperceptibly.

Then came land enclosure, urban growth, evangelicism, "the rigorous disciplining of labour under the new industrial capitalism" (ibid.), and a new view by the ruling classes of "plebian culture as morally offensive, socially subversive, and a general impediment to progress" (ibid.). The definition of what was deserved and worthwhile now became a focus of class hostility rather than of 'tolerance'. More than that, the definitional distinction between work and leisure became sharper, so much so that leisure became the obverse rather than the complement of work: for the poor and *nouveaux riches* alike, a little leisure became hard work's reward. So, by the middle of the nineteenth century an ethic of work had emerged whose virtue and legitimacy was defined by its opposition to an ethic of leisure. Time taken in leisure was time off work, and *vice versa*. The two were dichotomous. This is one aspect of a more general process of industrial capitalism by which work becomes categorized or set apart as an entity standing in opposition to another.

What I now describe from a rural area in coastal Kenya is another aspect of this definitional separation, asymmetry and conceptual dominance of industrial work, not however just in relation to leisure, but to other kinds of pre-industrial trade and craft work. Also, just as in pre-industrial English culture, work and leisure were often intertwined in ritual and religious festivities, both Christian and animistic and sometimes mixed, so the pre-capitalist notion of work among the people I have studied seems also to have been separated out from a comparable embeddedness in religious ideas. Here, then, is a religious and moral origin of the concept of labour as an embedded rather than discrete concept.

It is empirically proper to put this discussion in the context of the so-called great problem of unemployment in Africa. So-called because it is often more an ideological question of *how* unemployment and employment are defined in relationship to each other in a modern society that is more relevant than the presence or absence of a specific quota of jobs.

I want to remedy the view that African systems of labour division and definition are really so passive in the face of the shift to wage dependency. We may ask what part such cultural forms play in defining the 'new' capitalistic distinction between employment and unemployment (cf. Gutkind 1975). The point of answering this question is that it should help us understand the essence of any new ideologies which have developed along with the emergence of widespread wage dependency. We can view such ideologies not as pale reflections of the dictates of a ruling élite but as the time-hallowed instruments by which ordinary people debate their destinies, turning now in support of their rulers but at another time against them.

Dotted along the coast of Kenya, from a few miles north of Mombasa right up to Malindi just under a hundred miles away, are small groups of fishermen numbering anything between five and fifteen, who use only two or three items of equipment: a home-made spear gun (*bunduki*) made up of strips of rubber tyre inner-tube attached to a wooden 'bow' and a sharply pointed metal bolt or arrow (*mwitho* or *muvi*); and a goggling mask used without a snorkel. At certain times of the year these fishermen may use a locally made harpoon (*njoro*) instead of a spear-gun. The cost of the equipment comes to less than Shs.100. Very occasionally a man may invest another Shs.60 or so in a small fishing net, operable if necessary by a single man, but this is uncommon. These fishermen live with their families a few miles inland from the sea and walk out every day to fish, leaving their equipment hidden overnight in carefully selected bushes near the beaches.

Dotted along the whole of Kenya's coast, and well into neighbouring Tanzania, are the near-shore villages of an entirely different category of fishermen. These have a much wider range of capital equipment: small dug-out boats called (*ma*)*dau*, and other larger boats variously named; light and heavy nets each used for different kinds of catch; moveable fish traps made of wattle fibre, (*ma*)*hema*, and permanent fish traps staked out a hundred yards into the sea with best poles and

wattle, called *uzio* (*nyuzio*). The cost of all these and other items
runs into several thousands of shillings, which are raised, if necessary,
by a complex system of financial pooling and loans.

The 'capitalized' fishermen are all Muslim. The 'non-capitalized'
ones are not. This division is also spoken of in ethnic terms: the
Muslim fishermen are either *Digo*, *Gunya*, or *Pemba*; the non-Muslim
fishermen are referred to as *Giriama*, a category which hides a number
of differently named ethnic sub-divisions but is accepted by the men
themselves as a label used by outsiders. The Muslim fishermen speak
Swahili as their sole or main language, while the non-Muslim
Giriama know Swahili but use their vernacular as a main language.

This division into two main categories of fishermen has an
historical basis, which was entrenched during the colonial period.
Under an agreement made in 1895 with the Sultan of Zanzibar, the
British gave him suzerainty, under continuing British control, over
a notional 10-mile coastal strip of East Africa which includes the
area in Kenya with which I am dealing here. The area thus fell under
Muslim jurisdiction and British political control. Land in the coastal
strip was owned by Arabs, Swahili, and Muslim Africans, as well as
by the occasional European and Indian, but not by non-Muslim
Africans, including the Giriama (or non-Muslim Mijikenda as the
wider group comprising them is sometimes called). Before the 1895
agreement, non-Muslim Africans had worked on Muslim-owned
plantations and estates, either as slaves or "free" labour often tied
to the land. These workers and their progeny came to constitute
the so-called squatters of recent years, whose rights to land in the
coastal strip were constantly denied until Kenya's independence
in December 1963, after which a dramatic reversal in land rights
occurred.

Before independence a constant slogan uttered by those Muslims
(and this did not include all of them) who wanted political autonomy
for the coastal strip was that Muslims were "people of the sea", i.e.
depended on the sea as fishermen or port traders and merchants,
and that the non-Muslim Giriama were people of the (hinter)land.
Since independence, much of the land formerly part of the coastal
strip and held in freehold title by Muslims (mainly Arabs and
Swahili), has been converted by government into settlement schemes
consisting of 12 acre plots, most of which are now occupied by
non-Muslims, including many of the so-called former squatters.

Curiously, through these dramatic reversals of fortune, the same
slogan continues to be used: "Muslims are people of the sea:
Giriama are people of the land". Now, however, this formula is
expressed by both Muslims and Giriama. For Giriama it substantiates

their newly acquired rights to land, and for Muslims, many of them
faced by the loss of near-shore land as a result of considerable land
speculation by members of the national élite who are building hotels,
beach cottages, and acquiring fertile farmland (see Kenya
Government 1978), the slogan re-emphasizes their right to a village
site near the sea from which they can gain easy access to their
moored boats and equipment stored in caves or under cliffs, or
nearby houses, along the beaches.

As long as they retain such ease of access, the Muslim fishermen
have the techniques, skills, and capital equipment to earn more,
sometimes considerably more, than they would get, given their low
educational level, from regular monthly wage employment. It is
true that some areas have seen a decline in the number of young men
who have stayed in the family fishing tradition. Some have moved
instead into wage labour. But others do continue in it and this
Muslim occupational enclave is in no immediate danger of disappear-
ing and could well be re-invigorated with increasing numbers of
government loans enabling even more injection of capital. In short,
Muslim fishermen generally express neither a need to go into
monthly wage labour nor even a preference for it.

Among the Giriama fishermen, on whom I now concentrate, quite
'the opposite applies. With remarkable frequency and quite
independent of each other in different groups along the coast, each
occupying its small camp (*bandari*, literally meaning 'harbour'), one
is told that "fishing is not work" (*uu uvuvi si kazi*). The younger
fishermen say that they are doing it simply as a stop-gap solution
until they get regular monthly wage employment (*kazi ya mwezi*).
The older ones claim, referring back to the above political slogan,
that they regard fishing as simply a means of getting extra but non-
essential food and clothes, that farming is their "real" occupation,
and that they leave fishing to the Muslims, "for they are the people
of the sea".

And yet, when we look at the incomes earned by these non-
capitalized Giriama fishermen, they are certainly in excess of what
most of them could possibly earn in wage labour, even though they
do not reach the levels of the Muslim fishermen. On average during
the good fishing months, they can earn around Shs.600/– a month.
During the poor fishing months, this may drop to Shs.200/–,
producing an annual monthly average of about Shs.500/–. Even
assuming they could find monthly wage employment, it is unlikely
to exceed Shs.200/– per month in the local rural trading centre
or Shs.350/– in, say, Mombasa town. The effective value of these
wages is even less when the extra costs of urban housing and food

are deducted. Not only are the Giriama fishermen able to earn more from the craft they deprecate, they can also feed themselves from it, since a little of the catch is usually taken home for family consumption.

Plans, Control and Destiny

Two questions may be asked here. First, since they are already formed into loose groupings, why do the Giriama fishermen not pool sufficient money to buy, say, a boat and other equipment and go in for more profitable capital-intensive fishing? The reason given for not doing so is that they would have to become Muslim in order (a) to be able to buy the equipment from its Muslim makers who would not otherwise sell it to them, (b) to have mooring and storage rights near the shores, and (c) to acquire the considerable expertise required to fish in this more intensive manner and which would only be imparted to them if they became proven *bona fide* members of the Muslim fishing community. For practical reasons this kind of switch is not easy. It would mean repudiating Giriama culture and non-Muslim associates, and, anyway, conversion to Islam is normally on an individual rather than a group basis.

The second question, even allowing for the difficulty in being able to make the switch from non-capitalized to capitalized fishing, is: why do the Giriama fishermen persist in evaluating the occupation so lowly, lower than regular monthly wage employment (*kazi ya mwezi*), even though financially it ranks above it? And here, in answering this question, we encounter a number of mutually reinforcing ideas, part 'traditional' and part modern capitalist, which shape this preference for wage labour over fishing, and operate also in a range of other contexts.

First, constantly held virtues of permanent monthly wage employment are that (a) "you always know how much you will get at the end of the month" and (b) "you can plan your expenditure ahead of receiving your wage and know the limit of your expenditure". The idea of a regular fixed sum enabling one to plan not just one's immediate budget but one's very life, comes out in many other statements. One can plan ahead for the school fees of children and siblings, for building a house, buying clothes, and even saving for an expensive consumer article, or a shop, land, cattle or goats. Coupled then with the idea of planned budget, is that of saving (*ku-ika akiba*) a sum sufficiently large that it can be turned into productive capital, e.g. school fees, land, a shop, livestock, or even a vehicle for a transportation business. Though fishing provides a higher income on average than monthly wage employment, it is

irregular. There are lean months and good months whose beginning
and end cannot be predicted precisely. Within even these seasons,
there are good catches which alternate with bad ones. A man may
catch Shs.80/— or even Shs.100/— worth of fish one day and use
it all towards paying off a debt or buying some small item such as
food or clothes, expressing the view that tomorrow will produce
an even better catch because the shoals are large at present. But the
next day's catch may in fact yield very little, and the chance to
save has been lost. It is indeed much more difficult to accumulate
capital when income is irregular and when this income is only a little
above the family's subsistence needs.

We see then that while the Muslim fishermen re-invest the proceeds
of their capital, the Giriama fishermen also aim to acquire productive
capital — but they aim to do so by monthly wage employment rather
than by fishing. This alternative route to capital envisaged by the
Giriama fishermen is, of course, highly idealized: few actually take
it and even fewer complete it. Monthly wage employment is very
scarce. A report issued for 1977 stated that only 150,000
enumerated regular wage jobs had been created since 1973 in the
whole of Kenya, whose total population is 14 million and whose
school-leaving, wage-seeking proportion has annually exceeded that
figure of jobs during this period. Casual wage labour is more easily
obtainable, but it is regarded as having all the disadvantages of uncertainty and unpredictability associated with non-capitalized
fishing.

Indeed, there is here a second, more overriding set of ideas. These
are summarized in the opposition made by people between the two
phrases '*kazi ya mwezi*', monthly wage employment, and '*kazi ya
kibarua*', casual wage labour. Not only are these key verbal concepts,
each unravelling a series of other semantic associations, but they are
recognized as opposites, each dependent for its sense on the other.

Non-capitalized fishing while normally denied the status of 'work'
(*kazi*) at all, is in other contexts subsumed under the general rubric
of 'casual wage labour' (*kazi ya kibarua*). The phrase literally means
'letter work' and refers to the system once used at docks and other
employment centres of giving men work on a daily basis, providing
them with a chit (i.e. 'letter') which would be exchanged for cash at
the end of the day or specified number of days. Nowadays it is taken
to refer to most work in the so-called informal sectors of employment,
some of which is indeed highly transitory but much of which is in
effect long term, even though sporadic. Inevitably, *kazi ya mwezi*
has much higher status (*sifa*) than *kazi ya kibarua*, a point to which I
turn below in discussing a third set of ideas of relatively recent origin

— namely, school education.

At a higher level of abstraction, the distinction betwen *kazi ya mwezi* and *kazi ya kibarua* connotes a distinction between (a) income which is predictable and certain and which facilitates some degree of control over one's own and family's destiny, and (b) income which is unpredictable and uncertain (even though it may overall be higher) and which therefore reduces the degree of control over one's destiny. It is interesting that this folk distinction between preferences completely reverses the notion of many social scientists who see permanent monthly wage employment as leading to irreversible dependency and less control by the wage earner over his labour, and who see such 'casual work' as, say, fishing or even certain craft forms of informal sector employment as leaving the earner with more control. The social scientist might argue that such a folk preference for permanent wage employment actually hides or mystifies the earner's growing dependency. But in fact so few actually get permanent wage jobs that they become dependent, not on wage labour itself, but rather on the illusion of its availability. Moreover, it is a perfectly rational emic response to a situation of ecological and economic uncertainty which these fishermen attempt to resolve by acquiring, as they see it, the more planned control over their destinies that comes with permanent wages. Nevertheless, it is true that this preference for wage labour, however rational it is according to the information available to them, does create the conditions of acceptance of the third set of ideas — those which lead to the pursuit of school education as the *sine qua non* of worthwhile employment.

Thus, while among the capitalized Muslim fishermen (though not, incidentally, among other Muslims), a low proportion of children go to secular school (with a correspondingly large proportion attending Koranic school), among the Giriama fishermen, a much higher proportion receive schooling. Indeed, a few of the younger Giriama fishermen are themselves still paying their way through secondary school education, fishing only in the school holidays and at weekends, even though they are into their twenties. Whether for themselves or their children, these Giriama fishermen share a consistently favourable attitude to secular education, or 'European' education (*elimu ya kizungu*) as it is often called as distinct from Koranic education. We see again how the original and historically based religious distinction between the two categories of fishermen of Muslim versus non-Muslim becomes re-interpreted in present time as a difference of preferences between (a) the two types of education available in the coastal strip and in many ways in competition with each other; and (b) as described already, fishing and permanent wage labour.

Again, just as the Giriama fishermen have little chance of finding permanent wage labour and even less chance of converting this into the productive capital of land or shops, etc. which is their ultimate aim, so there is little chance of their being able to convert even secondary school education into permanent wage employment. Nearly all the members of these fishermen's families who are in secondary school education are at either Harambee (self-help) or 'cheap' private shcools. Their standards, especially in Coast Province, are at present very low, and examination results compare very unfavourably with government and expensive private schools which have places for only a minority of all the young men and women wishing to attend. Primary school education (up to seven years' schooling) offers no special advantages on the job market but is a necessary hurdle attempted by the many and successfully crossed by the few. It is still a very widely held belief in the coastal area, which until recently had few schools, that a substantial school education greatly increases its possessor's chances of acquiring, say, permanent white collar work or acceptance in a craft training programme. But in fact anything less than very high grades at Ordinary School Certificate level (11 years of schooling) does not significantly do so: the area in which I worked included a number of holders of low or medium grades school certificates who called themselves "jobless" and who were working in what they and their peers and relatives regarded as temporary work.

Conceptual Parallels

We find, moreover, that the folk-distinction between permanent *kazi ya mwezi* and temporary *kazi ya kibarua* goes further than reflecting the preference for permanent wage labour over non-capitalized fishing. There are other forms of economic enterprise which are similarly discussed or referred to in the same vein as *kazi ya kibarua*. Some concrete examples follow:

Case 1

A Giriama father had invested much money in his son's education, sending him to one of the many relatively cheap commercially run secondary schools in Mombasa. The son, though bright, finished in 1973 with three poor ordinary level certificates, with which he was able to get a temporary clerical job for a few months. Thereafter he failed to get a permanent job and so studied privately for some further qualifications in book-keeping and accounts. Then, satisfied that he had a thorough knowledge of basic commercial practices,

he set up business with a matrilateral cousin, a recently converted
Giriama Muslim. They sold vegetables, fruit and fish (dealt with by
the Muslim cousin) from a ramshackle wooden kiosk of about six
square metres. They worked hard and the business thrived,
representing as it did a neat compromise between non-Muslim and
Muslim interests and expectations. But the man's father refused
to accept this as "work". "This is not work", he would say. He
continued to urge his son to seek permanent wage employment.
When brought into the affair I was obliged to point out that the
young men earned more than they would as low or even middle-
grade clerks. The father was slightly appeased when the two young
men rented a permanently built shop from which to operate
their business. The move did not significantly increase custom, but
it did increase costs through the high rental required. It also appeased
the Kilifi District administration which was compelling traders to
abandon kiosks and to operate from shops of permanent structure.
The story is not over, however, for, still under pressure from his
father and now subscribing to the same view himself, the son
continues to spend hours and money on postage every week submitting applications for jobs advertised in the national press. His
aim, he says, is to obtain permanent wage employment as a way
of "securing" his own position and subsidizing the business. But in
fact, since he would need to employ at least two people to cover
the amount of work that he does in the shop, it is doubtful whether
his wage income would cover these and other extra expenses. In
the end, it might be the business which would be subsidizing his
position as permanent wage labourer, a situation likely to lead to
friction in a jointly run enterprise and possibly even to bankruptcy.
This case is not unusual. Many women's independent, low capital
enterprises are similarly denigrated, especially by men, being placed
in the almost residual category of the "informal sector" by planners,
government, and social scientists alike.

In short, then, while well-established trade or shop-owning are
ultimate aims among many Giriama, they are still seen as deriving
their security from the assumed security of permanent wage employment. Further, any enterprise carried out in circumstances which
fall short of official definitions of properly accredited "business"
(i.e. in permanent structures) tend to be defined by people themselves as "non-work": official and popular definitions here coincide.

Case 2

It is generally recognized that in many rural African societies women
form the backbone of agricultural production. This could not be more

true of Giriama society, in which women do most of the farming. But many women also specialize in other money-making enterprises: buying, fetching, carrying and selling palm wine over great distances, often by foot; making and selling *makuti*, the palm-thatch sections used for roofing houses; or growing, carrying, and selling agricultural produce, again often over great distances. Husbands sometimes help in these enterprises, depending on what their own economic activities are, but are not normally central to them. A large proportion of women's earnings are, however, used for the family's subsistence, some of the cash going first to the husband.

We get insights from conversations about employment: men and women may talk, for example, about a husband or son's wage employment chances, e.g. is it better for him to try in Mombasa or should he join a relative in a smaller town like Malindi? In these conversations, the remarks and assumptions are that for a relatively young man to stay in the homestead is "to do nothing like a woman". The same view came out just as strikingly, and quite unexpectedly, when I asked about people's occupations, using the word *kazi* for "work" (spelled the same as in Swahili but with a slight yet discernible difference of intonation). I sought information not just on those who had wage labour but also those who, like many women, earned often significant amounts in enterprises of the kind I have described above. Men doing temporary or permanent wage labour were always said to "have work", but a stock response concerning women was "Ah . . . she is just at the home", i.e. "is just a housewife" (*ni kwa nyumbani tu* and similar expressions). The inference is that domestically-based female labour not only falls into a different category from wage labour, which is understandable, but that it is evaluated below it, in spite of its economic importance for subsistence and even for releasing a permanent wage-earning husband's income for investment in productive capital.

Case 3

Similarly, a man who has no wage employment and who is not a farmer employing outsiders, yet is at the rural home farming for subsistence needs and even raising a few cash crops, is often described as "having no work" (*kana kazi*) which may be further elaborated as "he just sits/stays" (*anakeresi tu*). This phrase applies either to young or middle-aged men who are, it is known, currently seeking wage employment either of a casual or permanent kind, or to middle-aged or elderly men who are known either to have retired from such work or to have given up hopes of or even the wish for such work. And yet such people do not lie idle. For a start they are probably able to

feed themselves and possibly a few dependents from their small farming activities and, especially in the case of men who are now firmly
committed to rural 'retirement', may make useful incomes from
basket making. To take a good example, one man in the Gotani
area of Giriamaland is famed far beyond his immediate locality
for the strength, beauty, and originality of design of his baskets,
the craft secrets of which he wisely keeps to himself. He
justifiably asks higher prices for his baskets than do other men,
and no one disputes his superior craftsmanship. Yet his sons and
brothers, and people from other homesteads, would casually group
him together with those who "just sit", etc. in spontaneous conversations about those in the area who had or lacked "work"
(*kazi*) including wage employment.

Spontaneous and unchallenged examples of this mode of thinking
occur in many situations. I was once asked by a friend to witness
his sale of coconut and other trees to the new owner of some land
formerly occupied by the friend. The new owner had a supervisory,
factory job in Mombasa and ran his small farm through members
of his family, but spent little time on it himself. We managed to
catch him at the farm during the Easter break. He was just about
to spend his available money on hiring a tractor to plough the land,
a job that could not be delayed. He suggested we come back to
discuss the sale of trees at a later date, to which we agreed. He said
it had to be a Saturday or Sunday "because I am a working man"
(*ni mutu wa kazi*). Since these were the only days when he could
be available, this was a reasonable request. But the manner in which
it was said and unquestioningly accepted clearly carried the negative
implication that those available on their farms all week long were
by definition, "those who just stay" and have no "work". This and
comparable cases show that this classification between absentee
land-owners who "work" for wages and "non-working" farmers is
accepted even by those whom it effectively stigmatizes.

In other words, when wage employment, whether temporary or
permanent, is brought into the definition of "work" (*kazi*), it sets
itself up in opposition to women's or men's domestically-based
income-earning labour and then, so to speak, denies the latter status
as real labour. This conceptual opposition and consequent ranking
of income-earning activities parallels that made by Giriama fishermen between permanent wage labour and non-capitalized fishing.
The point about such opposition and ranking of activities is that they
are not accurate statements about *economic* value. Rather they are
'ideological' statements which, if you like, 'mystify' their relative
economic advantage, or, as I prefer to say, express the growing

dominance of a capitalist mode of production in which wage labour divorced from independent agricultural subsistence emerges as the essential component.

The Continuity of Traditional Definitions of Work

If we were to leave the analysis here, the conclusion would be that the ideology emanating from the dominant mode of production was irrisistibly imposing itself on the working population. But this view does not take account of the complex interaction of ideas in the Giriama people's own continuing definition of labour.

Thus, where the conversational context clearly excludes reference to wage employment, then these female and male enterprises may be referred to as "work" (*kazi*). This applies most clearly to women's roles before and after marriage. Before marriage, which for women normally occurs at about the age of fifteen, a girl is likely to live at a close relative's home as a *mu-kazi*. In this role she helps look after young children in the homestead. Unprompted, Giriama will give their own version of the semantics of the term. This role, they say, is so named because it is an unmarried girl's "work", and also prepares her for the "work" she will have when she marries. And a prospective bride's marriage prospects are indeed affected by how she is judged to have performed as a *mukazi*. Similarly, *muka-kazi* means co-wife and is recognized as referring to the expectation that co-wives shall "work" together, i.e. in harmony and not in conflict. Finally, when I have raised questions about how much bridewealth (*hunda*) was transacted for a par-ticular wife, I have heard such wives say that it is not for them to know how much bridewealth was given for them but that their "work" (*kazi*) is to farm, cook, and produce and raise children. Though artificial in the sense that normally such a question would not be directed at a woman, the consistency of this response suggests that when the frame of reference excludes wage labour, women subscribe to the ideal customary sexual division of labour and in doing so, credit themselves as "workers" in the same way that men regard them as such, when using, and where necessary elaborating on, the terms for child-nurse (*mu-kazi*) and co-wife (*muka-kazi*). Men are similarly credited as "workers" in such full-time and permanent customary roles as cattle/goat/sheep herder (*murisa*), palm-wine tapper (*mujema*), coconut-feller (*mukweraji*), and farmer (*mukulima*), when the reference excludes wage employment.

The use of the suffix *-kazi*, or a similar form, to denote a woman or female roles is in fact widespread in Bantu languages. It often has

further semantic associations of female reproductive fertility and of
female-induced fertility of the soil (reinforced by the notion that
women's "work" is focused on the land rather than on cattle-
herding and fishing). Most Giriama are unaware of the occurrence
of this female suffix in more distant Bantu languages and see it as
linked etymologically with the morphologically identical term
which we translate as work, and which possibly has a different origin
(though I consider this unlikely). For Swahili, Madan suggests that
the term may be of Hindi, Persian, or Arabic origin, but also
suggests its possible derivation in the Bantu verb *ku-kaa*: to reside,
stay in one place, endure. The term *mkazi* in Swahili actually means
a stay-at-home (*Standard Swahili-English Dictionary* 1939: 162, 181),
and is frequently the ideal characterization of a woman, especially
after marriage, whose village- or descent-group-based reproductive and
domestic roles ideally ensure socio-cultural continuity.[1] The common
associations of the one term seem to indicate an implicit understanding, even among men, that women's "work" is, in the end,
basic to socio-cultural continuity. As an implicit view of "work"
which is both "female" and "good" for socio-cultural continuity,
it negates the otherwise widespread culturally explicit symbolic
equation of "female" with "bad" (cf. Needham 1973). Whatever
its origin, the term *kazi* in Giriama is now the inevitable common
expression of overlapping ideas about what we translate as work:
kazi as the female suffix identifies the fertility of females and soil
as the *sine qua non* of cultural and social perpetuation; *kazi* as a
noun-phrase ambivalently identifies the traditional male and female
roles which ensure this continuity yet, in other conversations, subordinates the significance of these traditional roles to wage-
employment.

The Moral Struggle in Definitions of Work

Thus far in this paper I have moved from (a) an historically based
division, perpetuated in a religious idiom between Muslim capitalized
fishermen and non-Muslim Giriama non-capitalized fishermen; to
(b) a division of preferences among the Giriama for wage labour over
fishing, sanctified by an unquestioned belief in the power of secular
education; to (c) a symbolically powerful semantic distinction
between temporary wage employment (*kazi ya kibarua*) and
permanent monthly employment (*kazi ya mwezi*), with a preference
for the latter; to (d) a semantic rule which states (i) that, when
referred to in the same context as economically productive roles in
the domestic domain, including crafts, wage labour alone is credited
as "work" and achieves unquestioned sanctity as such; and (ii) that,

dissociated from any reference to wage labour, a perduring
'traditional' structure of economically productive roles among
Giriama is indisputably given customary work as "work" (*kazi*).

The four steps in this analysis are closely related to each other
and could, if space allowed, be expressed more abstractly. It is anyway clear that a concrete division between two social groups becomes
re-expressed several moves later as a semantic ambivalence in a single
vernacular word, *kazi*; and that the word *kazi* is applicable in some
contexts but not in others and so plays, by virtue of its negative
as well as positive connotation, a critical part in people's definition
of unemployment.

Going back to an earlier point, we might be tempted to see this
ambivalence as a direct product of the growing dominance of a
capitalist over a pre-capitalist made of production, and therefore
as an aspect of the mystification of the ensuing social inequalities.
This is, as it were, the term becoming ambivalent as a result of
contradictory pressures exerted on it from above. But this is only
half the answer. We must ask why it is that a single word and not a
plurality of words can have assumed such central importance. After
all, some other languages have numerous synonyms for work which
eliminate or reduce ambiguity. Compare, for instance, the general
semantic contrast in English between the use of the words
'enterprise' and 'labour'. It is certainly not that the Giriama language
(nor Swahili in which the term *kazi* is similarly central) is not rich
in vocabulary. There are a number of verbs to express "doing things",
from which different abstract nouns like "work" could easily be
extracted. It is rather that the word *kazi* already had for generations
past, and still has, central significance as a term ambivalently
denoting forces of good and evil in ritual contexts. To give a brief
example, when speaking to spirits, a diviner may beseech them to
"stop your work (*kazi*)" and then a sentence later, "to do your
work (*kazi*)". Taken out of context, this would be a contradictory
and meaningless appeal. But in fact the diviner is imploring the
spirit to stop inflicting the patient with sickness and to begin the
job of restoring him/her to normality. The appeal is backed up by
promises made by the diviner to the spirit, which is to receive certain
objects it requires in exchange for releasing the sick person from his
or her suffering. The diviner bargains with the spirit, perhaps by
substituting one "gift" for another in order to persuade the spirit to
stop "working" against humanity but rather for its (i.e. the patient's)
good.

The religious basis of this concept of "work" (*kazi*) sets up the
idea of "good" work being the necessary counterpart of "bad" work.

This nicely parallels the contrast (a) between wage labour which is exalted and domestic labour which is denigrated, and (b) between productive capital-intensive enterprises, to which wage labour is thought to lead and which is an ultimate ideal, and economic activities which have negligible capital and from which people are urged to escape. Wage labour and well-capitalized enterprises are both "good work"; domestic labour, home-based crafts and so-called informal sector activities are "bad work". This is of course frequently how colonial and some post-colonial governments have defined employment and unemployment respectively: economically productive "slums" are razed to the ground; "progressive" farmers are those who move from subsistence to commercial agriculture, often through the investment of capital given in the form of loans; officially acceptable traders are those who abandon cheaply built kiosks with their limited overheads and move into expensive, permanently built shops, and one official measure of "development" is any expansion in the officially enumerated labour force.

We have here a further parallel. The Giriama word for spirit is *pepo* and is sometimes used synonymously with the Swahili word, *shetani.* But the latter is also the word used by Christians and Muslims to mean the Devil (or devils if in the plural). The parallel, then, is that the "good work" of the spirit or devil in agreeing to release the patient from sickness in exchange for commodities offered by the diviner on behalf of the patient is spoken of with the same approval, through use of the word *kazi*, as is given to wage employment and capital-intensive enterprises which are "offered" by employers including government in exchange for educational qualifications and demonstrated skills. Both the devil and government constitute irrepressible forces. The difference is that the strength of the devil has been largely constant over the generations while that of government has grown immensely over the same period.

Marx would probably enjoy the analogy of capitalist government with the Devil but would be unlikely to agree to a pre-capitalist notion of "good" and "evil" work having a moral and religious basis and thereby playing a part in a people's own later definition of employment and unemployment as "worthy" and "unworthy" economic activities. He does see established religious thought as sanctifying the transformation of feudal serfdom into the "illusion" of free, mobile labour. But he does not see the hierarchical role distinctions between 'master' and 'slave' or 'serf', 'boss' and 'employee', or between 'wage labourer' and 'capitalist' on the one hand, and 'casual' or 'domestic workers' on the other as resting on a fundamental conceptual opposition of good and evil which is enshrined in religious language and reaches back to a people's cosmological core and so actually precedes any 'new' economic structure.

A comparable example of inherent ambivalence in the use of the term *kazi* may be found in such expressions as *ni kazi yao* ("that is their nature/habit") when referring to children fooling around, or to a drunkard acting likewise. The use of the term here for what we may translate as human nature combines disapproval of the antisocial dimensions of the act with tolerance of the state (i.e. drunkenness), or stage of development (i.e. childhood), of the actor. This ambivalence parallels the alternative notions of good and evil contained in religious uses of the term.[2]

Taken together, then, 'our' translation of 'work' for the term *kazi* is really just one aspect of its wider meaning of the paradox of human nature, which, by its unpredictability, threatens to destroy the conditions of socio-cultural continuity even as it creates them. The uses of the term *kazi* convey various possible meanings but together reveal the struggle to control human and extra-human capriciousness and thereby personal and collective destiny.

Conclusion

What I have described is the re-expression of a particular people's folk-definition of "work" in terms and contexts which are logically consistent with an increasingly dominant capitalist mode of production. The folk-definition is prior and adapts to the capitalist environment but is not created by it. We might have expected a different adaptive response in, say, neighbouring Tanzania, at least during that country's earlier days of enthusiasm for a contrasting ideology of anti-capitalism. It is doubtful that a semantic analysis of this kind is actually of any help at all to someone who wishes to plan for economic development, whether from a capitalist or anti-capitalist perspective. But it does at least help explain why a people may hold rationalities which are alien to the outside planner such as the evaluation of wage labour above a better-paid and independent livelihood in fishing or the denial of economically productive domestic or craft roles as being truly "work". One man's plan is another's ideology.

The Giriama were in fact in 1914 among the first peoples in Kenya to resist violently and valiantly the attempt of colonial administrators to force them into paid labour, at that time displaying clearly a view of wage labour and government as forces so "evil" as to require such a measure. The reversal in preference since then is best seen not as a conservative retreat but as part of a

cumulative cycle of responses, the next point on which may well be
a requestioning of the value of wage labour and now also of
monopoly capitalism. It goes almost without saying that there
exists in the established industrialized world a similar cyclical
questioning and re-questioning of ideological assumptions: the
aim of limitless growth followed by the aim of controlled growth
followed by a questioning by some of the very concept of growth
as the ultimate criterion of economic excellence, and so on.

A number of rural parts of up-country Kenya have been more
thoroughly incorporated than the coastal strip in the wage
economy for very much longer. In such areas, the ideological
assumptions of the wage economy are already being questioned by
a minority, though admittedly not always consistently nor always
through collective organizations like trade unions. Nevertheless
the signs of 'protest' are there. For historical reasons the rural areas
of coastal Kenya are at present increasingly accepting without
protest those ideological assumptions. Indeed, the most recent
politically extensive witchcraft-eradication movement occurring in
the area since independence (Parkin 1968, 1970; Brantley 1979),
far from protesting against the trappings of the expanding capitalist
mode of production, actually espoused them by urging people to
abandon traditional ritual and religion as well as Islam, and to
embrace the values of Christianity and 'Western' medicine and
education instead. Given the connection between traditional
definitions of employment and traditional religious beliefs, as I
have suggested, we can see how, quite unintentionally, such a
witchcraft-eradication movement actually embodies people's own
everyday statements, as I have outlined them. It redefines a scale
of worthiness in "work" in conformity with rather than in defiance
of wage employment. To repeat, religion is not here simply acting
as a conservative force but is laying the conditions for a later, perhaps
greater debate.

Notes

I wish to acknowledge helpful remarks made on versions of this paper in
seminars at Michigan State, Oxford, Sussex, Stockholm and York (Toronto)
Universities, at the L.S.E., and in the S.S.R.C. Conference on *The Politics of
the Common People*, convened by George Bond and Joan Vincent, as well as
in the A.S.A. Conference itself.

1. The Giriama term for wife of so-and-so is *mukaza-*. *Kukaza* in Giriama has
    the meaning of to persist, carry on, increase. *Kukaza* in Swahili is probably
    the causative form of *kukaa*, to reside or stay firm, as mentioned in the
    paper, and means to make fast or tighten, with the derived term *Mkazi*,

when referring to God, given in the *Standard Dictionary* as the upholder (of the world). The underlying notion of fixity, persistence and continuity, and the linking of this to womanhood in both languages, seems to me persuasively archetypal as, I think, more intensive semantic analysis will confirm.
2. I am grateful to Gill Shepherd and John Parry for seminal remarks on this point.

References

Bailey, P. 1978. *Leisure and class in Victorian England.* London: Routledge and Kegan Paul.

Brantley, C. 1979. An historical perspective of the Giriama and witchcraft control control. *Africa* **49**, 2, 112–33.

Gutkind, P.C.W. 1975. The view from below . . . the urban poor in Ibadan. *Cahiers d'Etudes Africaines* **10** (57), 5–53.

Kenya Government. 1978. *Report of the Parliamentary Select Committee on land ownership at the coastal strip.* Nairobi.

Inter-Territorial Language Committee of East Africa. 1939. *A standard Swahili-English dictionary*, (founded on that of Madan). London: Oxford University Press.

Lowerson, J. and Myerscough, J. 1977. *Time to spare in Victorian England.* Sussex: Harvester Press.

Malcolmson, R.W. 1973. *Popular recreations in English society 1700–1850.* Cambridge: Cambridge University Press.

Needham, R. (ed.). 1973. *Right and left.* Chicago and London: Chicago University Press.

Parkin, D. 1968. Medicines and men of influence. *Man* N.S. **3**, 424–39.

—— 1970. Politics of ritual syncretism: Islam among the non-Muslim Giriama of Kenya. *Africa* **40** (3), 218–233.

THE WORK OF MEN, WOMEN AND THE ANCESTORS:

Social Reproduction in the Periphery of Southern Africa

COLIN MURRAY

Every tradition forbids the asking of certain questions about what has really happened to you. (John Berger)

A social position is never solely created by theatrical notions; it owes more to the inescapable pressure of facts, the give and take of daily life. (Eileen Power)

Introduction

The rural periphery of southern Africa is characterized by its dependence on the export of labour to the industrial centres of South Africa. In a narrow sense the periphery comprises the black 'homelands' of South Africa and the independent enclave of Lesotho. In a wider sense it includes Botswana, Swaziland and southern Mozambique. This essay[1] is concerned with the barren mountain kingdom of Lesotho, whose acute economic dependence is simply illustrated. Firstly, perhaps 200,000 migrants from Lesotho are employed in South Africa, out of the country's total population of one and a quarter million. More than 130,000 men were employed in the mines alone in 1977, supplying a quarter of the industry's complement of black labour. Secondly, the earnings of these migrants far exceed Lesotho's Gross Domestic Product. Thirdly, according to a recent survey (van der Wiel 1977), about 70 per cent of mean rural household income is derived from migrant earnings. Only about 6 per cent is derived from domestic crop production. The population of the periphery in the narrow sense is aptly described as a rural proletariat which scratches about on the land.

The predicament of Basotho as inhabitants of an impoverished labour reserve is expressed in the universal and bitter complaint *mosebetsi ha o eo*, "there's no work (here)". Work (*mosebetsi*) in this sense refers to paid employment, opportunities for which within the country are minimal: they are effectively confined to a small administrative and commercial élite, two very small industrial sites and a number of handicraft enterprises. Most Basotho can only find employment as migrants who oscillate between the 'white' industrial areas of South Africa and their rural homes in Lesotho. Nine out of ten migrants are men. Women participate in the labour market under certain structural constraints. Firstly, entry into South Africa for the purpose of seeking work is illegal. Border controls established by legislation in 1963 effectively circumscribed access by Basotho women to the South African labour market, since labour contracts undertaken within Lesotho are not available to them. Secondly, the wages and conditions of such work as they do find nevertheless are appalling.[2] Thirdly, therefore, the decision by women to find employment in South Africa, despite the degrading conditions, social isolation and risk of arrest under the pass laws, is one of desperation. Women go because they have no alternative. Individual life stories illustrate the cycle of structural violence in which women may be trapped as a result of circumstances of default by migrant husbands or of their own inevitably clandestine search for work in the Republic.

South African influx control precludes migrants from taking their families with them to their places of work. The *de facto* rural population (those present at any one time) therefore exhibits the following demographic features: a high proportion of widows and female-headed households, a distorted sex ratio in the middle age ranges through the absence of male migrants, and a numerical preponderance in villages of the young, the female and the elderly. In many areas at least 40 per cent of rural households are headed by women, while 70 per cent of rural households are effectively managed by women. Many of these women are widows. Many others are the wives of absent migrants. Almost all of them assume a heavy onus of responsibility for managing household affairs, looking after children, the sick and the elderly, and for extracting what they can from the land.

These facts demonstrate a stark physical separation of the sphere of production from the sphere of reproduction. Empirically, however, the two spheres are vitally inter-connected. Migrants spend their working lives in repetitive periods of absence on labour contracts, interspersed with repetitive periods of 'rest' at home. Almost all adults spend part of their lives in South Africa. But migrants have no security in their places of work. By definition they cannot rear legitimate families there. Therefore they depend on their wives, mothers and other kin who remain at home and who assume primary responsibility for the reproduction and socialization of the next generation. Together with the sick, the elderly, the children and the unemployed, women who assume these responsibilities comprise the "superfluous appendages" to which the apologists of apartheid repeatedly refer. They provide the essential services that are subsumed by marxists under the phrase 'the reproduction of labour power' and that take up more than 6½ hours of the average woman-day.[3]

This vital empirical connection underlines the fallacy of adopting discrete theoretical frames of reference. On the one hand, it is obvious that an ethnographic investigation of the 'traditional' Sesotho division of labour between the sexes is quite inadequate for an understanding of the contemporary conditions of social reproduction in the labour reserve. On the other hand, it is equally obvious that an analysis of the political economy of apartheid in terms which relate only to the logic of capitalist accumulation does scant justice to the way in which Basotho apprehend their own experience. I have briefly outlined two conditions of social reproduction in the southern African periphery: these are wage labour, performed mainly by male oscillating migrants who remit cash earnings to their families, and non-wage labour, performed mainly by women left behind in the rural areas who assume primary responsibility for looking after their families. In Lesotho and other parts of the periphery, the "works" of the ancestors (*mesebetsi ea balimo*), the performance of proper obligations towards the dead, are also an indispensable condition of social reproduction. It should be emphasized that these conditions cannot be identified as material and ideological, respectively. The dichotomy of paid and unpaid labour, itself ideologically constructed. is susceptible to familiar ideological elaboration, in which home is separated from work, the family from the market place, and kinship relations from economic relations. The "works" of the ancestors in Lesotho, on the other hand, are expensive investments in custom: ritual expenditure involves the transfer of resources on a massive scale from urban areas to rural areas, and their dispersal outside the rural household within which a migrant's earnings are increasingly concentrated.

These investments in custom are made by migrant men, the conditions of whose existence are best understood within a theoretical perspective I define as the political economy of migrant labour. The implication of this is that I can only do justice to the elaborations of Sesotho culture by releasing it from the onus of explaining the behaviour of Basotho by itself, and by seeking to relate it to the dynamics of oscillation and to the process of differentiation that has been taking place in the periphery. Conversely, I can only do justice to the capacity of the Basotho to make their own history by accepting that the logic of their contemporary situation is not derivative from capitalism in the abstract but is derivative from the particular historical conditions under which Basotho have been incorporated, together with their distinctive culture and their relative political autonomy, into the system of racial and class oppression in South Africa.

The theoretical challenge posed by the ethnography of work in Lesotho is therefore the need to integrate custom into political economy. There are welcome precedents for this endeavour elsewhere in Africa. David Parkin (1972) has shown how, among the coastal Giriama of Kenya, heavy expenditure on bridewealth and funeral obligations has the effect of disguising patterns of economic accumulation within the reference points of a common language of custom. Van Binsbergen has argued, for the Nkoya of Zambia,

> At present . . . ritual . . . seems the most important and effective way
> to assert and maintain economic and kinship-political claims across
> the urban-rural gap, in addition to structuring the social process within
> the rural area itself. (1976: 216.)

Both writers are anxious to avoid the utilitarian reductionism that such arguments might imply, by stressing the authenticity of the ideas and actions of their informants, and by explicitly avoiding the imputation of ulterior motives. The particular stimulus of van Binsbergen's paper is his realization that models of religion in which action expresses ultimate values are quite inadequate to understanding the relationship of ritual behaviour to non-ritual behaviour in a *part-society* in which social relations are by definition governed by structures outside the terms of reference of that society's cosmology. But this does not mean that culture as a source of values and of action is not real and alive and important. Rather, its vitality must be understood in relation to the political and economic forces which to some extent shape it and which are, in turn, shaped by it. Custom is a repository of action, for creating and re-creating the conditions of existence. Whether its exploitation has positive or negative political implications can only be determined in specific historical circumstances.[4]

Labour and Value: Some Theoretical Considerations

Particularly in the circumstances of southern Africa, unpaid labour is subject to contradictory evaluations. On the one hand, the battery of discriminatory legislation known as the Pass Laws has been consistently based on the principle enunciated by the Stallard Commission of 1921:

> The native should only be allowed to enter the urban areas, which are essentially the white man's creation, when he is willing to enter and to minister to the needs of the white man and should depart therefrom when he ceases so to minister. (Transvaal, Province of, 1922.)

Black people in 'white' areas who are not engaged in wage employment are not 'economically active' and may therefore be 'endorsed out' to the 'homelands' without loss to the white economy. On the other hand, official South African declarations of their redundancy to the needs of the South African economy are belied by the long tradition of the 'subsistence wage' in central and southern Africa. Employers have always rationalized the 'subsistence wage' by reference to the partial livelihood that migrant workers' families are alleged to derive from cultivating the land in the African reserves; and by reference to the 'social services' available to migrants there, whose provision would otherwise, for a stabilized labour force, require expensive urban infrastructure.

Rationalizations of cheap labour by the apologists of apartheid are therefore self-contradictory. It is arguably more important to expose the inability of neo-classical economics, seen in its full ideological matrix as capitalism's self-image, to impute value to labour that has no price in the market place. For the neglect of unpaid labour is central to the practice of liberal economists who would dissociate themselves from the politics of Afrikaner nationalism and whose hard-headed 'realism', by contrast with the obstructive waffle of the rural sociologist, dominates the corridors of the international development agencies. For example, in a paper entitled "Approaches to the Conceptualization and Measurement of the Social Cost of Labour Migration from Lesotho" (Cobbe 1976), women are not mentioned at all. They are neither conceptualized nor measured. Economic costs, we are told, have mainly to do with the effects of migration on agricultural output and with the disutility to migrants of undertaking employment in a foreign country, far from home, etc. Cobbe himself has attempted to measure this disutility by comparing the 'shadow' wage rate with the real wage rate. "If one asks a worker with experience of migration the wage he last earned in the Republic, and the smallest wage for which he would have been willing to do the same work, but at home in Lesotho, the difference between the two should in fact measure, in rands and cents, the cost to that

individual of being a migrant worker rather than working at home."
(Cobbe 1976: 85.)

The precision implied in this exercise is quite spurious. It wholly
fails to take into account that a migrant makes his decision to
migrate not merely with reference to the differential that he
observes between domestically-generated income and his potential
earnings as a migrant, but also with reference to the distribution of
labour within the rural household.

The domestic circumstances of a migrant coal miner, Motlalepula,
illustrate this point. His wife 'Mapuleng died in December 1977.
Motlalepula could not undertake a further contract on the Natal
mine where he was usually employed because there was no one
he could trust to look after their four children (aged 8 to 15)
properly in his absence from Lesotho. The point is this. The
conventional economic analysis of Motlalepula's decision to
migrate or not to migrate proceeds by reference to the marginal
product of labour in agriculture. Could he earn more by taking up
a mine contract than he could supplement the household's
domestic income from agriculture by staying at home? These are
not in fact alternatives, since agricultural output partly depends
on cash investment from migrant earnings. Even if they were
alternatives, however, it can be seen that his dilemma has little to
do with choosing between them. It could be argued, rather more
plausibly, that the value of his wife's services was precisely the
difference between Motlalepula's putative income as a migrant
coal miner, that he could have earned in 1978 had his wife been
alive and well, and his real income in the informal sector at home
in 1978. I have absolute figures for neither income but the
difference between them was clearly very great. The obvious
solution to Motlalepula's dilemma, as the senior widow of the
family observed, is for him to marry again. He duly did so in
April 1979. This example demonstrates that a man's decision to
migrate is conditional on the presence of someone at home who
will carry out the essential tasks connected with the rearing of the
family. This consideration has often been ignored by economists
because a wife's domestic services have no price in the market
place and therefore their value is not directly measurable.

All methods of accountancy involve arbitrary assumptions of
one kind or another. But it is obviously more realistic to impute
some value to women's domestic labour rather than none at all.
Failure to take account of unpaid labour is still a critical source
of bias in development project proposals. Its allocation is often
unconceptualized, unmeasured and, literally, unrealized as a

result of methodological preoccupation with the market price of factors of production. It is fair to point out in mitigation that in recent years the 'new home economics' has decisively expanded the boundaries of neo-classical discourse, from the market place into the home, and that its influence is filtering through to southern Africa.[5] But the other limitations of neo-classical discourse still apply. In a paradigm that assumes harmony of interest between husband and wife and rational maximization of their pooled resources, a decision that the wife should remain at home to carry out household tasks, look after the family and so on is explained in terms of the fact that her labour in the market place would command a lower wage than that of her husband. Conversely, she commands a lower wage in the market place because she has spent a larger amount of time at home, and is therefore 'worth' less in terms of human capital investment — higher education, work training, experience etc. Such tautology demonstrates the inability of neo-classical economics to explain structures of inequality, precisely because it takes them for granted in the first place. It is a significant step forward to recognize that decisions about the allocation of labour time have reference to the household or conjugal unit and not simply to the individual. But it does not follow from this that the household or conjugal unit must exhibit internal harmony of interest. In the southern African periphery women very often assume the onus of managing the rural household but have very little control over the resources with which to manage it effectively. Such disjunction between power and responsibility is the source of much bitterness, frustration and marital disharmony.

It is interesting to note that the partial advance represented by the 'new home economics' has taken place in parallel with an effusion of interest in the political economy of domestic labour. The marxists are also unable to measure the value of domestic labour but their vigorous debates of recent years represent an attempt to transcend this difficulty in a theoretical context which Marx himself failed to elaborate.[6] The terms of the debate relate to domestic labour under fully-developed capitalism and are not therefore directly applicable to the rural proletariat of southern Africa which is not wholly 'freed' from the land. The pertinence of the controversy to the present discussion must be further qualified, firstly by the sensible recognition that 'subsistence' levels do not determine but are determined by wage levels (cf. Hubbard 1977); and secondly by the observation that the contemporary rationale of oscillating migration from the point of view of the South African

state and of the various 'fractions' of capital is much less any direct
economic subsidy of capital that it may provide and much more the
sophisticated machinery of influx control and labour bureaux,
which allows tight political control of the labour force, effective
export from 'white' areas of the reserve army of labour, and
political domination of the labour reserves by proxy, through
the Bantustan administrations.

The attempt by socialist feminists to theorize domestic labour,
'women's work' and capitalist accumulation is part of the ambitious
project of relating the sexual division of labour to the labour process.
Many of the issues which have arisen are presently unresolved
(Edholm, Harris and Young 1977; Kuhn and Wolpe 1978). But it
is possible to identify an approximate consensus on the following
propositions which are directly relevant to the question of whether
or not equal exchange takes place within the household or conjugal
unit in peripheral economies subordinated to capital. Firstly, the
value of unpaid domestic labour cannot be measured directly. But
it is functional to the interests of capital in that it makes a vital
contribution to the maintenance of reproduction of labour power
over time. Therefore it contributes to the surplus value appropriated
by capital. Secondly, the sexual division of labour is *not* explained
by demonstrating this functional contribution and an approximate
correspondence between 'women's work' and unpaid domestic labour.
Gender hierarchies cannot be reduced to particular relations of
production and reproduction. But they cannot be analyzed
independently of them. The implication of this is that an attempt
to discover the elementary form, as it were, of the sexual division
of labour must give way to an attempt to discover the transformations which have taken place through incorporation into social
formations in which the capitalist mode is dominant. Thirdly,
exchanges within the household or conjugal unit are non-
commensurable. As Edholm, Harris and Young put it in the Women's

> the sexual division of labour acquires an ideological function of
> rendering non-comparable the different tasks performed by men and
> women, and correspondingly the portions of the product that are
> assigned to each sex. (1977: 124.)

In this way, the ideological construction of gender roles as complementary both obscures the dependence of women upon men in
the conjugal relationship and legitimizes the unequal exchange
between them.

Migrant Labour: The Facts of Life

This discussion poses a number of empirical questions:

(1) What is the justification for identifying the household as the appropriate unit of analysis? The answer is essentially a pragmatic one, in terms of significant boundaries in flows of resources and expenditure.

(2) What is the evidence for inequality within households? It is possible to investigate this quantitatively, in terms of the distribution of cash earnings within the rural household (see below), and qualitatively, in terms of particular relationships between husbands and wives, mothers and sons, etc. (cf. Murray 1976).

(3) What is the evidence for inequality between households? This may be assessed in terms both of income distribution and of processes of class formation, with reference to contractual, reciprocal and other inter-household transactions. I present here only a brief summary, since I have reviewed this evidence elsewhere (Murray 1978).

(4) What are the aspects of Sesotho custom which represent the terms of the exchanges as non-commensurable, and therefore as complementary rather than as unequal?

I shall argue that heavy investment by migrants in the "works" of the ancestors obscures the increasing inequality of exchanges both within and between households.

By what criteria is the household defined? It is not a co-residential group, nor does it engage in joint activities, for the energies of household members are divided between industrial production in South Africa, on the one hand, and agricultural production and domestic reproduction in Lesotho, on the other hand. I distinguish accordingly between *de facto* houshold members — those present at the time of enumeration — and *de jure* household members — those present plus putative absentees. The *de facto* household is the unit of co-residence and consumption. It habitually employs a single cooking arrangement. In the terms used by Basotho, *de facto* household members comprise "those who eat from one pot" (*ba jang potong e le'ngoe*) or "those we live with" (*bao re lulang le bona*). But the *de facto* household is not self-sufficient. It depends above all on the earnings of absent migrants, who are often described as "those who make us live" (*ba re phelisang*). Collectively, the *de jure* household may be known as *ba h'eso*, "our family", but the use of this term varies with context and also refers to close relatives irrespective of household membership.

The simplest pragmatic approach to the definition of the household is to regard it as an aggregate of individuals within which are concentrated the flows of income and expenditure generated by the activities of those individuals. The most important source of

evidence in this respect is the effective distribution of migrants'
earnings, about which there is still a dearth of reliable information.
In a survey of 82 Basotho mining recruits in 1976, van der Wiel
(1977) found that 41 per cent of their cash earnings from their
previous contract had been spent on themselves, 31 per cent on
other household members, 19 per cent on communal items, and
9 per cent had been distributed in various ways outside the
migrant's household, including 5 per cent on bridewealth transactions. Although these mean figures obscure wide variation in
patterns of disposition they do reflect the concentration of
earnings within the *de jure* household and differential expenditure
within it in favour of the migrant himself and to the relative
disadvantage of his immediate dependents. They suggest that the
mutual dependence of husband and wife and the potential for
conflict between them have intensified. However, such quantitative
evidence should be interpreted with caution. One reason is that
the figure of 9 per cent of total cash earnings disposed outside the
migrant's own household would assume greater significance relative
to that proportion (approximately 70 per cent) of these earnings
which accrues to Lesotho. Another reason is that any sample of
migrants as opposed to rural households will obscure the more
important process of differentiation that is taking place
between rural households as a result of the intensification of general
dependence on migrant labour combined with the tendency for
migrants' earnings to be disposed largely within their own households. By no means all households, after all, have direct access to
migrant earnings. In my own household survey in northern Lesotho
in October 1974 I found that 'paid employees' (defined in a sense
that includes contract miners 'resting' at home) were distributed
between 48 households out of 73 (66 per cent). Recent evidence
reviewed elsewhere (Murray 1978) suggests, firstly, that there is
an approximate but consistent correlation between household size,
domestic productive capacity (in crops and livestock) and migrant
earning capacity; and, secondly, that about one quarter of rural
households, predominantly small female-headed households,
exhibit both a very low domestic productive capacity in absolute
terms and a negligible level of income from migrant earnings. This
evidence conflicts with the view endorsed by a World Bank
Mission and by the Second Five Year Plan (1975/76 — 1979/80)
that Basotho are all poor together. They are poor, but some are
very much poorer that others.

    For this reason at least it is very important to investigate
systematically the nature and significance of inter-household

income transfers. They are of various kinds: occasional remittances in cash and kind, bridewealth transfers, share-cropping arrangements, various other contractual and reciprocal arrangements connected with agriculture; and informal sector transfers which presently consist of beer-brewing, petty trading and 'concubinage' (*bonyatsi*) but which may be expanding, in circumstances of higher mine wages together with enforced marginalization of labour power, to soak up migrants' surplus cash. Many of these transactions assume the form of reciprocal kinship relations. Many do not. There is of course ample evidence relating to 'family' gatherings, court cases, mutual assistance, or merely patterns of 'visiting', etc. to identify aggregations of kin larger than the household and significant networks of kin outside those encapsulated within the household. But the inference from all the evidence to which I have briefly drawn attention is that an ethnographic investigation of inter-household kinship relations must comprehend the informal sector and the distribution of unpaid labour; and it must be undertaken within the framework of an analysis, whether in terms of income distribution or of class formation, of the structural differentiation that has been taking place in rural communities.

The anthropological method is indispensable to this endeavour. It requires surveys of household composition and detailed observation of transactions within and between households over time. The rural community in northern Lesotho which I studied in depth contained 73 households, a *de jure* population of 361 and a *de facto* population of 294. There were 65 people whom I classified as 'paid employees', of whom 52 were absent from home in October 1974, and 13 were present. Most of the 50 men were on mining contracts, while at least 7 out of the 15 women were in domestic service in South Africa. There were 41 male (56 per cent) household heads and 32 female (44 per cent); but 45 households (63 per cent) had no resident adult male (more than 17 years old); and women were effective managers in 51 households (70 per cent).

Women are therefore central to the processes of social reproduction in the periphery. But many are at an acute relative disadvantage in respect of inequality within households and inequality between households. In their capacity as married women and household managers, an extant conjugal relationship specifies a combination of heavy domestic responsibility with a variable degree of economic insecurity. Since effective household management depends above all on the reliability of cash remittances, it is not surprising that women's experience ranges from relative security to bitter frustration, acute personal stress and emotional desolation. In their capacity as

single women, the failure of a conjugal relationship exposes them
directly to the vicissitudes of a labour market heavily loaded
against them; and exposes their children to the vicissitudes of
rearing by more or less distant kin, to the high risk of malnutrition,
and to a vicious circle of deprivation.[7] In their capacity as widows,
they face the deprivations of old age under circumstances where
the capacity of the social relations of kinship to sustain their
traditional functions has been undermined, to the disadvantage of
the elderly, the sick and the unemployed. In some cases, however,
they emerge as senior women in large households containing subordinate migrants. They may become effective local entrepreneurs
in agriculture, village politics or family affairs (cf. Murray 1977:
Appendices 1 and 3).

Women's lives in the periphery are best understood as expressions
of a continuous tension which reflects the contradictory effects of
their participation in the economy of the labour reserve. On the
one hand they have little control over the earnings of migrants, and
are often unable for this reason to engage efficiently in domestic
agriculture. On the other hand the work that they do is an indispensable condition of social reproduction; and their physical
presence, in default of that of men, articulates structural relationships that, literally, constitute the rural social system. The 'position
of women' is an abstraction which obscures the diverse manifestations
of this contradiction.

The Work of Custom

The "inescapable pressure of facts, the give and take of daily life"
(Power 1975: 34) in Lesotho is most clearly demonstrated by
reference to the effects of oscillating migration. Constrained as they
are by the structures of apartheid and the imperative of migration,
Basotho also conduct their lives with reference to ideas and practices
which are recognized as "proper Sesotho", the repository of a long
tradition — the everyday observance of taboo, the fulfilment of
ritual obligations to the dead, and the invocation of Sesotho
customary law. The 'work of custom' refers to the way in which
these ideas and practices serve to reproduce social relations,
between the living and the dead, between men and women, between
categories of kin and affines.

In Sesotho customary law a married woman is the focal point of
'house' identity. Implicit in the substantive definition of a house
is its differentiation from other houses in respect of the operational
management of domestic resources and of rights of inheritance and
succession. A man has as many houses to administer as he has married

wives; and he must allocate property from his estate to each house in an equitable manner. This property is heritable in due course by the sons of each house; while that portion of a man's estate which has not been allocated to his various houses passes on his death to the principal heir (*mojalefa*), namely the eldest son of the senior house. The integrity of house property is governed by the principle "houses do not eat each other". This principle precludes the transfer of assets between houses, for bridewealth or other purposes, without the specific approval of the heir and of his mother in each of the houses concerned.

The analytical components of house identity therefore presuppose

(1) the practice of polygyny,
(2) significant heritable resources and/or
(3) eligibility for succession to office.

These features of the house-property complex are historically appropriate to distinguishing a wealthy stratum of polygynous aristocrats with vested interests in livestock and political office, from a rural proletariat of monogamous commoners without significant heritable resources, and ineligible for succession to office. Indeed, the concept of the jural independence of the house is such an integral aspect of the customary law in its presumption and practice that confusion may arise: either in cases of simple monogamy, where there is no necessary distinction between allocated and un-allocated property (thus begging the question of the balance between the widow's and heir's respective rights and obligations); or in cases of serial monogamy, where there may be difficulty in determining the number of houses with rights to inherit (cf. Poulter 1976). Such confusion reflects the historical bias of the customary law as a representation of rights and duties amongst the ruling aristocracy.

It follows from this that the provisions of the customary law do not adequately represent the 'position of women' as it were in abstract from particular historical circumstances. Such represent-ation must be qualified with reference to structural differentiation within the rural population and also with reference to the temporal phases of development of the domestic group. A woman starts off married life as a subordinate daughter-in-law (*ngoetsi*) in her husband's family. In her maturity, however, and provided there are children borne to the house established by her marriage, she is not only house keeper in the mundane sense but keeper of the interests of her house as against those of other houses within the agnatic family (*lelapa*). Some senior wives and widows exercise a great deal of autonomy and discretion, and may be formidable protagonists in family affairs. But their 'strength' in this position depends upon the importance of the issues at stake, which almost invariably relate to the disposition of property or office. Since the property-holding unit is the house and not the agnatic family as a whole, a woman's independent role as defender of the property interests of her own house is contingent on the presence of polygynous arrangements. Otherwise, her identity is submerged, as it were, in that of her husband, and the rule "houses do not eat each other" becomes redundant except in retrospective resolution of issues in the past. Given the statistical infrequency of polygyny today, the wider political relevance of the role of house keeper is effectively confined to circumstances of competition for office. But such competition by definition preoccupies the "owners" of the family (*beng ba lelapa*), the senior men acting through the family council. The logic of the house-property complex is that a woman's domestic autonomy is greatest where the interests of the wider agnatic family are most strongly articulated.

The two most striking aspects of the 'position of women' as represented in Sesotho formal or ritual discourse are that they are 'central' in respect of house identity and 'marginal' in respect of their status within the *lelapa* as a whole. These two aspects of women's position are structurally complementary, although the balance achieved by individual women varies in the course of the developmental cycle. The role of a woman as focal point of house identity presupposes the identity, in some sense, of the larger agnatic family. Likewise, a married woman is marginal in respect of her attachment both to her natal family (*moo a tsoetsoeng*, where she was born) and to her husband's family (*moo a nyetsoeng*, where she is married). Her 'central' role as house keeper and her 'marginal' role as daughter to one family and daughter-in-law to another family are both structural corollaries of the integrity of the agnatic *lelapa*. Ideas and practices which define the position of women in these respects therefore implicitly reinforce the integrity of the *lelapa*. Conversely, ideas and practices which define the integrity of the *lelapa* implicitly reinforce the position of women in these respects.

Funerals offer a striking illustration of this point. The *lelapa* is a group of people referred to as "the children of (one) person" where the focal ancestor is seldom more than three generations above the senior living generation. Its boundaries and internal structure can only be inferred, however, from observation of the contexts — funerals, marriages, feasts, disputes — in which individuals act in their capacity as members of the *lelapa*. Funerals are occasions fraught with potential embarrassment, because the order in which agnates of the deceased throw earth into the grave is a definitive statement of their relative seniority within the *lelapa*. The senior member of the junior generation throws earth first, followed by his collaterals in order of seniority; then the senior member of the generation next senior, followed by his collaterals; and so on, until the junior representative of the senior generation. Each funeral is, then, a public display of the rank order of houses within the *lelapa* and thus serves as a precedent for the next occasion. Any disagreement between agnates will result at worst in a public scandal and at best in subdued recriminations. Many *malapa*, however, are represented at funerals in attenuated form, as a result of demographic dispersion, or in 'ghost' form, by the presence of 'sisters' and daughters-in-law and the absence of linking males.

On marriage a woman experiences not merely a change of residence from her natal place to her husband's place but a change of personal identity. She is no longer known by the personal name of her childhood and adolescence; instead she is given a new name which usually takes the teknonymous form "Mother-of-So-and-So" in anticipation of her reproductive fulfilment. Ideas about the proper place of a daughter-in-law are reproduced through the observance of *hlonepho* (respect, avoidance) prohibitions which require a married woman to avoid calling the names of her father-in-law and other senior male agnates. She must also avoid homonyms of these. She rapidly learns the necessary verbal dexterity and discretion. The *hlonepho* prohibitions, which are still scrupulously observed today by most Basotho married women, are strikingly similar to those described by Caroline Humphrey (1978) for Mongol women, and they may be said to serve similar functions — 'suppressing attention' and dramatizing hierarchy within the agnatic family. In addition, in Lesotho a male child is often named after his paternal grandfather, so that it is not uncommon for a woman to be unable to call her son by his own name. She will either call him *ntate* (father) or use a nickname. The effect of this under circumstances of oscillating migration is that the elementary 'structure' of the *lelapa* may be rehearsed in the everyday behaviour of its daughter-in-law, since many of the linking males in the senior and middle generations are either dead or absent.

As daughter to one family and daughter-in-law to another, a married woman experiences conflicting moral claims upon her which are reflected in her ambivalent secular loyalties and in her mystical vulnerability to the ancestors (*balimo*) of both families.

Although she is progressively 'incorporated' into her husband's *lelapa*, she never loses her membership of her natal *lelapa* and may throughout her married life claim protection by her own kind from maltreatment by her husband or his kin. For example, she has the right to return to her own home following a marital dispute or trouble with her affines. If her husband is found to be at fault, he should approach his in-laws with the conciliatory gift of a sheep to precede a request for his wife's return. If, however, the conjural rift is a permanent one, a woman generally returns in any case to her natal home.

For the same reason, a married woman is susceptible to mystical attack where either family has neglected its obligations in respect of the marriage, since she is the only target available through whom the ancestors (*balimo*) can exert moral pressure on affines reluctant to fulfil their obligations. A common source of resentment is failure on the part of the wife's family to slaughter the ox of *tlhabiso* which constitutes acknowledgement of enough bridewealth cattle, usually at least ten, to fulfil the marriage contract.

Most Basotho take for granted the mystical capacity of the *balimo* to influence their lives, and the consequent necessity of performing their ritual obligations. The *balimo* may appear in dreams as a reminder to the living of those obligations, and they may inflict illness or misfortune on a member of a family which has lapsed in the moral conduct of its affairs. Such interference, with its implication of neglect, is occasionally resented by the living but it is generally accepted as legitimate and steps must be taken to propitiate the *balimo*. The most common way of doing this is the feast (*mokete oa balimo*) for "giving food to the ancestors". The "owner" may arrange the feast spontaneously to "make the ancestors happy", in retrospective thanks for "luck" (*mahlohonolo*) in the past or as an invocation of "luck" in the future. Or the ancestors may initiate the exchange with an admonitory nudge, appearing in dreams with the complaint, "We are hungry. Give us food".

The *mokete ao balimo* is a generalized expression of reciprocal goodwill. But there are many other more specific obligations. A departed spirit for whom no feast of "accompanying" (*phelehetso*) has been performed will wander in limbo and return to haunt the living with the complaint, again transmitted in a dream, "Where is my blanket? I am cold" — referring to the skin of the beast that must be slaughtered to provide a "blanket" for the deceased in the abode of the *balimo*. Arranging the feast of *phelehetso* is the obligation and prerogative of close agnates of the deceased, but it is often delayed for a long time through lack of means. Small stock are only grudgingly acceptable in this context. Otherwise, a sheep must be slaughtered to remove the death pollution (*ho tlosa sesila*) attaching to close kin following a death in the family. In a widow's case, the "filth" (*sesila*) symbolized by the mourning clothes is said to derive from the "sweat" of sexual congress and of co-operative labour. The ritual takes place at her natal home, and she must be washed with a solution of the gall in water into which pieces of the species of aloe known as *lekhala* have been placed. Her head is shaved, her nails cut and her black mourning clothes burned. Her own agnates must provide her with new clothes.

Basotho like to carry out their formal ritual obligations in order to maintain good relations with the ancestors and avoid gratuitous mystical interference in their lives. But the *balimo* may be offended by miserly, unreasonable or recalcitrant behaviour between kin, and may manifest their unease by inflicting illness on an individual who is not necessarily responsible for the offence. In this case the reason for the affliction is usually divined by a doctor rather than directly revealed in a dream, and the ritual *ho tsoara motho ka matsoho* — "holding someone by the hands" — must be performed to propitiate the ancestors and to induce harmony within the family.

All of these contexts of mystical influence relate to *taba tsa lelapa*, "family affairs". These are articulated in the agnatic idiom, although mystical interference by specified matrilateral ancestors is by no means uncommon. The rituals undertaken in fulfilment of the obligations of the living to the dead are referred to as "works" of the ancestors (*mesebetsi ea balimo*). A feast for the ancestors can be interpreted on several different levels. At the level of ideological representations, it is a matter of propitiating the dead and securing "good luck". It also formally constitutes relations of kinship, in that it celebrates the integrity of the agnatic *lelapa*. More prosaically, any feast worthy of the name requires the slaughter of an animal and many other associated expenses which must be met out of cash earnings. The feast described below is a typical example of a *mokete oa balimo*, the archetypal "work" of the ancestors. It demonstrates two points: firstly, moral responsibility for the proper conduct of such "works" is vested in men, as "owners" of family affairs; secondly, they are extremely expensive.

In October 1973 Phutsoa, a contract miner who had lost a finger in a mining accident, arranged a *mokete oa balimo* spontaneously for "luck", i.e. he had not been troubled in dreams. He slaughtered two beasts which he had bought with his own earnings, each costing about R70. One sheep was provided by the senior branch of the family, and contributions of beer were made by other members. His father's junior brother (*rangoane*) made a formal speech of introduction.

> I have been instructed by the sons of Lerama to tell you what this gathering is for. This young man, the "owner" here, Phutsoa of the Lerama family, made a little work (*mosebetsinyana*) of the family . . . He has cooked for Bafokeng (the clan), both living and departed. I think many of you, in the circumstances, do not know him, and I wanted to introduce him . . . Here he is, Phutsoa of the Lerama family, who has made this work . . . He has prepared himself, through his own goodwill, to make food here so that Bafokeng, and everyone who is gathered here together with Bafokeng, will be happy with him today and so this food will be eaten. I think if there is any-thing I have forgotten, the elders will remind me . . . they told me . . . I should simply praise this food, lest people say 'Hao! The sons of Mokotjo (his own branch) made a feast here with the sons of Lerama (the senior branch), now we don't know what it is about, what is being done . . . ' That's all.

The preparations for this "little work" were those of cutting fire-wood, brewing beer, cooking the meat and all the other food, and serving a large assembly of people. This was all done by the women of the family over a period of many days. The social credit for it accrued to Phutsoa as the "owner" of the feast, the one who paid the bills. He himself put in an appearance on the day of the feast only, being otherwise preoccupied, during this period of 'rest' at home, with his duties as instructor at a boys' initiation lodge. A senior widow commented on the division of labour on such occasions:

> Women surpass [do much more than] men! They brew beer, cook bread, they go into the cattle kraal to clean out the guts, they cook the beast as well; men . . . when they've finished killing [the beast], they just go and stand over there drinking beer . . . it's the mixed-up way we do things.

In summary she remarked *mosebetsi ke oa banna empa re ba feta tsebetsong*, which can be roughly translated "the work belongs to men but we [the women] do all the work".

Much more detailed evidence of a quantitative kind is obviously required to establish the proportion of earnings that Basotho spend on "works" of the ancestors and the significance that these represent in terms of inter-household income transfers. I hope to publish this elsewhere. Meanwhile it is obvious that, in view of the expenses involved, such "works" are heavily underwritten by migrants even where migrants themselves are not the nominal

"owners" of them. In general the scale of a feast or "work" of the
ancestors is directly related to the resources the "owner" can
command: these range from a minimum of sorghum beer alone
to a really good feast in which a beast has been killed, various forms
of alcohol lavishly provided and 'sweets' (cakes, custard, jellies, etc.)
made available. Participants comment on the quality of a feast with
minute discrimination: whether helpings were generous, whether the
beer ran out, whether people were served individually or collectively,
whether tobacco and cigarettes were freely available. They apportion
kudos accordingly. Feasts are occasions of relief from a diet of
starch and from the monotony of everyday life in a community
deprived of its most vigorous members.

Interpretation

Certain aspects of custom are obsolete or obsolescent. Public rain-
making no longer takes place. Only a minority of Basotho today
goes through initiation school. Other aspects of custom are in-
vigorated by the earnings of migrants. The number of medical
charlatans, for example, whose practice is thoroughly eclectic in
inspiration, has notoriously expanded in recent years. And the
proliferation of independent churches, in Lesotho as elsewhere in
southern Africa (cf. Werbner 1977), is a sociological phenomenon
with profound implications — congregations are predominantly
female — which I have no space to analyze here. For the most
part Basotho continue to carry out the important rituals of kinship,
the "works" of the ancestors. Why? We might merely observe that
they are necessary within the terms of references of Sesotho
custom. Sanctions apply in the form of many stories in which the
aetiology of illness and misfortune is affliction by the ancestors
for neglect of some moral obligation or other. I was assured that
Seventh Day Adventists and (recently) Jehovah's Witnesses would
incur, and in some cases already had incurred, vigorous ancestral
retribution for deliberate suspension of Sesotho funeral rites. But
this sort of answer, adequate in its own terms, is sociologically unsatisfactory because it fails to relate the fulfilment of custom to
the transformations that have taken place in the lives of its
practitioners.

    In the first part of this paper, I outlined the "inescapable
pressure of facts, the give and take of daily life" in relation to the
system of oscillating migration in which almost all Basotho must
participate. In the second part I sought to identify some of the
"theatrical notions" by reference to which Basotho men and
women seek to make sense of their lives. I would stress that the

distinction between the "inescapable pressure of facts" and "theatrical notions" which I have borrowed from Eileen Power is not that between infrastructure and superstructure, if the infrastructure is seen as outside the apprehension of the actors. Rather, it is that which Maurice Bloch drew in his Malinowski Lecture between "the systems by which we know the world" and "the systems by which we hide it" (1977: 290). It is absurd of course to suppose that the experience of Basotho is constrained by the internal logic of what is distinctively Sesotho. They know all about apartheid and its effects on every aspect of their lives. I use the phrase "the political economy of migrant labour" to analyze my own vicarious experience of these effects. But the fact that Basotho villagers are not familiar with the term of reference fashionable in academic discourse does not mean that they do not clearly comprehend a general connection between white wealth and black poverty, for example, or between urban prosperity in South Africa and rural desolation in Lesotho. They take an active interest in national politics; they are appropriately cynical about politicians, the international aid agencies and the motives of people who describe themselves as students of Sesotho history and customs. The mood on the campus of the National University reflects the volatile susceptibility of the present generation of Basotho youth to the radical currents of southern African historiography.

The implication of this is that the "academic theory of social structure" on which most anthropologists have been reared is an impoverished one, in two senses. In so far as it is given in the words of our informants, or displayed on ritual occasions, it is semantically impoverished in a way that is characteristic of formal discourse (Bloch 1974). In so far as it is drawn largely from the formal part of the discourse that is everyday life, and "forgets all about the other part of the discourse" (Bloch 1977: 286), it cannot explain why, for example, Basotho spend their lives going backwards and forwards between rural poverty in Lesotho and racial and class oppression in South Africa. This gives us a clue to its meaning, at two levels. At one level, Sesotho customary representations of the 'position of women' are misrepresentations of women's real contribution to social reproduction, in a way that I have tried to outline. At another level, anthropological 'models' of social structure also serve to mystify to the extent that they accept, at face value, the legitimacy of instituted hierarchy, say, between the sexes. Their impoverishment in these two senses is precisely the source of their potency, at these two levels.[8]

Yet the problem with Bloch's very interesting argument is that it offers no clear criteria for distinguishing 'common-sense' cognition, knowledge of the world, from ritual cognition, knowledge which mystifies the world. It is always easier to diagnose other people's false consciousness than our own. This difficulty is obvious at the most basic ethnographic level. I was both impressed and distressed by the characteristic response of Basotho to particular deaths. For example, my enquiries in September 1978 revealed that the death of 'Mapuleng in December 1977 was caused by peritonitis contracted because a careless government doctor sewed up a pair of forceps inside her following an operation for cervical cancer. Her neighbours "knew" this. But in their anxiety to offer solace they simultaneously invoked *mosebetsi oa Molimo*, the work of a God whose greater purposes were beyond their comprehension. Of course this is the difference familiar to anthropologists between the 'how' and the 'why' of misfortune but, failing an intellectual conviction that the latter is subsumed under the former, we can hardly have confidence that we have correctly distinguished the system by which Basotho know the world from the system by which they hide it. For the ideas and categories which are prominent in formal or ritual discourse are also those which are used to make sense of everyday experience. Harriet Ngubane (1977) found that illness among young Zulu children in the Vally of a Thousand Hills was often attributed to the resentment of ancestors that either the children concerned or their mothers had not been properly "introduced" to the ancestors through sacrifice of the appropriate goat. Whereas the doctor or the student of political economy will argue that the incidence of gastro-enteritis among young children is very high in the rural periphery because of poverty, ignorance and lack of hygiene, conditions largely imposed by the architects of apartheid. The first step towards a remedy is seen to lie in the substitution of the latter sort of knowledge for the former, as a pre-condition of the political action necessary to change those conditions of existence. Yet the ancestors are very much part of Zulu common-sense apprehension of the world. The Zulu also observe, in their own idiom, that social problems are attributable to faulty human relations. Are they not right? Misery in the rural periphery is generated by the inhumanity of the system in which they live and work.

Conclusion

By way of conclusion the following propositions are offered in a provisional attempts to integrate custom into political economy.

1) At one level, that of Sesotho formal discourse, ritual represents

an appropriate response to the existentially profound, albeit pervasive and mundane, problems of daily life. It also serves to constitute relations of kinship between the living and the dead, between men and women, that are in various ways contradicted by the prosaic experience of Basotho. Examples of such contradiction are the manifestation of the *lelapa* in 'ghost' form which may result from the absence of its linking agnates, or the fact that, despite their nominal jural subordination throughout their lives, women effectively manage a majority of rural households.

2) At another level, that of migrants' need to invest in the security of the rural social system, ritual expenditure serves to mitigate to some extent the effects of differential distribution between households of paid labour and unpaid labour. The credit for it, however, accrues to the "owner" of the "work", who incurs the expenditure, and not to those whose unpaid labour is a necessary condition of it.

3) In Sesotho formal discourse, the conditions of social reproduction are transposed into the terms of relations between the living and the dead, whose ritual regulation lies in the hands of men. At one level, this is inequitable, in that women are precluded from direct access to the ritual resolution of their problems. At another level, it mystifies the real contribution of women to social reproduction, in that such ritual resolution transposes their problems to a plane where their explanation lies both beyond question and beyond women's moral responsibility. Sesotho ritual discourse therefore inhibits understanding of, for example, the real causes of gastro-enteritis and tuberculosis, or of forms of depressive illness, described as being "gripped by spirit (of the ancestors)", to which both sexes are susceptible but whose incidence, capricious and unpredictable in moral terms, appears to be higher among women than it is among men. The problem of explaining such phenomena is very complex but I would argue that the vulnerability of women is attributable partly to pressures arising out of the circumstances described above (loneliness, insecurity et.); and partly to differential patterns of diagnosis, following a cultural logic in which men are defined as morally responsible and are able to take alternative ritual action *vis-à-vis* the ancestors, while women are defined as morally irresponsible and therefore have no access to other means of resolution. In other words, sex may be a significant variable, not only in the circumstances which predispose individuals to develop the symptoms of mystical affliction, but also in the process by which such symptoms are diagnosed and treated.

4) 'Men's work' and 'women's work' are both indispensable to

social reproduction in the periphery but they are differentially evaluated, both inside and outside Sesotho terms of reference. Nevertheless, a 'map' of social structure in Lesotho reveals women visibly 'exposed', demographically and sociologically, in a way that is at odds with the Sesotho customary representation of women as structurally marginal and morally irresponsible. Whereas migrant men are transient visitors, even strangers, in their own communities. One way of interpreting the investment by migrants of substantial resources in the "works" of the ancestors is that such "works" replicate conditions of social reproduction, through celebration of the integrity of the agnatic *lelapa*, in which men and women respectively resume their proper places. It follows from this that the meaning of the work of the ancestors cannot be confined to nor solely derived from the symbolic reverberations, the internal logic, of the Sesotho cultural code.

Notes

1. I should like to thank Judy Gay, Andrew Spiegel and Pepe Roberts for their helpful comments on an earlier draft. I carried out fieldwork in Lesotho from 1972—4, and made a further brief visit in September/ October 1978.
2. Domestic service in South Africa is the largest single category of employment available to migrant women from Lesotho. Wages in October 1972 varied from R14.78 per month in Bloemfontein to R28.93 per month in Cape Town, according to employers' estimates (SAIRR 1974: 312). I was told that wages in Lenasia, an Indian suburb of Johannesburg, were between R16 and R24 per month at the end of 1974 (R1.6 = £1).
3. Little systematic study has been carried out of the disposition of women's labour time, in Lesotho or any other part of the periphery. The figure cited here is derived from time budgets for 57 women at various seasons of the agricultural year, compiled by a team responsible for evaluating the effects of a rural water supply programme (Feachem *et al.* 1978). Observation of 79 woman-days revealed the following distribution of time in the average woman-day:

water collection	13 mins.,
household work (cleaning, washing, cooking, etc.)	391 mins.,
agricultural work	142 mins.,
social and leisure activity (eating, resting, visiting)	312 mins.

4. For telling examples of its negative political implications, see Ngugi wa Thiong'o's novel *Petals of Blood* (1977), in which he describes a conspiracy on the part of the new Kenyan bourgeoisie to administer to the Kikuyu peasantry a compulsory Tea Drinking ceremony, a cynical corruption of the Mau Mau oath; or Shula Marks' (1978) account of the way in which a growing threat of proletarian consciousness amongst Zulu workers reversed official attitudes towards the Zulu kingship.

5. For a representative sample of the 'new homes economics' see the *Journal of Political Economy* 81, 2 (II), March/April 1973, and 82, 2 (II), March/April 1974; and for a review of its development and current trends, see Cawhill (1976). One example of its influence in Lesotho is Wykstra's (1978) recent argument that crop yields in Lesotho are low partly because of an absolute shortage of female labour for the critical task of weeding. Another example of progressive accountancy is the recognition by the evaluation team referred to in note 4 (Feachem *et al.* 1978) that the introduction of piped water supplies has the sole significant benefit of reducing the time spent on drudgery, even though that time has negligible opportunity cost. It imputed a value to the time saved, 30 minutes per average woman-day, by relating the cost of a typical water supply, at R51 per adult woman, to the time saved over a period of ten years, discounted at a rate of ten per cent per annum, which amounted to 1,234 hours per adult woman. This works out at a rate of 4 cents an hour. This figure had no reference to the 'real' cost of women's labour time, whatever that is. But it has the merit of recognizing the utility to women of a reduction in drudgery; and its relevance in cost-benefit analysis is that, if women's labour time is valued at 4 cents an hour, then the piped water supply is 'economically' justifiable; if it is given no value at all, the provision of piped water may not be 'economically' justifiable, in view of the team's conclusion that there are no other benefits which derive directly from it.

6. Their starting point is the distinction between use-value and exchange-value. The value of a thing is the expression of the average social labour embodied in its production. Its value is not made apparent if it is produced directly for use but it is made apparent if it is exchanged with other commodities. This means that, while value does not derive from exchange-value, it is only realized in the form of exchange-value. Failing its realization in exchange-value, there is no way of measuring the value of domestic labour. Within the British contribution to the domestic labour debate there are two main 'tendencies': the 'orthodox' and the 'unorthodox' (cf. Smith 1978). The difference between them relates to such issues as (1) the nature of productive labour; (2) whether or not domestic labour creates value; (3) whether the value of labour power comprehends or excludes domestic labour; and (4) the political implications of the analysis. In so far as they are relevant to the present discussion, the difference between the two 'tendencies' may be conveniently illustrated by reference to the debate between Seccombe and Gardiner in the *New Left Review*. Seccombe (1974) argued that the value created by female labour in the home is embodied in the exchange value of the commodities to whose production it contributes — labour power, in the case of domestic labour under capitalism. This leads him to assert that the value created by the wife's domestic labour is reflected in the value of the wage she receives from her husband's pay packet. Gardiner rejected this view on the grounds that "the mystification of the wage form which Seccombe exposes and rejects in the case of wage labour is then applied unquestioningly to domestic labour" (1975: 50). Her criticism is based on Seccombe's alleged failure to acknowledge the

economic dependence of women upon men in marriage, and the unequal exchange which derives from the relationship. Behind this disagreement lies the question of whether the value of labour power is (a) the labour embodied in the reproduction and maintenance of labour power (i.e. including domestic labour); or (b) the value of commodities purchased by the wage and consumed by the worker's family. Proponents of the first view, who include Duncan Clarke and Harold Wolpe, writing about 'primitive accumulation' in southern Africa, use the phrase the value of labour power in a sense that appears synonymous with the historically determined subsistence level for a worker and his family, although there is ambiguity in alternative phrases such as the value of the commodities that comprise necessary consumption. Gardiner argued that domestic labour does not create value, in the marxist sense, and therefore she adopts the second view, which implies that the value of labour power is not synonymous with the historically determined subsistence level. There is, however, agreement that domestic labour contributes to surplus value. According to the first view, it allows labour power to exchange at a wage below its value. According to the second view, it allows the value of labour power to fall below the subsistence level.

7. Some of the costs of desertion and illegitimacy may be assessed from the results of research on malnutrition in the Ciskei and KwaZulu. The incidence of malnutrition was found to be highest where mothers had no support from fathers and where children were in the care of relatives other than their own parents (Thomas 1973; Schlemmer and Stopforth, 1974).

8... It might be helpful to give an example of slightly misplaced anthropological ingenuity that is pertinent to my problem in this paper. In her book *Body and Mind in Zulu Medicine*, Harriet Ngubane (1977) identified a structural homology between the interstitial or marginal role of Zulu women in the secular sphere and their marginal, and therefore dangerous and powerful, role in the mystical sphere. In the secular sphere, from the point of view of the men of a local descent group, their wives are outsiders, and such women are in an ambivalent position partly because they are never wholly incorporated into the descent group into which they have married but retain membership in significant respects in their natal descent groups, and partly because they are the foci of internal differentiation of the descent group into sets of half-siblings and sets of full siblings. In the mystical sphere, an intensity of pollution attaches to birth and death, both seen as processes of transition between this world and the other world, where ancestors belong. Women give birth and women are chief mourners. In this way women control both entry into and exit from the world of the living. Women are therefore structurally appropriate to serve as mediators of mystical influence between the world of the living and the world of the dead. This is why Zulu diviners, who experience mystical communion with the ancestors in the other world and interpret their moral authority to the living in this world, are women. Ngubane's analysis reveals a fascinating consistency of ideas concerning health, disease, imbalance in the universe and the mystical intervention of the ancestors. She also effected a pleasing compromise between well-known factions of the Cambridge anthropology department. In these respects her work is representative of an illustrious anthropological tradition. But, except in so far as alien spirits of 'colonialism' invade Zulu cosmology and afflict Zulu women, she does not relate the 'position of women' to the larger structures in which Zulu women necessarily participate and which generate the "inescapable pressure of facts" of life in the haphazard aggregate of bits and pieces that constitute KwaZulu.

References

Bloch, M. 1974. Symbols, song, dance and features of articulation: is religion an extreme form of traditional authority? *European Journal of Sociology* **XV** (1), 55–81.

—— 1977. The past and the present in the present. *Man* **12** (2), 278–292.

Cawhill, I. 1976. Economic perspectives on the family. *Daedalus* **106** (2), 115–125.

Cobbe, J. 1976. Approaches to conceptualization and measurement of the social cost of labour migration from Lesotho. In *South Africa today: a good host country to migrant workers?* Horison, Tvl.: Agency for Industrial Mission.

Edholm, F., Harris, O. and Young, K. 1977. Conceptualizing women. *Critique of Anthropology* **3** (9 and 10), 101–130.

Feachem, R.G.A. *et al.* 1978. *Water, health and development: an interdisciplinary evaluation.* Tri-Med Books.

Gardiner, J. 1975. Women's domestic labour. *New Left Review* **89**, 47–58.

Hubbard, M. 1977. Notes on the concept of subsistence in wage theory and policy. Mimeo, Department of Economics, University College of Botswana.

Humphrey, C. 1978. Women, taboo and the suppression of attention. In *Defining females*, S. Ardener (ed.). London: Croom Helm.

Kuhn, A. and Wolpe, A.M. 1978. *Feminism and materialism.* London: Routledge and Kegan Paul.

Marks, S. 1978. Natal, the Zulu royal family and the ideology of segregation. *Journal of Southern African Studies* **4** (2), 172–194.

Murray, C. 1976. *Keeping house in Lesotho.* Unpublished PhD. thesis, University of Cambridge.

—— 1977. High bridewealth, migrant labour and the position of women in Lesotho. *Journal of African Law* **21** (1), 79–96.

—— 1978. Migration, differentiation and the developmental cycle in Lesotho. In *Migration and the transformation of modern African society*, W. van Binsbergen and H. Meilink (eds.). Leiden: Afrika-Studiecentrum.

Ngubane, H. 1977. *Body and mind in Zulu medicine.* London: Academic Press.

Ngugi wa Thiong'o. 1977. *Petals of blood.* London: Heinemann.

Parkin, D. 1972. *Palms, wine and witnesses.* London: Inter-text Books.

Poulter, S. 1976. *Family law and litigation in Basotho society.* Oxford: Clarendon.

Power, E. 1975. *Medieval women*, M.M. Postan (ed.). Cambridge: C.U.P

SAIRR. 1974. *A survey of race relations in South Africa 1974*, vol. 28, M. Horrell (ed.). Johannesburg: South African Institute of Race Relations.

Schlemmer, L. and Stopforth, P. 1974. *A study of malnutrition in the Nqutu district of KwaZulu.* Durban: Institute for Social Research, Fact Paper No. 2.

Seccombe, W. 1974. The housewife and her labour under capitalism. *New Left Review* 83, 3–24.

Smith, P. 1978. Domestic labour and Marx's theory of value. In *Feminism and materialism*, A. Kuhn and A.M. Wolpe (eds.). London: Routledge and Kegan Paul.

Thomas, T. 1973. *Their doctor speaks.* Cape Town.

Transvaal, Province of. 1922. Report of the Local Government Commission (1921). (T.P. 1-1922). Pretoria. [Stallard Commission].

Van Binsbergen, W. 1976. Ritual, class and urban-rural relations: elements for a Zambian case study. *Cultures et Développement* 8 (2), 195–218.

Van der Wiel, A. 1977. *Migratory wage labour: its role in the economy of Lesotho.* Mazenod Book Centre.

Werbner, R. 1977. *Regional cults* (ASA 16). London: Academic Press.

Wykstra, R. 1978. *Farm labor in Lesotho: scarcity or surplus?* Lesotho Agricultural Sector Analysis Project, Discussion Paper No. 5. Maseru.

THE HIDDEN WORK OF EVERYDAY LIFE

CATO WADEL

Introduction

Work, as an activity and as a concept, has preoccupied many branches
of social science: it also pervades the daily life of most people. In
both cases it seems to be regarded as an "objective" category, that
is, as one whose essence does not vary with social and cultural
circumstances. Yet work is an ambiguous concept.

In this paper I shall approach work as a socially constructed
category. By this I mean that (1) activities we term work in our own
society are continuously changing: new types of activities are continuously included under the concept, while others are excluded, and
(2) the way in which we characterize work activities and distinguish
them from nonwork activities is continuously changing.

By using the term, "hidden work", I am myself participating in
social construction. For my suggestion is not only that there are
working activities we are less aware of, but also that there are
activities that have some major characteristics of work but which
we do not yet *call* work. The argument in this paper may thus be
seen to have a practical component in addition to the analytical
one — and I may as well state it at the outset.

I feel a need, as a social scientist, to refine and broaden the work
concept so as to give a more central place to the notion of work as
a source of cultural and social *values*. This view of work is a recognizable contribution of anthropology; however, it is not, in my view,
adequately taken into account in our analysis of work. I suggest
that the analysis of work as a social construction must take account
of a dialectic relation between changes in institutional arrangements
(e.g. allocation of work activities) and cognition (e.g. characterization
of work activities).

This dialectic may be approached through posing the following
questions:

1) Are our conceptions of work in some way influenced by
changes in our occupational structure? e.g. by the growth of the

service industries.

2) Will the fact that a decreasing proportion of our total population engages in paid work, and an increasing proportion has income without working (i.e. social security) have any influence on our work concept?

3) Will the amount and types of work we engage in outside the market (i.e. non-paid work) have any influence on our work concept? What is the relation between work inside and outside the market?

4) If we can isolate forms of individual and social value-creation which are based on activities we do *not* term work — does this conceptualization have any influence on what may be termed the "living conditions" of this form of value-creation?

It is of course not possible to answer these questions in a short paper: but I hope to be able to identify (1) some of the major diacritica of the activities we term work and (2) the social and cultural basis for the selection of those diacritica rather than others. Although in writing this paper I have had a cross-cultural anthropological perspective in mind, I restrict myself here to what may be termed Western industrial capitalist societies — something that an anthropology of work would have to include in order to be truly comparative. In conclusion, I attempt an assessment of the diacritica of our Western concept of work compared to those of so-called primitive society.

The Work Concept Among Economists

Neither anthropologists, nor sociologists nor political scientists have, to my knowledge, tried to develop a "sociological" concept of work. All three disciplines seem to have borrowed the work concept they normally use either from economists or their own folk culture — often taking "pieces" from both. A brief review of these two sources is therefore necessary.

There is very little discussion of the work concept among modern economists as compared with the discussions of the classical economists like Smith, Ricardo, Mill and Marx. It might also come as a surprise that in such a "classical" textbook as Paul Samuelson's *Economics* (8th ed. 1970) we do not find any definition of work or labour, although one has to assume that the author has some conception or other about what activities constitute work or labour.

The main reason for this but moderate interest in the concept of work among modern economists is that they have come to operate with a very *simple* concept — so simple indeed that it needs no definition. The simplicity consists of treating work/labour exclusively as those activities that are sold on the market for a price. In short, work, for all practical and theoretical purpose, is paid work. Economists have had no difficulties in including new types of activity (as well as new occupational groups) under their work concept, so long as this activity is sold on the market. Thus, they have been able to incorporate as work, one of the major changes in modern society, i.e. the increasing division of labour, without changing or refining their concept of work.

But with this close relation between the concept of work and the market, economics is left with a view of work that has a business administrative basis, not to say bias. Moreover, as long as it is business organizations (including organizations such as hospitals and government bureaucracies) and not "society" that demand and pay for work, "work" for the economists, is something that is left to these organizations to define.

Business organizations are likely to define work as those activities which they find necessary for whatever production is involved. Activities during "working time" which cannot be so related are generally not termed work: they are "leisure at work" or informal activity. As I shall argue later on, this informal activity may indeed be necessary for the "real" work to be carried out (see pp. 373–74). Perhaps more intriguing is the fact that most working people, on the shop floor and in the office, do produce other things than what is regarded as the product. These other things include such things as social relations, technical and social skills, attitudes and values. These "products" might be crucial for the functioning of the concrete business organization in question as well as for society at large. But such activities are not normally grasped by the economists because they put most of their attention (not to say all) on the pay for work and the product of work (in the narrow sense just outlined), not on the activities of work.

We can thus say that the work concept among economists has become subservient to other concepts which they more easily handle professionally. These include those that can be quantified, like pay and product, and those which may be said to be the institutional basis for our kind of economy, like business organization and market.

This development and use of concepts among economists may be said to reflect, if in an extreme way, the specific mode of our Western economy. Such a state of affairs could be regarded as a scientific virtue were it not for the "imperialistic" tendencies of economics, i.e. the tendency to equate the economy with the market-economy. It must be added that such tendencies among economists are connected with the failure of other social sciences to develop their own concept of work, or to take seriously the development of institutional economics (cf. Hernes 1978).

By thus delimiting their empirical and theoretical studies of work to paid work, and by entrusting the definition of what activities constitute work to business management, economists have disregarded the notion of work as a source of cultural and social value. Of course, they are aware that most people are also working outside markets and that large groups of people, e.g. housewives, work wholly outside markets. But economists have shown little interest in this non-paid work, except where it is at the same time also found on the market. Work which falls wholly out-side the market — work which, I shall argue, is criticial in the maintenance of major social institutions — has not been of interest to economists! (cf. Elkan, this volume.)

Note may also be taken of the fact that economists (and other social scientists) have not found "work" to be a necessary concept in their analysis of certain economic institutions. While work is a central concept in the analysis of production processes, it is not central, and in some cases not used at all, in the analysis of economic institutions like, for instance, the labour market. Yet we all know that it can take a person (e.g. one who is looking for a job) a lot of time, effort and activity to keep himself informed about the labour market. We also know that many people actually secure their employment through informal channels: that is to say the labour market is to a large extent maintained by what we may term "free" work.

We may conclude by stating that the economists' concept of work is professionally biased, narrow and shaped in relation to the specific field (the market) that economists have taken upon them-selves to study; what the general public and officialdom learn about "work" from the economists is accordingly restricted. The folk (i.e. lay) concept of work, by contrast, is much broader. However, there is also less agreement, among ordinary people, as to what work *is*. It is therefore somewhat hazardous for us to generalize about the folk work concept. Even so, I shall venture some generalizations in order to make the contrast with the economists' view of the matter — for it is by such means that we can begin to construct a sociological definition of the concept of work.

The Folk Work Concept

The folk or lay concept of work is in many respects identical with that of the economists; it is restricted to activities one is paid for (paid work); such work takes place at specific places (work place) and at specific times (work time/working hours). The question "What's your work?" usually means paid work.

This identification of work with paid work must also be said to dominate the tradition in sociology called "the sociology of work". This would not be so, I assume, in "an anthropology of work" — but then there is no tradition in anthropology in this field. The only writings I know of that may be said to be concerned with the establishment of an anthropology of work are Udy (1959 and 1970); but Udy restricts himself at the outset by stating that "we shall define work very simply as any purposive human effort to modify man's *physical* environment (my emphasis).

Even if the folk work concept in many contexts is identical with paid work, few people would restrict their use of the term to paid work; and we may note at the outset some of the transformations that happen in our society between paid work and leisure (work). When, for instance, yarn becomes so expensive that one may buy a sweater with the money needed to purchase the yarn for a knitted sweater, the housewife might regard her former work (knitting) as leisure (work). We may also register cases in the opposite direction. For example, gardening: what was earlier leisure activity can become through rising real-estate prices, an investment and thence, because it "pays", work. In other words, market-prices can determine what is work and what is leisure. Furthermore as an increasing amount of goods and services are being produced both commercially and domestically, and as costs of labour and materials fluctuate, we may expect lay definitions of what constitutes work to "fluctuate" as well.

This should seem-to suggest that the folk concept of work is sub-dued to the market. Thus the care of children and of sick or elderly persons, *within a family setting*, does not seem to have been regarded, in the past, as work proper (nor as leisure). However, the fact that these activities now can be bought on the market, or supplied by local authorities, coupled with the fact that more and more people make use of such professional services, seem to have led to a greater recognition and legitimation of them as work even when carried out within a family setting.[2] Then again, there are a large number of services that are *only* available outside the market; these are such that it is critically important *who* supplies the service — one's parents or children, neighbours, friends or colleagues. Even where this work is both private and personal it is nonetheless popularly recognized as work.

The folk concept work is thus much broader than the economists'.

The folk concept of work also differs from that of the economists by having a strong *moral* component. While both economists and people in general might agree that any work implies "costs" of various sorts, these costs are, to the economists, *only* costs; but the layman also attributes a "moral income" to work precisely *because* it involves costs.

Thus while economists in their way of thinking are bound to regard income and cost as exclusive categories, because they only operate with one type of "account", most people need not do so because they have at least two "accounts", an economic and a moral one. The fact that most people operate with two "accounts" for cost and income with regard to paid work, gives to this work a *raison d'être* beyond that of "making a living"; to have a job is commonly held as a pre-requisite for membership in the "moral community" . . . a fact that people on the "dole" all too often experience (cf. Wadel 1973).

All the same, the lay public seems to question the need of many forms of work in a way that the economist does not. Because the economist does not look for criteria of value beyond the market, all paid work must be necessary. By contrast, the lay public constantly take stands on the *social worth* of work and hence, in the final analysis, on the *necessity* of certain work activities (Williams, 1968: 2).

This tendency among the lay public is, undoubtedly, stronger today than ever before. It is to be accounted for by the increasing complexities (easily seen as increasing artificiality) in the once — basic principles of division of labour; by the increased amount of "paper work" jobs; and by the increased production of consumer luxuries (of things "we don't really need"). It is in these circumstances that people begin to "define" work by relatively trivial criteria such as its routine, its time and place (one goes from home *to* work) — instead of by reference to the social necessity of what they are doing and for what their labour produces.

To sum up this far: the folk work concept is much broader than that of the economists', but it is also more ambiguous and (subjectively) confusing. One way of looking at this is to say that the folk or lay concept is more "open" to changes in the institutional structure of western society than ever is the economists'. Or put another way, we can see the dialectic between institutional changes and cognition more clearly in the folk concept of work.

Towards an Institutional Definition of Work

If neither the folk nor the economists' models of work are sufficient, where are we to turn? What we require is a model that takes account of such work of everyday life that remains "hidden" and/or unacknowledged in both the lay and the economists' view of work. The first step towards the construction of such a model is a simple one: it is to recognize the central place the concept of "social institution" has in the social sciences, outside economics. The next step is more difficult: it is to deploy the writings about social institutions towards our specific concern. This may be seen as a task of conceptual translation. In short, our present concern involves a short excursus into the sociology of knowledge which is, however, anchored in the institutional approach to social life as exemplified in the disciplines of sociology, social anthropology, political science and, though to a lesser extent, social psychology.

These disciplines are distinguished by their concern with the creation and maintenance of social institutions, and with institutional change. Moreover, it is recognized that social institutions are created, maintained and changed, not on any *deus ex machina* basis but by social action — by the efforts of persons. Clearly, this is a critical point for us. At the same time it is the point at which the need for a shift in emphasis becomes apparent. For whereas the place that effort or action — that is, work — has in the making of institutions is, on the whole, left implicit, in my view, it is important that it be made explicit and its implications fully explored. As the situation is at present, it is the social *form* of institutions that has received the most attention: we write mostly about institutions as "end results" and not about the "work" that has gone into their achievement.

Concretely, we should ask in each case what work (activities and effort) is necessary for the creation/maintenance/change of an institution? I think we may expect to find various kinds of work that are overlooked by both layman and economists alike. The importance of the exercise is that it opens the possibility of demonstrating that whereas everyday activities which, when considered in isolation may appear "trivial" (even to the person who carries them out) and not merit the label work, when aggregated and considered in relation to formal work do constitute a prerequisite of effective institutional arrangements. Not least important among the contributions of such everyday work to society in general, is the generation of social values.

In the sections that now follow, I outline four areas or domains (among others) in which social scientists have provided some documentation of this process — but without proceeding to what I see as the next logical step: namely, arguing for a broader concept of work.

Studies of Informal Organization Within Formal Organizations

Though we are without a complete empirical overview of formal organizations in Western society, the insights we do have from a large number of studies, especially in sociology and political science, suggest that no formal organization exists without a parallel informal organization. Indeed, it has been convincingly argued in some cases that the formal organizational set-up would not "work" at all were it not for the informal organization (cf. e.g. Homans 1950, Gouldner 1954, Blau and Scott, 1962).[4]

I find it here more appropriate to talk about informal activities rather than informal organization; and we may notice that whereas all the formal activities within any formal organization are termed work, few, if any, of the informal activities are so termed. A major reason for not calling the various types of informal activity, work, would seem to be that these activities most often take place simultaneously with "ordinary" work. Another reason is that the informal activities are not considered "necessary" — the formal organization can fulfill its goals, it is held, without these activities. Thus, when people, for some reason or other, stop their ordinary work to engage in informal chat, they — and their employers and their colleagues — are likely to feel that they are "stealing" time away from their work.

What is surprising is that such informal activities have not been recognized and discussed *as work* in social science studies. Instead, we are likely to find them discussed under the rubric of informal organization — and the fact that people give time, thought and effort to produce and maintain these informal organizations is often lost. At all events, the work is left unanalyzed (in strong contrast to the detailed treatment afforded to the formal work activities).

As a matter of fact, recognition that informal activities *do* matter in industries has happened without the help of social research — chatting on the shop floor, for example, has become "institutionalized" through being formally allocated time and place and also function, as "co-ordinating chats" conducted within the instituted framework of a "meeting". *That* is recognized as work.

Perhaps the most important contribution of social science to the present problem is to be found in the domain of role theory. Goffman's (1961) essay on "role-distance" is a good example. He convinces us that the various role-distancing activities of the surgeon are, at the least "functional", perhaps even indispensable. Without them, particular (surgical) operations might be endangered; they may even benefit "surgery in general" (p. 135). The general theoretical contribution of role theory, in the present context, is to make possible what Goffman terms "moment-to-moment studies of behaviour". The focus is upon what people do, and have to do, in playing their roles.

Even if the relevance of informal activity to formal organization is recognized, it is generally assumed that their relevance is restricted to the specific work setting in which they occur: there is evidence however, as Goffman indicates, that the influence of informal activity is not necessarily so restricted.

Once again, I must enter a plea: this time it is for the *integration of role theory with work theory*. As the matter stands there is a more or less arbitrary separation of actions we term "work" from those actions, analyzed by role theorists, that are variously labelled under the catch-all term "impression management" (e.g. role-distance, deference and demeanor, joking, avoidance etc.). Both kinds of action, not just the one, must be recognized as work.

Community Studies

While they have not resulted in any "theory of community" the large number of studies in this genre have shown, at least, that the maintenance of neighbourhood and community requires *effort* on the part of the inhabitants. However, neither the researchers nor the informants themselves seem to categorize this effort as work.

As I indicated above, a certain ambiguity is associated with such neighbourly activities as visiting, "giving a helping hand", or simply listening to the worries of others. At the same time as they are trivialized through comparison with "real" work activities – and even "excused" in such phrases as "Well, this won't do: I must go and do some work" – people can get very upset when they believe they are being neglected by their neighbours. Indeed, doctors, psychiatrists, psychologists, and other social workers have documented how it is especially individuals who are not involved (either as givers or receivers) in such neighbourliness that are likely to have a precarious medical/mental state of health. Much the same argument has been made (and sustained I think) in respect to the dependence of families and (formal) local organizations on informal community relations and activities. Several factors suggest themselves when seeking an explanation as to why activities associated with informal community relations have not been associated with work:

1) they are not "planned" but *ad hoc* and sporadic;
2) they are of a "personal" character – the value of the activity depends on who does it as much as on what is done; and
3) they are of a "private" character – what is done is not really

open to the public view (cf. Paine 1969);

4) thus means and ends (or aims) are difficult to distinguish — the actions are likely to have as much intrinsic value as extrinsic (cf. Paine 1974).

But these are emic reasons (cf. discussion of the folk concept of work). That they are allowed to prevail as reasons for the exclusion of informal community relations from the domain of work in social science writings is, I suggest, a reflection of how "community research . . . lacks a firm theoretical basis" (Elias 1974: xv). While we may agree with Elias (1974: xxv) that,

> As societies become more differentiated and the hierarchy of levels of integration grows in size and complexity, communities develop into one of the lower levels of integration.

this still leaves open the problem as to what actions, effort and time is required to establish and maintain this lower level of integration, and with status we should give to these actions (cf. Thuen and Wadel (eds.) 1978).

Studies of Informal Political Activities

A characteristic feature of democratic societies in the West is the small small number of paid and full-time positions, what we may call professional positions, in politics. Without having the exact figure, a fair estimate is probably one tenth of a per cent of the number of paid and full-time positions in the economy. This imbalance between the polity and the economy does not seemtto bother us. Western democracy seems to "work" satisfactorily without too many people being involved full-time in politics; indeed, some might be of the opinion that too many full-time jobs in politics would be contrary to the idea of democracy.

Even so, the small number of full-time jobs in politics calls our attention to two matters of relevance here: first, democracy is a very "cheap" system in economic manpower terms, and second, we do not correlate paid work with work in politics, as we do in the economy.

Were we to follow conventional economic theory with regard to politics, we would have to try to explain the difference between these two sectors of public life in terms of a lack of demand for political or democratic "commodities". Further, we might be led to argue that, because the production of political/democratic commodities takes much less time than the production of economic commodities, we need much less manpower and work effort in politics. Both these factors may be operative but, quite certainly, they do not of themselves help us very much in explaining the difference between the work situation in the polity and the economy. Much more to the point is that the work effort going into politics is largely non-paid work and is, in addition, "hidden" work to a considerable extent.

The unpaid but "open" political work in western democracies is considerable: various estimates (e.g. Martinussen 1973) suggest that ten per cent or more of the adult population is so engaged at any one time (and at various levels of political life); even if most of this be part-time work, it surely compares favourably with the total effort put into politics by professional politicians.

"Hidden" unpaid political work is likely to amount to still more — but of course, we cannot know. We may postulate that every occupational position gives some opportunity for political work, but that the degree of opportunity will vary considerably. Much political work both within one's occupation and in one's "free time", is hidden even from the actors themselves, and includes activities which are normally not thought of as work at all — e.g. discussion, reading newspapers, listening to media reports and making up one's mind concerning a political issue. Such a situation means that we cannot depend on emic categories alone for an understanding of the political scene, or even for description of it.

To my knowledge, no studies have actually demonstrated that democratic institutions depend on informal (and sometimes "hidden") political activity among the citizens of a democracy.[5] To this extent we lack an empirical basis for a "theory of democracy": what has been termed classical democratic theory must, for the time being, be regarded as, in the main, a normative or ideal theory. My suggestion here is that we should regard democracy, *qua* normative system, as a *learning system.* An important task in analysis will be to provide an account of the various kinds of "input" into the system from non-professional, as well as professional, sectors of the population (cf. Bachrach 1969). Particular regard should be paid to the fact that "some issues are organized into politics while others are not" (Schattsneider 1960: 71, quoted in Bachrach and Baratz 1962), and as a corollary, that some political activities are regarded as work while others are not. For, I suggest, "backlashes" in the working of a democracy are associated with failures to include issues on the political agenda and/or to recognize informal political activities as genuine work activities.

Studies of Clients and Professionals

The three types of informal activities I have discussed so far — within

formal organizations, within local communities, and in politics —
might all be said to have had the same fate: they have been
neglected as forms of work. The activities of clients, on the other
hand, have been actively defined as non-work.

The normal definition of being a client is that of a "receiver" —
and only a receiver — of someone else's work.[6] But we all have
experiences of being clients in everyday life; and we all know that
being a client takes time, planning and effort. And yet we seem to
think of the activities we perform as clients as something less than
work. On the other hand, it should be clear to us that our activities
as clients constitute a necessary "input" for the maintenance of
central economic, political, religious and familial institutions in a
modern — and increasingly bureaucratized and professionalized —
society. Put another way, contemporary western society is organized
around institutions, and within each of them we find an overriding
status distribution between, on the one hand, working people or
professionals, and on the other, non-working people or clients (cf.
Table I).

Along with the growth of the welfare state, the client status has
attracted increasing attention of social scientists — from the perspective of this paper the most important questions that have been
raised have to do with the "production" of clients. The implication
of the present situation which especially intrigues me is that it
seems, in order for certain categories of people (professionals) to
have *their* activity recognized as work, other people will have to be
given the status of clients and so of non-workers. Supporting
evidence for this view of the modern world is a general understanding
among professionals and clients alike that clients cannot evaluate
the quality of the service they are given or need (Torgersen 1972).

Professional-client relationships thus seem to be based upon a
process of ascription of competence and incompetence. Its end
results will, of course, vary according to the specific institutional
setting: in the most extreme cases, competence and knowledge are
accumulated exclusively among the professionals, while among the
clients the ability to evaluate the professional service they receive
tends towards zero.

This trend we may term "clientization". And of relevance here
is that most, if not all, professional-client "models" seem to share
the basic assumptions that (i) a solution (for the client's problem)
exists prior to its implementation, (ii) the solution can be applied
uniformly in all cases, at least in broad outline, and (iii) the
management of the solution rests, in critical ways, with the
professional only. But these assumptions rest on theories of learning

TABLE I

The institutional world and its status dichotomy

Status dichotomy / Institution	Workers or professionals	Non-workers or clients
The economy	Workers Producers	Consumers
The polity	Professional politicians	Voters
The law	Judges Lawyers Police	Clients Citizens
The bureaucracy	Civil Servants Bureaucrats	Clients Citizens
Education	Teachers Professors	Pupils Students
Health	Doctors Nurses Social Workers	Patients
Religion	Ministers Preachers	Members of the congregation
Art and sports ·	Artists Players	Audiences
The family	Parents	Children

which, certainly in the long run, lend themselves to distortion (cf. Shon 1970: 137). For example, while the professional learning increases, the "total" (i.e. professional *and* client) learning decreases.

It is useful to consider the various "backlashes" recorded among various sorts of clients, as well as professionals, from this perspective. We seem to find an increasing number of professional groups voicing such sentiments about their clients as "they get more and more stupid" and "they are not able to take care of themselves"; as for the clients, an increasing number of them seem to look to "quacks", demagogues, or simply passivity, for their cure or solutions. Now one way to ensure that a society does not, as a result of increasing professionalization, get "surprises" in the form of what we have called backlashes, would be to treat professional-client relations as a mutual learning system. More concretely, we should recognize that clients always make a contribution and can be taught to make an even larger one to the professional-client relationship. In other words, we should recognize that these are client-related activities, and these activities should be regarded as work.

Conclusions

While many of the activities that are directed to the production of socially valued goods and services (and thus help to maintain institutions of social value) are widely recognized as work, there are, as we have seen, a number of such activities that are *not* so recognized. These latter activities share at least three characteristics:

1) the individual time and effort spent on them seem sporadic and less planned when compared to the activities we ordinarily term work;

2) the time and effort spent appears to be only vaguely, or not at all, connected with an institutional "product";

3) most people perhaps all, participate in these activities in their everyday life.

These circumstances encourage the view that such activities are not work because, they happen, anyway, in the "natural" course of events.

The question before us is, however, should social scientists also delimit the concept of work this way? The question is pressed upon as by the knowledge that a number of activities which are not termed work in common parlance are nevertheless necessary for the maintenance of widely valued institutions.

It is my view that if we do not conceptualize these everyday activities by an "active" and "functional" concept, we are guilty of withholding sociological insight from the public at large: insight which can help the public to place their everyday activities in a social context — and thereby help them to find *value* in what they do. The active concept that we choose for this purpose need not necessarily be "work"; however, it does seem an appropriate choice — as Williams (1976: 281−82) has said of work, it is "our most general word for doing something, and for something done".

Economists may be said to have made their insight into society more available than other social scientists. But by concentrating their attention on one sector of society, the market economy, and developing a coherent conceptual "kit" to analyse the creation of value exclusively within the sector, their insight is limited. They are not interested in the creation of values that are, in their view of the matter, non-economic. But note should also be taken here of how within the economy of a modern western society there are a number of social institutions (e.g. firms, money, markets) and conventions (e.g. the discrimination of households and firms) that makes it possible to measure "economic" values, whereas in practically all other sectors of society such measurement of value is either not possible or is extremely difficult.

We can formulate the problem that confronts us by posing more general questions: what characterizes social institutions and conventions that allows measurement of value? Have we somehow arrived at a position in Western society where we can identify and measure some forms of value but not others? Social scientists, including economists, have not been able to answer such questions on a general theoretical level. On the other hand, it has been possible to show that the creation of values in one sector, the economy, can be have negative as well as positive consequences for the creation of values in other sectors. This being the case, do we need (e.g. for fuller understanding of these consequences) a common set of trans-sector concepts? And is not "work" one of them? I say this with a particular problem in mind. It seems to me (as must be clear by now) that, in the West today, we have a "lop-sided" notion of what work is and is not. Not only that, but, in practical terms, the distribution of work, i.e. "jobs", is also dangerously lop-sided. The one follows the other and a consequence is that some social institutions — heretofore generally acknowledged as "valuable" — are increasingly difficult to maintain. Put another way: these institutions, if they are to be maintained, need to be supplied with more work.

It is especially in this connection that anthropological research, from so-called primitive societies, is relevant. For anthropology has demonstrated that while such societies, on the one hand, lack social institutions and conventions which make it possible to measure what we would call economic value, on the other hand, they abound with institutions, for the measurement of social (or non-economic) values. It should also be noted that many (or most?) of these societies lack a concept comparable to what we mean, in the West, by work (cf. Richards 1948; Sahlins 1972). What seems to characterize these societies is not that activities such as we term as work are not conceptualized, but that these activities are conceptualized *in association with* social relations. We may express this in a simplified manner by saying that activity A + social relation A; is covered by the concept A, while activity B + social relation B, is covered by the concept B, and so on. It would be unheard of in these societies to separate part of activity/relation A, and part of activity/relation B, and to denote either or both of these separate parts with a special term, say, work. Furthermore, production and consumption are not normally seen as contrastive activities; rather, consumption is built into production, and both closely associated with social relations. Thus production + consumption + social relations are collectively conceptualized. This is, for example, what the Naskapi indians mean when they talk about "caribou hunding on the barrens" (Henriksen 1973).

Anthropological research also provides key case-studies of how a concept of work may be introduced into a culture, or transformed. Thus Barth (1967) indicates how agricultural "help" activities, in connection with beer parties among the Darfur, came to be regarded as "work", when entrepreneurial activity integrated the production of beer and the activity of "help" into the market economy. In short, such case-studies help to make clearer how the concept of work has a "history", wherever it is found, and how the concept is always institutionally supported. These are, of course, very complex matters in respect of Western socities but that is, in itself, no reason to forget them. And the "dialectic" between changing institutional arrangements and concept formation, as highlighted in many anthropological studies, should make us aware of the historical nature of our own western concept of work.

Work in western industrial society has come to stand for what might be termed "middle-ground" activities — they are placed between the activities that maintain our most private relations and the activities that maintain our most public relations. The basic reason for this would seem to be our separation of our various institutions into the economy, the polity, the family, etc., and our insistence that the economy is our "focal institution" (Dubin 1976). It may be that the market economy itself has been the most responsible for this separation and superordination — as much has been suggested by Marx, Weber, Durkheim and Polanyi. But there also seems to be a parallel process in this development of the middle-ground placing of work; namely, that we have not thought of work as a *social* "thing". But this should be the starting point for any anthropological or sociological theory of work. By work as a social "thing", I mean not only that "what is and what is not work is socially defined" (Morgan and Ward 1970: 196) or that work is a socially constructed category, but that work is something that characterizes social relations. In other words, a sociological theory of work must treat work as a *relational* concept. Now, viewing work as a relational concept does not necessarily imply that we look upon everything we do as work, but there is the expectancy that work is an *aspect* (actual or potential) of all social relations. In other words, I want to see the view of work as a middleground activity expanded in two directions: it should include the mutual activities that go into maintaining personal and private relations and the collective activities that have to do with the maintenance of community, democracy and other valued social institutions.

Notes

1. This paper is a revised version of one published in *Tidsskrift for samfunnsforskning* (1977, **18**, *387–411)* under the title of *"Hva er arbeid? Noen refleksjoner om arbeid som aktivitet og begrep"* (What is work? Some reflections on work as activity and concept). In revising and translating the paper I have relied on Robert Paine for criticism and formulations.

2. In recent years unpaid "caring work" (Norw. *omsorgsarbeid*) has been officially recognized in Norway as work, and calculated as amounting to more than the total work effort put into Norwegian manufacturing industries (see "Levekarsundersøkelsen", NOU 1976, **28**, 36).

3. David C. Thorns (1971) writes ". . . there has been little systematic investigation of the question as to what, in the eyes of the "worker", constitutes work: how the worker himself would set out to define and describe the activity he terms work. One study which has been attempted along these lines is that of Weiss and Kahn with workers in Detroit" (p. 543). About his own investigation into two communities near Bristol and Nottingham, Thorns concludes: "The study of two suburban populations has shown clearly that considerable ambiguities exist as to what kind of activity constitutes 'work' for different individuals. It also demonstrates the necessity of distinguishing between views which give support to what are considered to be the prevailing acceptable views of work at the societal level produced by political and other mass media pressures and the actual views which individuals themselves hold" (p. 554).

4. Blau and Scott (1960: 6) write: "In every formal organization there arise informal organizations. The constituent groups of the organization, like all groups, develop their own practices, values, norms, and social relations as their members live and work together. The roots of these formal systems are embedded in the formal organization itself and nutured by the very formality of its arrangements. Official rules must be general to have sufficient scope to cover the multitude of situations that may arise. But the application of these general rules to particular cases often poses problems of judgement, and informal practices tend to emerge that provide solutions for these problems".

5. On the other hand, we may ask with Shubic (1967: 773): "In voting do we have criteria other than a blind faith in the 'stolid common sense of the yeomen'? The growth in the size of the electorate and in the numbers and complexities of issues is only exceeded by the torrents of writings in which the public may be buried if it so chooses. In the jungle of municipal politics, even the well-educated and relatively more articulate part of the population is woefully under-informed. At what point does a division of labour become a division of values and of social responsibilities?"

And further: "If we believe that our political and economic values are based on the individual who understands principles, knows what the issues are, and has an important level of knowledge and understanding of his fellow citizens, then the twentieth and twenty-first centuries pose problems never posed before".

6. A less partisan point of view has been suggested by Becker (1974 and 1976) in relation to works of art. He writes (1976: 41–42) that: "Although we conventionally select some one or a few . . . to whom the responsibility for the work (of art) is attributed, it is *sociologically* more sensible and useful to see the work as the joint creation of all (involved)" that is, "people who conceive the idea of the work . . . who execute it . . . who provide the necessary equipment . . . and people who make up the *audience* for the work" . . . since this "makes problematic the *co-ordination* of the activities of all these people" (my emphasis).

References

Bachrach, P. 1967. *The theory of democratic elitism.* Boston: Little, Brown.

Bachrach, P. and Baratz, M.S. 1962. Two faces of power. *The American Political Science Review* **LVI**, 947–52.

Barth, F. 1967. Economic spheres in Darfur. In *Themes in economic anthropology*, R. Firth (ed.). A.S.A. Monographs 6. London: Tavistock Publ.

Becker, H.S. 1974. Art as collective action. *Amer. Social. Review* **39** (6), 767–76.

——— 1976. Art worlds and social types. In *The production of culture*, R.A. Peterson (ed.). Beverly Hills/London: Sage Publications.

Blau, P.M. and Scott, W.R. 1963. *Formal organizations: a comparative approach.* London: Routledge and Kegan Paul Ltd.

Dubin, R. 1976. Work in modern society. In *Handbook of work, organization and society*, R. Dubin (ed.). Chicago: Rand McNally College Publishing Company.

Elias, N. 1974. Foreword – towards a theory of communities. In *The sociology of community. A selection of readings*, C. Bell and H. Newby (eds.). London: Frank·Cass and Co. Ltd.

Goffman, E. 1961. *Encounters.* New York: Bobbs Merrill.

Gouldner, A.W. 1954. *Patterns of industrial bureaucracy.* Glencoe, Ill.: The Free Press.

Henriksen, G. 1973. *Hunters in the barrens. The Naskapi indians on the edge of the white man's world.* St. John's: Institute of Social and Economic Research.

Hernes, G. 1978. *Mot en institusjonell økonomi.* In Hernes: *Blandings-administrasjon og forhandlingsøkonomi.* Tromsø-Oslo-Bergen: Universitetsforlaget.

Homans, G. 1950. *The human group.* New York: Harcourt, Brace and Co.

"*Levekarsundersøkelsen*" 1976. NOU 1976: 28. Oslo: Universitetsforlaget.

Martinussen, W. 1973. *Fjerndemokratiet.* Oslo: Gyldendel Norsk Forlag.

Morgan, D.H.J. and Ward, R. 1970. Work, industry and organizations. In *Introducing sociology*, P. Worsley *et al.* (ed.), Ch. 5. Penguin Books. (1st edition)

Paine, R. 1969. In search of friendship: an exploratory analysis in "middle-class" culture. *Man* **4** (4), 505—24.

—— 1974. *Second thoughts about Barth's "models"*. RAI Occasional Paper No. 32. London: Royal Anthropological Institute.

Richards, A.I. 1939. *Land, labour and diet in Northern Rhodesia*. London, Oxford: Oxford University Press.

—— 1948. *Hunger and work in savage society*. New York: The Free Press. (First published London: Routledge, 1932.)

Sahlins, M.D. 1972. *Stone age economics*. Chicago and New York: Aldine, Atherton Inc.

Samuelson, P. 1970. *Economics*. (8th edition). New York: McGraw-Hill.

Shon, D.A. 1973. *Beyond the stable state. Public and private learning in a changing society*. London: Penguin Books.

Shubic, M. 1967. Information, rationality and free choice in a future democratic society. *Daedalus* **96**, 771—8.

Thorns, D.C. 1971. Work and its definitions. *The Sociological Review, New Series* **19**, 543—55.

Thuen, T. and Wadel, C. (eds.). 1978. *Lokale samfunn og offentlig planlegging*. Tromsø-Oslo-Bergen: Universitetsforlaget.

Torgersen, U. 1972. *Profesjonssosiologi*. Tromsø-Oslo-Bergen: Universitetsforlaget.

Udy, S.H. Jr. 1959. *The organization of work*. New Haven: H.R.A.F.

—— 1970. *Work in traditional and modern societies*. Englewood Cliffs: Prentice Hall.

Wadel, C. 1973. *Now, whose fault is that? The struggle for self-esteem in the face of chronic unemployment*. St. John's: Institute of Social and Economic Research.

Weiss, R.S. and Kahn, R.L. 1960. Definitions of work and occupations. *Social Problems* **18** (2), 142—151.

Williams, R. 1968. The meanings of work. In *Work. Twenty personal accounts*, R. Fraser (ed.). London: Penguin Books.

—— 1976. *Keywords. A vocabulary of culture and society*. Glasgow: Fontana/Croom Helm.

Young, M. and Willmott, P. 1973. *The symmetrical family*. London: Penguin Books.

NOTES ON CONTRIBUTORS

Anthony P. COHEN
  Born 1946, England. Senior Lecturer in Anthropology, University of Manchester.
  Educated Southampton, (B.A., M.Sc., Ph.D. 1973). Previously appointed as
  Research Fellow, Memorial University of Newfoundland 1969–70, Asst.
  Prof. Queens University, Ontario, 1970–71.
    Chief Publications: *The Management of Myths* 1975.

Walter ELKAN
  Has been Professor of Economics and Chairman of the Department of
  Economics at Brunel University, London, since 1978. Previously worked
  at the University of Durham (1960–78) and the Makerere (Uganda)
  Institute of Social Research (1953–60) where most of his colleagues were
  social anthropologists. He has been back to East Africa several times since,
  spending 18 months at the Nairobi Institute for Development Studies in
  1973. He has worked briefly for short periods in many countries of Africa,
  the Caribbean and the Western Pacific — mostly small ones. His principal
  research interest is the economics of earning a living which encompasses
  "the informal sector".
    Publications include: *Migrants and Proletarians* (O.U.P.: 1960);
  Introduction to Development Economics (Penguin: 1973); and The East
  African Trade in Woodcarvings, *Africa*, 1958.

Leonard FAGIN
  Medico (Argentina) M.R.C. Psych. Born 1946, Argentina. Trained as a
  doctor in Buenos Aires, and came to work in the U.K. in 1972. Now a
  psychiatrist working at the London Hospital, Whitechapel. General
  interests are in Community Psychiatry; specifically concerned with
  helping families undergoing crisis situations and emotional distress.
  Dr Fagin is currently undertaking a research project with the Department
  of Health and Social Security on *Families and Unemployment*, taking
  samples from South Wales, the Midlands, Tyneside and the London area.

Sir Raymond William FIRTH
  Born 1901, New Zealand. Emeritus Prof. of Anth. in the U. of London.
  Educated Auckland Un. Coll. (M.A. Econ. 1922; Dip. Soc. Sci. 1923),

U. London (Ph.D. Anth. 1927). Taught at Sydney, NSW, 1930–32; London, LSE, 1933–68.

Author of numerous books and papers in economic anthropology, among which see: *Economics of the New Zealand Maori* 1959; *Malay Fishermen* 1966; *Elements of Social Organization* 1971.

Morris A. FRED

Born 1946, Waco, Texas. Educated University of California, Berkeley (B.A. Political Science 1968; Ph.D. Anthropology 1975). Fieldwork in Taipei, Taiwan (1971–72) and Sweden (1978–9). Asst. Professor of Social Anthropology, Stockholm University (1976–78).

Author of articles concerning Christian sect studied in Taiwan.

Stephen F. GUDEMAN

Born 1939, USA. Professor of Anth., Univ. of Minnesota, Minneapolis, Minnesota, U.S.A. Educated at Harvard (A.B. Social Relations 1961; M.B.A. 1965), Cambridge (M.A. Soc. Anth. 1963; Ph.D. 1970). Taught at U. Minnesota, 1969–78. Institute for Advanced Study, Princeton, New Jersey 1978–79.

Author of: The Compadrazgo as a Reflection of the Natural and Spiritual Person, *Proceedings of the RAI* 1971; Spiritual Relationships and Selecting a Godparent, *Man* 1975; *Relationships, Residence and the Individual* 1976; Saints, Symbols and Ceremonies, *American Ethnologist* 1976; *The Demise of a Rural Economy*, 1978; Anthropological Economics, The Question of Distribution, *Annual Review of Anthropology* 1978.

Geoffrey Ainsworth HARRISON

Born 1927, England. Educated Trinity College, Cambridge, B.A.; Christ Church, Oxford, M.A., D.Phil.; University of London, B.Sc., Honorary Ph.D. University of Adelaide. Departmental Demonstrator, Oxford University 1953–54. Lecturer in Physical Anthropology, University of Liverpool 1954–63, Reader in Physical Anthropology, University of Oxford 1963–76. Professor of Biological Anthropology 1976–. Fellow of Linacre College, Oxford 1965–. Visiting Fellow, Australian National University 1969 and 1974. Visiting Professor of Anthropology, University of Harvard 1973–4, President of Royal Anthropological Institute 1969–71.

Co-author of: *Human Biology* 1964 and some 150 scientific papers in the fields of human evolution, human genetics and human ecology.

Joseph Buist LOUDON

Born 1921, UK. Sen. Lect. in Soc. Anth., U.C. Swansea, Wales, UK. Educated Oxford (B.A. Nat. Sci. 1943; M.A. Nat. Sci. 1947; B.M., B.Ch. Medicine and Surgery 1946), U. London (Dip. Soc. Anth. 1956). Has worked as a Medical Practitioner, 1946–56. WHO, Consultant, Western Pacific, 1956. LSE, Asst. Lect. Anth. 1956–57. Medical R.C. Member, Scientific Staff, 1957–64; U.C. Swansea, 1964–.

Author of: Psychogenic Disorder and Social Conflict among the Zulu, in

Culture and Mental Health, (ed.) M.K. Opler 1959; Religious Order and Mental Disorder, in *The Social Anthropology of Complex Societies*, (ASA) (ed.) M.P. Banton 1965; Teasing and Socialization on Tristan Da Cunha, in *Socialization, the Approach from Social Anthropology*, (ASA) (ed.) P. Mayer 1970; White Farmers and Black Labour-Tenants, *African Soc. Res. Doc.* 1970; (ed.) *Social Anthropology and Medicine*, (ASA) 1976; On Body Products, in *The Anthropology of the Body* (ASA) (ed.) J.A.R. Blacking 1977.

Gerald MARS

Born 1933, UK. Reader in Occup. Studies, Director, Centre for Occup. Research, Middlesex Polytechnic, Enfield, Middx. Educated at Cambridge (B.A. Econ. and Soc. Anth. 1962); London (LSE) (Ph.D. Soc. Anth. 1972). Previously worked at NISER, Newfoundland, 1962–64. Nuffield/Fellow at Inst. Criminology, Cambridge 1973–75. Tavistock Inst. 1972–.

Author of: *Room for Reform?* (with P. Mitchell) 1976; *Solving Manpower Problems in Hotels and Restaurants* (with P. Mitchell and D. Bryant) 1979; Crime at Work (with Stuart Henry), *Sociology* 1978; Hotel Pilferage, in *The Sociology of the Work Place* (ed.) M. Warner, London 1973; Dock Pilferage, in *Deviance and Social Control* (eds.) P. Rock and M. McIntosh 1974.

Leonard MARS

Born 1941, UK. Lect. in Soc. Anth., U.C. Swansea, Wales. Educated at Edinburgh (M.A. Soc. Anth. 1965); Manchester (Ph.D. Soc. Anth. 1970). Manchester, Res. Ass. 1966–68. Associate, 1968–70. Fellow, 1970–72.

Author of: A Village at War, *New Society* 1973; The Position of the Administration in an Israeli Co-operative Village, *Sociologia Ruralis* 1976; Politics and Administration in the Israeli Port of Ashdod, *I.D.S. Bulletin* 1978.

Colin MURRAY

Born 1948, UK. Research Fellow, University of Liverpool. Educated at Cambridge (B.A., Soc. Anth. 1970; Ph.D. Soc. Anth. 1976). Taught at LSE 1976–78.

Author of: Sex, Smoking and the Shades: A Sotho Symbolic Idiom, in *Religion and Social Change in Southern Africa* (eds.) M.G. Whisson and M. West 1975; High Bridewealth, Migrant Labour and the Position of Women in Lesotho, *J. African Law* 1977; Migration, Differentiation and the Developmental Cycle in Lesotho, in *Migration and Rural Development in Tropical Africa* (eds.) Meilink and Van Binsbergen 1978.

Sutti ORTIZ

Born 1929, Argentina. Living in Ohio, U.S.A. Educated at U. London (Ph.D. Anthrop. 1963). Has held appointments in LSE (Lecturer, 1963–69). Case Western Reserve (Assoc. Prof. 1969–72). Oberlin College (Vis. Assoc. Prof. 1975–76). LSE (Academic Visitor, 1977–78).

Author of: *Uncertainties in Peasant Farming* 1973; Colombian Rural
Market Organization, *Man* 1967; Reflections on the concept of Peasant and
Peasant Cognitive Systems, in T. Shanin (ed.) *Peasants and Peasant Societies*
1971; The Effect of Risk Aversion Strategies on Subsistence and Cash Crop
Decisions, in *Risk and Uncertainty in Agriculture* (ed.) Roumasset 1967;
Expectation and Forecast in the Face of Uncertainty, *Man* 1978.

David John PARKIN
Born 1940, England. Reader in Anth., School of Oriental and African
Studies, University of London. Educated at London (SOAS) (B.A. 1962;
Ph.D. 1965). Has previously worked in East African Inst. Soc. Research
1962–64. SOAS (Assist. Lect. Soc. Anth. 1964–65. Lecturer 1965–71).
Sussex 1971–72; Nairobi U., 1968–69.
Author of: Voluntary Associations as Institutions of Adaptation, *Man*
1966; *Town and Country in Central and Eastern Africa* 1975 (ed.);
Politics of Ritual Syncretism, *Africa* 1970; Congregational and
Interpersonal Ideologies in Political Ethnicity, *Urban Ethnicity* (ed.) A.
Cohen 1974; The Rhetoric of Responsibility, in *Political Language and
Oratory in Traditional Society* (ed.) M. Bloch 1975; *The Power of Culture:
definitions of political response among the Luo* 1979.

Enid SCHILDKROUT
Born 1941, U.S.A. Asst. Curator, Dept. Anth., American Museum of Natural
History, NY, U.S.A. Educated at Sarah Lawrence Col. (B.A. 1963); Newnham,
Cambridge (B.A. Hons. 1965; Ph.D. 1970). Previously appointed in SUNY
(Purchase) Adjunct Prof. 1975. Sir George William U. Montreal (Vis. Asst.
Prof. Anth. 1973); McGill U. (Vis. Asst. Prof. Anth. 1972–73). U. Illinois
at Urbana Champaign (Asst. Prof. Anth. 1970–73).
Author of: Ethnicity, Kinship and Joking among Urban Immigrants in
Ghana, in Du Toit and H. Safa (eds.) *Migration and Ethnicity* 1975;
Economics and Cultural Integration in the Domestic Context in Kumasi, in
J. Goody (ed.) *The Changing Social Structure of Ghana* 1975; Ethnicity and
Generational Differences among Urban Immigrants in Ghana, in *Urban
Ethnicity* (ed.) A. Cohen (ASA) 1974; Islam and Politics in Ghana, *Anth.
Papers of Amer. Museum of Natural History* 1974; The Fostering of
Children in Urban Ghana, *Urban Anthropology* 1973; Government and
Chiefs in Kumasi, in M. Crowder and O. Ikime (eds.) *West African
Chiefs* 1970.

Erik Gabriel SCHWIMMER
Born 1923, The Netherlands. Educated at Victoria University College,
New Zealand and University of British Columbia, Canada (Ph.D. Anthropology).
Taught at University of Toronto 1968–74– now Professeur titulaire,
Université Laval, Québec.
Author: *The World of the Maori* 1965; *Exchange in the Social Structure
of the Orokaiva* 1973; *Les frères-ennemis; analyses de la communication inter-
ethnique en Papouasie* (in press). Ed. of *Yearbook of Symbolic Anthropology.*

Mary SEARLE-CHATTERJEE
Born 1942, London. Studied at Nottingham University (B.A.); Benares Hindu University (M.A.); Manchester (M.A. Econ.), Benares (Ph.D.). Lecturer in Sociology at Benares from 1974–77.

Author of: *Reversible Sex Roles: the special case of Benares Sweepers* (in press).

Cato WADEL
Born 1936 in Oslo, Norway. Professor of Social Science, University of Tromsø, Norway. M.A. in social anthropology, University of Bergen, 1966. Assistant professor Memorial University of Newfoundland 1967–70; ammanuensis University of Oslo 1970–72; Professor, University of Tromsø 1974–.

Published books: *Marginal adaptations and modernization in Newfoundland* 1969; *North Atlantic fishermen* 1972 (co-ed. with R.A. Andersen); *Now, whose fault is that? The struggle for self-esteem in the face of chronic unemployment* 1973; *Trygdeliv og arbeidsliv* 1978; *Lokale samfunn og offentlig planlegging* 1978 (co-ed. with T. Thuen).

Sandra WALLMAN
Born 1934, London. Visiting Professor of Social Anthropology, University of Stockholm, Sweden. Educated at the University of London, LSE (B.Sc. 1961– Ph.D. 1965). Previously appointed in the University of Toronto (Lecturer, Assistant/Associate Professor of Anthropology 1965–75); University of Amsterdam (Visiting Professor of Anthropology 1973); University of Bristol (Senior Lecturer and Research Program Leader for SSRC-RUER 1975–).

Publications include the volumes: *Take Out Hunger* (LSE Monographs 1965); *Perceptions of Development* (ed.); *Ethnicity at Work* (ed.) 1979; and papers in applied anthropology, boundary marking and resource management.

INDEX OF NAMES